THE SEARCH FOR MEDIEVAL MUSIC
IN AFRICA AND GERMANY,
1891–1961

NEW
MATERIAL
HISTORIES
of
MUSIC

NEW MATERIAL HISTORIES OF MUSIC

A series edited by James Q. Davies and Nicholas Mathew

Also Published in the Series

Musical Vitalities: Ventures in a Biotic Aesthetics of Music
Holly Watkins

Sex, Death, and Minuets: Anna Magdalena Bach and Her Musical Notebooks
David Yearsley

The Voice as Something More: Essays toward Materiality
Edited by Martha Feldman and Judith T. Zeitlin

Listening to China: Sound and the Sino-Western Encounter, 1770–1839
Thomas Irvine

THE SEARCH FOR MEDIEVAL MUSIC
IN AFRICA AND GERMANY,
1891–1961

Scholars, Singers, Missionaries

ANNA MARIA BUSSE BERGER

THE UNIVERSITY OF CHICAGO PRESS

CHICAGO AND LONDON

The University of Chicago Press, Chicago 60637
The University of Chicago Press, Ltd., London
© 2020 by The University of Chicago
Published 2020
Printed in the United States of America

29 28 27 26 25 24 23 22 21 20   1 2 3 4 5

ISBN-13: 978-0-226-74034-8 (cloth)
ISBN-13: 978-0-226-74048-5 (e-book)
DOI: https://doi.org/10.7208/chicago/9780226740485.001.0001

This book has been supported by the Martin Picker Endowment and Publications
Endowment of the American Musicological Society, supported in part by the National
Endowment for the Humanities and the Andrew W. Mellon Foundation. It has also
been supported by a publication grant from the University of California, Davis.

Library of Congress Cataloging-in-Publication Data

Names: Berger, Anna Maria Busse, author.
Title: The search for medieval music in Africa and Germany, 1891–1961 :
    scholars, singers, missionaries / Anna Maria Busse Berger.
Other titles: New material histories of music.
Description: Chicago ; London : The University of Chicago Press, 2020. |
    Series: New material histories of music | Includes bibliographical
    references and index.
Identifiers: LCCN 2020013472 | ISBN 9780226740348 (cloth) |
    ISBN 9780226740485 (ebook)
Subjects: LCSH: Musicology—Germany—History. | Mission music—German East
    Africa—History and criticism. | Missions—German East Africa—History—
    20th century. | Ethnomusicology—Germany—History. | Ethnomusicology—
    German East Africa—History. | Musicologists—Germany. | Music—
    15th century—History and criticism. | Medievalism—Germany. | Music—
    Social aspects—Germany. | Music and youth—Germany—History—20th century.
Classification: LCC ML3797.2.G47 B47 2020 | DDC 780.72/1—dc23
LC record available at https://lccn.loc.gov/2020013472

∞ This paper meets the requirements of ANSI/NISO Z39.48–1992
(Permanence of Paper).

For my parents

Joseph Busse (1907–1972)

Erika Busse (1910–2003)

and my sisters

Katharina Peters-Rellensmann *1937 in Mbeya

Luise Böß *1939 in Rungwe

Dorothea Woydack *1950 in Hamburg

CONTENTS

FIGURES

Introduction

When I was nine years old my father was asked by the Lutheran World Federation to become director of a seminary to educate future Lutheran Church leaders from all over Africa. As a result, I spent two years in Tanzania, in the Kilimanjaro area. These two years transformed my life and undoubtedly were the very beginning of this project. I remember that when we arrived with the boat in Mombasa, we went to the Holy Ghost Cathedral and listened to Mass. It so happened that just six months earlier we had visited the Benedictine abbey Kloster Beuron in Germany, and there I had heard Gregorian chant for the first time. I could not believe how different Gregorian chant sounded in Mombasa! A week later we attended a Chagga service in Marangu, Tanzania, where the several-hundred-member-strong congregation sang Lutheran chorales. Again they sounded completely different from what I was used to from Germany. My father, who was usually able to answer all of my questions, was not helpful: he just said that Africans sang "differently." My curiosity was aroused.

In 2004 I began to explore the archive of the Moravian Church in Herrnhut, in East Germany. Moravians were the earliest Protestant missionaries to work outside Europe; they started their activities in 1732, when the first Moravian missionaries went to St. Thomas (in the U.S. Virgin Islands) and Greenland. Other German missionary societies essentially imitated the Moravians. Looking through the various materials collected in Herrnhut, I realized that the archive was a gold mine. It contains copious correspondence between the missionaries in the field and the German center, as well as numerous diaries of the missionaries dating from the earliest years of missionary activity. Much of this material remains unexplored. It became clear to me that the Moravian archive alone would keep scores of historians busy for years.

In the end, I decided to concentrate on music in mission stations in Tanzania because I knew the country and had good contacts there. Even then, there was so much material that I had to limit myself to only a few mission societies. Since German East Africa was a colony and the relationship between the colonial administrators and the missionaries formed an important part of my research, I decided to concentrate on four mission societies that were there more or less from the beginning in 1891, when German East Africa became a German colony, and remained involved through the 1950s and 1960s, that is, through the whole colonial period (Tanganyika became independent in 1961). I eventually decided on three Protestant mission societies and one Catholic: the Moravians, the Leipzig Mission, the Bethel Mission, and the Missionsbenediktiner from St. Ottilien in Bavaria. These societies maintain rich archives, with extensive letters, diaries, and publications by missionaries. I also conducted research in Tanzania. In some cases families of the missionaries provided me with additional documents.

In studying these materials, I came to realize that many missionaries had done serious scholarly research, especially in African languages, and had been in close contact with the Africanists Carl Meinhof (Hamburg University) and Diedrich Westermann (Friedrich Wilhelm University, forerunner of Humboldt University in Berlin), who helped them with Bible translations, grammars, and dictionaries. Still more surprising to me was the discovery that many missionaries had been involved not only in linguistics, but also in ethnomusicological research. They made recordings for the Berlin Phonogramm-Archiv,[1] and they read articles and books by such scholars as Erich Moritz von Hornbostel, Marius Schneider, and the Hamburg comparative musicologist Wilhelm Heinitz.[2] Subsequently, I discovered that scholarly activity was not limited to a closed club involving only white missionaries: a little-known African scholar and composer, Nicholas Ballanta, had given a lecture at a missionary conference in Le Zoute, Belgium, in 1926, as a result of which the Bethel Mission Society tried to introduce African music into the service. Clearly, comparative musicology loomed large in the mind of many missionaries.

The other discovery I made is perhaps equally surprising. It is commonly believed that missionaries introduced Christianity into indigenous societies and that they were in the service of colonial governments. While this is undoubtedly true, it is only part of the story. On the one hand, the relationship between missionaries and colonial administrations was often more complicated than has been recognized; on the other, Christianity was just one component of the culture that informed missionaries' activities. Many missionaries come from the youth movement known as *Wandervogel*,

which later became the *Jugendmusik*- and *Singbewegung*. So did some secular colonists, such as the imperial navy officer Hans Paasche (who, by the
way, also made recordings for the Berlin Phonogramm-Archiv). Stationed in
German East Africa between 1904 and 1908, he was forced to fight on the
German side in the Maji Maji Rebellion. The experience was so traumatic
that he became a pacifist and an anticolonialist. After he resigned from the
navy, he spent several years in East Africa, a country he loved. Like his
friends from the *Wandervogel*, he hated modernity and loved the Middle
Ages and old folk songs (which he sang accompanying himself on the lute).
He considered the African way of life ideal. His fictitious epistolary novel
Die Forschungsreise des Afrikaners Lukanga Mukara, a big bestseller from
1921, shows both his alienation from modernity and Western culture and
his love for Africa. Similarly, many missionaries who came from the movement shared the belief that only in Africa could one still find an intact community (*Gemeinschaft*) where people looked out for one another, in contrast to the impersonal society (*Gesellschaft*) of modern Europe. Thus, like
Paasche, they did not consider living in Africa a sacrifice; for them it was an
ideal community. All of these movements (the *Wandervogel* and the *Jugendmusik*- and *Singbewegung*) are characterized by a passion for folk and medieval music, and a dislike for modernity and its culture. Last but not least,
they all promoted participatory music making, as opposed to the concert
life of the bourgeois. In Africa, everyone took part in the ritual: there was
no such thing as a concert, with its division of participants into musicians
and listeners.

Gradually, I realized that if I wanted to do justice to the research done
by these missionaries, I had to know where they came from. What was their
background? What motivated them? As a medievalist, I had long been interested in the origins of medieval musicology, and I was astonished to discover
that these two interests—the music of missionaries in Africa and the origins of medieval musicology—are intertwined. At the beginning of the last
century little was known about medieval music: the notation was incom-
pletely understood, the surviving sources were not evaluated, and the theorists had barely been studied. We have long known that Friedrich Ludwig
and his devoted students began systematically to explore medieval polyphony at the beginning of the last century through an analysis of the sources.[3]
However, at very much the same time, comparative musicologists were
also interested in medieval music, approaching the field through comparisons with music of what they called "primitive" societies.[4] In fact, their approach was somewhat like that of Milman Parry and Albert Lord, who went
to the Balkans between 1933 and 1935 to study and record contemporary

oral poetry in order to find out how Greek poetry might have been orally transmitted.[5] Lord and Parry's work is well-known, but few people know that comparative musicologists used a similar approach.[6]

Thus, while I originally wanted to write a book on the efforts of German missionaries to introduce European church music in East Africa and to describe the music they found there, the project evolved into a history of early twentieth-century music scholarship in Germany and one of its colonies. The result is a different kind of music history from that generally associated with Germany. There will be very little on high culture or on composers and concert life. Instead, I will examine musical events in Germany in which thousands of people, not just the cultural elite, participated. I include several chapters on individuals, both scholars and missionaries, most of them completely unknown, and yet, I believe, of importance if we want to understand what happened musically in the first half of the twentieth century. And not only musically: this was a period of traumatic political upheaval, and so I have tried to account for the political attitudes and behaviors of the people I write about both during colonial times and during the Nazi period.

The book consists of three parts: part I addresses comparative musicology; part II discusses the *Wandervogel, Jugendmusik-,* and *Singbewegung* movements (essentially a who's who of German musicology in this period); and part III tells the story of musical activities at the German mission stations in what is now Tanzania. Central to all three parts is a concern with medieval music, ethnographic research, and communal music making. The actors in all three parts were in contact with each other.

I begin part I with the origins of comparative musicology in Berlin, an undertaking largely inspired by Carl Stumpf, who recruited a group of scientists from a variety of backgrounds: Otto Abraham (medicine), Erich Moritz von Hornbostel (chemistry), and Curt Sachs (art history). Hornbostel collected orally transmitted music from all over the world in the Berlin Phonogramm-Archiv in order to analyze and classify it. The significance of the collection (more than sixteen thousand recordings on thirty thousand cylinders and discs) can be recognized from the fact that since 1999 it has been on the UNESCO Memory of the World Register.[7] Much of the musical repertoire recorded between 1893 and 1952 is now extinct or has substantially changed.

Hornbostel modeled his research on that of comparative linguistics done a hundred years earlier, also in Berlin, under the guidance of Wilhelm von Humboldt. The result was a new discipline called comparative musicology. The central questions were similar to those of comparative linguistics:

while linguists searched for the origins of language and established language trees, musicologists searched for the origins of music and the relationship of various musics to one another.[8] Linguists used grammars to compare languages; musicologists analyzed and compared transcriptions of recorded music. Just as Humboldt had used grammars compiled by missionaries, the Berlin Phonogramm-Archiv asked missionaries and travelers to make recordings for the institution. And yet, it became quickly clear that while linguists were able successfully to construct language trees, musics did not lend themselves to the kind of comparisons.

How did Hornbostel and his students try to approach the question of the origins of music? While Greek was of central importance for the Indo-Europeanists, since in their opinion it was the oldest written language, musicologists concentrated on comparisons of "exotic" musics to European medieval music, since the latter was the earliest notated music. They found that both were pentatonic (based on a five-note scale) and that both used similar techniques when performing polyphony. These findings had far-reaching consequences. Music history textbooks from the first half of the twentieth century routinely lumped medieval music and non-European musics together, using the same terminology to describe them. Moreover, many comparative musicologists believed that they could understand and reconstruct European medieval music through a study of "exotic" musics.

Comparative musicology is based on comparisons, so comparative musicologists needed to identify shared features when they compared non-European with medieval music. Virtually all scholars observed parallels in the use of the modes; they also often compared polyphonic techniques. The interplay of orality and literacy was an important topic, as was the role of improvisation and of various notational systems that might be compared to medieval notation.

I concentrate on six comparative musicologists, beginning with Hornbostel, who also defined the field of African music with his article "African Negro Music."[9] Naturally, the field has undergone major changes since Hornbostel's days. Today increased knowledge of Africa's musical heterogeneity and cultural diversity leaves most scholars reluctant to write about "African" music in general. Ethnomusicologists have moved away from an older philosophy of salvage ethnography and have for the most part abandoned attempts to preserve only what appears to be an older or more homogenous repertoire. Instead, scholars have come to value and study musical hybridity, understanding that music is an interactive medium that often cuts across cultural boundaries. In the 1920s and 1930s, however, Hornbostel's articles served both as a clarion call for Africanist research in music from the perspective of the new field of comparative musicology and as a critique of current missionary practice with respect to indigenous music in Africa. My primary goals are (1) to analyze the writings of Hornbostel and other comparative musicologists, and (2) to examine the effect these writings had on German missionaries in African colonies. While there will be an occasional discussion of the evolution of ethnomusicological research's theoretical underpinnings, I will not engage with these issues at great length, since the primary orientation of my book is historical rather than theoretical.

The following chapters in part I are on Hornbostel's student and successor Marius Schneider, the most influential ethnomusicologist in post-1945 Germany; then, Georg Schünemann, who was also instrumental in helping to realize the goals of the *Jugendbewegung* in Weimar Germany; Jacques Handschin and Manfred Bukofzer (both of whom were primarily historical musicologists, but also made major contributions to comparative musicology); and finally, the African scholar Nicholas G. J. Ballanta. It is no accident that Schneider, Schünemann, Handschin, and Bukofzer were also, even primarily, medievalists. Hornbostel established the agenda of the field, Schneider and Schünemann attempted to use comparative methodology to learn how medieval music really worked and sounded, and Handschin and Bukofzer contributed to the demise of the field by proving that Hornbostel's central contribution, the "theory of the blown fifth" (*Blasquintentheorie*) relied on faulty measurements; Handschin also challenged the evolutionary modes of thinking that informed much of comparative musicology. Surprisingly, while the historical musicologists from part I who were interacting with comparatists, including Handschin, were convinced that medieval polyphony was largely improvised, none of the historical musicologists treated in part II shared this view.

A separate chapter is devoted to the fascinating case of the little-known African scholar Nicholas Ballanta, the first recipient of a Guggenheim Fellowship in music, who had been sent from Africa via New York to Berlin to study with Hornbostel on the recommendation of the anthropologist Franz Boas. His relationship with Hornbostel was an unhappy one: the recordings Ballanta made for the Phonogramm-Archiv mysteriously disappeared, and Hornbostel believed that Ballanta had never sent them. Ballanta published a number of original articles in journals that were (and still are) difficult to access and thus were not read by musicologists. His book was never published because of a devastating and clearly biased review by the comparative musicologist George Herzog. And yet, much of his research on African music was written before Hornbostel's seminal 1928 article on the subject. He was the only scholar to state explicitly that African music had nothing in common with medieval music. And his lecture at the International Mission Conference in Le Zoute in 1928 had a profound influence on one mission society.

Part II deals with the *Wandervogel*, a youth movement that swept Germany in the first half of the twentieth century and involved all social classes, all political movements, and all religious denominations. The movement started before World War I as a youth group in the Berlin neighborhood of Steglitz, and then in the 1920s and 1930s two new groups replaced the original *Wandervogel*. One, the *Jugendmusikbewegung*, had a more socialist leaning and resulted in exceedingly popular sing-alongs all across Germany. While much has been written about concerts of new music in Berlin, virtually nothing has been written about mass sing-alongs in the city's many parks, where some three to four thousand people from all political parties participated. Thanks to this movement, German music education was fundamentally reformed and became one of the best systems in the world. The other movement, the *Singbewegung*, was mainly Protestant and characterized by singing retreats in the countryside. Both movements shared an intense dislike for modernity, popular entertainment music, and the bourgeois concert hall. What they practiced instead was participatory music making that involved both early music and folk music. There was a longing for the Middle Ages and "primitive" societies, where people looked out for each other—for *Gemeinschaft*.

Not surprisingly, research into music of the Middle Ages and folk music took center stage. The great medievalist Friedrich Ludwig, the first ordinarius in musicology in Germany, was too old to participate in the movements, but all of his most consequential students were involved, foremost among them Heinrich Besseler, Joseph Müller-Blattau, Walter Blankenburg, and Konrad Ameln. Others were Wilibald Gurlitt, Friedrich Blume, and Hans-Joachim Moser, leaders of musicology from the 1930s through the 1960s and teachers of the next generation of German and German Jewish scholars who fled Germany for the United States. The first performances of Notre Dame polyphony took place in 1922 and 1924 in Karlsruhe and Hamburg, and most of Ludwig's and Gurlitt's students participated. (The performers were not listed on the program, because the point of the events was participatory music making.) Two important publishing houses were established, Bärenreiter and Möseler (formerly Kallmeyer; I will refer to this firm hereinafter as Kallmeyer-Möseler), essentially in order to provide music for the singers and performers. These publishing houses also issued many of their books, including Herman Reichenbach's widely read *Formenlehre*, which related all musical forms back to Gregorian chant. The German

Volksliedarchiv in Freiburg was founded in 1914; the Staatliches Institut für Musikforschung, Abteilung Volksmusik followed in Berlin in 1935.

Theodor W. Adorno was among those who was highly critical of the movement after the war because participatory music making had become a hallmark of Nazi cultural life. Many of the leaders became members of the Nationalsozialistiche Deutsche Arbeitspartei (NSDAP; the Nazi Party) and embraced Hitler wholeheartedly. But there were also many Jewish members who emigrated to the United States or Palestine, and many who were so deeply affected by their participation in early-music performances in the 1920s that they devoted their life to early-music scholarship (for example, Konrad Ameln and Werner Blankenburg).

The last part deals with four different mission societies. The work of Jesuit missionaries and British and American Protestant missionaries has been much studied, yet non-Germans have had few opportunities to learn about the background of German Protestant missionaries. They were markedly different from those in England or the United States in that they were inspired by Nikolaus Ludwig Graf von Zinzendorf, the leader of the Moravian Church, and considered missionary activity their main purpose in life. They were less interested in spreading Western civilization than in "saving souls." In the nineteenth century another German theologian, Gustav Warneck, deeply influenced by Johann Gottfried Herder (1744–1803), put his stamp on German mission activities. These missionaries were taught to preserve as much of the local culture as possible and were encouraged to do linguistic and ethnographic research. Grammars and dictionaries of local languages were made and sent to Wilhelm von Humboldt in Berlin, and the Bible and hymns were translated. In many cases attempts were made to preserve local folklore and culture. Very little of this work is known today.

With respect to all missionary societies, I have tried to answer two questions: First, what kind of scholarly research did they do in music? And second, what music was performed in the service? I am not concerned with the theological contents of missionary activity or conversion. All three Protestant mission societies (the Moravians, the Leipzig Mission, and the Bethel Mission) did important research on local music, many made recordings, collected local fairy tales and sayings, and tried to introduce local music in the 1930s. German Catholic missionaries made recordings for Hornbostel and Schneider, but the Pope's *motu proprio* prevented them from introducing any local music into the service. All mission societies, with one exception, believed that medieval and African music were similar. And since most missionaries came from the *Jugendmusik-* and *Singbewegung*, they believed in participatory music making.

In each chapter I center in on a few missionaries and their contributions. The Moravian Traugott Bachmann did fundamental linguistic work (Bible translation and beginning work on the Nhiya grammar) and made recordings for Hornbostel that were transcribed and analyzed by numerous comparative musicologists. He was probably the first missionary to try to introduce local music and dance into the religious service in the early 1900s. Franz Ferdinand Rietzsch, another Moravian, steeped in the *Singbewegung*, was probably the best-trained musician among the missionaries, with a strong background in comparative musicology. Not only did he do fundamental research on Nyakyusa music long before Gerhard Kubik, but he also tried to introduce fifteenth-century polyphony into the service because he believed it was similar to Nyakyusa polyphony. He failed spectacularly.

The Leipzig missionary Bruno Gutmann (1876–1966) was perhaps the most important scholar among the missionaries, with volumes of fundamental work on the Wachagga and numerous honorary doctorates for his research. Even though he did not have a strong background in music, he came under the influence of the *Singbewegung* in the 1920s and published extensively with the movement's publisher Bärenreiter. He was invited to gatherings and talked and wrote with great conviction about the Wachagga, a culture that was similar to how he imagined medieval society to have been, with close family and community ties and rituals marking important life events. As a result, he transformed the Chagga rituals into Christian ones and translated hundreds of Lutheran chorales into Chagga. Both rituals and chorales are alive and well and remain much loved to this day.

Otto Hagena, a missionary for the Bethel Mission, was the best educated of the missionaries, having attended Friedrich Nietzsche's old school, Schulpforta. As a result he made major contributions to the translation of the New Testament from Greek to Haya, and he also gave a detailed and exceptionally complex account of Haya music in the 1920a and 1930s. Nevertheless, even though he would have loved to introduce Haya music into the service, it proved beyond his abilities. Before Hagena came to missionize and study them, the Hayas had the reputation of being completely "unmusical" and "resistant" to Western music. Hagena taught them Lutheran chorales with such success that one of his students, Josiah Kibira, who became the first black president of the Lutheran World Federation in 1970, insisted on continuing the Lutheran tradition even when later missionaries wanted to introduce local music into the service.

As for the Catholic missionaries from St. Ottilien, I do not concentrate on a single figure. Their beginnings were unhappy because they were close to colonial administrators, a circumstance that led to several of their missionaries being killed because the local population associated them with the colonial government. They even sent back one of their missionaries because he stood up to the German military on behalf of a member of his congregation. In the beginning, their attitude to local music was similarly dismissive; but, in addition, Catholics all over the world were also hampered by the pope's *motu proprio*. Nevertheless, they shared the common belief that African music was similar to medieval music and therefore felt fully justified introducing Gregorian chant everywhere and with great success. Also, the Catholic missionaries noticed the importance of participatory music making in Africa, commenting that Gregorian chant was therefore particularly appropriate.

Most astonishing is the story of how eventually something akin to local music was introduced in the mission stations. Marius Schneider transcribed Ngoni music from the phonograms provided by Catholic missionaries in his *Geschichte der Mehrstimmigkeit*. When the book was published in 1934, he sent a copy to Peramiho in Tanganyika. A few years later, in the late 1930s and '40s, another missionary, Jean Baptiste Wolf, found the book in the Peramiho library, looked at Ngoni songs, and noticed that they were similar to some Gregorian chant melodies he knew. He then took his *Graduale Romanum*, looked for antiphons that were melodically similar to the Ngoni songs transcribed by Schneider, and provided them with a Swahili text. They were sung with great success all over Tanganyika. Eventually a student of Wolf's, Stephan Mbunga, was sent to study with Marius Schneider in Cologne. Upon his return, and after he became rector of the Peramiho Seminary in 1968, he was finally able to introduce local music and dance into the service. The circle closes: Hornbostel and Schneider commissioned recordings from the Benedictine missionaries, and the Benedictines, in turn, used transcriptions of these recordings to perform "local" music. What better example than this to show that comparative musicology and music in the mission stations must be studied together!

In this book I uncover the remarkable interaction between the activities of missionaries, on the one hand, and the early twentieth-century scholarship on and performance of medieval and non-European music, on the other, as well as the lively interaction between early medievalists and ethnomusicologists (interactions that later disappeared). My book is fundamentally an attempt to bring this triangle back to life.

PART I

The Search for the Origins of Music: Comparative Musicology

Comparative musicology should unearth from collected and critically classified material the common factors and the context of musical development in all parts of the world, clarify differences on the basis of particular cultural relationships, and finally, by extrapolation, draw conclusions regarding origins.
—Otto Abraham and Erich Moritz von Hornbostel, "Über die Verbreitung des Phonographen für die vergleichende Musikwissenschaft" (1904)

Instead of accounts based on myths, we can now use the results from comparative musicology. If we want to investigate the problems of Greek and medieval music, and if the relationship between art and folk music is not to be based entirely on speculation, this is the only way to go. It is not necessary to place the music of "uncivilized" people as well as the art of Asian "culture people" [Kulturvölker], which we can now study thanks to phonograph recordings, on an equal footing with our music. Instead, we can see them as precursors of our musical development. And with systematic summaries of separate studies, it will be possible to create a foundation for the beginnings of music history which derives from a music that is alive and practiced rather than descriptions based on laborious and unreliable constructions.
—Georg Schünemann,"Über die Beziehungen der vergleichenden Musikwissenschaft zur Musikgeschichte" (1920)

If we want to understand the history of the German music scholarship and culture in the first half of the twentieth century, we need to consider the new field of comparative musicology. While ethnomusicologists have written fundamental studies of comparative musicology, these studies have neglected the influence comparative musicology had on historical musicology. And while we know that the field started in Berlin at Friedrich Wilhelm University, there is still much to be learned about the aims and goals of the discipline. We can begin by asking how comparative musicology affected German musical life. In this part of the book, I shall summarize the contributions of some of the most important comparative musicologists and attempt to determine their agenda and impact. I shall also address the reasons for the eventual demise of the discipline.

In 1900 Carl Stumpf was appointed chair of the psychology department at Friedrich Wilhelm University. In the same year a music-theater group from Siam visited Berlin, and Stumpf, together with Otto Abraham, a physician, made a recording of them.[1] Stumpf realized very quickly that only with a large number of recordings could he conduct serious research into musics from different cultures. Thus, he set out to establish the Phonogramm-Archiv in Berlin, which was to collect performances of orally transmitted music from all over the world in order to analyze, compare, and classify it. Since he was a psychologist, he was also interested in the psychological effect of music. Significantly, he also called for an investigation of musical instruments. Stumpf was joined in 1905 by Erich Moritz von Hornbostel, who took over the Berlin Phonogramm-Archiv in 1906 and ran it until he was forced to emigrate in 1933. This collection forms an important basis for the research undertaken in this book.

Stumpf and Hornbostel are considered among the founders of the new discipline of comparative musicology, which eventually developed into ethnomusicology. They analyzed their recordings for three distinct purposes: to determine scales and tone systems, to transcribe and analyze musical structures, and to create a classification system for musical instruments. Where did Hornbostel and Stumpf get the idea to compare musics of different cultures to one another? And what were the questions they wanted to find answers for? In a lecture from 24 March 1905 given at the meeting of the International Musicological Society in Vienna, Hornbostel begins by stressing that "the most noble means of scientific knowledge is comparison."[2] The comparison of different things makes it possible to recognize similarities and to deduce laws from them. Even though most scholarship is based on comparisons, he singles out anatomy and comparative linguistics as particular models for comparative musicology.[3] While it might seem surprising to us that a musicologist is modeling his work on that of anatomists, we shall see that Hornbostel got this idea from nineteenth-century German scholars. Comparative anatomy creates new classifications and also inspires one to do investigations in completely new fields. It also makes it possible to define research as scientific rather than humanistic. Indeed, this was one of the main reasons comparative linguists saw themselves as analogous to anatomists. Hornbostel writes:

> First philology studied the separate languages individually, then comparative linguistics started to spin connecting threads between them. Also here the idea of evolution had to occur all on its own, as a scout that led to new groupings. Languages of the so-called primitive people, which had thus far received little attention, were suddenly of particular interest. Within the known language areas of the civilized lands [Kulturländer], dialects were carefully studied, and thus it became possible to compare a constantly increasing amount of material.[4]

Hornbostel has an even more detailed description of the parallels in his 1904 article, "Über die Verbreitung des Phonographen für die vergleichende Musikwissenschaft" (On the Use of the Phonograph in Comparative Musicology).

> In the same way that philology initially researched individual languages with respect to the separate categories of vocabulary, laws of inflection, and syntax, so until recently has musicology involved itself exclusively with the history of our European musical system and European forms of composition. But whereas philology completely adopted the comparative method within a short time, musicology has ventured only a few tentative steps in the new direction, and it would be premature to speak of comparative musicology as an established cultural discipline. In fact, surveys of music history usually do contain a fleeting sketch of the circumstances of foreign music; however, the consideration is advanced primarily from an artistic, subjective-aesthetic point of view, and the struggle toward scientific objectivity is a most recent phenomenon.[5]

Hornbostel shows a detailed knowledge of the methods of comparative linguistics, observing that scholars compared languages with respect to vocabulary, inflection, and syntax.[6] As we consider what the corresponding categories for music might be, I suggest that comparative linguistics could have set the agenda for Hornbostel and his colleagues and students. In what follows, I will not give an overview of the entire field, but instead concentrate on topics that have had an impact on comparative musicology.

CHAPTER ONE

Comparative Musicology and
Comparative Linguistics

In 1769 the Prussian Academy invited scholars to participate in a competition to answer the question of whether man could have invented language all on his own, and if so, how he went about it.[1] The winning entry was composed by the twenty-six-year-old Lutheran pastor Johann Gottfried Herder, who wrote an article entitled "Abhandlung über den Ursprung der Spache" (Treatise on the Origin of Language), published in 1772.[2] The text is generally considered the beginning of comparative linguistics.[3] Herder argued that the language and thought of a people are intrinsically linked. While the idea that language is the tool of human thinking had been voiced before, understanding language as the content and form of human thinking was new.[4] Herder suggested that language and thought originated at the same time, depended on each other, and evolved together through successive stages of growth. The logical consequence was that one could only understand a culture by knowing the language well.[5] As Isaiah Berlin recognized, for Herder each collective individuality "has its own aims and standards, which will themselves inevitably be superseded by other goals and values. . . . Each of these systems is objectively valid in its own day, in the course of 'Nature's long year' which brings all things to pass. All cultures are equal in the sight of God, each in its own time and place."[6] As a result, Herder called for a thorough investigation of differences between languages, systems of thought, and cultures.[7] The questions addressed in Herder's essays, including the question of the origins of language, became the most important questions of the new discipline. In the nineteenth century there were two groups of comparative linguists, which will be discussed separately. Both were equally interested in the question of the origins of language.

THE INDO-EUROPEANISTS

Historians of linguistics generally place the next important step in the development of the discipline in late eighteenth-century India. The relationship between Indian and Western European languages had fascinated people since the sixteenth century. Between 1583 and 1588 the Florentine merchant Filippo Sassetti had noticed similarities between Sanskrit and Italian words. Over the next two hundred years numerous missionaries published articles in obscure missionary journals, commenting on the similarities between Persian, Greek, and Latin number words, and had made rudimentary grammars of Sanskrit.[8] But the first serious contribution on the topic was by Sir William Jones (1746–1794), a judge in the British court in India, who spoke thirteen languages fluently and twenty-eight more passably. In a 1786 paper read at the Royal Asiatic Society in Calcutta, Jones was able to show that Sanskrit is related to Latin, Greek, and the Germanic languages:

> The Sanskrit language, whatever be its antiquity, is of a wonderful structure; more perfect than the Greek, more copious than the Latin, and more exquisitely refined than either; yet bearing to both of them a stronger affinity, both in the roots of verbs and in the forms of grammar, than could possibly have been produced by accident; so strong indeed, that no philologer could examine all three without believing them to have sprung from some common source, which perhaps no longer exists. There is a similar reason, though not quite so forcible, for supposing that both the Gothic and the Celtic had the same origin with the Sanskrit.[9]

Here Jones describes the two methods used by linguists to establish relationships: a comparison of words and a comparison of grammars.

In 1808 Friedrich von Schlegel (1772–1829) published *Über die Sprache und Weisheit der Indier*, in which he similarly argued that Sanskrit was the source of all of these languages.[10] He advocated the study of the "inner structures" of languages in order to establish their genetic relationships, again an area of utmost importance for comparative musicologists, and coined the term *vergleichende Grammatik* (comparative grammar).[11]

Schlegel was characteristic of most nineteenth-century comparative linguists in that he concentrated particularly on comparisons of Sanskrit to Greek and Latin.[12] Their interest in Greek and Latin is easy to explain. These are Indo-European languages that were spoken 3500 years ago and are still spoken today (in modern versions); moreover, they exist in writing. It was clear from the beginning that their alphabets, syntaxes, lexica, and literary genres had a major impact on all Indo-European languages. We have in them written documents of a culture that was fairly close to their Indo-European origins. Nineteenth-century philologists felt that ancient Greek was perhaps closest to what they were looking for in their quest to find the Proto-Indo-European language, because Greek was considered "a highly refined (and evolved) means of expressing an author's thought."[13] In particular, Greek stems were found to be closely related to those of Indo-European languages.

Three important scholars dominated the field in the beginning of the nineteenth century: the Danish linguist Rasmus Rask (1787–1832), who published only in Danish, with the result that the importance of his work went unrecognized at first; Jacob Grimm (1785–1863); and Franz Bopp (1791–1867). Wilhelm von Humboldt (1767–1835) belongs to the same generation, but we shall discuss him separately, because his thinking was not in line with those in the mainstream of German comparative linguistics. Even though the ideas presented by these three scholars were formulated at the beginning of the nineteenth century, they went on to dominate much of nineteenth-century German thought.[14]

Rask is really the inventor of what came to be known as Grimm's law. He systematically compared word forms and concluded:

> If there is found between two languages agreement in the forms of indispensable words to such an extent that rules of letter changes can be discovered for passing from one to the other, then there is a basic relationship between these languages.[15]

Rask started with Icelandic, then moved on to Germanic languages and compared them to Slavic, Greek, and Latin. As a result, he was able to formulate clear rules for the relationships between the languages.[16] He found that lexical matching between different languages is unreliable because of constant interactions among individuals. On the other hand, grammatical agreement is a very reliable method of determining whether the languages are related, "since a language that has been mixed with another one, will only very rarely or never take a form or inflexion from it."[17] He observed that languages with the most artificial grammar are the oldest and least contaminated, because the grammatic inflexions wear off in the newer languages. Thus, he found that Danish grammar is considerably simpler than that of Icelandic, English grammar is simpler than that of Anglo-Saxon, Italian grammar is simpler than that of Latin, and German grammar is simpler than that of Gothic. Icelandic, a language that is almost identical to medieval

Old Norse, provided Rask with the basis for comparison, just as Greek had done for other linguists.[18] This is a point of importance for comparative musicologists.[19]

Grimm, known to us as the author of the *Deutsches Wörterbuch* and, together with his younger brother, Wilhelm, as the compiler of *Kinder- und Hausmärchen*, included the so-called Grimm's law in his 1822 edition of his *Deutsche Grammatik*. He formulated the law after reading Rask's book. Because this law governs the Proto-Indo-European stop consonants as they were transformed into Proto-Germanic consonants, Grimm was able to describe the stages of the consonant changes from Greek to Latin to Gothic to Old High German. For example, Greek *p* became Gothic *f* and Old High German *b* (*v*). Grimm's law stands to this day, even though Grimm himself had observed that there are numerous exceptions to it. These exceptions are now explained by Verner's law, after the Danish linguist Karl Verner.

Bopp is considered the founder of Indo-European studies. With the support of Wilhelm von Humboldt, in 1821 he became the first chairman of Sanskrit and comparative grammar at Friedrich Wilhelm University in Berlin. In his fundamental book *Über das Conjugationssystem der Sanskritsprache in Vergleichung mit jenem der griechischen, lateinischen, persischen und germanischen Sprache* (On the System of Conjugation of the Sanskrit Language Compared with Those in Greek, Latin, Persian and Germanic Languages; 1816) he tried to reconstruct the original grammatical structure of Indo-European, which he believed had disintegrated in all of the languages derived from it. Bopp arrived at his conclusions by compiling comparative grammars, concentrating first on conjugations and then declensions. Concerning conjugations, he writes:

> If we want to truly understand these very important sentences for the history of languages, it is above all necessary that we become acquainted with the conjugation system of the Indo-European languages, then compare the conjugations of the Greek, the Roman, the Germanic, and the Persian languages. In this way we are able to understand their special character, but also recognize at the same time the gradual and stepwise destruction of the simple language organism and observe the striving to substitute it with mechanical connections. From these there comes the appearance of a new organism, of which the elements were no longer recognized.[20]

In his book *Vergleichende Grammatik des Sanskrit, Zend, Griechischen, Lateinischen, Litauischen, Altslavischen, Gotischen und Deutschen* (1833),

Bopp compares eight languages, and not only the verbs but also other word forms.[21] It is quite characteristic that he wants to turn comparative linguistics into a science; he explicitly states that his field is equal to anatomy and physics, a comparison Hornbostel also makes in the paper mentioned above.[22]

Like Grimm, Bopp is convinced that the original languages had a superior grammar (he calls grammar *Organismus*) that gradually deteriorated in the derived languages. "Languages . . . are to be regarded as natural organisms that develop on their own according to specific laws, evolve carrying within themselves an inner life principle, and die off little by little by no longer comprehending themselves; they gradually discard, mutilate, or abuse parts or forms that were originally significant, and gradually use them for purposes for which they were not appropriate."[23] Because the original Indo-European language and its close relatives Latin and Greek were considered to have the most perfect grammars, and also because they were transmitted in writing, they were taken as a benchmark for comparisons of other language families, even though these had completely different structures. As a result, the younger languages were found to be wanting.

August Schleicher (1821–1868) was probably the most important linguist from the middle of the nineteenth century. He devised what he called *Stammbaumtheorie* (family-tree theory) that included classifications similar to those of botanical taxonomy.[24] But he might have also been influenced by his teacher Friedrich Ritschl, a distinguished philologist and Nietzsche's teacher, who established stemmata between manuscripts that are quite similar to his *Stammbäume*.[25] Of course, his *Stammbäume* have been adjusted since his book appeared, but scholars have long agreed that they have the advantage that you can see at a glance the history of the language family and the relationships of the languages to each other.

Not surprisingly, Schleicher was heavily influenced by Charles Darwin's *The Origin of Species* (1859), even though he was adamant that he had written his book *Compendium of the Comparative Grammar of the Indogermanic Languages* before Darwin's book appeared.[26] Like Bopp, he considered himself a scientist and believed that he had used scientific methods in his research. He drew a comparison between Darwin's theory of evolution and comparative linguistics and believed that "the diffusion of different languages over the earth's surface and their contacts and conflicts could be likened to the struggle for existence in the world of living things, in which the Indo-European languages were victorious."[27] Here we have another assertion that even though other language groups exist, the Indo-European group is the original and most refined one.

In sum, we have seen that in the first half of the nineteenth century comparative linguists approached the central question of the origins of language by concentrating mainly on Indo-European languages. The study of Greek in particular was considered an important tool in trying to establish language relationships. Linguists used essentially two methods to compare languages: first, a comparison of lists of words that languages share; and second, a comparison of grammars. Concerning the former, these linguists arrived at laws that governed the changes of consonants that occurred between languages. Concerning the latter, Rask observed that the older languages have more complex grammars than the more recent ones, that is, Icelandic is more complex than Danish, Norse more complex than English, and so on. There was further general agreement that Indo-European languages were superior to other language families, especially with regard to their grammatical structure. Especially in the second half of the nineteenth century, linguists considered themselves scientists and believed that their methods were comparable to those of anatomists.

WILHELM VON HUMBOLDT AND THE BEGINNINGS OF ANTHROPOLOGY

Wilhelm von Humboldt was interested in finding the origins of language, but he did not concentrate only on Indo-European languages. As a result, his language theory is different from that of his contemporaries and opened up an entirely new level of thinking that led directly to the development of anthropology. Many of his ideas, especially those about non-Indo-European languages, came to be fully understood only many years after his death.

Like Herder, Humboldt believed that language conditions thought: "Language is, as it were, the outer appearance of the spirit of a people; the language is their spirit and the spirit their language; we can never think of them sufficiently as identical."[28] Language categories determine our thinking, because "in every language lies its specific view of the world."[29] The organization and structure of a language is understood not through its grammar but "from an analysis of the procedures language employs in its generation of speech."[30] When Humboldt visited Spain to learn the language of the Basques, he noticed that they had words he would not have been able to translate one-to-one into German, for example, words for the hard physical labor done by women, or words for the ball games played by men.[31] Humboldt gives a specific example: he observed that in Sanskrit there are three different terms for elephant, each of which creates a different image of the elephant: "the one who drank twice," "the one who has two teeth," and "the one who has one hand." All of these words are untranslatable, a point that becomes important for missionaries when they try to translate biblical images.

In addition, Humboldt carried out extensive comparative research. While previous scholars had mainly concentrated on Indo-European languages, Humboldt was interested in every language he could access. Of course he knew Greek and Latin, Sanskrit, all the Romance languages, English, Old Icelandic, Lithuanian, Polish, Slovenian, Serbo-Croatian, Armenian, and Hungarian. In addition, he could read Hebrew, Arabic, and Coptic, as well as such Asian languages as Chinese, Japanese, Siamese, and Tamil. These were all languages familiar to other linguists too. He is exceptional in that he established language families thus far completely unknown to his colleagues. During his stay in Paris, according to the Humboldt scholar Kurt Mueller-Vollmer, he began to explore the Basque language, "an idiom whose origin and structure had defied hitherto all attempts at an explanation by historians, philosophers and linguists following conventional methodologies."[32] After extensive research trips to Spain in 1799 and 1801, in 1821 he published *Prüfung der Untersuchungen über die Urbewohner Hispaniens vermittelst der vaskischen Sprache* (*Examination of the Original Inhabitants of Spain through the Basque Language*), the first of a number of scholarly texts showing that Basque descended from a separate pre-Indo-European language.[33]

Next Humboldt turned to South, Central, and North American languages, and after 1827 to the languages of the Pacific Coast, from the east coast of Africa to Hawaii and the South Sea Islands. These languages are now called Austronesian languages, and until his publications no one knew that this language group even existed.

How did he accomplish all of this? Even getting access to grammars and dictionaries of these obscure languages was then a significant challenge. First, his brother, Alexander von Humboldt (1769–1859), helped him buy the majority of his linguistic materials. Second, in Rome he befriended the Spaniard Lorenzo Hervás, himself a linguist as well as the former chief of the Jesuit missions in the Americas and head of the Papal Quirinal Library. As a result, Humboldt was given full access to all of Hervás's Native American grammars. Third, Humboldt regularly corresponded with missionaries, encouraging them to compile grammars and dictionaries, and never failed to cite their work in his publications. The Moravian missionaries Theophilus Salomo G. Schumann and Christlieb Quandt, both active in Suriname, were helpful to him.[34] However, his most important missionary contact was the Moravian David Zeisberger (1721–1808), who knew many Native American languages and produced the Onondaga dictionaries and also, and more important, a grammar of the Delaware language.[35] In addition, Humboldt contacted not only the Moravian missionaries themselves, but also their widows, as well as the South German Jesuit missionaries.[36]

Humboldt's publications on non-European languages are impressive. All together he wrote twenty-four grammars of Native American languages based on notes from missionaries, each one mentioned by name.[37] In 1811 he published his first book on Native American languages, *Essai sur les langues du Nouveau Continent* (Essay on the Languages of the New Continent).[38] He died before he finished his greatest work, a study of the Kawi language on the island of Java that includes a discussion of the entire Austronesian group of the Pacific. His research associate Eduard Buschmann brought it out in 1836–39 under the title *Über die Kavi-Sprache*.

There are two important points in Humboldt's approach to comparative linguistics that were at odds with that of his Indo-Europeanist colleagues, and both were to become important for comparative musicologists. First, in contrast to Schlegel, Bopp, and Schleicher, Humboldt does not believe that a grammar deteriorates—that, say, Icelandic is better than Danish—nor does he think that certain languages have "superior" grammars. He argues repeatedly that every language has its own grammar, and that of, say, Italian is no worse than the grammar of the Latin from which Italian derives. And second, in comparing grammars of different language groups he believes it unjustifiable to compare them to Latin and French (or Greek) grammars and as a result find them wanting.[39] It cannot be overemphasized that Humboldt is different from other nineteenth-century linguists in that he has "a decidedly non-Eurocentric orientation." While he was also interested in the origins of languages, he acknowledged that there were many language groups, and languages derived from these groups were no less authentic than the original ones. Similarly, simpler and later grammars are not better than the original ones. Both of these points will become increasingly important for comparative musicologists after Hornbostel.

The reaction to Humboldt's ideas as published by Buschmann was, unsurprisingly, mixed. While Bopp finds much to praise, he tries to undermine Humboldt's main theory of the independence of Austronesian family. For him, these languages are derived from Sanskrit and have "lost their grammar."[40] In return, Buschmann defended Humboldt and warns of the imperialistic attitude of Indo-European studies. He reiterated Humboldt's principle that "every language is its own world and excludes in the stable moment another language."[41] According to Buschmann, Humboldt believed that language classification could only show histories of individual languages, not their genetic relationships.[42]

After Bopp's death the Indo-European scholar August Pott in 1880 did at least acknowledge that the Austronesian languages form a separate group—not, however, on the basis of linguistic arguments, but rather for racial reasons. The languages are different because "there is a deep gulf between Malaysians and Caucasians, human races that are incompatible, and thus the gulf is insurmountable."[43]

There were, however, a small number of scholars in Germany who continued to admire Humboldt's work. The Berlin comparative linguist Heyman Steinthal (1823–1899) tried to keep Humboldt's ideas alive by publishing his most important writings on language.[44] Steinthal received access to Humboldt's Nachlass after Buschmann's death. Moreover, he became one of the founders of *Völkerpsychologie*,[45] which he derived directly from Humboldt's framework of comparative linguistics.[46] In 1860 he and his friend Moritz Lazarus (1824–1903) founded the *Zeitschrift für Völkerpsychologie und Sprachwissenschaft* (Journal for Comparative Folk Psychology and Linguistics), which ran until 1890. According to Steinthal, a "psychologist of the people" (*Völkerpsychologe*) was to do two things: describe in great detail the manifestations of the specific people and establish "the laws that governed the psychological development of a people" (19, 23–24). They were joined by Wilhelm Wundt (1832–1920), professor of psychology at the University of Leipzig, who argued that psychological phenomena originated in the community of the folk, not in the individual. Wundt was one of the most powerful professors in Germany and attracted large crowds in his lectures, among them two missionaries to be discussed later in this book who both studied in Leipzig under him, Bruno Gutmann and Meinulf Küsters (1890–1947).[47] Küsters even wrote an article on Wundt.[48] Wundt investigates "cultural products" (*Erzeugnisse*) of the "totality of the spiritual life" (*geistiges Gesamtleben*). In this "totality of spiritual life" he looked for what he called *Sitten*, by which he means language, art, myth, and customs.[49] The individual can act only as part of a social group, not separately.

The German-born anthropologist Franz Boas (1858–1942) got to know Humboldt's work through Steinthal, whom he met when he served as an assistant in the Königliches Museum für Völkerkunde in Berlin in the 1880s. Steinthal helped Boas when he was trying to understand Inuit linguistic material.[50] Boas had traveled in 1883 to the Baffin Islands in order to collect geographic and geological material about the islands, but when he was forced to spend a winter there he got to know the Inuit well, and his interest

shifted to anthropology.[51] So Humboldt's work on Native American languages must have been a great help to him, because in the following years
he did extensive research on them. To quote Matti Bunzl, "Like Wilhelm
von Humboldt seventy-five years before, Boas began to relish the diversity
of American Indian languages for its own sake."[52] While Humboldt never
managed to finish his book on Native American languages, Boas did, and it
is very much along the lines of Humboldt's language theory. As had Humboldt, Boas explained the vocabulary of a people as a product of the "chief
interest of a people." Thus, many Native American languages lacked terms
for abstract concepts because, wrote Boas, they simply did not need them.[53]
Similarly, "Boas' critique of evolutionism and its racialist concomitants, as
well as of his linguistic relativism and his cultural historicism" harks back
to the Humboldt brothers and their students.[54]

Boas had a direct connection to comparative musicologists, since he was
a friend of Hornbostel. Bruno Nettl reports that his teacher George Herzog
(1901–1983) was sent to Columbia University (where Boas had been a professor of anthropology since 1896) by Hornbostel specifically because Boas
wanted the assistance of a music specialist.[55]

In this chapter we have seen two different comparative linguistics traditions emerge. Both were interested in exploring the origins of language, but
they did so in different ways. First, the Indo-European comparative linguists
worked with many different languages, conducted systematic comparisons
of words and grammars, and were able to establish a Indo-European proto-
language from which many others were derived. One gets the impression
that this tradition was profoundly shaped by the biblical account of the Tower
of Babel. There was a definite value judgment associated with this language
group: the Proto-Indo-European language was the most perfect creation, which,
unfortunately, deteriorated over the course of time in the languages derived
from it.

The second group consists of Humboldt and his followers. They had
none of the Eurocentric viewpoints of their colleagues. Humboldt was interested in all languages and did not believe that Indo-European languages
were superior to other groups. As a result, he refuses to measure the grammars of other languages against Latin and Greek and never observes a dete-
rioration of grammars. He was inventive in his use of informers, especially
in his employment of missionaries to help him compile his grammars.

I have provided this summary of history of linguistics because I believe
that musicologists and ethnomusicologists today are unaware of the extent to which the founding fathers of their discipline were influenced by
linguists, borrowing many of their concerns, questions, and methods. The

influence can be observed in the writings of all three comparative musicologists discussed here in four different areas. First, they all subscribed to the *Kulturkreislehre*, a term for which we do not have a standard English translation but is probably best rendered as "culture-circle doctrine." To quote Albrecht Schneider, the main authority on the topic, "Basically, *Kulturkreislehre* held that cultural parallels (obvious similarities of material goods, social institutions, etc.) are the result of migrations that took place in the remote past or more recent times."[56] Scholars who subscribed to *Kulturkreislehre* were convinced that cultural traits could be grouped into "geographical circles of distribution."[57] These circles were arranged chronologically: the largest circles would include the oldest traits, and the small ones the most recent. Musicologists would classify and arrange items such as musical instruments, melodies, and polyphony in circles of different sizes.[58] In other words, all believed in evolution, just like Schleicher and the linguists following him.

Second, they were all concerned with the origins of music. As we will see in the next chapter, Hornbostel derived from the Indo-Europeanists his concern with original, authentic music, uncontaminated by outside influences. In addition, he considered himself primarily a scientist like Bopp and Schleicher and regularly compared his work to that of an anatomist. But Hornbostel was also strongly influenced by Humboldt: there is no evidence that he thought that European music was more valuable than non-European. And he was intellectually and personally close to Boas. Marius Schneider and Schünemann, on the other hand, were doing research in comparative musicology because they hoped to learn more about medieval music. Under the Nazis, after 1933, research into Indo-European questions became increasingly important, but not even Schneider, who stayed in Germany for most of the war, was interested in tracing the beginnings of music to Indo-European culture. None voiced the opinion that older music was better or more complex than more recent music, in contrast to the Indo-Europeanists, who were convinced that the older languages, such as Indo-European and Greek and Latin, have complex grammars that deteriorated in their descendants. None disapproved of hybrid music; rather, they saw it as a natural development. In addition, Hornbostel's students did not adopt his scientific mode of writing.

Third, Hornbostel and Schneider must have learned from Humboldt and other linguists and anthropologists to use missionaries (as well as travelers, and colonial administrators) as informants. The Africanist Meinhof was particularly useful in helping identify missionaries that would be useful for this purpose.

Fourth, we have observed that comparative linguists concentrated particularly on languages that existed in written form one (in the case of Icelandic) or many (in the case of Greek) thousands of years ago in order to trace
the development of language. And this brings us to one of the main topics
of the book: the attempt to construct a parallel between medieval music
and non-Western music. Hornbostel, Schneider, and Schünemann similarly
tried to understand the origins of music by comparing their recordings to
medieval music, whether Gregorian chant or early polyphony. We will see
throughout this book how they fare with this project.

Jacques Handschin (1886–1955), on the other hand, is close to the followers of Humboldt (see chap. 5). His books show none of the Eurocentric
traces so common in other music histories; he was opposed to the very idea
of invidious comparison and insisted that every culture should be studied
in its own terms. And finally, like Humboldt, he was very careful to avoid
evolutionist language.

CHAPTER TWO

Erich Moritz von Hornbostel

Erich Moritz von Hornbostel (1877–1935) was one of the founders of musicology. An immensely curious man, he absorbed not only comparative linguistics and anthropology, but also Pater Wilhelm Schmidt's *Kulturkreislehre*, as well as research in acoustics, psychology, and physiology. In addition, there are several fundamental essays about the methodology of the newly founded discipline of comparative musicology,[1] as well as papers on musical aesthetics and instruments.[2] His research is characterized by objective scientific methods very similar to those of the comparative linguists Bopp and Schleicher. In fact, as we saw in chapter 1, he frequently refers directly to comparative linguistics as a model for comparative musicology.[3]

Much of his research is still valid today—for instance, the instrument classification he developed together with Curt Sachs. The great exception is his "theory of the blown fifth," which was demolished during his lifetime by his former student Manfred Bukofzer and his friend Jacques Handschin (fig. 2.1), as we will see in chapter 5. He never wrote a comprehensive book, instead presenting his research in numerous essays. There have been excellent studies of his output, so I will concentrate only on a few areas that are particularly relevant to my subject: the origins of music and its relationship to medieval music; his attitude to the orality-literacy relationship and how it shaped his view of Western medieval music; the influence comparative linguistics had on his work; and his view of authenticity.

LIFE

Hornbostel was born on 25 February 1877 in Vienna. His father was a prominent Viennese lawyer and his mother, Helene, née Magnus, an excellent singer.[4] Brahms was a regular guest in the family home. He earned a doctorate

Figure 2.1. Erich Moritz von Hornbostel and Jacques Handschin in front of the Berlin
castle. Courtesy of Allard Pierson, Universiteit van Amsterdam, collectie Jaap Kunst,
foto 164.034.

in chemistry from the University of Vienna in 1899 and then started working at Friedrich Wilhelm University in Berlin, in the Institute of Physical
Chemistry. In 1905 he became an assistant to Carl Stumpf in the Psychological Institute. After a research trip to North America to study the music of
Native Americans in 1906, he took over the Berlin Phonogramm-Archiv. He
remained its director until his forced emigration in 1933 because of his Jewish mother.

Hornbostel was related to the great art historian Aby Warburg:[5] Hornbostel's mother was the aunt of Alice Magnus, the wife of Max Warburg, who

was the younger brother of Aby Warburg. The families were very close; Alice lived with the Hornbostels in Vienna for some time, and there are numerous letters in the Berlin Phonogramm-Archiv from Hornbostel to Max Warburg as well as several letters from Hornbostel to Aby Warburg, now in the Warburg Institute in London. It seems that Hornbostel's decision to give up chemistry and switch to musicology was inspired by Aby Warburg, as he wrote in a long letter to him in 1925.[6] When Hornbostel visited America in 1906 and stayed with the Native Americans, he sent a postcard to Aby Warburg about "the Indians."[7] It is entirely possible that he concentrated on "the Indians" in the first place because his older relative had done so.[8]

He received the title of "Professor" in 1917, even though he had not yet completed a *Habilitationsschrift*. (His *Habilitation*, entitled *Studien zur Form der ostasiatischen Musik*, was completed only in 1923.)[9] During World War I he worked together with his friend the psychologist Max Wertheimer on the physical and psychological basis of sound detectors. Since he came from a well-to-do family, he made a decision to invest much of his personal savings into the Berlin Phonogramm-Archiv.[10] After his emigration in 1933 he taught at the New School for Social Research in New York. But he could not tolerate the climate and moved to Cambridge, England, where he died in November 1935, not yet sixty years old. Among his students were Hans Hickmann, Robert Lachmann, Marius Schneider, Mieczyslaw Kolinski, Georg Herzog, Walter Wiora, Heinrich Husmann, and Manfred Bukofzer. In addition, he was a close friend of the great medievalist Jacques Handschin.

RESEARCH

Like his predecessors in linguistics, Hornbostel sought to collect enormous amount of material, in his case recordings rather than grammars, and search it for "the common factors and the context of musical development in all parts of the world, clarify differences on the basis of particular cultural relationships, and finally, by extrapolation, draw conclusions regarding origins."[11] Hornbostel's efforts to procure recordings were continuous and wideranging. His correspondence in the Berlin Phonogramm-Archiv shows that he followed Humboldt by writing to practically all the major mission societies and colonial administrators in Germany, asking them to identify missionaries who could do the recordings for him. The African linguist Meinhof was particularly helpful in this respect. Hornbostel would send them phonographs, along with instructions, for free, provided they would send back recordings.[12] I have found letters to missionaries from the Herrnhut Mission (Traugott Bachmann), the Leipzig Mission (Bruno Gutmann; the recordings

were eventually made by Elisabeth Seesemann), and the Missionsbenediktiner (Meinulf Küsters). In his article "African Negro Music" (1928) he
identifies missionaries as the main source of his recordings.[13] Note, however, that Hornbostel's article also had a major impact on a number of missionaries to whom he did not write, in particular Franz Ferdinand Rietzsch
(see chap. 10).

Hornbostel set his research agenda by following the example of his
mentor Carl Stumpf, author of the important article "Lieder der Bellakula-
Indianer" (1886) and of a monograph on the origins of music entitled *Die
Anfänge der Musik*.[14] Stumpf had already suggested that one could find useful information concerning music's origins by studying the music of "less
cultivated people":

> That the study of the melodies of less cultivated people allows us to get
> valuable information for research of music history is generally recog-
> nized by scholars of this discipline. In addition, psychological-aesthetic
> research can also be of advantage for investigation because the basis of
> the feeling for music cannot be separated from its historical develop-
> ment. Also, the juxtaposition of their music with ours increases the un-
> derstanding of agents common to both and thus helps analysis. These
> studies will gradually also gain anthropological importance, in addition to
> the music-theoretical one, by showing identifying markers for relationships
> or contact between now-separated tribes.[15]

Even though Hornbostel followed his mentor's agenda, he was nevertheless fully aware that music of "less cultivated people" also had a historical dimension and that it could have changed through the centuries.
In his influential study "Melodie und Skala" (1913), he reasoned that although many had tried to understand the musical system of classical antiquity by studying the music in written traditions of "cultural nations"
(*Kulturvölker*), one also has to realize that the music of these people has undergone transformations over the years. Instead, he recommended the study
of "culturally poor" (*kulturarme*) people:

> One is therefore justified, in following the cultural history of anthropol-
> ogy, even when one does not want to think of culturally poor people as
> born late and without history, who are only now starting to repeat this
> development; one should rather think of them as having been separated
> early, as a people who have multiplied their original property through

their isolation in a slow and one-sided way, and have given up less of the old while even less of the new came from the outside.[16]

In other words, there is a common ancestry, but "cultural nations" have developed longer and further than "primitive cultures."

Hornbostel's search for the origins of music was frequently combined with references to ancient music theory and medieval music. Just as the linguists concentrated particularly on Greek as the oldest Indo-European language transmitted in writing, Hornbostel and his colleagues and students were particularly interested in medieval music, the oldest notated musical repertoire. There were an extraordinary number of distinguished medievalists among his students and collaborators (Schneider, Husmann, Bukofzer, and Handschin), and even those who were not medievalists by training often showed an excellent grasp of medieval studies.

Hornbostel drew parallels between music of the "less developed peoples" and European medieval music throughout his entire output.[17] Five different parallels can be distinguished: first, and most important, Hornbostel believed that both exotic and medieval music are primarily melodic, while later Western music is harmonic. As a result, bringing us to the second point, he and many other scholars tried to apply concepts from medieval church modes to non-Western music. Hornbostel, unlike many who follow him, was more careful than others in applying these concepts and was fully aware of the fact that the scales and tunings of the non-Western peoples vary considerably; he never claimed that all cultures have the same tonal system. Third, he was the first to publish extensively on forms of improvised polyphony, be it in Africa or in Iceland, and he noted a remarkable similarity between these and early medieval polyphony. Fourth, he observed that the most "primitive" people have only two or three note patterns, which then evolve into pentatonicism. Similarly, a number of musicologists, especially in the 1920s, argued that Gregorian chant was originally pentatonic. And fifth, the question of authenticity looms large in Hornbostel's output. Because he was trying to explain the origins of music, he was always trying to find music that demonstrated little influence of later European music; in other words, he wanted what he considered to be the authentic musical language, untouched by the outside world.[18] This is a recurrent theme both in his letters to the missionaries and in his publications. (We find the same concern with authenticity with historical musicologists of part II, especially Friedrich Ludwig, Wilibald Gurlitt, and their students).[19] We shall examine these claims in order.

Claim 1—Melodic versus harmonic music. The main reason Hornbostel drew a comparison between "exotic" music and medieval music is that he believed that both are primarily melodic, while considering Western music after 1600 to be harmonic. In his 1910 article "Über vergleichende akustische und musikpsychologische Untersuchungen" (On Comparative Acoustic and Music-Psychological Investigations), he wrote about the "absolute rule of melody" (*Alleinherrschaft der Melodie*) characteristic of medieval music as well as music in "primitive countries."[20] The most detailed discussion comes in his article "African Negro Music": "In the first place, of course, the general distinctions between native and European music became evident. The main difference is this: our music (since about A.D. 1600) is built on harmony, all other music is pure melody. In fact, it is non-European music that has made us remember what pure melody really is."[21] For Hornbostel, early music was still melodic until roughly 1600, which is one of the main reasons he constantly drew a parallel between chant and medieval polyphony.[22]

Claim 2—Modes. Hornbostel began to make the comparison between African tonal systems and medieval church modes in his 1909 article "Wanyamwezi-Gesänge," where he identified both "church modes" and organal techniques from the Middle Ages in Wanyamwezi music (which will be discussed below).[23] Again, Hornbostel was too good a scholar not to recognize that the concept of scale cannot really be applied to the music of "natural people." Because the music is orally transmitted and improvised, the singers do not have a permanent memory of pitch, and as a result they vary the pitches considerably. In fact, he went so far as to say that we Europeans have to get used to the idea that in "primitive melodies" we can only distinguish between two kinds of motion: by step and by leap.[24] And he gave the example of the major third, which is often heard by non-Europeans as a stepwise interval. This is followed by a cautious description of Wanyamwezi "scales," which can be distinguished from one another similar to the way medieval church modes are distinguished, depending on where the half steps lie.

In "African Negro Music" he explained the difference between a major and minor scale as compared to ecclesiastical modes: "Mode—in the sense in which we speak of the ecclesiastical modes—is vitally different from scale. A scale fixes the relative pitch of the notes, and therefore the intervals, without taking account of their melodic function; a mode, on the contrary, only determines the melodic function of the notes, whereas their relative pitch and the size of the intervals are merely an outcome of that function."[25]

There is also an important but passing reference to church modes in his 1930 article "Phonographierte isländische Zwiegesänge" (Icelandic Polyphony), even though he was not discussing Africa. Thirty of the forty-two pieces that he discussed are in *fa-modus*, that is, Lydian. His modal analysis of the songs is impressive for its time, and on a par with those of chant specialists of his generation.[26] Hornbostel noted that most organa are in the *fa* mode; but he complained in a footnote about "bad definitions of church modes" then in use and the difficulty of assigning a song to one particular mode. This was the first publication Hornbostel sent to his friend Handschin, who completely agreed with Hornbostel that the discussion of church modes needed to be clarified by chant scholars.[27]

Claim 3—Improvisation. This perhaps most important point concerns the origins not simply of music in general, but of polyphony. Was polyphony invented in the medieval West, or did it originate in many areas of the world independently of one another? Hornbostel was one of the first major scholars to devote extensive thought to this issue.[28] Even though his 1909 article is entitled "Über die Mehrstimmigkeit in der aussereuropäischen Musik" (On Polyphony in Non-European Music) he drew parallels to medieval music:[29]

> Only thanks to the phonograph have we managed to get access to truly original material, which allows us to learn how people without notation and under different circumstances of material and mental culture gradually develop polyphony from the simplest beginnings to more complicated forms. The analogies of these forms to those transmitted to us from the early Middle Ages are so striking that we are justified in drawing a parallel between the old European development and the exotic one, in spite of certain differences which result from different melodic traditions. It is now possible to determine the temporary succession of exotic forms of polyphony on the one hand, and to fill in the gaps in the European tradition on the other.[30]

He then outlined the following three stages:

1. He called the first group the *harmonic series*. It consists of parallel fifths and fourths and is frequently encountered in East Africa and also in Indonesia. According to Hornbostel, parallel organum of the fifth and fourth now has to be considered one of the most "primitive" forms of polyphony. As a result, "the early medieval organum can no longer be interpreted as a mistake resulting from an incorrect interpretation of Greek music theory."[31]

2. The second group is called *polyphonic series*, and is older than the harmonic. The bordun is the simplest form, and it is not necessarily instrumental in origin. And it also occurs in "culture nations."

3. He called the third stage *beginnings of harmonic-polyphonic forms*, and it requires that certain dyads are formed intentionally while others are avoided.[32] This technique originates from the bordun and came about because the singers gradually became aware of dissonances and started to avoid them. He concluded:

We have thus reached the highest developed forms of exotic polyphony researched thus far. According to our present knowledge, the development of polyphony with musically illiterate people comes to a stop around the same time when Europe reaches a point at which mensural notation becomes codified, and therefore more creative musicians have access to a memory tool, without which we would not have come further than the musical Middle Ages.[33]

Hornbostel addressed here an important issue, namely the role notation played in the development of Western music, something almost entirely absent in the discussion of Friedrich Ludwig's explanation of early notation (see chap. 7). Only with notation could you clearly work out the rules governing dissonance. Only by writing or visualizing the notes could counterpoint be developed.[34] Note also that he dates the development of written polyphony from the invention of mensural notation, that is, at the earliest, the middle of the thirteenth-century Franconian notation. He must therefore have considered Notre Dame polyphony to have been improvised, which places him very much in opposition to historical musicologists of his and the next two generations, who considered it the first written and worked-out polyphony.[35]

In his 1909 article "Wanyamwezi-Gesänge," Hornbostel discussed the music of a Bantu tribe in the Tabora area. He also identified organal techniques similar to those from the Middle Ages in Wanyamwezi music. (Other places where this kind of singing is found are the Andaman Islands, East India, Sumatra, Japan, and New Guinea.) In a section entitled "Harmonie" he began by summarizing the improvisation techniques of the ninth-century treatise *Musica enchiriadis* (he understood it to be from the tenth century until Handschin corrected him in a letter dated 18 July 1930), which recommends improvisation with parallel octaves, fifths, and fourths, the only difference being that with the Wanyamwezi the main part is below the added voice. Hornbostel's description of the text differs radically from those of historical musicologists. While Hornbostel found that the text describes a common practice and sees it as part of an improvisational technique found all over the world,[36] and especially among the Wanyamwezi, historical musicologists have elevated the text to a high platform as the first to explain the sensational new concept of polyphony. In contrast, Hornbostel would prefer another explanation of the origins of this polyphony, and wonders whether it was already used by the Greeks. Did the Wanyamwezi, who worked as porters, perhaps hear it from the Europeans? He concluded that this is unlikely, because there are people in Togo who have had no contact with Europeans yet who also practice this kind of polyphony.[37]

Hornbostel's 1930 article, "Phonographierte isländische Zwiegesänge," is a particularly impressive comparison of medieval polyphony with living organum practice. The comparative linguist Rasmus Rask, as we have seen, had studied Icelandic (which has much in common with Northern European languages as they were in the Middle Ages) and compared it to other Northern European languages that were derived from Icelandic. As a result he was able to formulate what is now called Grimm's law.[38] So for Hornbostel the idea of comparing Icelandic polyphony to medieval polyphony must have been particularly exciting. It was the first article he sent to Handschin, clearly hoping for input.

The songs have been recorded by Jón Leifs,[39] an Icelandic musician. Hornbostel writes, "Whoever listens to the phonograms, which are analyzed here, will have the impression that what we have here are early medieval songs."[40] Hornbostel noted further that the pieces are very similar to those published by Bjarni Dorsteinsson in 1906–9—in other words, they seem to change little from performance to performance.[41] The *tvisöngvar* are sung at an extremely slow tempo. Hornbostel observed that also the organum in the *Musica enchiriadis* were intended to be performed in *modesta morositate*.[42] There follows a detailed analysis of rhythm, meter, and mode. Next he analyzed the dyads and triads and observes that they are mainly parallel fifths, but also present other intervals that arrive from polyphonic movements of the parts. There are voice crossings that come into existence through the change of the organum voice from top fifth to lower fifth by passing through the unison.

The central question for Hornbostel is where these organa originated. He mentioned again the long-held notion that organal singing came to Iceland through the Church, but he thinks that belief can now be proven wrong thanks to the research of comparative musicologists:

But we know today that singing in parallel fifth is not a particularly complicated affair. Quite the opposite: it is so natural that it is done everywhere and even by the most primitive people, such as, for example, the Andamanese [aboriginal people from the Andaman Islands] or people in Tierra del Fuego. To this we must add another step: we notice the fullness of the fifth sound in comparison to the unison or octave, and it is saved for this very reason for the end as a final effect. Also this discovery was made by the "natural people," the East African negroes [sic]. . . . Since a historical connection to European organum can hardly be made, these cases prove at the very least the possibility of its natural creation from folk song.[43]

Hornbostel concluded that organum originated in secular music (which is probably older than the sacred monody) and referred briefly to Handschin's hypothesis that it might have come from "Joculatores."[44]

Handschin answered in a letter that was finished on 18 July 1930 (the date on the first page is illegible): he now believes that the people of late antiquity knew polyphonic song, even though it was probably primarily instrumental.[45] He added that *Musica enchiriadis* goes back to the ninth century. Finally, he is happy that also Hornbostel finds church modes badly defined and tells him that the tritone does occasionally occur in chant.

In short, Hornbostel's articles assert forcefully that early medieval polyphony used techniques similar to those found all over the world; polyphony was not a uniquely Western phenomenon. Indeed, there are a number of scholars who continue to argue that polyphony was very much part of origins of music.[46] And yet, as Bruno Nettl has shown, after 1950 ethnomusicologists largely lost interest in the subject; Alan Merriam is quoted as telling Nettl, "There's no point in the concern about origins of music, we will never know anyway."[47] Yet, the questions asked and the methods used by Hornbostel could have been used to throw light on early European music, and yet, they were completely ignored by historical musicologists (that is, Ludwig and his students). Only Handschin argued that much of medieval polyphony was improvised (see chapter 5).

Claim 4—Pentatonicism. The idea that in "primitive" societies melodies had only a small range of three to four tones that could then be expanded to pentatonic melodies was first discussed at length by Hornbostel's teacher Stumpf.[48] In his 1913 article "Melodie und Skala," Hornbostel also talked about the music of the Wedda, who only use two or three neighboring notes within the range of no more than a minor third.[49] Hornbostel had already described pentatonic scales in his 1905 article "Die Probleme der

vergleichenden Musikwissenschaft" (p. 89), and, unusually for this generation of scholars, he warned the reader not to consider pentatonic scales necessarily as an earlier evolutionary stage than, say, heptatonic scales. Indeed,
he points out that they often coexist.[50] Among music historians, the most
detailed discussion of pentatonicism in medieval music is found in Herman
Reichenbach's *Formenlehre* (1929), in which he connected pentatonicism to
the church modes. In his analysis of chant he concluded that most of Gregorian chant was originally pentatonic.[51]

Claim 5—Authenticity. like other comparative musicologists of his generation Hornbostel was extremely concerned about finding authentic, original music. In this he is like comparative linguists a hundred years earlier. He
must have expressed the wish to the Missionsbenediktiner Meinulf Küsters,
because the latter wrote to Hornbostel, "I made these recordings wherever
possible in an area that Europeans would visit only briefly. By the way, after
initial shyness the blacks enjoyed the gramophone to such an extent that
they would walk for days from their home just in order to see this instrument
and to speak into it."[52] Hornbostel expressed the need for music untouched
by European influences in many articles,[53] but perhaps most eloquently in
"African Negro Music." The article shows Hornbostel's concern about current missionary practices and can be read as an attempt to keep European
music out of Africa. According to Hornbostel, "No race is so well prepared
for, and so susceptible to, European influence as the Negro. How dangerous
this influence is in music as elsewhere can be judged from present conditions
among the Zulus, who have hardly preserved any African characteristics even
in their melodies. The harmony of thirds and triads necessarily destroys the
faculty for conceiving the melodic tonality, which is based entirely on the
relation of fourths and fifths; and so the large variety of shades represented by
the modes is reduced to nothing."[54]

He was also critical of Islamic influence on African music.[55] Nettl
showed that this view was still prominent in the field throughout the
1950s, while now the discipline is more concerned with the "relationship
of cultures as expressed in music."[56] In fact, Nettl writes, "what Hornbostel
feared—that the world's musics would become an unholy mix—has come
to pass."[57]

Similarly, historical musicologists, in particular those concerned with
performance practice, were—then and for generations to come—concerned
with finding the true, authentic, and earliest version of a piece of music.
The scholar most responsible for developing the tools of manuscript studies
in the early twentieth century was above all Friedrich Ludwig.[58] The quest
for historically correct performances, that is, authenticity, dominated early

music performances until the 1980s at the latest, when scholars began to realize that there is no such thing as a historically correct performance.[59]

In sum, Hornbostel established the field of comparative musicology in a series of highly original articles and set the agenda for future generations. Most of his students essentially just refined and developed his ideas. He was fundamentally influenced by comparative linguists; like them, he tried to apply the strictest scientific methods and wrote the same scientific prose. Like the linguist Schleicher, he believed in evolution (*Kulturkreislehre*),[60] and he looked for parallels between medieval music and "primitive music" (although he never argued that "exotic music" should be studied mainly in order to gather more information on music of the Middle Ages). His views on the improvisation of polyphonic music influenced the next generation of comparative musicologists and were highly relevant to medieval polyphony but seem to have had little influence on Ludwig and his students. As we will see, "African Negro Music" defined the field of African comparative musicology and had a profound influence on numerous missionaries in Africa, in terms of both the music they collected and that which they performed during the religious service.[61]

CHAPTER THREE

Marius Schneider

Marius Schneider (1903–1982) is perhaps the most controversial of the comparative musicologists.[1] He is particularly interesting because he is both a medievalist and a comparative musicologist. For Americans and Israelis who are aware of him, any mention of his name brings up contempt for both the man and the scholar, while among Germans the reaction is mixed: some consider him an imaginative scholar and dedicated teacher, but others find his work deeply flawed.[2] On the one hand, numerous distinguished comparative musicologists, among them his former colleague from Berlin, George Herzog, have accused him of writing under the influence of Nazi ideology and infusing his publications with racial prejudices.[3] Bruno Nettl, a singularly judicious scholar, similarly believed Schneider's publications to be problematic and upon meeting him in person had his poor opinion confirmed.[4] Moreover, the Berlin composer Walter Zimmermann, who had studied ethnomusicology with Schneider in Cologne, was confronted in Jerusalem by the musicologist Ruth Katz, of Hebrew University, who told him about Schneider's racial theories and the fact that Schneider signed his letters to Robert Lachmann with "Heil Hitler." Zimmermann then wrote an entire book on Marius Schneider to see for himself whether his research would show that Katz was right.[5]

On the other hand, Schneider's career did not flourish under the Nazis; in 1944, when he was forty-one years old, he left Germany for Barcelona, where he stayed until 1955. Throughout the Nazi period he cited his Jewish teachers and colleagues in his publications, and he studied mainly music that the Nazis disliked. A deeply religious Catholic, he exhibited courage in professing his faith openly under the Third Reich. Moreover, he left behind a great number of loyal students, who were inspired by him when he became professor of ethnomusicology at the University of Cologne in 1955.[6]

Among them were the Catholic priest Stephan Mbunga and the Bethel missionary Werner Both, each of whom was able to introduce local music in their respective services thanks to Schneider's influence. (See part III, chaps. 12 and 13.) I will begin my evaluation of Schneider by discussing the problematic biographical issues and then turn to the scholarship.

LIFE

Schneider (fig. 3.1) was born in 1903 in Alsace. As a result, he had both French and German citizenship and was fully bilingual. At first he was equally involved with performance and musicology. He studied piano at the Strasbourg Conservatory and musicology and German philology at Friedrich Ludwig's old University of Strasbourg from 1922 to 1924. In 1924 he enrolled at the Conservatoire National de Paris as a student of Alfred Cortot as well as at the Sorbonne as a student of André Pirro. From 1927 on he was in Berlin with Johannes Wolf, Arnold Schering, and Hornbostel.[7] His 1930 dissertation, "Die Ars Nova des 14. Jahrhunderts in Frankreich und Italien" (The Fourteenth-Century Ars Nova in France and Italy) written under the supervision of Johannes Wolf, was published by the *Jugendmusikbewegung* publisher Kallmeyer in 1931. His study *Geschichte der Mehrstimmigkeit* (History of Polyphony), the first volume of which deals with the music of "primitive" peoples and the second with early medieval polyphony, followed in 1934–35.

In 1931 Schneider became an assistant to Hornbostel, who at this point already had serious health problems. Schneider substituted for him in the winter semester of 1931–32 and the summer semester of 1933. Bernhard Bleibinger provides much information on the finances of the Berlin archive, which were in poor shape because the *Demonstrationssammlung* (a collection of recordings demonstrating different musics) did not make as much money as expected.[8] Most of their funds went to supply scholars and missionaries with phonographs (four per year). After Hornbostel's emigration in 1933, Schneider took over the archive, and in 1934 he became the director. The first issue that Schneider had to face was the question of what to do with all of the recordings in the Phonogramm-Archiv, which was then housed in the Hochschule für Musik (HdK; now the Universität der Künste [UdK]).[9] The issue was a thorny one because Hornbostel considered these recordings his personal property; he had, after all, invested much of his personal income in collecting them.[10] Stumpf presented Schneider with two possibilities. The first solution was the one Stumpf preferred, namely, to return the entire collection to Hornbostel. This, however, would mean that the collection would go abroad. The second solution was to add the collec-

Figure 3.1. Marius Schneider.
From Bleibinger, *Marius
Schneider und der Simbolismo,*
393.

tion to the existing *Lautarchiv* at Friedrich Wilhelm University.[11] Schneider
opted for a third solution: to supply Hornbostel with copies made of all the
recordings and transport the originals in 1934 to the Ethnologisches Museum (Ethnological Museum; part of the Staatliche Museen zu Berlin) in
the Dahlem borough of Berlin. He wrote to the HdK director, Fritz Stein, on
19 July 1933 "that this suggestion will, without a doubt, be fair to both parties. Under no circumstances can we consider the possibility of giving the
archive away, since the archive has approximately doubled in size since it
was taken over by the state, and the old collection was mainly paid for with
money from the Simson Foundation and not Hornbostel's private funds."[12]

    In other words, Schneider argued that most recordings came to the ar-
chive after it passed to the state and were not privately financed by Hornbostel. It is clear from the correspondence that Hornbostel had expected to be
able to take the collection with him to New York and had already instructed
collectors to send additional recordings directly to him there. As Bleibinger
points out, had Hornbostel come to the United States with the recordings,

it would have been much easier for him to get a job.[13] So Schneider's decision must have been distressing to Hornbostel, and it is probably one of the reasons that some of Hornbostel's students, such as Ruth Katz's professor, Robert Lachmann, were critical of Schneider.[14]

Possibly the most serious charge against Schneider is that in 1936 he denounced the Polish scholar Marek Kwiek to the Gestapo as a spy.[15] It appears that when he did so, he knew that Kwiek already left Germany eighteen months earlier, so he seems to have been in no danger of arrest. Germans were never suspicious of Kwiek, and he was not persecuted by them after the invasion of Poland in 1939 or, for that matter, by the Communist authorities after 1945. Nevertheless, such an action is morally unacceptable under any circumstances, and it remains unclear why Schneider denounced his colleague.

It is perhaps unsurprising that for the rest of his life Schneider, even though he was viewed with suspicion in postwar Germany and abroad, considered himself a victim of the Nazi regime. This is mainly because his *Habilitation* was rejected by Friedrich Wilhelm University. (He claims that the Nazis deprived him of his *Habilitation* after he received it.) He submitted his *Studien zur Geschichte der Mehrstimmigkeit* in 1934, and after a lengthy deliberation it was denied on 9 September 1936. A letter by the group of professors asked to evaluate his *Habilitation* questions his "national orientation," considers him an opponent of National Socialism, and finds that he would have a deleterious influence on the students because he fundamentally lacks a proper "national orientation" (*völkische Einstellung*).[16] He was particularly criticized for not realizing that polyphony is exclusively "Nordic-Germanic."[17] Nevertheless, Bleibinger shows that Schneider was supported by Heinrich Besseler, who also asked Handschin to make sure that Schneider's *Habilitation* was accepted, even though Handschin thought it was "a terrible book." And, indeed, Handschin waited until 1939 to publish his negative review.[18]

Instead of caving in, Schneider reacted by writing an enthusiastic article on Gregorian chant, which he knew would not go down well with Nazi authorities; throughout it, the reader cannot fail to notice his deep religiosity. As a result, the matter of his *Habilitation* was dropped until after the war. I will discuss the contents of *Geschichte der Mehrstimmigkeit* later but will note here that there are three obvious reasons his *Habilitation* did not find favor with the Nazi faculty at Friedrich Wilhelm University. First, throughout the book he refers to publications by his Jewish colleagues, in particular Hornbostel, but also Curt Sachs and Robert Lachmann; second, he deals with music of "primitive" cultures and strongly suggests that Western polyphony must have once used similar techniques; and third, he was in close contact with Catholic missionaries in Africa, who made many of the recordings that he analyzes.

The next compromising event in Schneider's life was his participation in the Reichsmusiktage in 1938 with a lecture on the Indo-European question. He asks in a letter for funds for his research: "There is no other institute that connects research on music and race as intimately as ours, and therefore fulfills all the cultural issues of Adolf Hitler. . . . After we have now received a large onetime grant to save our old Indo-European collections, the Indo-European question will receive a thorough investigation in the next two years. . . . If we want to help effect a breakthrough of Adolf Hitler's thoughts in every area, the financial assistance must be increased."[19] Despite his letter, Schneider failed to receive funding.

In the following years Schneider, who held the position of research assistant (*wissenschaftlicher Mitarbeiter*), repeatedly applied for a promotion to curator at the Phonogramm-Archiv, but all his requests were denied. His allies were Blume, Besseler, and the ethnomusicologist Kurt Huber. Herbert Gerigk, responsible in the Amt Rosenberg for music, was not supportive and wrote to the Sicherheitshauptamt on 25 October 1939:

> We urgently need an ideological and cultural-political evaluation of the musicologist Marius Schneider. . . . Dr. Schneider is suspected to be strictly Catholic and to also carry forward these tendencies in his scholarly work. It would be useful to find out to what extent this tendency can be documented also in the private life of Schneider, who, according to our sources, is neither a member of the Party nor of any organization. The Phonogramm-Archiv, which is directed by him, is supported by "Christian missions," especially Catholic researchers who travel. One can assume these connections only happened because of Schneider's association with Rome.[20]

Gerigk is certainly wrong about his assumption that Schneider initiated contact with the Catholic missionaries. As we have seen, Hornbostel wrote to both Catholic and Protestant missionaries, including P. Meinulf Küsters.[21]

From 1940 to 1943 Schneider was a member of the Germany's official military intelligence agency (Abwehr des Oberkommandos der Wehrmacht) under Wilhelm Canaris and responsible for radio broadcasts and prisoners of war in North Africa. There is no proof that he took part in any war crimes.[22] Schneider evidently used his time in North Africa for research, and then, when he returned to Berlin in 1943, he applied for the position of curator

at the Institut für Musikforschung. In numerous letters Gerigk accuses
Schneider of being a deeply religious Catholic and of refusing to participate
in anti-Semitic publications; all the letters question his commitment to
National Socialism.[23] The person who denounced him and to whom Gerigk
refers was the French musicologist Guillaume de Van.[24]

When he was denied the job, Schneider moved to Barcelona in early 1944
thanks to an invitation by Higini Anglès. Again, there are a lot of rumors
about why he left Berlin and moved to Barcelona, all of which have been un-
tangled with remarkable perseverance by Bleibinger. Anglès wrote in letters
that he was very happy to have been able to "save him" during the war—an
ambiguous formulation. Was he saved because he was in danger of being ar-
rested? Or was he saved because life in Berlin during the war was dangerous?[25]

In 1947 Schneider started teaching at Barcelona University, and in 1955
he became a professor of ethnomusicology in Cologne thanks to the strong
support of Anglès and Karl Gustav Fellerer.[26] He remained in Cologne until
his retirement in 1968 and died in Munich in 1983.

In short, there are three points that might be held against him. The first
is the fact that he transferred the contents of the Phonogramm-Archiv to
Dahlem and failed to return them to Hornbostel after he emigrated, though
he did supply his colleague with copies. His justification was that he was
convinced that most of the recordings were not purchased by Hornbostel
himself. The second is that he denounced a Polish scholar to the Gestapo.
And the third is that he signed his letters with "Heil Hitler" and tried to
ingratiate himself with the Nazi party in order to further his career.

And yet, we can also conclude that his biography does not show him to
be a committed Nazi. It seems unlikely, for a number of reasons, that he
was ever a collaborator: his article on Gregorian chant, his continuing to
work on African music, his cultivation of African missionaries, and his constantly citing of his Jewish teachers and colleagues, all despite the obvious
disapproval of Nazi authorities. Finally, it is unlikely that Besseler would
have used Schneider as a witness for his defense after the war if there was
any shade of suspicion of Schneider's having been a collaborator.[27]

SCHOLARSHIP

THE ARS NOVA DISSERTATION

Schneider is particularly interesting because he wrote his dissertation on
a historical medieval topic, music of the Italian and French *ars nova*,[28] with
Johannes Wolf (1869–1947), best known for his *Geschichte der Mensuralno-*

tation von 1250–1460, in which many manuscripts were made available in original notation and transcription for the first time.[29] Wolf was an honorary professor at Friedrich Wilhelm University, director of the Early Music Collection, and, from 1917 on, director of the entire music collection of Preussische Staatsbibliothek in Berlin. For us it is particularly noteworthy that he was close to comparative musicologists and was one of the editors of the *Sammelbände für vergleichende Musikwissenschaft*. Wolf also behaved well after 1933, resigning from the Deutsche Gesellschaft für Musikforschung because of Alfred Einstein's dismissal.[30] Schneider's other teachers included the main ordinarius at Friedrich Wilhelm University from 1928, Arnold Schering (1877–1941), Curt Sachs (1881–1959), and especially Hornbostel. His dissertation is very different from the publications of Friedrich Ludwig and his students. While Ludwig's students were very much concerned with musical manuscripts, Schneider was not. Instead, he clearly showed the influence of comparative musicology from the very beginning in two areas. First, he is one of the earliest scholars to espouse and give very detailed support of what Daniel Leech-Wilkinson has called the "Oriental hypothesis."[31] The introduction gives us a good idea of his views: "Only in the 15th century was the culture of the Middle Ages, a crossing of Hellenistic and oriental elements, abandoned in order to create the true European culture. We will see strong Hellenistic and oriental influence in every part of life, in the government, philosophy, literature, and art. In the course of this study we will often refer to the connections to oriental music practice."[32] And second, in contrast to historical musicologists, especially Ludwig and his students, Schneider believed that there was a lot of polyphonic improvisation going on in the fourteenth century, both in Italy and France. While the first point was certainly wrong, it nevertheless continued to exert strong influence on performers after World War II; in contrast, the second was correct and almost entirely ignored.

Leech-Wilkinson argues that the Oriental hypothesis might have originated with Schering and cites a remarkable passage from his 1931 book *Aufführungspraxis alter Musik* in which he suggested improvisatory elements

> both in the treatment of the voice itself (nasal and guttural tone color, falsetto, trembling of the voice, pulling intervals up and down, staccati, etc.) and in the performance (sprinklings of improvised melismas [*flores armonici*], hockets, trills [*reverberations*], appoggiaturas, grace notes, etc.). We rightly accept today that the various ornamentations, loop, and slide notes that neumatic notation knows have been nothing other than attempts of the West to record improvised Oriental singing style in the

form of writing. Their actual performance was assured through the living on of oral tradition.[33]

While Schering had only a few remarks on this topic, Schneider presented a full account of these "Oriental influences." Leech-Wilkinson shows
in fascinating detail how Schneider's hypothesis was realized by early music
performers, especially in the 1950s and '60s. Most groups who performed
medieval music did not play on medieval instruments (instrument makers
had not yet constructed them), but on Renaissance or Arab ones.[34] The British musicologist Thurston Dart talked about instruments that were added
from the "mountains of Sardinia and Sicily" and Catalan bands that had a
medieval flavor.[35] But perhaps the most prominent representative of the Oriental school was Thomas Binkley, with his Studio der frühen Musik, who
taught at the Schola Cantorum in Basel from 1973 to 1977 and educated numerous students in the Oriental style. Today's most famous representative
is Marcel Pérès with his group Ensemble Organum. Leech-Wilkinson has
shown that there is little to prove this hypothesis except "living oral tradition," as quoted by Schering above.

Now to the second point, Schneider's belief that improvisation was common in both French and Italian fourteenth-century music: Schneider argued
that manuscripts of fourteenth-century music indicate only a small part of
what was performed, that much of the music was never notated in the first
place and was orally transmitted. Possibly under Hornbostel's influence,
he came to believe that musicians in "primitive cultures" were similar to
those of the thirteenth and fourteenth centuries.[36] Also, he reasoned, even
those pieces that have been transmitted in writing do not really show how
the music was performed:

> During this period, in which improvisation was in full bloom, the no-
> tated composition was in essence only a scaffolding from which the
> piece was constructed. Sometimes one would add a voice, at other times
> one would leave it out, or one would add hockets where none were no-
> tated. . . . We know with certainty that the addition of borduns was wide-
> spread, yet we do not possess a single manuscript where it was indicated.
> In fact, up to the seventeenth century much of what was performed was
> not notated, as we are used to do today.[37]

Schneider's statement is in complete opposition to Ludwig, whose research concentrated on manuscripts of medieval polyphony in order to find out
where Renaissance polyphony came from. The idea that much of fourteenth-

century polyphony was improvised did not even enter into his picture. Similarly, Schneider added a remarkably modern statement, one that leaves little doubt he was fully aware of the importance that notation played in the development of polyphony: "No one can deny that notational techniques had a major influence on the music itself."[38] Unfortunately—and this remains my central criticism of his research—he never went into any detail regarding this point.

Since 2005, I and a number of other scholars have argued that most of medieval polyphony was essentially improvised, and that only a small portion was written down.[39] We also know that the notated text in manuscripts was not always held in the same reverence with which we treat it today. Schneider was surely right in arguing that voices were added and removed ad libitum. So why did the Oriental hypothesis become so influential, while no one seems to have paid any attention to Schneider's ideas on improvisation? The answer is simple: Schneider was not a good scholar. He gave no evidence whatsoever to support his claims. It is not enough to assert that music was improvised without offering any explanation of how it was done and what kind of training musicians received that made such improvisation possible.[40] His remarks on medieval music theory, in particular compositional process, are superficial and show that he is not in the least interested in understanding fourteenth-century compositional processes:

> The impersonal character of these works [i.e., music theory] also explains the bizarre way in which one deals with compositions. Depending on whether you have instruments or voices available, you add or leave out a part or even improvise an additional part. . . . The medieval musician does not compose his motets as the modern artist does, who can put his genius to work because he has a secure technical knowledge [or ability]. A motet of the *ars nova* is just "put together" [*zurechtgebaut*] in the most primitive sense of the word. We get a clear picture of this through the technique of isorhythm, which can only be understood intellectually and through the treatise by Aegidius de Murino, printed by Coussemaker.[41]

He looked at fourteenth-century composers from a twentieth-century perspective and did not even try to put himself into their shoes. Nor did he seem to be aware of one of the most important counterpoint treatises from the early fourteenth century by Petrus dictus Palma ociosa. Edited by Wolf, it explains in great detail how memorization and composition interacted in the compositional process.[42] For every mensuration sign, Petrus lists music

examples to choose from that were clearly memorized and used by impro-
visers or composers.[43] These formulas are strikingly similar to voice parts
in Vitry motets.

Most remarkable is that he paid no attention to all of the scholarship
done by Ludwig. He lists a number of his articles in the bibliography at the
end but seems not to have digested them. In any case, they had no impact
on his thinking. This avoidance might be connected with a devastating review Ludwig had published of Wolf's *Geschichte der Mensuralnotation* in
1904, but if Schneider had been a serious medievalist, he would not have
ignored Ludwig's work.[44] In short, it is no wonder that other scholars took
no notice of Schneider's remarks on improvisation in fourteenth-century
music.

Geschichte der Mehrstimmigkeit

Schneider's *Geschichte der Mehrstimmigkeit* consists of two volumes: part 1,
Die Naturvölker (The Primitive People), and part 2, *Die Anfänge in Europa*
(The Beginnings in Europe). These encapsulate more extensively than any
other scholarly effort one of the central issues of this book: the belief that
medieval music shared many traits with music in "primitive" cultures.
Schneider concentrated on one particular area, the origins of polyphony, but
in the process also touched on the evolution of the tonal system. The topic
of the origin of polyphony is very much associated with Schneider, even
though he only refined the observations and ideas of his teacher Hornbostel.
Hornbostel's publications were generally treated with respect and admiration (with the exception of the *Blasquintentheorie*), so it is surprising that
few have recognized that the main ideas in Schneider's study are derived
from Hornbostel's article.[45] Originally Schneider had planned a third book
entitled "Von Perotin bis Bach," but, as he explained in the introduction to
the 1969 reprint of *Geschichte der Mehrstimmigkeit*, this manuscript was
lost during the war.[46]

Because the original edition of Schneider's book was burned during the
war, the two volumes were for decades difficult to access; thus, in 1969 the
book was reissued in a new edition, including a new introduction, with
photographic reprints of the first two parts.

Schneider clearly outlined the questions he wants to address in the introduction to volume 1: he was concerned with the origins and early development of polyphony,[47] and he was particularly interested in the relationship of medieval to non-Western polyphony. The tenth-century theorist
Hucbald is mentioned as the first to have discussed organum, but Schneider

stressed that medieval theory and manuscript sources are not helpful in explaining how improvisation happened. He concluded: "The only possibility of exploring the early history (of polyphony) in an indirect way consists in investigating the gradual development of *analogous* recent music forms in the various 'primitive' people."[48]

The main point of his study is to understand medieval polyphony, not to deliver a detailed discussion of *all* "primitive" polyphony. It is striking that his idea lines up neatly with the work of Milman Parry and Albert Lord, who went to Yugoslavia between 1933 and 1935 to study and record oral poetry in order to find out how Greek poetry had been orally transmitted, even though he was clearly not aware of their work.[49]

Schneider acknowledged that his methodology would cause doubt among many scholars: "The fact that the author uses music of primitive people in order to explain the early history of European-medieval music culture will be accepted only with great reluctance by most readers from a methodological point of view. For that reason, I want to stress right at the beginning that I am not looking for any kind of direct cultural-historical relationships between exotic and medieval music circles. That would be a hopeless undertaking."[50] Instead, Schneider wanted to show purely technical parallels between the two practices.

So how did Schneider go about this? He combined the polyphonic techniques described by Hornbostel with stylistic categories from Stumpf. From Hornbostel he borrowed three techniques: harmonic series (i.e., parallel fifths and fourths), polyphonic series (among which is bordun), and "beginnings of harmonic-polyphonic forms" (i.e., intentionally formed dyads); and from Stumpf's *Anfänge der Musik* he took three additional categories: organum, bordun, and heterophony.[51] To these he added a new concept he himself had developed: *Tonalitätskreise* (circles of tonality), which he then associated, following a suggestion made previously by Hornbostel, with stages from *Kulturkreislehre*. Just as for Hornbostel and Stumpf, so too for Schneider these categories are considered stages in the evolution of polyphony, which ultimately ends in functional harmony.

As the quotations above make clear, Schneider was fully aware that no direct relationship between medieval and exotic music could be demonstrated. He also did not believe that one could discover in some people the "original polyphony" and then transfer this to all cultures.[52] His argument is similar to that of Hornbostel: namely, that the techniques that exotic and medieval music share are so striking that, even though they are not derived from each other, performers in both instances "unconsciously" apply the same rules.[53] In other words, he appears remarkably modern in his idea that elements of polyphonic singing could have sprung up independently from one another in different places. Expanding on and renaming what Hornbostel described, Schneider identified four elements in polyphony: melody, variation, tonality, and the relationship of polyphony and harmony. So far, his ideas are uncontroversial. But his next idea, that of *Tonalitätskreise*, met with such resistance from other scholars that he substantially simplified it in the 1969 edition of *Geschichte der Mehrstimmigkeit* and did not mention it at all in his 1961 article on the subject, "Wurzeln und Anfänge der abendländischen Mehrstimmigkeit" (Roots and Beginnings of Western Polyphony), first presented at the IMS Conference that year in New York.

The concept of *Tonalitätskreis* can once again be traced back to Hornbostel, namely to his article "Melodie und Skala," wherein he derives tonal systems from an analysis of the melodies that are generally framed by fourths and fifths.[54] For Schneider, scales have their origin in a central interval, say, F–G, that is combined with fifths and fourths relationships. For example, F–G is combined with the fourth below and above into C–F–G–C; Schneider then derives from the three fifths the three scales: F–C becomes C–D–F–G–A–C; C–G becomes G–A–C–D–E–F–G; and G–D becomes D–E–F–G–A–B–C–D; these then become four circles of tonality.[55] He then combined these three *Tonalitätskreise* with *Kulturkreise* (note that circle 3 is a later version of circle 2, which is why we have three *Tonalitätskreise* and four *Kulturkreise*):

> 1st circle: F–G ("primitive" cultures in South Asia and South America)[56]
> 2nd circle: (D)–F–G–A–C–D ("less primitive people" of Indonesia, Papua New Guinea, and Melanesia)
> 3rd circle: G–A–B–C–D–E–F–G, a later version of the second circle (Samoa)
> 4th circle: C–D–F–G–A–B–C (can be expanded in various ways and occurs in "more advanced" cultures in Africa)

These circles are based on a detailed analysis of the recordings. Thus, for example, music examples in the first circle generally have a small range, sometimes of only two or three notes, with F and G as the central tones.

The second volume deals with medieval polyphony and uses exactly the same concepts. Schneider stressed at the beginning that a direct influence from exotic music seems highly unlikely, but that similar developments occurred independently of one another in different parts of the world.[57] Again, he distinguished between melodies that stress the fourth and are tetrachordal (found in early French and Italian music), and melodies that are pentatonic, stressing the third and fifth (found in early English and northern French music). And, of course, there are mixtures. A third circle comprises St. Martial and blends both types; a fourth group is called "the German circle" (*Der deutsche Kreis*). The last one uses thirds and fifths regularly, and the significance of *Tonalitätskreise* has almost been lost.[58]

In a 1941 article entitled "Kaukasische Parallelen zur mittelalterlichen Mehrstimmigkeit" (Caucasian Parallels to Medieval Polyphony), Schneider argued that medieval polyphony must have derived from Caucasian polyphony: "The diffusion shows that the Middle Ages have adopted here a Caucasian technique. Of course, they did not take it over word for word; this new art form had to be adapted to liturgical needs. Only in this way one can explain the curious fragmentations of a continuous liturgical cantus firmus. . . . This technique was then transferred to existing liturgical melodies."[59] Schneider did not believe that the transfusion came through Byzantium; rather, he thought that it spread through the Balkan countries. Unfortunately, once again Schneider presented little proof of his theory apart from the fact that both use parallel fifths, borduns, diminution of tenors, and the use of similar motifs. Failing to cite evidence, he observed that "such similarities of technical characteristics have thus far not been demonstrated anywhere else."[60] The article concludes with numerous musical examples.[61]

In 1961 Schneider summarized his view on the origins of polyphony once more in an article entitled "Wurzeln und Anfänge der abendländischen Mehrstimmigkeit." He now observed a connection between Indian ragas and medieval *color*,[62] as well as also major influences from Mediterranean polyphony: "In *ars antiqua* the Caucasian elements prevails, in *ars nova* (especially in Italy) the new Mediterranean."[63] Italian *ars nova* is, according to Schneider, imitating Hindu-Persian music. He again concluded the article with numerous music examples, all taken out of context and with very little explanation, which were supposed to prove his point.

Virtually all reviewers rejected his theory of *Tonalitätskreise*. Their criticisms concentrated less on the analysis itself and more on the term *Tonalitätskreis*, which could easily be confused with *Kulturkreis*. For that reason, Handschin suggested replacing *Tonalitätskreis* with *Tonalitäts-System*.[64] As Schneider made clear, he had not originally planned to associate the circles of tonality and culture: "The classification according to specific circles was originally done for purely musical reasons. Afterward, the organization of the material was found to coincide with the classification of the peoples, so that the first circle corresponded to very primitive cultures in South Asia and South America, the second to the Papuan, Melanesian, and primitive Malayan, the third to Samoan, and the fourth to African peoples."[65]

It seems that it was Hornbostel who insisted that *Tonalitätskreise* be matched with *Kulturkreise*.[66] Perhaps Schneider himself realized that the evolutionary thinking associated with *Kulturkreislehre* could no longer be supported, for he toned down the concept and did not even mention it in his later work, concentrating instead on his categories of polyphony.

In general, the main result of his classification into *Tonalitätskreise*, both in exotic and medieval music, is that Schneider believed he could demonstrate a gradual evolution from the pentatonic via the hexatonic to the heptatonic scale. Even though he disagreed in some details with Hugo Riemann, this was very much in line with what Riemann and Oskar Fleischer thought about the evolution of music in the first half of the twentieth century.[67]

Both volumes are arranged the same way: they present analyses followed by an appendix that includes 221 transcriptions in the first volume and 172 in the second, all without text and in modern notation. The transcriptions in the first volume must have been especially useful, because very little was known about exotic music. And yet, they were also misleading, since they were taken completely out of context and forced into our modern Western notational system, which certainly does not work for most African music.[68] Like Humboldt in his language studies, Schneider was careful to note who did the recordings, and three of our missionaries are regularly mentioned here: Traugott Bachmann (from the Herrnhuter Mission; see chap. 10), Elisabeth Seesemann (from the Leipzig Mission; she worked at the request of Bruno Gutmann; see chapter 11), and Meinulf Küsters (from St. Ottilien; see chap. 13). Even though he had argued in his dissertation that he believed that much of fourteenth-century polyphony was improvised, he did not include in *Geschichte der Mehrstimmigkeit* any explanation of how this could have been done.

So how should this study be judged? The central question looming behind the work of Hornbostel and Schneider was whether polyphony was found not only in medieval Europe, but also elsewhere.[69] It cannot be stressed enough that we now do indeed know that similar improvisational techniques appeared independently from one another at various places around the world.[70] So, despite their shortcomings, Hornbostel and Schneider were correct that medieval polyphony existed in a larger cultural context.

The most important point that Schneider has managed to convey is that early medieval polyphony was improvised, as was polyphony among "primitive" people. He expanded substantially on Hornbostel's 1911 article, "Über Mehrstimmigkeit in der außereuropäischen Musik," and transcribed many more examples. The idea that medieval polyphony was improvised must have been both disturbing and laughable to historical musicologists, who tried to put Western polyphony on a pedestal and saw in Leonin and Perotin the direct ancestors of Josquin and Palestrina. The condescending statement by Hans-Heinrich Eggebrecht in the article "Polyphonie" from the 12th edition of the *Riemann Musiklexikon* is indicative: "The common term 'Mehrstimmigkeit,' which is used without any thought—even if there seems to be no other word available—is problematic in describing non-European and ancient sound production, since the latter does not have a simultaneity of several voices as a point of departure."[71]

But even more enlightened reviewers were not kind to the book. While Handschin thought that Schneider's transcriptions of "exotic" music were valuable, because the music was so little known, he did not think the same of the medieval examples, which he considered inaccurate and not clearly marked; he was bothered by the fact that Schneider published only excerpts and never indicated his sources properly.[72] Handschin ended by lamenting that it was unfortunate that the book had not been written "by a real music historian"[73]— quite a remarkable statement considering that Schneider wrote his dissertation in historical musicology with Johannes Wolf and Arnold Schering.

The results of Schneider's study are no longer of interest to either musicologists or ethnomusicologists, for several reasons. To begin with, the issue of *Kulturkreislehre* and the evolutionary principles associated with it that can no longer be supported.[74] Furthermore, in a book on the origins of polyphony one would expect to learn something about improvisational techniques. While Schneider gives many examples, one does not really learn how musicians were trained. Since the early years of the twenty-first century scholars have made tremendous progress in explaining how improvisation was done, both in Africa and in medieval Europe. How has this change in understanding come about? Classicists, especially Milman Parry and Albert Lord, have had a lot to do with it. In their influential study of South Slovenian epic poetry, they tried to discover how poems were improvised, identifying formulas that the poets had memorized. The first, pivotal article by Parry appeared in 1930.[75] Then, in several papers and books published between 1960 and 1980, Jack Goody demonstrated that orality and literacy are not mutually exclusive—quite the contrary: written texts allow one to analyze and memorize in a new way.

Finally, Schneider's assertions—it is hard to call them theories, because they were never theorized—also became irrelevant when literary scholars and historians described methods by which long texts could be memorized word for word through subdivision and classification of the material. It was precisely these techniques that allowed musicians in Africa or in medieval Europe to improvise. Any kind of improvisation, in either written or oral societies, depends on the memorization of formulas. Once one has committed whatever formulas are used to memory, one can either improvise or compose. Paul Berliner has shown this in fascinating detail, first in *The Soul of Mbira* (1978) and later in his 1994 book *Thinking in Jazz: The Infinite Art of Improvisation*.[76] Similarly, Klaus-Peter Brenner's book on harp and xylophone patterns in the Central African Republic shows that formulas and structures are systematically memorized.[77] Exactly the same procedures were used to improvise thirteenth- and fourteenth-century medieval polyphony: the Vatican Organum Treatise shows the same kind of formulas as Notre Dame polyphony,[78] and it is clear that they were memorized by the singers, who would then either improvise or compose organa.[79]

There is one group whom Schneider has continued to influence: missionaries. Having learned from his *Geschichte der Mehrstimmigkeit* that there was a gradual evolution from pentatonicism to hexatonic and heptatonic music, and that Gregorian chant was originally pentatonic, readers of his book in mission stations felt justified in introducing Gregorian chant and polyphony based on pentatonic scales.[80] Two music scholars who studied with him, the missionary Werner Both and the African priest Stephan Mbunga, were encouraged by Schneider to introduce local music that was largely pentatonic (see part III). And what is perhaps most significant, Werner Both probably would not have made his valuable recordings without Schneider's seminars.

MUSIC AND RACE

The most serious allegations against Schneider's scholarship have been made by George Herzog (another former Hornbostel student), Ruth Katz, and Bruno Nettl, all of whom have discussed his use of racial theories during and even after the Nazi period. I turn now to the publications in question.

Schneider's 1937 article, "Ethnologische Musikforschung," summarized his views succinctly: "Musical race criteria can only be found to a limited extent through analysis of the formal structure (that is, scales, succession of intervals, structure of the piece, etc.). These formal elements can be transferred, but the vocal timbre [*Stimmklang*] and the delivery [*Vortragsweise*] seem to be inherited."[81] The first sentence, however charged it appears to us today, actually contradicted popular Nazi lore that melodic structures were tied to races. The prevailing Nazi opinion was that major triads were of Nordic origin.[82] Schneider clearly disagreed with this thesis and rejects Riemann's and Lederer's hypothesis that the major chord was originally Nordic.[83] In most of his publications, he argued instead that there are in fact cultural connections—for example, between hunting songs in different cultures. He did admit to melodic similarities among Indo-European peoples, who are linguistically related. (However, according to Nettl, even Herzog assumed that people who are linguistically related have similar music.[84]) In other words, he did not believe that scales, triads, and musical structures were racially determined because musical elements can easily travel.

Schneider's second sentence is problematic to us today: he believed that sound production and delivery were probably dependent on race.[85] But before concluding that this view stems from racial theories propagated by the Nazis, we should note that this view can be traced back to his teacher, Hornbostel, and was shared by most other comparative musicologists in the 1920s and 1930s.[86] Indeed, it can be traced to comparative anatomists of the nineteenth century and Jacob Grimm.[87] Racism in scholarship predates the arrival of the Nazis.

Schneider gave a lecture on race and music ("Grundsätzliches zur musikalischen Rassenforschung unter besonderer Berücksichtigung der Indogermanenfrage") on 28 May 1938 at the Reichsmusiktag in Düsseldorf. While the presentation is not preserved, Bleibinger has reconstructed it from Friedrich Blume's book *Das Rasseproblem in der Musik* (The Problem of Race in Music), which includes extensive citations from Schneider's paper.[88] Again, he reiterated the views summarized above.

In 1946, while still in Barcelona, Schneider published *A propósito del influjo árabe-Ensayo del etnografía musical de la España medieval*, in which he repeated this racially biased view of sound production. The book attempted to answer the question of Arab influence on Spanish music in the Middle Ages, concentrating especially on Spanish folk music. Schneider was particularly critical of a study written by the Spanish scholar Julián Ribera entitled *La música de las Cantigas* (1922); he believed that Ribera's claims of an Arab influence on European music were tenuous.

The whole matter was brought to the attention of an international readership in 1951, when Herzog wrote a devastating review of the book in *Journal of the American Musicological Society*. Herzog argued that Schneider's book was based on the following three assumptions that concern music in "very simple civilizations" but also apply "beyond this restricted perspective":

(1) the individual singer's own versions of melodies traditionally current in his group are shaped by his *physical constitution*; (2) related to this,

the particular musical style of this group, especially the musical rhythm, is due to its *race* (in the sense of its physical type and ancestry); (3) in contradiction to the latter, the author also states that style and rhythm are due to the general mode of life, such as hunting versus pastoralism.[89]

A central term that Schneider had not used before and that occurs in the article is *cephalic index*, which comes from a theory based on measurements of human skulls. Schneider argued that races with similar cephalic indices can easily appropriate one another's melodies, while people with different cephalic indices can do so only with great difficulty.[90] The cephalic index was first described by the Swedish anatomist Anders Retzius (1796–1860), who distinguished between long-headed, medium-headed, and short-headed groups.[91] The concept made its way into the writings of one of the most important popularizers of racial theories in Nazi Germany, Hans F. K. Günther (1891–1968), whose 1922 *Rassenkunde des deutschen Volkes* (Racial Types of the German People; Hitler owned four different editions) was extremely influential.[92] Even though scholars thought of Günther as a popular author, he was often cited in scholarly publications. It is not clear whether Schneider read Günther, but there is little doubt that cephalic index was a concept known to most scholars in Nazi Germany.

Let us try to untangle the issues of vocal timbre (*Stimmklang*), manner of singing (*Vortragsweise*), and cephalic index. Most comparative musicologists, especially those in Vienna, thought about voice quality in racial terms.[93] The Viennese comparative musicologist Richard Wallaschek (1860–1917) wrote in 1903 that "the difference between people with and without harmonic music . . . is not a difference of development, but of race."[94] Similar statements were made by Robert Lach (1901–1971).[95] As mentioned earlier, even Hornbostel believed that the manner of singing was possibly hereditary. In one of his last articles, "Fuegian Songs,"[96] written in Cambridge, England, in 1936, he writes: "The most conspicuous factor contributing to the character of Indian music is the *manner of singing*. It will be readily apprehended when hearing Indian singers (or records); but it is almost impossible to analyze the immediate impression and to convey to someone else a clear notion by enumerating its 'elements.' Bearing this in mind, we may describe Indian singing by such epithets as emphatic, pathetic, impressive, grave, solemn, dignified, weighty, stern, etc."[97] A little later he comments in a footnote on the difference between the Yahgan and the Ona Indians: "Physically the Yahgan are clearly different from the Ona. There is no space here to discuss the problem whether the manner of singing is a hereditary physical character, as the voice quality and the general motor behavior undoubtedly are, or a mere traditional custom."[98] Hornbostel never mentioned the cephalic index, but he did believe it possible that the manner of singing was affected by race.

Where did comparative musicologists get the notion that vocal timbre (*Stimmklang*) might depend on racial characteristics? That comparative musicology was modeled on comparative linguistics and comparative anatomy is significant. The main professor of anatomy at Friedrich Wilhelm University in Berlin was Johannes Müller, whose *Handbook of Human Physiology* (1834–40) was the leading textbook in nineteenth-century Germany. Jacob Grimm knew Müller personally.[99] Müller dissected human and bird cadavers in order to study how they produced their sounds. We can draw a direct line from Müller to Hornbostel, who was similarly interested in the production of sounds in birds. As a result of Müller's research, Grimm wondered whether speech sounds were not related to race: "To ask a still stronger question, would the anatomist succeed in exhibiting pertinent external traces in the speech organs of those people who used decidedly harsh gutturals, or who have, like the Slavs, used strong sibilant combinations?"[100] In short, it is no wonder that comparative musicologists considered it possible that sound quality was related to race; Schneider was in the good company of his teacher and colleagues who were not Nazis.[101] Hornbostel's close friend Jaap Kunst cites a long list of comparative musicologists for whom "race is characterized by its style of interpretation."[102]

Nevertheless, it is understandable that after the war Herzog associated racial theories with Nazi ideology. There were numerous party members whose area of research became *Musikbiologie*. Wilhelm Heinitz, who was an important influence on the Moravian missionary Franz Rietzsch, is a well-known example (see chap. 10).[103]

Herzog delivered a magisterial rebuttal of what he considered Schneider's racist theories in his review citing Franz Boas's important study of cephalic index. Between 1910 and 1912, Boas undertook a study of immigrant children in New York in which he found that the immigrants' cephalic indices differed considerably from those of their children, concluding from this that race had little to do with the cephalic index. The study, first published as an article in 1912,[104] was also included in Boas's book *The Mind of Primitive Man* (1911; rev. ed., 1938). Of course, Schneider should have read the study, but, as we know from his other work, he tended not to read English-language secondary literature. The study might not have been easily available in Germany or Spain after 1933.

Herzog tried to separate Schneider from the first generation of comparative musicologists, arguing that Schneider came to do shoddy scholarship
as a result of Nazi ideology:

> Dr. Schneider is one of the few men trained in the excellent German
> school of comparative musicology established by Carl Stumpf, E. M. von
> Hornbostel, and Curt Sachs. We are indebted to him for a number of ex-
> cellent studies which he published before the war. However, the works
> reviewed here reveal all too clearly the effects of prolonged exposure to
> a mode of thinking in which, because of political expediency, concepts
> are ill-defined and terminology becomes fuzzy; where hypotheses are
> treated as established truths, but evidence or proof are treated as negli-
> gible. No lasting intellectual structure can be built on such quicksand.
> Now that some years have passed since Germany's intellectual isola-
> tion, it is much to be hoped that Dr. Schneider's writings will reflect
> once more that tradition of lucid scientific endeavor which was choked
> off in Germany of 1935.[105]

Under the influence of the horrors of Nazi Germany, Herzog seems to have
forgotten that Hornbostel and his colleagues also thought it was possible
that sound production could be influenced by hereditary factors. And yet,
undeniably, Herzog has a point. It was one thing to be a racist in 1908,
another in 1938, and yet another in 1946. A thoughtful man would have
noticed by 1946 what these racial categories imply.

When trying to assess his scholarship, one is struck by how deeply he
was influenced by Hornbostel. Most of his theories can be traced directly
back to his teacher, whom he never fails to cite. Even his most controversial
hypotheses, the relationship of the *Kulturkreislehre* and *Tonalitätskreise*,
as well as his ideas on voice quality, can be traced back directly to Hornbostel. In assessing his scholarship, we can conclude that his thinking,
rather than intellectually deviant, was a predictable or at least understandable working-out of the thinking of others in his field. Most important, he
lacked the moral sense to understand that with the Nazis' rise to power, the
racially motivated theories so prevalent in comparative musicology up till
then could no longer be supported.

CHAPTER FOUR

Georg Schünemann

More than any other scholar, Georg Schünemann (1884–1945; fig. 4.1) epitomizes the close relationship between historical musicology, comparative musicology, medieval music, and *Jugendmusikbewegung*; he published significant works in all four areas. Moreover, he was an important academic administrator who was instrumental in the 1920s in transforming Germany's into one of the world's premiere music education systems.

Figure 4.1. Georg Schünemann (*center*) recording prisoners of war (1915–18), Carl Stumpf (*right*) in Frankfurt an der Oder. Courtesy of Berlin Phonogramm-Archiv.

LIFE

A native of Berlin, Schünemann spent his entire life there, even though in 1920 he was offered a professorship at Heidelberg University.[1] His dissertation, "Zur Geschichte des Taktschlagens und der Textbehandlung in der Mensuralmusik" (A History of Beating the *tactus* and Treatment of Text in Mensural Music [1908]), supervised by Hermann Kretzschmar and Johannes Wolf, treated a difficult topic.[2] From 1906 he was the assistant in Carl Stumpf's Psychological Institute, which exposed him to the work done in the Berlin Phonogramm-Archiv. During World War I he was asked to make recordings of prisoners of war, which resulted in his *Habilitation* on the music of the German settlers in Russia, published in 1923.[3]

In 1920 he became the first vice rector, and in 1932 the rector, of the Berlin Musikhochschule, a position he held until 1933. During his tenure he was a close collaborator of Leo Kestenberg, a leader of the *Jugendmusikbewegung*, who was in charge of cultural politics in Germany in the Weimar years. Schünemann helped him institute an academic program for German schools.[4] As a result, German music teachers were placed on an equal footing with teachers of academic subjects, and all German children got a grounding not only in singing, but in music theory and history.[5]

Throughout his career Schünemann always stressed the importance of early music (he was by all accounts a good flutist). The Berlin Musikhochschule had an excellent early music program, with regular concerts of medieval and Renaissance music, both vocal and instrumental.[6]

Students at the Berlin Musikhochschule were regularly exposed to non-Western music as a result of Schünemann's interest in the subject. For example, Schünemann wrote a letter on 15 October 1929 to the Phonogramm-Archiv (still located in the Stadtschloss in the center of Berlin, even though it had been attached to the Musikhochschule since 1922) in which he asks for someone to talk to choral conductors about polyphony and tonal systems from Java, Burma, the Wanyamwezi, Russia, and Mingrelia (a part of Georgia).[7] He regularly scheduled concerts of Indian music (1925),[8] Turkish music (1926), and Javanese music and dance (1935).[9] Then he invited lecturers, including Pichu Sambamoorthy, a professor of Indian music in Madras, to speak about South Indian music (1931),[10] and he asked the Polish scholar Stefan Lubienski to lecture on Japanese music (1926).[11] I suspect strongly that only a few of these programs were saved and that there must have been many more such events.

The Berlin Musikhochschule was probably the top music conservatory in Germany, a school where the composers Ernst Krenek, Paul Hindemith, and Franz Schreker taught (Arnold Schoenberg and Hans Pfitzner gave master classes in the Prussian Academy of Arts), as well as the pianists Artur Schnabel, Egon Petri, and Edwin Fischer, the cellist Emanuel Feuermann, the conductor Fritz Busch, and the violinists Carl Flesch, Max Rostal, and Georg Kulenkampff. George Szell and Alois Hába were also students there.[12] I know of no other conservatory at the time where students and teachers were exposed to non-Western music to this extent. One cannot help but wonder what impact these concerts and lectures had on the students.[13]

After Hitler's election to power in 1933, Schünemann followed the orders to terminate all Jewish faculty, an action some of his Jewish colleagues (Kestenberg, for example) understandably found unforgivable.[14] At the same time, Schünemann himself was viewed with suspicion by the Nazis for his association with socialists and Jews and was fired a few months later. But lacking both strength of character and opportunity to leave the country or resist the regime, he joined the NSDAP, a move that allowed him to continue to be employed in important positions: first as director of the musical instrument collection, and from 1935 on as director of the music division of the Prussian State Library. During the war he also worked for the infamous department known as Amt Rosenberg, named after the chief Nazi ideologue Alfred Rosenberg.[15] This office supervised cultural politics and organized the systematic plunder of art as well as music manuscripts and musical instruments throughout occupied Europe. Schünemann died at age sixty-one in 1945, shortly before the end of the war.

SCHOLARSHIP

Schünemann's dissertation, published in 1908, is among the first studies of the recurring beat in mensural music, variably called *mensura, tactus,* or *battuta*.[16] It is a much more serious scholarly study than anything by Schneider. Schünemann had read and summarized all known theorists between 1300 and 1600 and arrived at clear recommendations as to how the changes of mensuration and proportion signs in medieval and Renaissance polyphony should be performed.[17] There are numerous transcriptions of pieces by composers such as Dunstaple and Josquin, who were at this point little known. He recommends substituting bar lines with small lines at the top of the staff and discusses in detail the text underlay found in the sources. This scholarly background is relevant to his later advocacy of early music at the Berlin Musikhochschule and his interest in relating it to non-Western music in his later publications.

Schünemann's *Habilitation* on the music of German colonists in Russia (who were prisoners of war in World War I) constitutes one of the first major studies in comparative musicology.[18] The idea for recording prisoners of war came from the English teacher Wilhelm Doegen, who came up with the plan to collect recordings of their various languages and dialects.[19] In 1915 Carl Stumpf took over as director of the Prussian Royal Phonographic Commission, a committee that included specialists in anthropology, music, and oriental studies, as well as in English, Romance, Indian, and African languages and comparative linguistics. The following year Schünemann became the director—without salary, but with the advantage that he did not have to serve at the front. Altogether he recorded 1030 phonograms, of which some were transferred to recording.

Hornbostel repeatedly called attention to the fact that comparative musicology was modeled on comparative linguistics. We have seen that the Danish linguist Rasmus Rask was able to arrive at what was later called Grimm's law by comparing Icelandic to other northern Germanic languages. The prisoner-of-war recordings of German colonists presented the exhilarating possibility of studying German songs as they were sung in the eighteenth and early nineteenth centuries: German settlers had emigrated to Russia between 1760 and around 1820 and had lived in German colonies—that is, in areas offering limited contact with their Russian neighbors. The central question would have been: could one perhaps arrive at similar rules in music as in linguistics?

Schünemann transcribed all of the recordings himself (with some help from Adolf Lane, who had lived in the Russian colonies for years).[20] A comparison of the same songs sung by different colonists resulted in his not-altogether-surprising conclusion that there are strong differences between settlers in different areas. Schünemann always attempted to search for influences of the local Russian music with the ultimate goal of deriving laws similar to those established by the linguists, an enterprise that proved unsuccessful.[21] For Schünemann, the most interesting recordings were from Germans living in southern Russia, Siberia, and St. Petersburg:

> They have preserved their original German culture and have for the most part not been threatened by industry and metropolitan culture in their way of life. Many of them, such as the Volga settlers, were practically closed off from any contact with their home country. They still speak their old dialect and sing their old German songs, which they have transmitted from generation to generation. The song makes them remember their old home and their own history, it is their everlasting possession, which has endured one and a half centuries and is preserved by all and

learned anew even today, in spite of the Russian surroundings and influences. We have to thank these colonists from the Volga, from southern Russia, from Siberia and the settlements close to St. Petersburg for this collection. It includes folk songs, art songs, religious songs, and songs of the Moravian Brethren.[22]

Schünemann not only listed melodic and rhythmic variants, but also described modifications of tonal systems. Particularly noteworthy is a chapter on delivery, where he observes such strong Russian elements that at first he thought the melodies were Russian.[23] He ends his study with the caution that further research is needed in order to arrive at laws concerning the variations encountered, a point also echoed by Stumpf in his otherwise excellent evaluation of the *Habilitation*.[24]

His dissertation and *Habilitation* allowed him to write his important 1920 article, "Über die Beziehungen der vergleichenden Musikwissenschaft zur Musikgeschichte" (On the Relationship of Comparative Musicology to Music History), in which he advocates the study of non-Western music to fill in the gaps of knowledge regarding ancient and medieval music.[25] His main point is familiar to us, but it cannot be stressed enough that he was one of the first scholars to make it:[26]

Instead of accounts based on myths, we can now use the results from comparative musicology. If we want to investigate the problems of Greek and medieval music and if the relationship between art and folk music is not to be based entirely on speculation, this is the only way to go. It is not necessary to place the music of uncivilized people as well as the art of Asian culture people [*Kulturvölker*], which we can now study thanks to phonogram recordings, on an equal footing with our music. Instead, we can see them as precursors of our musical development. And with systematic summaries of separate studies, it will be possible to create a foundation for the beginnings of music history that derives from a music that is alive and practiced rather than from descriptions based on laborious and unreliable constructions.[27]

According to Schünemann, there are numerous analogies and agreements between the musics of indigenous people and Western music that had thus far been more or less ignored by music historians. He is quite open about the fact that his interest in non-Western music is purely historical, and that studying the music of indigenous cultures does not mean that their music is of equal value; rather, he believes, like Schneider, that results from comparative musicology can help us reconstruct our own music history.

Schünemann's article epitomizes much of the research of the first twenty years of comparative musicology. For example, he draws a comparison between the chromatic tones in Arab music and Gregorian chant, which he believes might have also used these inflections.[28] Concerning notation, he cites Hucbald's concern about the lack of an unambiguous notational system and makes a comparison with Chinese music, which, however, gives only the general outline, not the details, of the pieces.[29] Most interesting are his remarks about folk song and polyphony: concerning the former, his position contrasts with that of historical musicologists, who try to find the true and original version of a melody (as we will see in part II). Probably as a result of his study of the German folk songs of prisoners of war, he writes: "If you really want to find creative and original elements for melodic variations in various notated versions to this day, you can look at the folk song in German areas. It is really the same creative moment that is at work with indigenous people when they constantly create new variations."[30] In other words, he does not believe it is meaningful to search for the one authentic version. Folk songs are, rather, about demonstrating one's creativity.

He is similarly progressive with regard to polyphony. While historical musicologists will generally write that polyphony was "invented" by the theorist who wrote *Musica enchiriadis*, and Ludwig simply assumed that Notre Dame polyphony was transmitted in writing, Schünemann writes that "polyphony is as old as music itself" and summarizes research done by Hornbostel.[31] He was one of the first scholars to call attention to Georgian polyphony, which he relates to medieval polyphony. It is likely that he heard the music, especially Migrelian polyphony, when he made the prisoner-of-war recordings.[32]

Schünemann had always planned to do more research in comparative musicology, but his administrative career left him no time. Yet, even these few publications show that he was an imaginative scholar in historical and comparative musicology, bringing them together in original ways. It is unfortunate that none of the historical musicologists to be discussed in part II (Friedrich Ludwig, Heinrich Besseler, Konrad Ameln) paid much attention to his publications. If Ludwig had read Schünemann, he would not have insisted on authentic versions of Notre Dame polyphony and Ameln would not have been so concerned to find the one "correct" version of Lutheran chorales. They would have been less obsessed with authenticity and paid more attention to the processes of creation and transmission of the music they studied.

CHAPTER FIVE

Two Crossover Musicologists:
Jacques Handschin and Manfred Bukofzer

In July 1928 the forty-three-year-old Jacques Handschin (1886–1955) wrote to Hornbostel, nine years older, asking if he could buy phonograms for Basel University's Department of Musicology. The recordings were duly sent, and Handschin and Hornbostel started to send each other scholarly articles; eventually a close friendship developed. Even though Handschin was not yet a professor, he was known as a rising star in medieval musicology, with a particular specialty in medieval polyphony (see again fig. 2.1).

Manfred Bukofzer (1910–1955; fig. 5.1) was a student of both Hornbostel and Handschin and studied both historical and comparative musicology in the early 1930s in Berlin. Today most musicologists only know of Bukofzer and Handschin as scholars of medieval music.[1] Yet their influence on the field of comparative musicology was perhaps even more consequential, because, more than any other scholars of their generation, they are responsible for undermining it.

LIVES

Jacques Handschin was born in Moscow of Swiss parents. Against his parents' wishes, he became a virtuoso organist and then a professor of organ at the St. Petersburg conservatory. After the revolution the political situation became untenable, so Handschin emigrated to Switzerland in 1921. He continued to work as an organist throughout his life, but his main interest became musicology.[2] He never enrolled in any university or attended lectures and was largely self-taught.[3] Both his dissertation and his *Habilitation* deal with early medieval polyphony. It is because of his early reputation as a medievalist that Hornbostel was particularly interested in getting Handschin's reactions to his publications on Icelandic and non-Western polyphony. In

Figure 5.1. Manfred Bukofzer.
Courtesy of Jean Gray Hargrove
Music Library, University of
California, Berkeley.

1935 Handschin became the main musicology professor in Basel, where he stayed until his death.

Manfred Bukofzer studied with the most important German historical and comparative musicologists in the 1920s and 1930s: first with Heinrich Besseler in Heidelberg (1928–30), then at Friedrich Wilhelm University with Arnold Schering, Friedrich Blume, Johannes Wolf, Curt Sachs, as well as with Hornbostel (1930–33). In addition, he studied composition with Paul Hindemith and piano and conducting at the Berlin Musikhochschule, which gave him a good background for directing his Collegium Musicum in Berkeley later on. During his Berlin years he also sang in choirs of politically engaged socialists,[4] like so many of his generation. As we will see in part II, these large choirs were established all over Germany; they were formed in churches, factories, youth groups, and student organizations and are all about participatory music making. This all puts him squarely into the company of the *Jugendmusik-* and *Singbewegung*.

In 1933 the Jewish Bukofzer fled Germany. Besseler, who had recognized his talent early on, made sure that Handschin would accept him as a doctoral student at Basel, where he finished his dissertation, entitled "Geschichte des englischen Diskants und des fauxbourdon nach den theoretischen Quellen" (A History of English Discant and Fauxbourdon According to the Theoretical Sources) under Handschin's supervision in 1936.[5]

The next years saw him as a visiting lecturer at Oxford, Cambridge, and the Warburg Institute in London, until his emigration to the United States in 1939.[6] He first taught at Case Western Reserve University in Cleveland, then, from 1941 on, at the University of California, Berkeley. He was considered a rising star and had guest professorships at the University of Chicago, the University of Southern California, and the University of Washington, as well as an offer from Harvard, which he turned down. He died of multiple myeloma at the age of only forty-five in 1955, the same year that his old teacher Handschin died.

THE ATTRACTION OF COMPARATIVE MUSICOLOGY FOR HANDSCHIN AND BUKOFZER

Handschin's relationship to comparative musicology is complicated. The ideas he shared with his Berlin friend and colleague Hornbostel established his early interest. During his Russian years he read every available musicological publication on non-Western music and often wrote about them.[7] There were many interesting ethnomusicologists active in Russia during the nineteenth and early twentieth centuries.[8] Russian composers in the St. Petersburg Conservatory, many of them friends of Handschin, were very interested in folk-song collections. So it is no wonder that he approached Hornbostel, the preeminent scholar of comparative musicology, who used the strictest scholarly methods to investigate non-European music.

Handschin's interest in comparative musicology first manifested itself as a deep interest in theories about orality and literacy. In contrast to the more doctrinaire views of most historical musicologists of his generation, he did not believe that notated music was necessarily better than orally transmitted music.[9] Handschin is among very few historical musicologists who do not have the slightest doubt that medieval polyphony was mostly improvised, a point of view that has only found acceptance in recent years. He places the beginning of polyphony not with *Musica enchiriadis*, nor even Notre Dame polyphony, but at the latest with the early Christian Church:[10] "We have to imagine that polyphony was a matter given over to the singers, that is, performance practice. The voice added to the given melody was sel-dom notated; for the most part it was improvised by the singers who only had the melody in front of their eyes."[11]

Bukofzer was similarly open to ideas of comparative musicology. The topic of his dissertation, which examined theoretical sources from England and the Continent, had essentially to do with improvisational techniques. He translated and analyzed all fifteenth-century sight treatises and concluded that English descant was largely improvised.[12] Moreover, he argued that this style is different from Continental fauxbourdon practice. His work kept the next generation of scholars busy with fifteenth-century English music.[13] Pre-cisely because he read all medieval theorists carefully (unlike Schneider), he was able to speak with authority about parallels to non-Western music. Thus, he writes in a 1940 article entitled "Popular Polyphony in the Middle Ages" that the third does *not* occur naturally in early polyphony, while parallel fifths and fourths are much more popular, both in medieval theory and in Icelandic *tvisöngvar* and non-Western music. He concludes, however, that medieval canons are different from non-Western polyphony in that they con-sciously work out the imitation, very likely in writing.

THE UNDERMINING OF COMPARATIVE MUSICOLOGY

After a period of initial attraction, Handschin contributed in a major way to the demise of comparative musicology, a fact that is perhaps not fully realized by ethnomusicologists. We can begin with Hornbostel's "theory of blown fifths." Hornbostel believed that this theory was his most important contribution to musicology. Let me quote from Hornbostel's earliest ex-planation of the theory, published in a 1919 article by P. G. Schmidt in the journal *Anthropos*:

The Northwest Brazilian panpipes allow you to derive a particular sys-tem of tuning: one takes a pipe in such a way that the first overblown tone (a twelfth) agrees with the fundamental of the model pipe. Then you continue in this way, bringing new tones into other octaves, and where necessary possibly doubling the octave. The overblown tone is not the pure fifth, but for physical reasons a slightly lower fifth (twelfth) of the fundamental. The lowering of the fifth is dependent on the width of the pipe and also on other accidental (botanical) factors. This lower-ing is so small that it can be more or less ignored. As a result, we get a theoretical system of a descending circle of slightly smaller fifths, the overblown-fifth circle. If you complete the circle of fifths of 678 cents

(= one-hundredth of a tempered halftone, the pure fifth = 702 cents), then you reach your starting tone after 23 steps: 678 × 23 = 15.594; 1200 × 13 = 15.600 = 13 octaves; difference = 6 cents = ¼ Pythagorean comma, so unnoticeable.)[14]

Or, to put it differently, he derived a circle of blown fifths, all smaller (678 cents) than the pure fifth (702 cents), from overblowing a stopped bamboo pipe. The second tone derived from the first overblown fifth, is in turn over-blown, and results in the third, and so on.

Hornbostel believed the circle of blown fifths and the pitch system as-sociated with it to be universal.[15] In this article he argued that he does not think that the system originated either in Brazil or in the Solomon Islands, but was used by the ancient Chinese. He associates it further with Indone-sia, Thailand, Japan, the Arab countries, and Africa.[16] He even suggests this tuning system for the ancient Greek aulos. The theory was taken up with great enthusiasm all over the world precisely because it was thought to be applicable to many music cultures.

In 1935 Bukofzer tried unsuccessfully to reproduce Hornbostel's mea-surements with much better equipment. He concluded that Hornbostel must have made a mistake and that the overblown fifth was not a constant size, but variable. It is ironic that Hornbostel, of all people, a scholar known for his strict scientific methods, would have made such a fundamental mistake when measuring acoustic pitches.

Handschin and Bukofzer contradict each other as to how it happened that Bukofzer discovered Hornbostel's mistake. Handschin writes in *Der Toncharakter*:

> Since I was close to this researcher [Hornbostel] (who died much too early) and I admired him in many ways, I found it hard to doubt his fa-vorite theory of overblown fifths. And nevertheless, the muddle of his ex-planation, in which facts and attempts at explanation were not clearly separated, . . . all of this had to give me doubts. Thus, I asked a colleague in my department, Dr. M. Bukofzer, to investigate the acoustic claims from which this theory originates: the overblown fifth of covered pipes (after the octave has been removed) is diminished and measures approxi-mately 678 cents (instead of 702). The experiment, which was executed in the Department of Physics at the University of Basel, leads to a nega-tive result: the variety of acoustical results was so enormous that one cannot talk about a constant lowering of the fifth or even a lowering by 24 cents.[17]

Throughout his publications Handschin is one of the first scholars to criticize the idea of "absolute pitch," both in the Middle Ages and in non-European countries.[18] He writes in *Der Toncharakter*: 'Thus one could call Hornbostel's theory really "the zenith of his craze for absolute pitch."' And a little later he continues, "The greatest weakness [of the theory] is its highly speculative character. From an old high culture, it asks, unrealistically, for improbable wonderworks of fine tuning, which cannot even be delivered with our technical tools with precision, and which can only be executed through calculation."[19]

Bukofzer's report on how he discovered Hornbostel's mistake is different from Handschin's. He writes in his article "Blasquinte" in *Musik in Geschichte und Gegenwart* that he originally shared the worldwide enthusiasm for Hornbostel's theory, which for the first time made it possible to connect tone systems from all over the world with one another.[20] The only reason he did the experiments in the physics department in Basel was that he wanted to apply Hornbostel's theory to panpipes in the South Sea Islands. There is no mention of Handschin's asking him to investigate the matter further. In fact, Bukofzer writes, "The opposing remarks of Handschin on this matter are wrong."[21]

Even though Bukofzer published his first articles on the theory of blown fifths in 1936 and 1937, respectively,[22] Handschin managed to inform Hornbostel about Bukofzer's observations in 1935, shortly before his death on 28 November. Hornbostel's reply is relaxed and not at all unfriendly:

> Oh, you bad man! You constantly visit frivolous Paris and don't come to bourgeois and decent Cambridge! We even have a beautiful manuscript here in the Fitzwilliam Museum (as Sachs just told me—you see, he is visiting) . . . The experiments of your Bukofzer don't unsettle me in the slightest. I know from my own experience that you can get enormous differences when you overblow a pipe. . . . But if you see that the Southeast Asian 7-step scale and its Indonesian ancestor as well as the different slendro scales with their absolute pitch can all be systematically derived from a system of 23 tones (I have just found a probably very old additional scale) then it is impossible to consider the 23-tone system as actually nonexistent, and it seems to me less important whether we take one or another hypothesis for its origin.[23]

Hornbostel was clearly not convinced that Bukofzer had found proof to refuting his theory. And he seems to believe that how the twenty-three-tone system is achieved, whether by overblowing or some other means, is unimportant: the main point is that it exists. Hornbostel had a playful attitude to his theories; he did not take this dispute personally and did not want it to affect his relationship with Handschin.

It took many years for scholars to reach a consensus that Hornbostel's "theory of the blown fifths" could no longer be defended.[24] But Bukofzer's publication made a serious dent in the structural underpinnings of comparative musicology. Jaap Kunst and Heinrich Husmann still tried to defend or modify the theory in the 1960s, but their work was poorly received.[25] Hornbostel and his followers considered the theory of blown fifths to apply universally. They believed that there had been a single point of musical genesis (in this case, musical scales) that then spread from its point of origin (China) all over the world. This was a proof of *Kulturkreislehre*. When the theory was proven wrong, belief in a universal music also took a serious hit.[26] Handschin certainly did not believe in it and repeatedly demonstrated that comparing musical cultures to one another would yield unsatisfactory results.

This brings us to the final and perhaps most important difference between Handschin and comparative musicologists: Handschin is remarkably free of evolutionary thinking, especially in his later publications. His *Musikgeschichte im Überblick* (1948) must be the only music history in which all periods are treated with equal thoroughness.[27] His approach to non-Western music is similarly free of evolutionary thinking, and he warns that we might not like, say, Chinese music simply because we are unfamiliar with it.[28] Remarkably, *Musikgeschichte im Überblick* includes chapters on early Chinese, Japanese, and Arab music.

Handschin believes that one cannot draw conclusions about any one culture by comparing it with another. To give a few examples: Carl Stumpf had used the comparative method in explaining the concept of heterophony in Greek antiquity by comparing it to the Siamese orchestra he recorded in Berlin in 1900. He concluded that heterophony applies in both cases and is nothing but ornamented unison.[29] According to Handschin, the much-admired Stumpf misunderstood what Greek heterophony actually was, arguing that it is not an "ornamented unison" but rather a "consonant dyad with ornamentations."[30]

Handschin is similarly critical of attempts to draw conclusions from the study of "exotic" music about the transmission of Gregorian chant and about medieval polyphony.[31] Concerning the latter, he doesn't even bother to refute Schneider's discussion of parallels between "primitive" and medieval polyphony in his *Geschichte der Mehrstimmigkeit*. Instead, he discusses the more sophisticated parallels the comparative musicologist and

Hornbostel student Robert Lachmann (1892–1939) tried to draw between
orally transmitted music that uses specific symbols to indicate formulas
characteristic of specific scales, on the one hand, and Gregorian chant transmitted by neumes, on the other.[32] Thus, the music of Yemenite Jews is organized according to fifteen melodies, which use melodic formulas that have
since the sixth century been indicated through specific cantillation symbols. Handschin, who considers Lachmann an otherwise reliable researcher,
is dismissive of his suggestion that the cantillation symbols function similarly to the medieval neumes:

> The latter [the use of the cantillation symbols], as I have explained else-
> where, has resulted in the absurd claim made by representatives of mod-
> ern "comparative musicology" that neumes only indicate the melody
> approximately, so that the singers of Saint Gregory only reproduce ap-
> proximately the up and down of the melody, in other words, that they
> had no certainty as to the tones they were singing—while quite the op-
> posite was true, they had to know their tonal system and their scales
> much better than someone who sings according to exact notation.[33]

In short, he would have agreed with Kenneth Levy, who also argued that
singers knew their chant exactly.

Similarly, many comparative musicologists were convinced that pentatonic scales are earlier than heptatonic scales.[34] Handschin dismisses this
notion in *Der Toncharakter*:

> Most believe that pentatonicism is older than heptatonicism because it
> so eminently "plausible," because pentatonicism is simpler and there-
> fore should be the older system, and that heptatonicism grew out of it. I
> really don't see any arguments in favor of this theory, and in particular, I
> don't see any reason for the claim made by gullible musicologists that the
> music of the Babylonians and Sumerians must have been pentatonic.[35]

Handschin then gives many examples where pentatonicism and heptatoni-
cism are found side by side and cannot be so clearly distinguished. He is
convinced that this theory is a result of evolutionary thinking, which he
abhors.[36]

In this chapter, what we have witnessed is nothing less than two eminent historical musicologists paving the way for the demise of comparative musicology. First, Bukofzer showed that Hornbostel's beloved theory
of blown fifths was based on incorrect measurements. Subsequently, Hand-

schin questioned the idea of musical universals. Then, even though he was more interested in non-Western music than any other historical musicologist of his generation—or perhaps precisely because he had these interests—Handschin did not believe in the evolutionary underpinnings of comparative musicology. Thus, any kind of comparison of different cultures was highly suspect to him, and he did not believe that such comparisons could lead to convincing results. We have seen that with the exception of Nicholas Ballanta, who will be discussed in the next chapter, all comparative musicologists believed that medieval music could be understood through comparison with music in "primitive" cultures. Handschin effectively put an end to such research projects. In the end, Handschin, a historical musicologist, in *Musikgeschichte im Überblick* (1948) and *Der Toncharakter* (1948) contributed greatly to the noncomparatist, nonevolutionary, but relativistic modern agenda of ethnomusicology long before Nettl (1964), Alan P. Merriam (1964), or Mantle Hood (1971) wrote their defining books on the field of ethnomusicology, books that marked a clear separation of ethnomusicology from comparative musicology.[37]

CHAPTER SIX

Nicholas G. J. Ballanta

Even though Nicholas Ballanta (1893–1962; fig. 6.1) was a comparative musicologist, he differed from all the others of his generation. He was among a small number of African scholars who described African music in the 1920s.[1] While Hornbostel gave the first description of African music from a Western scholarly perspective, Ballanta tried to do the same from an African point of view. And while Hornbostel's article really set the agenda for African music research for the next decades, Ballanta's publications attracted very little attention.[2] As Tobias Robert Klein has shown in fascinating detail, Ballanta anticipated many of the findings of Hornbostel's 1928 article, as well as those of Gerhard Kubik and Simha Arom in the 1960s and 1970s. Ballanta's book, "The Aesthetics of African Music," went unpublished for a number of reasons,[3] the main one being a devastating review of the manuscript by Hornbostel's student, the distinguished comparative musicologist George Herzog.[4] Ballanta published a number of articles, and there are also some unpublished lectures at the Guggenheim Foundation that summarize Ballanta's view of African music. His work is pertinent to the present study for a couple of reasons. First, his description of African music differed in many ways from those of Western scholars. Second, he had a strong influence on one of the mission societies studied here after he gave a talk at the International Missionary Conference in Le Zoute, Belgium, in 1926, before he went to Berlin.

LIFE

Ballanta was born on 14 March 1893 in Sierra Leone.[5] In his first scholarly publication, "An African Scale," he included a detailed biography of his life up to 1922:

Figure 6.1. Nicholas G. J. Ballanta (*second from left*), in Sierra Leone, no date.
Courtesy of Dyke Kiel.

By 1911, I was appointed organist of St. Patrick's Church in Sierra Leone, and in that year I gained a Church Missionary Society's scholarship to prepare for the ministry. As I did not wish to enter the church, I abandoned the scholarship. I submitted an anthem to Novello in London in 1912, but it was returned with the remark that it should be corrected. As yet I had not studied harmony and counterpoint, etc. I then began the study of harmony in 1913 and I had to study by myself, there being no teachers in the theory of music in Sierra Leone. I studied first Ralph Dunstan's elementary harmony; followed by that by Vincent, and then I read Prout and many others in counterpoint. I studied Pearce, Prout, Bridge and several others, and read also books on form, free counterpoint, fugue etc., all by myself. In 1917 I presented myself as a candidate in music at Durham University [UK] and was successful in the first examination for the degree of Bachelor of Music. I have not yet presented myself for the final examination on account of financial difficulties. I came to this country with the hopes of having some of my works performed before going to England to take the final examination.[6]

He came to the United States in 1921 and began to use the name Ballanta instead of Taylor, a name given to his grandfather by missionaries.[7] After a stay in Boston, where he conducted his composition "African Rhapsody" at Symphony Hall, he began studying in 1922 with a scholarship at the Institute of Musical Art (which later became Juilliard) and graduated in 1924. Among his sponsors were the conductor Walter Damrosch and his brother Frank Damrosch, director of the Institute of Musical Art, and, most important, the businessman and philanthropist George Foster Peabody (1852–1938), who eventually financed many of his travels, equipment, and instruments.[8] With Peabody's support he was able to publish a collection of transcribed spirituals from St. Helena.[9]

Ballanta was the first ever Guggenheim Fellow in music research (1927), and his fellowship was renewed for a second year in 1928. That this completely unknown African became the first recipient in music of such a prestigious grant depended on the support of Peabody, who wrote countless letters on Ballanta's behalf, supported him for years, and got his friends to write letters of recommendation for his Guggenheim application. Peabody came from a modest background and made his fortune from the Edison Electric Company, retiring in 1906 and spending the rest of his life on philanthropic activities.[10] His support for African American institutions was particularly strong, and he served on the board of trustees for the American Church Institute for Negroes and Hampton University, a historically black college in Virginia.[11]

Ballanta's application for the Guggenheim was supported by letters of reference from five distinguished and influential men: Peabody; Frank Damrosch, his former teacher from the Institute of Musical Art;[12] Henry Frick, undoubtedly an acquaintance of Peabody; Charles Miller from Ann Arbor, Michigan;[13] and, most important, the Columbia University anthropologist Franz Boas. Boas wrote in his letter that he had a long conversation with Ballanta. Since he was the only serious academic among the referees, it fell to him to recommend that Ballanta get more training in comparative musicology. He suggested that Ballanta spend some time in Berlin studying with his old friend Hornbostel, "who is undoubtedly our best authority on this subject and who has given many years to the study of the music of primitive people the world over."[14]

Ballanta left for Berlin in 1926, before commencing his Guggenheim, to study with Hornbostel during the academic year 1926–27, in which he was probably financed by Peabody. Peabody was also responsible for his visit to the Missionary Conference in Le Zoute, Belgium. There he must have delivered an impressive paper, because the associate director of the Bethel Mission in Germany, Walther Trittelvitz (discussed in part III, chap. 12), completely changed course and tried to have African music sung in churches instead of Lutheran chorales. Why would Peabody send Ballanta to a missionary conference? In the 1920s, missionaries were among the most admired people in the United States.[15] Peabody was a progressive philanthropist, so he may have understood that a lecture by an African music specialist to world mission leaders might help preserve African music.

Ballanta's departure for Berlin was mentioned in the *New York Times* on 6 July 1926 in an article entitled "Negro Music" that described Ballanta's previous trip to Africa, financed by Peabody, which helped prepare his Guggenheim application: "Since his return to West Africa in the autumn of 1924 Mr. Ballanta-Taylor, who studied at the New York Institute of Music Art under Dr. Damrosch, has visited Gambia, Senegal, French Guinea, Portuguese Guinea, Liberia, the Gold Coast, Nigeria, and Sierra Leone. He has spent much time in the bush."[16] His Guggenheim application from 17 July 1926 presents his main ideas. Among them are:

1. African music consists of duple time "worked out into an endless variety of detail in the subdivisions of beat."
2. Melody is "calculated by a system of fourths either forward or backward."
3. Instrumental music uses an interval "called the neutral third which is neither major nor minor but midway giving seventeen sounds in the octave."
4. He asks whether any of these conceptions are "noticeable in any of the older systems of Europe."
5. He also asks, "Does any people in Europe, aside from scientific music, possess the neutral third?"

He further wants to investigate, with the help of Diedrich Westermann, a professor of African languages at the Friedrich Wilhelm University, the relationship of tonal languages to melodies.[17] During his last visit to West Africa, he collected "some 2000 examples of African songs in different languages" and would now also like to visit South and East Africa. The latter statement was mentioned several times by Peabody in his correspondence with Henry Allen Moe, principal administrator of the Guggenheim Foundation. Peabody was strongly supportive of this plan.

The only real specialist consulted by the Guggenheim Foundation was Boas, who directed Ballanta to Hornbostel. The musical adviser for the Guggenheim Foundation was Thomas Whitney Surette (1861–1941), a music educator and composer. The lack of specialists in comparative musicology in the United States would haunt Ballanta once Peabody began trying to find scholars who could evaluate Ballanta's book manuscript. And Ballanta

might well have believed that he knew more about African music than anyone on the East Coast of the United States.

We have no reports on Ballanta's Berlin stay, but Klein has given a detailed summary of the correspondence between Hornbostel and Ballanta,
which is preserved in the Berlin Phonogramm-Archiv.[18] To summarize: Ballanta received a phonograph from Hornbostel, who expected to get recordings in return. In 1928 Hornbostel inquired where the recordings were.[19]
Ballanta's answers show that he was having trouble doing his research.[20] According to Ballanta, numerous letters and packages from him to Hornbostel
had been lost in the mail, and he could not get to the Congo (where he was
supposed to record music for his Guggenheim fellowships) because European governments had erected barriers that made it impossible to travel
from one country to another. Ballanta was reluctant to use the phonographs
for other recordings since the fellowship was intended for the Congo. Hornbostel assures him that any recordings are fine as long as they don't show
influence of "white music."[21] By 1931 Ballanta's money from the Guggenheim Fellowships had run out, and he asked Hornbostel for financial help.
He included in his letter a list of the twenty recordings he had made in
Grand Bassa and sent to Berlin.[22] Hornbostel answered on 8 October 1931
that he never received the recordings, and so he did not send Ballanta any
money.[23] As we will see later, Hornbostel did not believe that Ballanta ever
sent the recordings. And there the correspondence ends.

There is an extensive correspondence in the Guggenheim Foundation
on Ballanta's unpublished "Aesthetics of African Music." He submitted the
manuscript to Oxford University Press in 1929. Oxford notified Ballanta
and Peabody that the book required serious editing, something they were
not willing to pay for, but they would be happy to publish the book with
a subvention for editing. At first Peabody was supportive, asking for cost
estimates. Privately, though, Oxford's editor, Geoffrey Cumberlege, wrote
to Moe on 23 August 1928, "Personally I don't think it is going to be worth
publishing but in order to satisfy Mr. Peabody I am getting expert opinions on it."[24] But then, in a letter to Moe dated 19 October 1928, Peabody
modified his opinion: "But Mr. Ballanta is a native, I gather. . . . Must the
great ideas of those who have no facility of expression be bottled forever?"[25]

Eventually three factors contributed to the book's not being published.
Since there were no comparative musicologists in America and few Africa
specialists, Peabody and Moe got in touch with Thomas Jesse Jones (1873–
1950) of the Phelps-Stokes Fund,[26] which was responsible for identifying
projects in Africa worthy of support.[27] He wrote to Peabody on 2 November
1934 that he was no specialist in music and recommended two experts:[28]

It seems to me well written but the technical phrases of it are out of my sphere and I cannot, therefore, pass an opinion on it. As a layman I have the same wonder about his technical observation as I have had about his former theories; namely that I feel a certain doubt as to the accuracy of his deductions. I hope therefore that the manuscript will be submitted to some experts in African music. . . . You will recall that our experiences with Mr. Ballanta in the past has [sic] been quite unsatisfactory. We have endeavored to place him at Achimota. We have tried to have him work at the Booker Washington Institute in Liberia. You arranged for him to study with Prof. Erich von Hornbostel at the University of Berlin. In all of these efforts the results were not satisfactory. My present feeling is that it would not be wise to send any funds to Mr. Ballanta. His past record seems to indicate that the only help that can be given to him is for results achieved in the form of writings that are completed and approved by authorities in music. In connection with this whole matter, I would also suggest that since Dr. von Hornbostel is now in this country, it may be worth while to submit the manuscript to him.[29]

Jones's advice was followed. Peabody invited Hornbostel to his home in Saratoga Springs and wrote to Moe on 4 November 1934, "We found him [Hornbostel] quite out of patience with Mr. Ballanta for his failure to send him records [a reference to the recordings Ballanta was supposed to have made]."[30] Jones informed Peabody on the same day that he had heard from Alvin Johnson that Hornbostel was ill in London and therefore unable to evaluate the book.[31] In the end, Hornbostel's student George Herzog was consulted. He wrote two devastating reviews of the manuscript, dated 13 November 1936 and 12 January 1939.[32] Moe sent the review to Ballanta on 28 September 1938 with the words, "There is nothing I can add." Ballanta still hoped for a subvention from the Guggenheim Foundation. However, on 15 March 1939 (after the Foundation had received the second review by Herzog), he received a letter from the Foundation stating that it had decided not to fund the project. In sum, Oxford would have published the book with a substantial subvention, which would have included major editing of the book. Jones's negative opinion of Ballanta, Hornbostel's conviction that Ballanta never sent the recordings he had agreed to make, and Herzog's negative review of Ballanta's scholarship resulted in the withdrawal of support from both Peabody and the Guggenheim Foundation.

In the 1930s Ballanta was a member of the Advisory Committee on Education of Liberia, and in the 1940s and 1950s he taught at a grammar school in Freetown.[33] His death in Sierra Leone in 1962 received only a short obituary by Alan Merriam in *Ethnomusicology*,[34] in which he is mentioned as a scholar of West African and American Negro Music and his book *Saint Helena Spirituals* is praised because it contains the first detailed analysis of rhythm in African American folk songs. Merriam calls it a "pioneer work in its attempt to show objectively the similarities between West African music and the spirituals."[35]

In sum, Ballanta was educated as a composer of Western music in New York. He never really studied comparative musicology, aside from a few months with Hornbostel in Berlin. Even though Boas recommended that he study with Hornbostel, there is no evidence that he profited much from his short stay. Whatever knowledge he had about African music, he acquired on his own. It would not have helped that until 1928 most articles by Hornbostel and Stumpf were written in German, a language Ballanta did not know. It is therefore unsurprising that he lacked the terminological and methodological background that Herzog expected from a serious scholar. The British historian Andrew D. Roberts sums up Ballanta's life: "Little of Ballanta's research on African music saw the light of day, and there the file ends. It is a depressing story which throws light not only on the 'confusion' of an African intellectual but on the still primitive state of Western scholarship regarding African music. One feels Ballanta had been floating around for almost 20 years on a tide of well-meaning ignorance, when what he really needed, by 1924 was the discipline of a doctoral programme."[36] The problem was that at this point there simply was no serious Ph.D. program in comparative musicology in the United States or Great Britain.

RESEARCH

Ballanta published three short articles during his lifetime: "An African Scale," "Gathering Folk Tunes in the African Country," and "Music of the African Races." All were published in journals for the general public that are difficult to access and probably were read by only a few people, and certainly not by musicologists. Then there is the unpublished book manuscript. Of interest to us is also the collection of spirituals entitled *Saint Helena Spirituals*. Finally, there are a number of lectures, which he sent from Africa to Moe at the Guggenheim Foundation.

We have two widely divergent interpretations of Ballanta's work: on the one hand, George Herzog, who himself did extensive fieldwork in Africa,[37] wrote a truly devastating review of the book manuscript "The Aesthetics of African Music." On the other, we have a detailed and thoughtful essay by the German scholar Tobias Robert Klein, who considers Ballanta an unfairly ignored pioneer of African music research. (Klein was unaware of Herzog's review.) However, Klein only read the articles and did not have access to the book. How are we to deal with these widely divergent viewpoints? And how should we regard his scholarship, published and unpublished?

Ballanta's articles were based on research he did with various tribes in West Africa. Like Hornbostel he aimed to explain to his readers what made African music so different from European music.[38] Thus far we have seen that because musicologists had not yet developed a vocabulary to deal with non-Western music, they regularly compared African music to medieval music. Medieval music was the only music they knew that was not based on major and minor modes. Scholars regularly "discovered" church modes in Africa and drew a comparison to medieval organum when describing African polyphony.

Strikingly, Ballanta is the only comparative musicologist of his generation who never made this comparison. Quite the contrary: he stated clearly that medieval modes were not a useful concept for understanding African music. He wrote at the beginning of his first article:

> One great difference between African music and that of the Caucasian races is that of the leading tone. The African, untouched by European musical influence, does not at any time use the note a semitone below as the lower auxiliary note to any principal tone. When one's ear has been trained so to use the lower auxiliary, he is bewildered to find that the music of his own people does not fit itself easily to the rules given by his tutors. It is true that some of the ecclesiastical modes possess this peculiarity—that is, a note which is a whole tone below the final. It is also true that some composers usually approach the cadence in the major key through the minor seventh; *but these composers do not write in native African scales, nor does the study of the ecclesiastical modes assist one in his quest for some data to work upon any more than an assiduous study of Greek literature furthers one's progress in the mastering of, say, the Mendi language or any other African language.* The only avenue open to me, therefore, was to embark upon the task of studying the native scales or any one of them and the best mode of treatment.[39]

Ballanta rejected any parallel to medieval music and believed that African music had to be analyzed on its own terms. In this vein he wrote to George Herzog a letter dated 8 September 1930 (years before Herzog evaluated Ballanta's manuscript), now in the Berlin Phonogramm-Archiv: "I thank you very much for your letter and the expression of opinion about my work.

I am mainly engaged in the music of my race which I desire to place on
proper footing for the purposes of development before I die. I have studied
the music from different countries on the West Coast and I am convinced
that in the musical perception of the African there is something which
should not only be preserved but also developed."[40] Clearly, Ballanta was an
independent thinker who did not believe that African music was on a lower
level than Western music. As we have seen, it took Europeans many years
to refute any parallel to medieval music and church modes.

In his 1930 article "Music of the African Races," Ballanta opined that
Western and African music showed some similarities long ago but then
both developed in different directions:

> It is interesting to observe that on account of these different perceptions
> the African is able to appreciate and understand other systems of music.
> Although the perception of the African to-day presents the same features
> as that of Western music in days gone by, the European has, by confining
> himself to the development of one form to the exclusion of others, lost
> the perception of the latter.[41]

In what follows, he explained that Europeans failed to develop their rhythmic language. His description of African rhythm is perceptive and gives an
early account of African polyrhythm:

> The fundamental of rhythmic perception is duple time throughout. Each
> beat of this duple time may be divided into two, three, or four parts.
> When more than one rhythmic instrument take part, or when the chorus
> is accompanied by hand clapping or other rhythmic devices, these differ-
> ent divisions of the beat are brought into effect. One part may divide the
> beat into twos, another into threes, another into four parts and a further
> division into six parts, giving intricate rhythmic effects in which synco-
> pation plays an important feature. This rhythmic device is so highly de-
> veloped that whole phrases may be syncopated: that is to say, they may
> be shifted from strong to weak pulses at pleasure without disturbing the
> rhythmic balance, although at the same time other parts are doing the
> same things or their opposites.[42]

Similarly, in his earlier article "Gathering Folk Tunes," he stressed the pri-
macy of duple time and found that other meters that occur simultaneously
are related to this one:

Duple time is the only time used by Africans. Although music apparently abounds in triple, quintuple and septuple times, yet the African does not regard them as such because he regards a group of three, five or seven equal values as coming under one beat. It is the beat or throb that is divided, not the measure.[43]

Ballanta used the term "cross rhythm" to describe what he observed in Yoruba music before A. M. Jones:[44] "The highest class of the artistic dance is with the Yorubas. Tempo moderate; 2–4 time combined with 6–8, 3–4 with 9–8 and 18–16, two bars being perceived being perceived as one whole bar of 6–4. Cross rhythms in abundance."[45]

In both "Gathering Folk-Tunes in the African Country"(1926) and "Music of the African Races"(1930), Ballanta expressed a similar concern to that Hornbostel voiced about the loss of authentic African music because of European influences.[46] Like Hornbostel, he was a comparative musicologist, and he was particularly interested in the relationship between speech tones and melodic contours. In his Guggenheim application he mentioned that he would like to do research on speech tones with Diedrich Westermann in Berlin. He showed in much greater detail than Hornbostel how dangerous it could be if European missionaries who did not know the languages well (especially if these languages are tonal) set English hymns to, say, Yoruba words (fig. 6.2):

In Ex. m I give a typical line translated from the English Hymnal. The tones of the words are suggested by the notes above them and the different meanings assigned to different tones. It is essential that, in order to get the precise meaning, the exact intonation should be followed, but when the line was sung to the English hymn tune a different meaning from what is intended is conveyed. The language is Yoruba. Such a line would be rendered by the Yorubas themselves as indicated in Ex. n. The short grace notes are necessary to fix the tones of the words, and at the same time to produce a beautiful melody.[47]

The original hymn text that the missionary intended to translate was: "Awake my soul and with the sun." The Yoruba text that he created with the intonation of the melody was "Ji, o-kan mi ba o-run ji," which translates as "Meaning Steal, soul of mine, steal in my sleep"—clearly not what the missionary intended.[48]

Ballanta's description of African tonal systems has been analyzed in

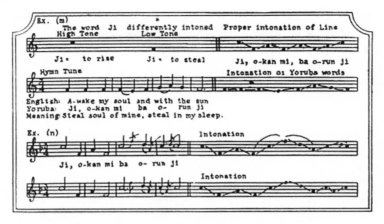

Figure 6.2. Ballanta, "Gathering Folk Tunes," 11.

some detail by Klein and J. H. Kwabena Nketia, so I will only give a general outline here. Ballanta's main agenda was to explain to Europeans and Americans the ways in which African scales and melodies differ from European ones. Like other scholars from this period, he commented on the fact that there are no leading tones in African music, as we have seen in the quotation above. Since Ballanta was eager to describe a tonal system that would include all African music, he adds "inflections."[49] In his article "An African Scale," he listed a pentatonic scale with the pitches C–D–E–G–A that is found in many "inflections." He observed inflections of both a quarter tone and a semitone.[50] While in his earlier articles he still transcribed the music he discussed, in "Music of the African Races" (1930) he explains why transcriptions are not possible: "The most important is the five-tone scale; but there are so many inflections of the tones of that scale that the fundamental character has been altered. It is not easy to note down African music by existing musical notation, as the signs would convey a different idea from what they intended to represent. A wholly different notation is necessary to do this properly."[51] It seems likely to me that he was referring here to the irregular tunings Kubik and others observed in African xylophones of both equidistant pentatonic and hexatonic scales.[52] Similarly, as we will see, one of our missionaries (Hagena, chap. 12) described how the Haya often connect leaps with small intervals that are difficult to reproduce or notate. Because Ballanta heard these "inflections," he was one of the first scholars to argue that the Western notational system was inadequate for African music, since there are many more pitches than the staff can accommodate. Klein has described in detail the seventeen-note scale Ballanta would like to adopt for African music, and Peabody even paid for a seventeen-note reed organ made to Ballanta's specifications.[53]

Ballanta also observed that while Western music is based on the circle of fifths and triads, "the perfect fourth is the basis of harmonic combination [in African music], that is, where two parts sing together tone by tone."[54] He lamented the fact that "in cities at the Coast . . . African musical perception is lost" because of "the substitution of the perfect fifth for the perfect fourth as [the] interval of association."[55] As Klein has pointed out, Gerhard Kubik made the same point in his 1985 article "African Tone Systems."[56]

Ballanta's book essentially reiterates much of the material discussed in his articles, but distributed over three different chapters: the introduction, "Musical Instruments and Drums," and "The Song." He provides much information on instruments and rituals that is unavailable elsewhere. Moreover, he includes 350 transcribed musical examples at the end. In the early 1930s there were few examples of African music available, so this trove of transcriptions alone would have warranted publication.

It is not difficult to understand why Herzog was exasperated by the manuscript. The prose is even more stilted than in the articles. The problems begin in the preface. Ballanta starts with a description of a Bambara flute player who would play a tone somewhere between B-flat and B-natural that he, Ballanta, was unable to reproduce on the harmonium. We know from his earlier articles that he was trying to describe the inflections mentioned above, but the fact that he is trying to match the pitches to the harmonium indicates that he does not realize that there is no such thing as absolute pitch, and Herzog of course noticed this mistake. His description of "beauty" in African music as compared to that of the West is naive and full of clichés.

Herzog applied the same standards to Ballanta as he would have to an American or German scholar. He could not bring himself to support a "native scholar who tries to do anthropological work without the proper training." In his 1936 report for the Guggenheim Foundation, he writes:

> Instead of an illuminating account by a native West African, it is an example of how easily a "native," when educated in Western terminology and thought, accepts and muddles this terminology and thought. Very little sound writing has been offered so far on African music. . . . A careful perusal of the manuscript indicates that Mr. Ballanta, unfortunately, does not qualify as a speaker for the music of his people. He has apparently learned a certain amount of theoretical background of our own

music, and some of the ideas which have resulted from this background
to primitive music.[57]

In the 1939 review he claims that much of what Ballanta writes is derived
from Hornbostel but becomes muddled in the process:

> Undoubtedly the native musician, if trained in our music, can contrib-
> ute something significant to our understanding of music, or of his own.
> It is precisely the realization of what the contribution of someone like
> Mr. Ballanta-Taylor could be which makes me feel that he fails. He
> stated that Africans today are floundering; I fear that he himself is an
> example of this floundering. We have had similar cases in Anthropology
> when the "trained" native has been left stranded with an imperfect grasp
> of Western technique and estrangement of his own culture.[58]

His main concern is, of course, that Ballanta has not undergone rigor-
ous training—he seems to be an amateur. His use of terminology is "facile"
and "imprecise." Many concepts Ballanta uses "have been discarded" in
the most recent scholarship. Despite the time the two men spent together,
Ballanta is unaware of the fundamental research Hornbostel did on African
music. He talks about African music, in general, when there are major differences within Africa. Polyphony is never mentioned in his book, even
though it is "especially highly developed in West Africa," and "the discussion of tonal analysis (pp. 17–27) is garbled throughout." He seems not to
know that "the standard relationships of 5ths and 4ths" are predominant
not only in Africa but in most "primitive music." The concept of form
is hardly covered at all. Drumming is also discussed insufficiently, "considering the very complex rhythmical forms that have been reported and
recorded." Herzog believes that there are serious problems with Ballanta's
transcriptions: "They are written in conventional musical notation, without signs for tones not found in our tone-system. The placement of bar lines
is often wrong." He believes that the melodies are incomplete and sketchy
and therefore the musical material "in the manuscript cannot qualify . . . as
material that would stand a serious critical text."

These statements make clear that Ballanta's book can in no way be compared to those of Hornbostel or his students. Herzog's view is characteristic
of the first generation of comparative musicologists, who introduced rigor-
ous methods into the discipline. He concludes that publication of the book
would "do more harm than good, as it reaffirms from a native and 'thus'

authoritative source all the popular misconceptions and myths that have had and still have their influences on the layman as well as on the music theoretician."[59]

And yet, many of Herzog's reproaches are unjust: for example, Hornbostel's article groundbreaking article "African Negro Music" also talks about African music in general. Similarly, most scholars of Ballanta's generation did transcriptions without indicating which tones are not found in the tonal system. In fact, I found them no worse than those Marius Schneider. And even though he does not include a systematic discussion of polyphony, there are many musical examples of polyphonic music that are similar to Schneider's. In his discussion of drumming and rhythms, he is far ahead of his time, as explained earlier.

In short, Ballanta's publications, imperfect as they are, reveal information about music in West Africa that cannot be found elsewhere. Let me draw a parallel to medieval music theorists. If Herzog's standards had been applied to theorists of the thirteenth, fourteenth, and fifteenth centuries, only Johannes Tinctoris would have been published, and perhaps Franco of Cologne, but without musical examples, which often seem to be wrong. Any medievalist will confirm that a careful reading of the less systematic authors reveals much important material. Herzog, who suffered from bipolar disorder, had quite a reputation for writing devastating and frequently unjust reviews, and very few of his graduate students managed to finish their dissertations. To quote David McAllister on Herzog as an adviser: "The campus was littered with failed Herzog students."[60] From Ballanta's point of view (and ours), it is most unfortunate that his manuscript was sent to Herzog. A more generous reviewer might have helped Ballanta revise the manuscript for publication, as was most likely done with his published articles and the introduction to the *Saint Helena Spirituals*.

Even though Ballanta was not a trained musicologist, as Hornbostel and his students were, and was certainly "muddled" in some of his writings, there is a lot of merit to his work that Herzog failed to see. He was the first scholar to state clearly that medieval church modes are not a useful concept for African music, at a time when most scholars in the West still believed they could understand the former via the latter. His main goal was to develop a separate set of tools for understanding African music. The Western concepts of dissonance and consonance do not apply to African music (which lacks a leading tone). He argued that African rhythm was more "developed" than European rhythm.[61] He believed that the Western notational system was inadequate to notate the music he heard in Africa because there are many additional "inflections," even if he did not notate them in his musical examples. Finally, in a talk that made an immediate impact, in 1926 (two years before the publication of Hornbostel's "African Negro Music") he argued persuasively at the Missionary Conference in Le Zoute, Belgium, that missionaries must promote African music rather than Western hymns.

.

PART II

Bringing Medieval Music to Life: Jugendmusik- *and* Singbewegung

A difference between the Maasai and the Germans . . . became obvious when the performance [in the concert] started. The Germans had two groups of people: the performers and the spectators, and there were more of the latter than the former. In Maasailand, almost everyone participated in a ceremony, except those who were unable to for one reason or another, such as those who were too old or too young.
—Tepilit Ole Saitoti, *The Worlds of a Maasai Warrior: An Autobiography*

It is deceptive to believe that community occurs and alienation is averted when a few people get together for something. The extent to which genuine relationships and human intimacy are still possible nowadays—and this includes any kind of planned conservation—does little to change the underlying social calamity. On the contrary: planned "primary groups" (Charles Cooley) violate their own concept. They are themselves part of the administered world. Many who were young at the time may have welcomed in the Hitler Youth the kind of community experiences that many leaders of the youth music movement yearn for nowadays. Yet that community was entirely bad and fake, mobilizing as it did the forces of closeness and connection for the purposes of suppression and power. The relation of the individual to communities is subject to the dynamic of history.
—Theodor W. Adorno, *Dissonanzen: Musik in der verwalteten Welt*

What do an imperial navy officer (Hans Paasche), a German missionary in Tanganyika (Bruno Gutmann), and a German musicologist and editor of the premier German publishing house Bärenreiter (Konrad Ameln) have in common? At first glance they make an unlikely group, and yet they all come from the German youth movement *Jugendbewegung* (in music the *Jugendmusik-* and *Singbewegung*) that grew to dominate German musical life in the first half of the twentieth century. They all shared a dislike for modernity, wanted to sing old folk songs and chorales, and longed for the Middle Ages and a sense of community, which they thought they could find in "primitive societies."

This movement goes back to the early twentieth-century German *Wandervogel*, which was intended to revive the singing of folk music from all over the world; they also combined music with a rediscovery of the Middle Ages and of nature. In what follows I will try to explain where this yearning for the Middle Ages, this passion for simple life or "primitive" society and folk music, came from and how it contributed greatly to the founding of our discipline of musicology while also fundamentally transforming everyday musical life. It is no exaggeration to say that this movement profoundly affected every German in the first half of the last century. It was this background that explains why many of the missionaries to be discussed in part III did not consider their life in Africa a sacrifice but loved the simple life they encountered and wrote passionately about the people who lived it and their musical culture.

This part also deals with the recovery of medieval music, but the scholars discussed here employed entirely different means from those in part I. At the beginning of the twentieth century, no one knew what medieval music sounded like. In chapter 7 I will describe how historical musicologists, almost all of whom came out of the movement, first systematically transcribed the manuscripts and then organized the first performances of medieval music in the 1920s. The recovery of medieval music began with Friedrich Ludwig, who was too old to be a member of the *Wandervogel* and the *Jugendmusikbewegung* but whose students were leaders of the movement, and continues with his younger contemporary in Freiburg, Wilibald Gurlitt, and the two men's many students, concentrating especially on their fascination with medieval music and their belief in community spirit (*Gemeinschaftssinn*), both of which were particularly strong in Ludwig's and Gurlitt's student Heinrich Besseler. I will then move on in chapter 8 to discuss the *Wandervogel*, *Jugendmusik-*, and *Singbewegung*, again concentrating on Fritz Jöde's and Herman Reichenbach's passion for early and non-Western music, as well as their advocacy of participatory music making.

CHAPTER SEVEN

The First Performances of Medieval Music and the Historians Behind Them

THE PERFORMANCES IN KARLSRUHE (1922) AND HAMBURG (1924)

Until 1922, when the Freiburg musicologist Wilibald Gurlitt organized the first concerts of medieval music at the Badische Kunsthalle in Karlsruhe, scholars had only very vague ideas of what medieval music really sounded like. It is no exaggeration to say that these performances had a major impact on German cultural life. A great many members of the *Jugendmusik-* and *Singbewegung* were involved in these performances. Ameln wrote to Heinrich Schumann, who was compiling the volume *Die deutsche Jugendmusikbewegung in Dokumenten ihrer Zeit von den Anfängen bis 1933* (The German Youth Music Movement in Documents of Its Time from the Beginnings to 1933), about the central importance of the Karlsruhe and Hamburg performances: "I have really experienced the very beginnings: Music of the Middle Ages in Karlsruhe and Hamburg with the Institute of Musicology of the University of Freiburg, of which Höckner and Reichenbach were a part."[1] They also changed the course of musicology: Heinrich Besseler would likely have never written his *Habilitation* on medieval music without them.[2] Moreover, from this moment on, scholars, led by Gurlitt, strove for "authenticity" in performances of early music.[3]

In the first concert, the audience heard Notre Dame organa, thirteenth-century motets from the Bamberg Codex, the Kyrie and Christe from Machaut's *Messe de Notre Dame*, and two motets by Guillaume Dufay. Ludwig's review of these concerts is full of praise for his colleague Gurlitt and is worth citing:

> The Freiburg musicology department, taking as a point of departure the early chamber music of the seventeenth and eighteenth centuries, which they are partly able to perform on original instruments, the repertoire of

their "Praetorius Organ," the vocal music of the baroque and Renaissance period and of the Netherlandish motets and chansons of the fifteenth century, very soon found the way back to the Middle Ages, to the Italian art of the Trecento, to the estampie, the old French motet, to Leonin and to Perotin, and to Gregorian chant.[4]

The Karlsruhe performance was followed by another one of medieval music at the Hamburger Musikhalle in 1924, also directed by Gurlitt, with a program consisting again of Notre Dame polyphony, anonymous thirteenth-century motets, chansons by Adam de la Halle, a piece by Francesco Landini, a motet by Machaut, a song from the *Lochamer Liederbuch*, and chansons by Dunstaple, Binchois, and Dufay.[5] The ensemble that participated included two recorders, two violas, a viola da gamba, and a small choir.

These performances would not have taken place without the fundamental work of Ludwig, who not only provided the transcriptions for both concerts but also in 1923 published the Gradual "Alleluja Pascha nostrum" in *Zeitschrift für Musikwissenschaft*; it was performed at one of the concerts.[6]

FRIEDRICH LUDWIG

Friedrich Ludwig (1872–1930), by training a historian and musicologist, was one of the founders of historical musicology.[7] He was a student of Gustav Jacobsthal (1845–1912) in Strasbourg, the first German *ordinarius* in musicology; Ludwig wrote his *Habilitation* with Jacobsthal and eventually became his successor upon his retirement in 1910.[8] Jacobsthal, whose intellectual formation was shaped by the romantic Palestrina revival, became Ludwig's most important intellectual influence. After World War I, Ludwig had to leave Strasbourg. In 1920 he was appointed the chair of musicology at Göttingen, where he remained until his death in 1930, serving as rector of the university in 1929–30.

The Palestrina revival goes back to the Lutheran pastor Johann Gottfried Herder, who felt that *a cappella* music of the Renaissance affected listeners in a deeper way than dramatic or orchestral music.[9] Both Jacobsthal and Ludwig were completely uninterested in any music later than Bach, so in a way Ludwig was an ideal mentor for the scholars who were instrumental in establishing the *Singbewegung*. With the notable exception of Besseler, they had little interest in music of the nineteenth and twentieth centuries.

Ludwig's teacher and other members of the Palestrina movement had edited and performed music of Palestrina, Lassus, and seventeenth-century composers. As a result, by the time Ludwig appeared on the scene scholars had a good idea of how Renaissance polyphony sounded. What they did not know about was medieval polyphony. No one had really managed to fully understand modal notation, and the scholarly community had only very vague ideas about the structure of medieval motets. The concept of isorhythm was as yet unknown. This is exactly where Ludwig came in: he set out to explore medieval polyphony in order to find out where his favorite composers, Palestrina, Lassus, and Schütz, came from.

Ludwig introduced unprecedented standards of scholarship into the field of musicology. This was the main reason Gurlitt sent Besseler to study with Ludwig, convinced that only Ludwig could teach students how to deal with medieval sources.[10] Other students of Ludwig in Göttingen were Werner Blankenburg, Konrad Ameln, Christhard Mahrenholz, Heinrich Spitta, Heinrich Husmann, and Higini Anglès.[11] Joseph Müller-Blattau and Friedrich Gennrich had been Ludwig's students at Strasbourg.

Ludwig's primary goal was the description and analysis of sources of medieval polyphony. His most famous book is the *Repertorium organorum recentioris et motetorum vetustissimi stili* of 1910—to this day, over a century later, still the most authoritative catalog of and book on thirteenth-century organa and motets. He gives the first detailed account of modal notation, lists all concordances in the thirteenth-century repertoire, orders them chronologically, and tries to establish which was the original and which was a copy. In other words, he was as concerned with the original or "authentic" version as Hornbostel. He also includes detailed descriptions of all the sources of the period. The accuracy and ingeniousness with which the project was executed make it to this day a model for the discipline of musicology.

The second part of the *Repertorium*, a catalog of thirteenth-century motets, although finished and typeset in 1911, was not published until 1961, by Ludwig's student Friedrich Gennrich, for two reasons: first, Ludwig was a perfectionist and wanted to wait to see what Jacobsthal had written on motets; and second, after World War I he became overburdened with administrative duties and had no time for scholarship.[12]

Ludwig was able to identify isorhythm, and he published three volumes of the works of Guillaume de Machaut.[13] The fourth volume of Machaut's *Missa de Notre Dame* was edited by Heinrich Besseler from Ludwig's notes in 1954.[14] In addition, in 1924 Ludwig published a synthesis of all of his previous work in Guido Adler's *Handbuch der Musikgeschichte* (Handbook of Music History; updated in 1929 and reprinted in 1961).[15] Finally, his papers, which are now held by the Niedersächsische Staats- und Landesbibliothek in Göttingen, include diplomatic and modern transcriptions of most known manuscripts of the thirteenth through fifteenth centuries.

Why did Ludwig publish so little material from his Nachlass? I believe that at the beginning of his career he felt that there was no interest in medieval music. He wrote in 1905, "The main reason to work and publish medieval music is not a practical but a scholarly one."[16] In 1905 the *Wandervogel* movement had just gotten started, so a longing for the Middle Ages was not yet common.

This all changed when interest in the Middle Ages surged in the 1920s.[17] To give just one example, the circle around the German poet Stefan George met regularly in Heidelberg between 1920 and his death in 1933, and the Middle Ages played an important role in their discussions and publications. Ernst Kantorowicz's first book, *Kaiser Friedrich der Zweite* (1927), was an enormous success (it was one of Hitler's favorites), and it would not have been written without George and his circle.[18]

So it is no wonder that Ludwig's attitude also changed. In an article on Perotin from 1921, Ludwig stressed that the primary goal of musicological research was to bring music of the past back to life. He regretted that so little of Notre Dame polyphony was available in modern transcription.[19] Soon scholars and musicians all over Germany started to perform medieval music. Ludwig was not much of a practical musician, but his student Besseler was. He organized regular singing of early music in Göttingen for the students, as described by Walter Blankenburg: "The *Singbewegung* took place when we sat down for a time on a daily basis around a table to sing something together, for example Josquin's 'Missa Pange lingua,' which at that point did not exist in a practical new edition, (as we did in 1925 under the direction of Heinrich Besseler)."[20] More important, Ludwig joined forces with Gurlitt, who taught at Freiburg im Breisgau from 1920 on and organized these performances.

Even Ludwig, whose research is characterized by meticulous analysis of sources, was swept up by the new spirit of the *Jugendbewegung*. In his review of Gurlitt's performances of the *Alleluia Pascha nostrum*, he states his conviction that in the Middle Ages a strong community spirit was present: "The whole demonstrates a very attractive picture of the medieval community spirit [*Gemeinschaftssinn*], of a perpetual common striving in the service of the holy work, a loving recreation on the communal task without a radical break with the old, and this, even though there are new artistic departures that happen . . . and even though Leonin's and Perotin's artistic personalities can be clearly distinguished, there is an image of a harmonic confluence."[21] Ludwig laments that this communal spirit has been lost in modern society.

WILIBALD GURLITT

Wilibald Gurlitt (1889–1963), brother of the art historian and art dealer Hildebrand Gurlitt (1895–1956) and of the expressionist artist Cornelia Gurlitt (1890–1919),[22] wrote a dissertation under Hugo Riemann on Michael Praetorius and taught from 1920 on at the University of Freiburg. In 1929 he was promoted to full professor, and he went on to assemble a large number of talented students mainly interested in early music. He initiated the reconstruction of an organ described by Praetorius in his *Organographia* of 1619 and formed a collegium musicum to perform early music, in particular medieval music.[23] Because Gurlitt had a Jewish grandmother and was married to a Jewish woman, in 1933 the Nazis removed him as director of the Collegium Musicum, and in 1937 from his professorship. After 1945 he returned to Freiburg.

Gurlitt was another scholar who combined his interest in early music with curiosity about non-Western music, possibly under the influence of his brother, whose collection included many artists fascinated by "primitive" art. (Hildebrand began his career in the Weimar years as a promoter of German expressionist painters.) In a 1967 letter that Ludwig's former student Hilmar Höckner wrote to Ekkehart Pfannenstiel (1896–1986),[24] he describes how he met the Gurlitt student Herman Reichenbach (1898–1958), who was to become one of the leaders of the *Jugendmusikbewegung*. He recalled how Gurlitt selected topics for their dissertations in the 1920s:

> And I was writing my first book on a topic given to me by Gurlitt; (at first he had wanted me to write a major comprehensive study about the music of "primitive people"). We met regularly in seminars and especially in the collegium musicum two evenings a week (collegium vocale and instrumentale). No one was allowed to be absent. We sang early choir music from old part books with old clefs. Many Netherlandish compositions, Josquin, Lassus. Also motets from the thirteenth century.[25]

RUDOLF VON FICKER

The Karlsruhe and Hamburg concerts led to many performances of medieval music all over Europe, and not all were concerned with authenticity.

Rudolf von Ficker conducted a performance of the organum work *Sederunt* in the Vienna Court Chapel and in Paris's Salle Pleyel in 1929. He ascribed the piece to Perotin (even though there is no attribution in any of the manuscripts)[26] and reorchestrated it in a completely new setting, very different from either Ludwig's or Gurlitt's.[27] Von Ficker's opinions of "Nordic" polyphony can no longer be defended. His interpretation of medieval polyphony differed sharply from that of Ludwig, Besseler, and Gurlitt: he believed that what medieval notation represented was a basic framework, and that it was up to the performers to develop it to a full sound in the cathedral.[28] Von Ficker arranged Ludwig's transcription for monumental performing forces: boys' choir, mixed choir, four oboes, three bassoons, two trumpets, two trombones, three violas, celesta, glockenspiel, and triangle. The performances were a huge success and were reviewed enthusiastically by Carl Orff and Alfred Einstein.[29]

In 1930 von Ficker published his piano reduction of the edition with Vienna Universal Edition and dedicated it to Ludwig; he added numerous dynamic markings as well as ritardandi and accelerandi and sprinkled it with such indications as "langsam, schwebend," "allmählich nachlassen," and "sehr langsam."[30] Orff heard the performance in 1930 in Munich and believed it was what medieval music must have sounded like. Anyone who has heard Eugen Jochum's performance of von Ficker's arrangement of *Sederunt* cannot fail to recognize it as a model for the *Carmina burana* (1935–36).[31]

HEINRICH BESSELER, MEDIEVAL MUSIC, AND *GEMEINSCHAFTSMUSIK*

The most influential musicologist to come out of the *Jugendbewegung* was Heinrich Besseler (1900–1969; fig. 7.1).[32]

In his 1923 dissertation *Beiträge zur Stilgeschichte der deutschen Suite im siebzehnten Jahrhundert* (Contributions to the Stylistic History of the German Suite in the Seventeenth Century), written under Gurlitt in Freiburg, he outlines for the first time his concept of *Umgangsmusik* or *Gebrauchsmusik*: it is defined as music that is "based not on listening, but on participation (dancing, singing, playing)."[33] According to Besseler, modern music began with the transition from "participation music" (*Umgangsmusik*) to "presentation music" (*Darbietungsmusik*).[34] Besseler's sympathies are clearly with "participatory" music making, hence his love of early music. He argued that active listening gradually developed in the seventeenth and eighteenth centuries.[35]

Figure 7.1. Heinrich Besseler, no date. From *Festschrift Heinrich Besseler zum sechzigsten Geburtstag*, 2.

In 1925 Besseler completed his *Habilitation*, entitled *Die Motettenkomposition von Petrus de Cruce bis Philipp von Vitry (etwa 1250–1350)* (Motet Composition from Petrus de Cruce to Philippe de Vitry), and followed it with two significant articles entitled "Studien zur Musik des Mittelalters" (Studies about Medieval Music; 1925 and 1926),[36] in which he expanded considerably on the idea of *Gebrauchsmusik*.[37] In his review of Gurlitt's Hamburg performances of medieval music, he writes that, just as with medieval art, so can medieval music only be understood through the intellectual conditions of the period. And, according to Besseler, Gurlitt is trying to reproduce in his performances this fundamental community spirit that is present in the Middle Ages:

> His [Gurlitt's] contemplation takes its point of departure from historical situatedness of medieval existence [*Dasein*]. All of life, creation, and receiving happens in the community [*Gemeinschaft*], which is offered to the individual as a staggered empire of corporation and estates, centered on the all-embracing circle of the Church. The environment is based on

tradition and authority, and in the end always related to the religious center, and it includes all elements as part of one organism; for this reason
the overbearing art which demands to give meaning to life from itself,
is impossible in the Middle Ages.[38]

A little later in the same review he writes that motets such as those in
the Montpellier Codex are "not meant to be listened to, but to be sung or
to be participated in: they are not to be taken in by the listener as a uniform sound structure, rather their musical meaning is fulfilled in a lively
relationship between the performers."[39] Thus, none of the performers are
mentioned by name, although we know who they were, since they all became leaders of the *Jugendmusik-* and *Singbewegung* (see chap. 8).[40] Their
identities are irrelevant; only the fact that they sing together in a group matters. In other words, Besseler is very much attempting to get away from the
modern bourgeois concert hall in which the classical and Romantic repertoire are listened to; what attracts him to the Middle Ages is the spirit of
participatory music making, which did not require an audience. As several
scholars have shown, the essential concepts deployed by Besseler, such as
the distinction between "participation" and "presentation," derive from Martin Heidegger's phenomenology.[41]

Between 1927 and 1934 Ernst von Bücken's *Handbuch der Musikwissenschaft* appeared, with Besseler writing the first volume entitled *Die Musik des
Mittelalters und der Renaissance* (Music of the Middle Ages and the Renaissance), reissued numerous times—a truly masterful picture of early music that
shaped our view of the Middle Ages until at least the 1960s.[42] As we will see,
Besseler's volume even made it to Africa: Besseler's publications on medieval
music were among those consulted by missionary Franz Rietzsch's sister in an
attempt to understand Nyakyusa polyphony (see chap. 10). Again, one of his
central concerns is the relationship of early music to that of the present time
(the opening chapter is entitled "Alte Musik und Gegenwart"). He includes
in the category "early music" the Palestrina revival as well as the musical re-
newal of early music by members of the *Jugendmusik-* and *Singbewegung*.

After his appointment as *außerordentlicher Professor* (extraordinary professor) in Heidelberg in 1928, Besseler established a collegium musicum
there as well.[43] In the 1920s and 1930s he participated regularly in meetings
of the *Jugendmusik-* and *Singbewegung*, giving lectures and attending services in churches and outdoors.[44] Moreover, most of his graduate students
and assistants (some of them women) wrote dissertations and *Habilita-
tionen* on early music:[45] Hans Eppstein (Gombert and Bach), Manfred Bukofzer (*Die Geschichte des englischen Diskant*), Helen Hewitt (*Harmonice*

musices Odhecaton A), Fritz Dietrich (seventeenth-century organ music), Erna Dannemann (*Die französische Musiktradition vor dem Auftreten Dufays*), Ernst Hermann Meyer (*Die deutsche mehrstimmige Sonata im 17. Jahrhundert*), Wolfgang Stephan (*Die burgundisch-niederländische Motette zur Zeit Ockeghems*), Walther Lipphardt (*Die altdeutschen Marienklagen*), Edith Gerson-Kiwi (*Studien zur volkstümlichen Liedmusik Italiens im 16. Jahrhundert*), Edward Lowinsky (*Motettenstil Orlando di Lassos und sein Verhältnis zur Motette der vorausgehenden niederländischen Generation*), Laurence Feininger (*Die Frühgeschichte des Kanons bis Josquin des Prez um 1500*), Siegfried Hermelinck (*Das Präludium in Bachs Klaviermusik*, though he is more famous for his *Habilitation* on modes from 1959), and Peter Gülke (*Liedprinzip und Polyphonie in der Chanson des 15. Jahrhunderts*).[46] Seven of his students (Eppstein, Bukofzer, Gerson-Kiwi, Lowinsky, Meyer, Hans Hermann Rosenwald, and Artur Schloßberg) were Jewish, and Feininger was half Jewish. In every case Besseler went against Nazi regulations, making sure that they finished their dissertations. All remained devoted to him after the war.[47]

While Besseler never published anything on non-Western or ancient music, Thomas Schipperges has uncovered among Besseler's papers a remarkable correspondence that shows not only that he thought he had something to say on the topic, but also that he was ready to denigrate his distinguished colleague, the comparative musicologist Curt Sachs, who had contributed to Bücken's *Handbuch der Musikwissenschaft* a volume entitled *Die Musik der Antike* (1928). The book also included essays by Wilhelm Heinitz on musical instruments, Robert Lachmann on non-European music, "Natur- und Kulturvölker," and Peter Panoff on old Slavonic folk and church music.[48] Sachs was Jewish and as a result lost his job in Berlin in 1933; he immigrated first to Paris and then, in 1937, to New York, where he taught at New York University.[49] Since books written by Jews could not be sold in Nazi Germany, in 1941 the publisher asked Besseler if he was interested in writing a new volume of *Musik der Antike*. Besseler jumped at the occasion and suggested that he rewrite not only Sachs's article (he accuses Sachs of espousing a "monomaniacal" point of view of the Near East [*Vorderorient*]); instead, he writes,

one would have to depict the foundation of all of Western music, antiquity and the Orient, as well as Nordic antiquity and European folk music (not the exotic one). . . . If one were to organize the new volume of *Musik der Antike* in this way, it would also result in a better connection with my description of the Middle Ages. I am even wondering whether the entire section "Christian Late Antiquity" (pp. 25–64 of my volume) would not fit better into the new introductory volume, and this would make room for the treatment of sixteenth-century music, which was given short shrift in my volume.[50]

Nothing came of the suggestion, but in 1949 Sachs, by that time president of the American Musicological Society, wrote to Besseler. Besseler's answer to Sachs, fully quoted by Schipperges, is the standard one he gave to all Jewish émigrés: that he is deeply shocked by the horrible things that happened in Germany, and that he knew nothing about them. No mention, of course, of the intended volume on comparative musicology.[51]

Last but not least, it might be worth mentioning that Besseler was friendly with a number of scholars who were either close to comparative musicology (Jacques Handschin), or were themselves comparative musicologists (Marius Schneider and Kurt Huber, who, as a member of the resistance group Weisse Rose, was executed in 1943).[52] In a report on a conference organized in 1936 at the Staatliches Institut für Deutsche Musikforschung in Frankfurt an der Oder, papers by both Huber on folk music and Schneider on comparative musicology are repeatedly singled out for praise for their superb, clear presentations.[53] Besseler cited both Huber and Schneider after 1945 to argue in defense of his behavior during the Nazi period.[54]

In Besseler, then, we have a great scholar and intellectual who transformed the study of early music. Not only did he help institute and popularize early music performances, but he gave the whole field intellectual prestige by associating it with Heidegger's philosophy and the ideas that grew out of the *Jugendbewegung*. As we will see in the next section, *Gemeinschaftsmusik* was embraced by everyone—academics, students, factory workers, Lutherans, Catholics, and Jews. He educated several generations of musicologists who specialized in early music and edited early music (particularly noteworthy is his collected edition of Dufay) that was crucial for early music groups.[55]

The question now is, how did all of these erudite publications and exclusive performances of medieval music trickle down to popular culture in Germany in the 1920s and '30s?

CHAPTER EIGHT

The *Jugendmusik-* and *Singbewegung* Ideology, Leaders, and Publishers

M ost accounts of musical activities in Germany in the early twentieth century distinguish between the *Wandervogel,* the *Jugendmusikbewegung,* and the *Singbewegung.* They all share a passion for participatory music making, the singing of folk songs (especially if the folk songs are old), a longing for the supposedly communal Middle Ages, and a dislike for supposedly individualistic modernity.

THE *WANDERVOGEL*

Wandervogel participants went on long hikes and sang campfire songs accompanied by lute or guitar, songs collected by the medical student Hans Breuer from the Steglitz borough of Berlin and published in 1909 under the title *Der Zupfgeigenhansl,* a name that defies translation.[1] This anthology became one of music history's great best sellers, with millions of copies sold. When people left Germany they took it with them. The booklet found its way to Israel, the United States, and the mission archive in Rungwe, Tanzania. As late as the 1950s and '60s, every German schoolchild was expected to own a copy. The *Wandervögel* deeply enjoyed hiking and nature, finding civilization rotten and corrupt. An early member, Hans Blüher, who published a history of the *Wandervogel* in 1912, wrote: "Steglitz was the place of origin of a youth movement . . . ; they took the idea of traveling minstrels and students from the Middle Ages and transformed it into a modern concept that was healthy and self-aggrandizing. And once the occasion arose, all of Germany was swept with Romantic enthusiasm for the movement; young people were offended by the older generation and roared through the forests."[2]

Hans Paasche (1881–1920), the German naval officer mentioned above and a leader of the *Wandervogel,* was typical of many in the movement, even though his biography is not. Paasche was stationed in German East Africa from 1904 to 1908 and forced to fight against Africans in the Maji Maji Rebellion. The experience turned him into a lifelong pacifist and a vocal critic of German colonial politics. In 1907 he wrote a book entitled *Im Morgenlicht* (In the Morning Light), which not only describes his experiences as a big-game hunter in Africa but also includes a lot of important ethnographic information. After leaving the military in 1909, he married a woman named Ellen Wittig. The couple went on a long honeymoon to East Africa, where they penned together a manuscript entitled "Die Hochzeitsreise zu den Quellen des Nils" (The Honeymoon to the Sources of the Nile), which was never published and is now lost. In 1912–13 he wrote his most important book, *Die Forschungsreise des Afrikaners Lukanga Mukara* (The Research Trip of the African Lukanga Mukara), a description of a well-educated African's impression of an imaginary trip through Germany. Paasche's wife died in 1918 during the great flu pandemic, and he was killed in 1920 by a right-wing commando of sixty armed men, leaving behind the couple's four small children.

Paasche epitomizes in a number of ways the spirit of the main characters I am discussing. To begin with, he was a strong advocate of the *Wandervogel* philosophy: he abhorred modernity and civilization and became an admirer of African life. He wrote in his diaries that in Africa the Middle Ages stretches into the present. A teetotaler and vegetarian, he went everywhere, in typical *Wandervogel* tradition, with his song collections and lute. He has been called the first member of Germany's Green Party,[3] because he criticized the killing of animals, the use of feathers in fashion, and the noise and pollution of big cities. In 1913 he was one of three thousand participants who sang and danced in circles at the famous *Jugendbewegung* meeting at the Hohen Meißner.[4] After his murder, his friends erected a monument in his honor at Burg Ludwigstein (between Göttingen and Kassel), the reconstructed medieval castle that became the center of youth movement activities and now houses the movement's archive. Not surprisingly, Ludwigstein was considered by the youth movement a Holy Grail, a "dreamworld of the future form of communal living," which unites youth of all confessions and political parties.[5]

Second, Paasche made twenty-nine recordings of East African songs and instrumental music for Hornbostel between 1909 and 1910 that are now part of the Berlin Phonogramm-Archiv. They are among the earliest recordings of East African music.[6] (His earlier recordings are now lost.) In contrast to the missionaries, he did not include much information on the music, yet he was fully aware of the importance of documenting these local traditions and was full of admiration for every detail of African life and rituals.

Third, his fictional letters that make up his *Forschungsreise des Afrikaners Lukanga Mukara* illuminate probably better than anything else the alienation from modernization and Western culture that members of the youth movement experienced and also explain their fascination with Africa. The first six letters appeared as a serial in the youth movement journal *Der Vortrupp;* the book was published the year after Paasche's murder and became a best seller. The letters are clearly modeled on Charles de Montesquieu's *Lettres persanes* from 1721. Lukanga comes from the island of Ukara in Lake Victoria, where the Bethel missionaries Ernst Johannsen and Otto Hagena (see chap. 12) were active. The message Paasche tries to convey is loud and clear: African culture is much better than German.

To give a few examples: Mukara describes the smoke everywhere in Germany, clearly a symptom of industrialization: "In Germany there is a lot of smoke. But it is not the kind of smoke that a hiker likes to look at and about which your heart beats faster. It is not a smoke in fresh air, it is a smoke in the haze, yes, smoke in the smoke. Led in long stony tubes to the sky; but the sky doesn't want it."[7] Smoke, of course, results in diseases; the Germans are stuck indoors, without fresh air. He goes on to describe the life of factory workers: "That is what I saw when I followed the smoke. A terrible noise, which is bigger than the thunderstorms in spring, men and women are standing and moving their hands in front of machines. . . . They do work which will never be finished, and they do the same work for years. How much better is it in Kitara [his kingdom in Africa]! There, every season has its own work."[8]

In his last letter Mukara finally meets people he approves of, namely members of the *Wandervogel*, who appreciate nature, hike, sing folk songs, and dance: "The season was cold, but we became warm while walking and swam in the brook under tall trees. Then we went to a meadow and found many people there, as many as there are blades of grass. They spoke in a circle and held hands, they sang and danced, they danced with bare feet as we do in Kitara."[9]

Several of our missionaries belonged to the same generation as Paasche, and they too detested Western civilization and glorified African culture. Again, for them, spending a life in Africa was not felt to be a sacrifice or part of a colonial enterprise. Quite the opposite: some much preferred their life there to European civilization (especially Bachmann, Rietzsch [chap. 10], and Gutmann [chap. 11]) and tried desperately to preserve African culture.

Of the various branches of the *Wandervogel*, one in particular needs to be mentioned: Wingolf, a group that Thomas Mann immortalized in his 1947 novel *Dr. Faustus*. The main character, Adrian Leverkühn, is a member of a theological fraternity that Mann calls Winfried (i.e., Wingolf). Mann's consultant, the theologian Paul Tillich, wrote about his time with the fraternity:

> What I became as a theologian, a philosopher, and a human being I owe partly to my professors, but to a larger extent to the fraternity, where theological and philosophical debates after midnight and personal talks before sunrise remained decisive for my entire life. Music played a big part, and the Romantic relationship to nature . . . I owe above all to the hikes through Thuringia and to the Wartburg in those years, in community with my fraternity brothers.[10]

Wartburg, the medieval castle where the so-called *Sängerkrieg* supposedly took place in the thirteenth century (the *Sängerkrieg* is fictional, but Walther von der Vogelweide and Wolfram von Eschenbach are said to have participated), and the castle in which Luther translated the Bible, is an ideal place for reinventing the Middle Ages. Virtually all missionaries of the Bethel Mission (chap. 12) came from the Wingolf fraternity.

The longing for the simple life went hand in hand with a longing for the Middle Ages and old folk song, which was, of course, romanticized. This fascination with the Middle Ages did not begin with the *Wandervogel* but had a precedent in Romanticism, as, for example, in Richard Wagner's choosing to set *Tannhäuser* in the Wartburg. *Wandervögel* hiked around Germany in the search for old folk songs, which they called *echte* [genuine] *Volkslieder*.[11] The idea of collecting old folk songs is, of course, not very different from what Achim von Arnim and Clemens Brentano had done with their collection *Des Knaben Wunderhorn* a century earlier. This is exactly what the mission inspector Walther Trittelvitz had in mind when he wanted his Haya missionaries to collect Haya "folk songs" (chap. 12). New is the stress on participatory music making, as well as the antimodernist and antitechnological angle. Remarkable, too, is that this movement swept through the entire country, all religious denominations, and all social classes.

THE *JUGENDMUSIK-* AND *SINGBEWEGUNG,* THE LEADERS, AND THE PUBLISHERS

Many followers of the *Wandervogel* movement joined in the related *Jugendbewegung*, which was split into numerous subgroups, two of which are particularly important for us: the *Jugendmusikbewegung*, which was founded in 1917 when Fritz Jöde (1887–1970) and Herman Reichenbach (1898–1958) founded the *Musikantengilde*, an amateur music society.[12] Kallmeyer-Möseler, in Wolfenbüttel, published most of their music, journals, and books. Jöde and Reichenbach had important positions in Weimar Germany and helped build Germany's music education system.

Equally important is the *Singbewegung*, which grew out of the *Wandervogel* and the *Jugendmusikbewegung* and shared many of their goals. Its origins are usually located in the Finkensteiner Woche of 1923, organized by Walther Hensel in the Moravian town of Finkenstein.

THE *JUGENDMUSIKBEWEGUNG*

Fritz Jöde has received extensive attention in German secondary literature. An extraordinarily charismatic and energetic elementary-school teacher from Hamburg with no advanced degree (he studied a bit with Hermann Abert in Leipzig), he conducted sing-alongs in Berlin in the 1920s and '30s in which thousands participated. From 1923 on he was professor of *Volksmusikerziehung* at the Staatliche Akademie für Kirchen- und Schulmusik in Berlin, a special school for the education of teachers that is now part of Universität der Künste.[13] In 1923 he founded the first *Jugendmusikschule* in Germany in Berlin, and in 1925, the first *Volksmusikschule*, with his friend Reichenbach appointed as the first director.

After 1933 Jöde was viewed with suspicion because of his socialist sympathies and friendship with Jews (Reichenbach and Leo Kestenberg), and he lost his job in 1936. Somehow he managed to get a job in a radio station in Munich, and from 1939 to 1945 he taught at the Mozarteum in Salzburg. His record during the Nazi period is not blameless: after 1933 he recommended to his colleagues from the *Jugendmusikbewegung* that they continue their musical work under National Socialism, and he wrote that the spirit of the *Jugendmusikbewegung* should now reach the entire German *Volk* through Hitler Youth (*Hitlerjugend*).[14] Thus, it is perhaps not surprising that he joined the NSDAP in 1940, only to leave it in 1943.[15] After World War II he was the director of music education at the Hamburg Musikhochschule, and from 1953 on he was also director of the Internationales Institut für Kirchen- and Schulmusik in Trossingen.

Like Besseler, Jöde disliked popular music and jazz (although after the war his attitude toward the latter changed). Similarly, his passion for *Gemeinschaftsmusik* became so intense that he took an active dislike to what he called *bürgerliche Kunstheuchelei* (bourgeois art hypocrisy) in concert halls. He was introduced to early music by Reichenbach and published a lot of polyphonic music, mainly with Kallmeyer/Möseler.[16] For example, in the preface to his edition of "Alte Madrigale und andere a capella-Gesänge aus dem 16. und 17. Jahrhundert" (Old Madrigals and Other A Capella Songs from the 16th and 17th Centuries) he is highly critical of the harmonic language of the nineteenth century and compares it unfavorably to madrigal-style polyphony.[17] Jöde edited the important *Jugendmusikbewegung* journals *Die Laute* (1919–23) and *Die Musikantengilde* (1923–31) in addition to making numerous editions of vocal and instrumental music.[18] In short, Jöde turned Besseler's scholarship into practice. In his sing-alongs he regularly combined early medieval as well as fifteenth- and sixteenth-century German songs with folk songs.[19]

By all accounts, Herman Reichenbach (fig. 8.1) was the major intellectual force of the movement, and yet he has been almost entirely forgotten.[20] Like Jöde, Reichenbach was born in Hamburg, though more than a decade later.[21] Reichenbach studied musicology, mathematics, and physics in Vienna, Freiburg, and Berlin. He participated in the performances of medieval music in Karlsruhe and Hamburg and eventually wrote a dissertation entitled "Wandel im Musikinstrumentarium vom Barock zur Klassik" (The Evolution of Musical Instruments from the Baroque to the Classical Period; 1922).[22] According to various accounts by his *Jugendmusikbewegung* friends, these formative years of study under Gurlitt first introduced him to medieval music, and he transmitted his passion for this repertoire to his friends in the movement. In fact, he made sure that an entire generation of youth understood that medieval music was central to understanding any kind of Western music.[23]

After he finished his dissertation, in 1924 Reichenbach became a research assistant (Wissenschaftlicher Assistant) to Ernst Kurth, whose writings were of great importance for the movement.[24] In 1925 he was appointed director of the Volksmusikschule Berlin-Charlottenburg, where he remained until 1933. There are numerous letters in the archive in Burg Ludwigstein that describe his remarkable activities there. In 1930 he became director of the Music Division of the Central Institute for Education and Teaching (Direktor der Musikabteilung am Zentralinstitut für Erziehung und Unterricht) in Berlin. In other words, he held one of the most important music-education positions in Weimar Germany.

A friend of Walter Benjamin and Adorno, Reichenbach had always had left-wing sympathies, but after 1933 he joined the Sozialistischer Studentenbund, a social democratic organization, which was immediately banned by the Nazis. His friendship with Otto Grotewohl (1894–1964), the first prime minister of the German Democratic Republic, must have started in this period. As soon as the Nazis came to power in 1933 he was fired from his Berlin

Figure 8.1a. Herman Reichenbach. Courtesy of Herman Reichenbach Jr.

Figure 8.1b. The Reichenbach siblings. *Left to right*: The journalist Bernhard Reichenbach, Wendelin Reichenbach, the philosopher Hans Reichenbach, and Herman Reichenbach. Courtesy of Herman Reichenbach Jr.

positions for racial and political reasons and forced to emigrate. The next years found him in Czechoslovakia,[25] where he conducted an orchestra among Wolga Germans in a town called Pokrowsk or, perhaps more commonly, Engels. By this time he was thoroughly disillusioned with communism, and in 1938 he managed to emigrate to the United States. Much to his chagrin, he could not get a teaching position in musicology or music, only in physics. He taught first at Mary Washington College at Fredricksburg, Virginia, then from 1948 on at Wilson College at Chambersburg, Pennsylvania. His last job was at Anderson College in Indiana, where he died in 1958 of a heart attack.

His American years were unhappy ones. His wife was half Chinese, and she and their daughter were not allowed to live with him in Virginia because of the state's antimiscegenation laws. It is quite ironic that he was forced into exile because he was Jewish according to Nuremberg race laws (his son told me that his father never considered himself Jewish) and then, in the United States, was not allowed to live with his wife because they were of different races.[26] He would have loved to teach music rather than physics, and he had trouble making friends. The most moving statement comes at the end of Jöde's obituary, written in the form of a letter to his old friend, where he quotes Reichenbach: "But what is the significance of all of these academic appointments [in the United States] when you consider the words with which you said goodbye to me in 1956 after your last visit: 'If only there were some kind of position for me back home! One is so terribly alone over there.' It was too late."[27]

Many émigrés returned to Germany after the war, and most of those who stayed in the United States did not want to return.[28] So why was it not possible for Reichenbach to get a job in Germany? He could have returned to the German Democratic Republic: his friend Otto Grotewohl had offered him a position, but he turned it down because he was thoroughly disillusioned with communism after his stay in the Soviet Union in the 1930s. I find it hard to believe that Jöde, who remained very influential after the war, could not have found a good job for his old friend. There was an enormous shortage of music teachers in *Gymnasien* after the war, and *Jugendmusikschulen*, all of which needed directors, had been founded throughout Germany. His experience from the Weimar years would have made him an ideal candidate for the directorship of such a school. There are many possible reasons for Jöde's reluctance. By all accounts Reichenbach was a quiet scholar and a mediocre administrator.[29] He never wrote a *Habilitation*, which made it impossible for him to get a university appointment. But Jöde's reluctance might also be connected with some shame he may have felt over his wartime life as a Nazi collaborator. In contrast to many others, he at least addressed his Nazi past in his obituary for Reichenbach:

> Politics also separated us as people. It had to be bitter for you; it had to appear as a betrayal against you that the largest part of your friends believed that they had to preserve the movement through the new times. We were soon forced to realize that this was impossible, and everyone has had to reckon with himself over the past. But of us all you had it hardest, because you now drifted around the world for years, because you were politically and humanly suspicious to the new rulers, and you, who had been expelled from your home, were only looking for one thing: to settle down somewhere away from home, and to find again the same kind of work as what we had done together.[30]

The central concept of the *Jugendmusikbewegung* is *Gemeinschaft*, or comradeship—being there for one another and helping one another. One cannot help but wonder where all of Reichenbach's friends were when he wanted to return to Germany after the war.

Reichenbach was important for the *Jugendmusikbewegung* for a couple of reasons: (1) he published numerous articles on what the *Jugendmusikbewegung* was all about, many republished in the volume *Die deutsche Jugendmusikbewegung in Dokumenten ihrer Zeit*; and (2) the first part of his *Formenlehre* (1929; the second part was never published) was without a doubt the most important theory book of the movement. Its influence would soon reach all the way to Africa. A detailed discussion of *Formenlehre* follows below.[31]

THE *SINGBEWEGUNG*

The *Singbewegung* had a more religious and nationalistic (*völkisch*) orientation than the *Jugendmusikbewegung*, advocating from the beginning the performance of Lutheran music, in particular that of Hans-Leo Hassler, Leonard Lechner, Michael Praetorius, Johann Hermann Schein, Samuel Scheidt, and most important, Heinrich Schütz. Many distinguished musicologists came out of the *Singbewegung*, including Konrad Ameln, Friedrich Blume, Werner Blankenburg, Wilhelm Ehmann, Christhard Mahrenholz, and Oskar Söhnken.[32] Blume and Blankenburg, in particular, regularly drew a direct line to Martin Luther's liturgy and the Lutheran chorales—the origin of participatory music making. Blankenburg also stressed the origin of congregational singing in the early Moravian churches.[33] Surprisingly, since it was primarily a Protestant movement, Gregorian chant was also promoted. Yet not all members were Protestants: Joseph Müller-Blattau was part of the Anthroposophical Society, and the chant scholar Walther Lipphardt (1906–1981) was a Catholic.

Walther Hensel (1887–1956), a native of Moravia,[34] and his wife, Olga Pokorny, a singer, speech therapist, and voice teacher, were the original founders of the movement, which started after a sing-along in the Moravian village of Finkenstein.[35] There is little doubt that he, like many members of *Singbewegung*, was a supporter of the Nazi regime, even though he eventually ran into problems with it.[36] Like Jöde, he was a charismatic conductor with a major following who introduced thousands to his two passions: medieval music and folk music. The *Singbewegung* would not have existed without him. He was not a serious scholar but more of a Romantic dreamer who tried to follow in Herder's and Grimm's footsteps.[37]

Konrad Ameln (1899–1994) represents the spirit of the *Singbewegung* better than anyone else. He was a student of Ludwig and Gurlitt and participated in the performances in Karlsruhe and Hamburg.[38] His dissertation with Gurlitt, "Geschichte der Melodie 'Innsbruck, ich muss dich lassen' und 'Ach Gott, vom Himmel sieh darein'" (1929), set the agenda for the rest of his life in that he became the leading expert on Lutheran chorales. He was one of the editors of the interdenominational hymnal *Das deutsche Kirchenlied* (The German Chorale), in which he tried to find the original, "authentic" versions of the chorales. His association with Bärenreiter was close from the beginning: he edited the *Singbewegung* journal *Singgemeinde* from 1925 to 1933. His edition of Christmas carols, entitled *Das Quempas-Heft* (1930, 1934, 1962, and 1965), became another big best seller and can be found in many Lutheran homes.[39] He edited many volumes of Leonhard Lechner's output. Like his mentors Ludwig and Gurlitt, he really liked music only from the fifteenth to eighteenth centuries and did much to restore it to the Lutheran service.[40]

Surprisingly, Ameln was also interested in non-European music. When the missionary Franz Rietzsch wrote to Bärenreiter asking if they could help him find literature on pentatonicism in polyphony, he received an answer from Ameln, who was working on precisely this topic and, according to Rietzsch, expressed the hope that African polyphony would show the way (see chap. 10, p. 163). Rietzsch and Ameln became close friends and regular correspondents, and after the war Ameln sent packages to the Rietzsch family. Under the GDR in the 1950s and '60s, Rietzsch was regularly sent to archives to check out manuscripts for Ameln.[41]

Ameln's publications had enormous influence: in 1925 he published the facsimile of the *Lochamer Liederbuch* (which includes forty-five notated songs that were quickly adopted by the singers), followed soon thereafter by the *Glogauer Liederbuch* (1937) and the *Schedelsches Liederbuch* (1933), and later the facsimile of a 1531 hymnbook of the Moravian composer-compiler Michael Weisse (1957). He was also an important performer, for example participating regularly in performances in Burg Ludwigstein. For his concerts in his hometown of Lüdenscheid he collaborated with one of the founding members of the Schola Cantorum Basiliensis, the viola da gamba player August Wenzinger, and the recorder player and flutist Ferdinand Conrad to create "authentic" performances.

The Berneuchen Movement, part of the Lutheran Liturgical Movement, was established to reinvigorate the church service and counter the influence of liberal theology. Several members were also close to the *Singbewegung*. This movement was also concerned with authenticity: worshippers returned to the traditional Lutheran liturgy (including the sung Mass Ordinary that Martin Luther adapted from the Catholic rite). Franz Rietzsch was a passionate admirer of the group, whose members met annually at the manor Berneuchen in Neumark, now in Poland. The most famous member was the theologian and old Wingolf member Paul Tillich.[42] While most members of the *Singbewegung* had National Socialist sympathies, the Berneuchen circle was closer to the Confessing Church (Bekennende Kirche), and a few of the members were active in the resistance.[43] The family of Maria von Wedemeyer, the theologian Dietrich Bonhoeffer's fiancée, was part of the group, but Bonhoeffer remained ambivalent and is reputed to have said, "Only those who cry out on behalf of the Jews are also allowed to sing Gregorian chant."[44]

THE PUBLISHERS: KALLMEYER-MÖSELER AND BÄRENREITER

Both Kallmeyer/Möseler and Bärenreiter were established essentially to provide music for the *Jugendmusik*- and *Singbewegung*.[45] Kallmeyer-Möseler published the journals *Die Laute*, later called *Die Musikantengilde*, and, most important, the series *Das Chorwerk*, edited by Friedrich Blume, which provided generations of singers in schools and in choirs with excellent editions of early music. The founder of the German publishing house Bärenreiter, Karl Vötterle, was an enthusiastic *Singbewegung* participant and a close friend of Walther Hensel, and he soon started issuing his first publication, the *Finkensteiner Blätter*. Bärenreiter also published the journals *Die Singgemeinde* and *Musik und Kirche* as well as numerous collected editions and facsimiles, among them the works of Heinrich Schütz.

Both Kallmeyer-Möseler and Bärenreiter became major publishing houses under the Nazi government after 1933, even though before 1933 the Kallmeyer authors regularly wrote that music rose above all political parties and confessions. An anonymous author from the movement wrote:

> I don't want to end this report without . . . pointing out the entirely nonpartisan and interdenominational nature of our musical work. It is almost impossible for many of us who are active in a political party to believe in nonpartisanship in our daily life in these conflicting times, so we are constantly attacked from the Right and the Left. But it has to be stressed again and again that we are seriously trying to avoid politics altogether.[46]

All of this changed in 1933. Georg Kallmeyer, who died in 1945, published *Musikblätter der Hitlerjugend* (Song Sheets of the Hitler Youth), as well as *Wir Mädel singen* (We Girls Sing) and cantatas for Nazi festivities. He wrote in 1938:

> The most beautiful event was the spring of songs, which came to bloom in the young people who were deeply moved by the new ideology and this was reflected in the "Song Sheets of the Hitler Youth" that appeared in my publishing house, several million copies of which were distributed all over Germany. It was one of the great pleasures of my life to see that the inner stream of my earlier work thus flowed into this enormous new come-into-being.[47]

Concerning Bärenreiter, there is a revealing letter by Herbert Just dated 11 March 1970 and written in preparation for the volume *Die Jugendmusikbewegung*. Karl Vötterle and Richard Baum, the owner and editor, respectively, of Bärenreiter, were not in favor of including the years 1933–45. They argued that one would have to cite publications that would compromise people who are now active in German musical life.[48] As a result, the volume ends in 1933. *Die Jugendmusikbewegung* includes at the end short biographies of the most important members of the movement. Not surprisingly, many were tainted by close association with the Nazis (Ameln, Ehmann, Jöde, and Heinrich Spitta, among others), but not one of these associations is mentioned.

THE MOVEMENTS IN THEORY AND PRACTICE

There are three central elements characteristic of the *Jugendmusik-* and *Singbewegung*: a rediscovery of medieval music; a passionate interest in folk music, be it German, European, or non-European; and a belief in *Gemein-schaftsmusik*, that is, participatory singing and playing. Both early music and folk music are the quintessential participatory music and are a logical consequence of *Gemeinschaftsmusik*. All of this is combined with a dislike for the concert hall, modernity, and anything popular (such as popular music), as well as anything American.

THE *JUGENDMUSIKBEWEGUNG* AND THE MIDDLE AGES

The passionate interest in music of the Middle Ages can be seen in the publications, editions of music, and programs of all groups in the movement. However, the only member of the movement to present a coherent scholarly analysis of medieval music and its relationship to the later repertoire was Reichenbach. He argues in his *Formenlehre* that medieval music and music theory are central to musical forms in general. In fact, he based his entire theory of form on church modes, more specifically pentatonic modes. Reichenbach explains why he starts his *Formenlehre* with church modes:

> I see the historical foundation [of musical forms] in the medieval system of church modes. Their importance lies not only in modes as scalar concepts, but in the fact that they are categories of formal traditions. They are the melodic "Urgestalten," of which every work in existence is just a variant. The reason I had to explain all of this in such detail is that this understanding of church modes is fundamentally different from their usual description.[49]

He begins by describing the church modes as we know them and explains that they are defined by the final, the range, and the reciting tone, as well as the species of fourth and fifth, citing all the usual literature.[50] This is followed by a most unusual and surprising chapter entitled "Pentatonik."[51] He summarizes his basic argument in the very first sentence: "Medieval music theorists could have based their music just as well on a pentatonic modal system as on the Greek one."[52] He argues that it is generally accepted that Gregorian chant has pentatonic roots. Reichenbach even includes a table (33–34) about the occurrences of half steps in the *Graduale Romanum* of church modes, which shows clearly that they are uncommon. His sources for this supposition are, for the most part, two books: Oskar Fleischer's *Neumen-Studien* (1897) and Hugo Riemann's *Folkloristische Tonalitätsstudien* (1916). To a lesser extent, he also referred to Peter Wagner's work.[53] Both Fleischer and Wagner believed that pentatonic scales in chant derived

Pentatonisch   Kirchentonig

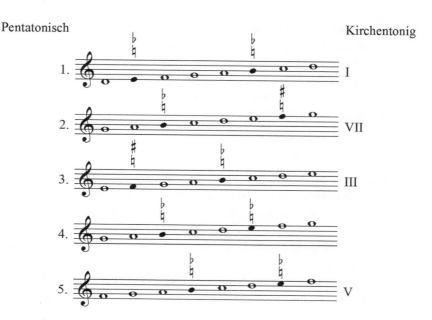

Figure 8.2. Reichenbach's pentatonic modes. From his *Formenlehre*, 31.

from "Nordic influences," although Reichenbach admits that Wagner no longer subscribed to the theory that all chant is pentatonic, because old Roman chant was not pentatonic.[54] For the pentatonic nature of "Nordic music" he cites "the important essay by Joseph Müller-Blattau on the question of racial music."[55] He concludes this passage: "Present-day ethnomusicological research has resulted in the conclusion that the pentatonic scale is the foundation of almost all music cultures, not just the oriental, but also the Germanic. The pentatonic scale is something like the 'Urskala' of all music."[56] Reichenbach then lists his five pentatonic scales (fig. 8.2) and relates them to church modes (he adds the half steps that can occur in, say, Chinese music as black notes in his table; they can be low or high depending on the tonal system; see table 8.1 in Reichenbach, *Formenlehre*, 81). Throughout he includes examples of pentatonic Gregorian chant and folk music from around the world.

The idea of pentatonicism as a possible musical universal continues to have numerous distinguished advocates, among them Jacques Chailley and Bruno Nettl.[57] The Tanzanian priest, composer, and ethnomusicologist Stephan Mbunga argued in 1963 that it is common to all cultures (see chap. 13), and in 1979 the Danish chant scholar Finn Egeland Hansen dedicated an entire book to the hypothesis that Gregorian chant was originally pentatonic.[58]

The material in Reichenbach's book was taught at music schools and singing retreats all over Germany, and Rietzsch owned a copy of the book (see chap. 10). Thus, every participant knew his church modes inside out, was familiar with the different pentatonic scales, and knew that non-Western music could be based on a tonal system other the major-minor one. Most important, every student of Reichenbach's *Formenlehre* must have understood that medieval and non-Western music have something in common. This explains the familiarity with which many missionaries and mission administrators (in particular Rietzsch [chap. 10], Trittelvitz and Hagena [chap. 12]) discuss early and non-Western music. Similarly, medieval music theory was firmly established in the curriculum of teacher-training colleges, where Ameln taught for years.

The fascination with music of the Middle Ages is present in other publications of the *Jugendmusik*- and *Singbewegung* as well. Hensel's *Finkensteiner Blätter*, intended for a general audience, appeared every month. In the very first volume Hensel published a short article entitled "Vom gregorianischen Choral" (On Gregorian Chant). Not only is Gregorian chant considered the origin of all music, but it is based on a central concept that can be traced back to what Ernst Kurth calls "linear monophony" (*lineare Einstimmigkeit*).[59]

JUGENDMUSIKBEWEGUNG AND FOLK MUSIC

We have seen earlier that the idea of collecting folk songs in the spirit of Achim von Arnim and Clemens Brentano was a central element of the *Wandervogel* ideology. As a result, serious scholars at numerous institutions explored the subject. The German Volksliedarchiv in Freiburg in Breisgau was founded in 1914 originally with the intention of collecting folk songs, and eventually it became an important research institution.[60] The choice of Freiburg for a folk-song collection was unsurprising: it was home to Martin Heidegger and later Gurlitt and Besseler, all strongly influenced by the movement. The musicologist Walter Wiora, a highly original student of both Hornbostel and Gurlitt, was active for many years in the Freiburg Institute and fundamentally reshaped the field of folk-music research.[61] Similarly, in 1935 the Staatliches Institut für Musikforschung, Abteilung Volksmusik, was founded and directed between 1937 and 1938 by Besseler's and Schneider's friend Kurt Huber.[62] Another scholar who did important work on orality in the Balkans and connected it to medieval music was the musicologist Gustav Becking, a friend of Hensel and a professor at the German

University in Prague, where he also conducted a collegium musicum.[63] He wrote an important article on the oral transmission of epics in Montenegro in an attempt to explain how early music was transmitted orally;[64] his work anticipates that of Leo Treitler.[65] Becking, a member of the NSDAP, was shot in 1945 by the Czechs.

The 1920s and '30s saw serious research into orally transmitted music, many of it done by members of the movement and/or former students of Hornbostel and Stumpf. The central character in Berlin was Georg Schüne-mann (see chap. 4, pp. 60–64). Schünemann was not officially a member of the *Jugendmusikbewegung*, yet he shared many of their interests and helped realize their music-pedagogical ambitions in his collaboration with Leo Kestenberg.

As we have seen, folk music was equally central for performing members of the *Jugendmusik-* and *Singbewegung*. Jöde had a strong interest in folk music. In 1937 he went on an extensive trip to the Balkans. In preparation for his journey, he went to visit Kurt Huber, who was then at the Staatliches Institut für Musikforschung.[66]

Wherever he went he tried to find local music, which he would then adapt for choir. The archive at Burg Ludwigstein has most of these publications, and it is astonishing how many "nations" are represented: Norway, Ukraine, Turkey, Tuscany, Andalusia, Russia, Lithuania, Korea, Chile, and North American Native Americans (by his friend Reichenbach), to name just a few. Some were probably transcribed from listening. He often includes a summary or translation of the text in the original language. Frequently, he expressed his conviction that folk songs outside of Germany were closer to the original medieval version.[67]

Hensel, under the influence of Herder and Grimm, repeatedly told his singers that only through folk music could you understand different peoples, an idea that recurs regularly with the missionaries we will soon consider. But what was new in the twentieth century was the realization that folk singing is really a prime example of *Gemeinschaftsmusik*, a collective experience that was originally created by an individual, taken up by a community, and orally transmitted over centuries by groups of singers.

Thus, the first question members would always ask themselves was, what was the age of the song? If it was old it was considered worthy of consideration; if it was of nineteenth-century vintage, less so. Next, what kind of changes did it undergo? Hensel's main contribution lies in folk-song collections in which he tries to establish what is the original version of a song and to distinguish between *echte* (original) and *unechte* (not original) *Volks-*

lieder. Many of his articles are simply entitled "Vom wahren Volkslied" (About the True Folk Song).[68] His goal was to save the population from the swamp of what he calls *Unkultur* (roughly translated as "complete lack of culture") through folk song.[69]

Noteworthy also is the fact that Ameln was interested in non-European music. As the editor of *Die Singgemeinde*, he published two articles by Bruno Gutmann on the Wachagga (1928; see chap. 11) and one by Gertrud Weißenbruch, the daughter of a missionary, on music in Sumatra (1931–32). The Sumatra article even includes transcriptions of songs, clearly reproduced in the hope of having choirs sing them. In addition, Bärenreiter published several books by Gutmann on participatory music making among the Wachagga. In all of these articles the music is transcribed by missionaries, and there is no concern with "authenticity," as there is with Hornbostel and his students. The primary objective is to have these songs performed in Germany.

The interest in the search for the true and original, whether medieval folk song or chorale, goes hand in hand with a passionate dislike for recent and contemporary popular music and hymns by the American Ira D. Sankey, known as "Sankey hymns," known in German as *Reichslieder*.[70] Fritz Reusch, a music educator and the first director of the Spandauer Kirchenmusikschule, a *Singbewegung* institution founded in 1929, cites extensively from what he calls *Kitschlieder*, which are full of "thick, sentimental emotions," both musically and textually (he gives several highly entertaining examples).[71] Reusch and his colleagues are critical of these songs because they are American, date to the nineteenth century, and come from fundamentalist Protestants, in particular groups such as the Salvation Army.

THE *JUGENDMUSIKBEWEGUNG* AND *GEMEINSCHAFTSMUSIK*

So what were these sing-alongs and retreats really like? What did participants find so appealing about participatory music making? For many of us, these events are difficult to imagine. Two colorful accounts give an inkling. The first was written by Jöde's collaborator Ekkehart Pfannenstiel, who described how Jacques Handschin attended an amateur choir rehearsal in 1928 in Berlin. The choir consisted of, believe it or not, five hundred insurance agents:

> After the choir rehearsal . . . an older gentleman with a goatee came to me and introduced himself: "Jacques Handschin." "Ekkehart Pfannenstiel.

Excuse me, but are you the distinguished musicologist from Switzer-land?" "Well, what I experienced here, deserves the attribute distin-guished just as much."[72]

A few weeks later Handschin sent Pfannenstiel an article published in a Swiss journal in which he wrote:

> I am closing the review with a picture observed in Berlin. On a Sunday afternoon an "open singing lesson" of a youth association of a large in-surance agency for employees took place in a large, friendly room. In the middle there was a small group of instrumentalists (no piano), and here, on a pedestal, was the director of the whole choir [Jöde]. The singing lesson begins with an Italian praise of music that is apparently familiar to the participants. Then many new songs are learned, and how they are being learned. Without blackboard and chalk, without first playing them on the piano, the conductor draws the melody with an expressive hand gesture in the air, demanding that they hear it within themselves, and lo and behold, the melody is understood. . . . There is a special spirit in these choir rehearsals. If you could remove from the word "religious" anything that is associated with the Church, then I would say that this community spirit is of a religious nature.[73]

Handschin also notes, in the spirit of Besseler, that polyphonic music is "the true representative of 'community in action,' and early music as a whole stands in for the connection between music and lifestyle that has been lost in our time to a concert life that is much too dominating."[74]

The second account is by Reichenbach and describes a sing-along in 1930, also conducted by Jöde in the Jungfernheide Park, in the Charlotten-burg borough of Berlin, that was attended by four thousand people from all political parties and religious denominations (fig. 8.3):

> For some years now, every summer the "Volksmusikschule der Musikan-tengilde e.V." of Charlottenburg has arranged a sing-along for all Berlin youth interested in music. The event, which takes place in the large am-phitheater of the open-air theater of the Jungfernheide Park, has now ac-quired a tradition. . . . One cannot escape this experience if one is pres-ent; when a huge crowd of four thousand festively dressed people starts to come alive, when calls, criticism, cheering, and jokes are thrown around, and finally everyone is united by singing together. . . .

Figure 8.3. Sing-along at Berlin Jungfernheide in 1930, attended by four thousand people. Courtesy of Archiv der deutschen Jugendbewegung, Burg Ludwigstein, Witzenhausen.

And this sing-along is a major occasion. One has only to look at the sociological composition of the participants, and to compare them to the audience of an orchestral concert, with the audiences at a political event, with the audience of a modern theater, film, or dance premiere. . . . The majority of participants are from the *Jugendbewegung*. Many arrive in groups directly from the Saturday–Sunday excursion. The banners of all parties and confessions are represented ranging from swastikas to the Soviet star without there being the slightest trouble. This is a fact that cannot be ignored. . . . And in between there sit men and women from all social classes; they have been invited by one of the sponsors, the Charlottenburg Education Department. Only one class is missing, the one that is generally called by humorous magazines the typical Berliner, and that is the intellectual snob.[75]

Reichenbach believed that communal singing would bridge political divides. In fact, most members of the *Jugendmusikbewegung* were desperately aware of the political tensions that were tearing the country apart in the early 1930s and tried to use music to overcome political and confessional divisions.

The *Singbewegung* sing-alongs were more intimate affairs, even though the organizers also reached a large number of singers: by all accounts some two thousand sing-alongs, in which more than a million singers participated, took place all over Germany between 1923 and 1945. In addition, there were also meetings in other European countries and even in Africa.[76] The Moravian Church hosted many gatherings in their settlements, such as Bad Boll, Gnadenfrei, Königsfeld, Herrnhut, Neudietendorf, and Niesky, as did Bethel, the headquarters of the Bethel mission. An invitation to a meeting on 15–22 September 1937 in the Moravian headquarters in Herrnhut reads:

> Now a new kind of singing has come to life in the Protestant Church. The Reformation songs suddenly speak to the man of today. . . . We ask you to come to make this living source more productive also for the Moravians. This is why we have asked Pastor Gölz from Wankheim near Tübingen to direct our Herrnhuter Singwoche. Anybody who has a wish to sing and make music within the Christian Church can participate. Therefore members of the official Protestant State Church are also welcome. Experience has also shown that singing and making music together bridges the differences between young and old.[77]

No alcohol or smoking was allowed,[78] and singers stayed in youth hostels or slept on haystacks. The daily schedule looked something like this: wake up, physical exercise, morning celebration (usually outside in a circle; fig. 8.4), breathing and voice exercises, music theory, choral singing, lunch, afternoon rest; the rest of the afternoon was like the morning. After dinner there were music, reading aloud, storytelling, and an end-of-the-day celebration. Sometimes musicologists, such as Besseler, were invited to give lectures on medieval music. For example, a meeting held on 3–7 October 1926 in Brieselang, near Berlin, for teachers and students included the following lectures:

> Friedrich Blume: Heinrich Schütz and Protestant church music
> Heinrich Kaminski: the church modes as the origins of music
> Hans Mersmann: vocal polyphony in the sixteenth century
> F. von Baußern: folk song and chorale
> Herman Reichenbach: music theory in the Middle Ages
> Wilibald Gurlitt: the *Jugendbewegung* and new music.[79]

Food was modest, mainly tea and bread. Men had to be at least eighteen years old, women seventeen. The *Singbewegung* gatherings usually took place in nature, and the participants liked to form circles.

In Gottes freier Natur sammelt sich die Singgemeinde zum Kreis und läßt die alten Weisen erschallen

Figure 8.4. Morning celebration in a circle of a *Singbewegung* gathering. Courtesy of Archiv der deutschen Jugendbewegung, Burg Ludwigstein, Witzenhausen.

While this meeting was geared toward teachers, many sing-alongs included amateurs. The list of participants is remarkably diverse for the *Jugendmusik-* and *Singbewegung*. Attendees might include, as you would expect, a lot of students, but also salesmen, housekeepers, teachers, pastors, social workers, and various craftsmen, such as tailors. In addition, there were also plenty of *Volksmusikschulen* (folk-music schools) for amateurs. Especially noteworthy are the ones in Berlin: one in Charlottenburg, directed by Herman Reichenbach, and another in Neukölln, a working-class neighborhood with many socialists.[80] In fact, Bukofzer was part of a socialist choir in his Berlin years.[81]

Perhaps Reichenbach put it best when he summarized the new spirit of the movement in an article published in *Melos* in 1925: "Thus, responsibility to the community is to be understood not as an order to subordination, but as consciousness to be a part of a whole that gives you tasks to fulfill."[82] Participatory music making is always contrasted with formal concerts; the latter are full of "vanity, rivalry, criticism, and the isolation that comes with being a specialist."[83] Reichenbach continued:

At larger places they are now founding music schools, where music is taught along the lines of participatory music understanding. . . . We can no longer deny that there is now a generation of people who no longer go . . . to a concert, and have not . . . graduated from a conservatory. But they are able to sight-read a Bach choral fugue, they have their Schein Suite in their head, and their life is anchored in music.[84]

The idea of *Gemeinschaftsmusik* was appealing to socialists and Nazis alike, so it is not surprising that most leaders of the *Singbewegung* would hold important administrative positions after 1933, either with the Nazi government or with the Nazi branch of the Lutheran Church, Deutsche Christen.[85] No testimony to the power of these events is as striking as the account of Inge Scholl, the sister of Hans and Sophie Scholl, who were members of the resistance group Weisse Rose. She describes the impact of this participatory singing when it was transferred to *Hitlerjugend*: "But there was something else which attracted us with mysterious power and carried us along: the compact band of youth with their blowing flags, their eyes turned forward, and their drumbeat and song. Was this not something overwhelming, this companionship? Thus, it was no wonder that all of us, Hans and Sophie and all of us, became members of the Hitler Youth."[86] The Scholls quickly became disillusioned with the *Hitlerjugend* because of the authoritarian ways of the group leaders; they joined instead a forbidden group of the *Jugendbewegung* called Bündische Jugend. Sophie and Hans Scholl, as well as the ethnomusicologist Kurt Huber, were all executed in 1943.[87]

We have seen in this chapter how an entire country was swept up in the discovery of participatory music making: scholars who specialized in early music; choir conductors and singers; and explorers, colonial administrators, and missionaries who sought the premodern life they associated with participatory music in "primitive" societies, especially in Africa. Bourgeois concert life was frowned upon as the opposite of the old, "genuine" song and chorale that they believed might be found in the Middle Ages. Even though we have seen that comparative musicologists were generally convinced that medieval polyphony was improvised—indeed, Schünemann even saw creativity at work in the transmission of folk songs—none of the followers of the *Jugendmusikbewegung* were much interested in improvisation. They longed for the "pure and original" versions of early music and were in favor of "authentic" performances. We will see in part III how missionaries reinterpreted this longing for the Middle Ages in German East Africa, later called Tanganyika.

PART III

Music in the German Mission Stations in East Africa: Some Case Studies

In 1928 Erich Moritz von Hornbostel published an article in the first issue of the British ethnographic journal *Africa* on the impact of missionary activities on African music. His main impetus was to save the last remnants of foreign singing and language from the spread of European culture.[1] Thus, he wrote a number of articles in hopes that missionaries would read them. Hornbostel was not alone: Marius Schneider, Wilhelm Heinitz, and the Sierra Leone scholar Nicholas Taylor Ballanta were also addressing articles and lectures to missionaries. All were aware of the fact that missionaries were doing important ethnographic and linguistic work in Africa.[2]

I would like to summarize briefly the main points of Hornbostel's paper, since it had a defining influence on one of the missionaries discussed in this part, Franz Ferdinand Rietzsch.[3] So what were Hornbostel's recommendations? The answer can be found at the end of the text, where he lists three musical possibilities for missionaries in Africa:

1. Africans can sing the hymns "such as they are, with their texts in a European language."

2. "The Negroes are encouraged to produce songs, tunes, and words *'à l'européenne.'*" The result would be an output of "spirituals." In both cases they would "rapidly forget their own music, and Africa would become what North, Central, and large parts of South America and Polynesia (and of Africa itself) already are: that is a mere European colony as far as music is concerned."

3. "The Negroes are encouraged to sing and play in their own natural manner, that is to say, in the African manner. To what extent one can be broad-minded in this respect, as far as the Christian church and

school are concerned, I am not competent to judge. From a musical point of view, one cannot be broad-minded enough."[4]

Hornbostel's first option should probably be adjusted somewhat: I know of no instance among German Protestant missionaries of hymns being sung in German. Instead, they translated the hymns into the local languages, often without much regard for either local cultures or tonal languages. Catholic missionaries, on the other hand, also sang in Latin. German Lutheran and Moravian missionaries usually concentrated on old Lutheran chorales, although in 1907 doubts were raised as to whether the Africans were really "ready" for translated texts by the seventeenth-century German poet Paul Gerhardt.[5] English and American missionaries preferred Sankey hymns, also translated into African languages, which were used systematically and with great success as a missionary tool all over the world.[6]

Hornbostel's dislike for option 2 obviously stems from his fear that African music will die out if it is not preserved as is. And it also implies that whatever new music resulted from this practice could never be "authentic" in the way preexisting local practices were, nor could it ever become a new and important kind of music in its own right.[7] It is therefore unsurprising that he promulgated the third option, even though there cannot have been many who would have supported local music this early.

And yet, upon perusing the archives of the Berlin Phonogramm-Archiv I discovered that Hornbostel and Marius Schneider were in touch with a number of missionaries. Similarly, I found in the archives of four different German mission societies evidence that missionaries tried to put the suggestions made by Hornbostel, Schneider, Wilhelm Heinitz, and Ballanta into practice. The stories of these missionaries are worth telling, for a number of reasons:

- First, they describe the music of various African tribes that is now mostly extinct and anticipate many of the findings made in the 1960s and '70s by the Austrian ethnomusicologist Gerhard Kubik. Thus, anyone studying the music of Tanzania will have to take their research into consideration.
- Like Hornbostel, German missionaries were convinced that African music was similar to medieval music. Thus, they introduced Gregorian chant, Reformation-style chorales, and medieval polyphony in the belief that these were similar to African music.
- Scholars and musicians alike disliked modern society and technology and favored participatory music making, which they believed

was characteristic of all early music as well as non-Western music. Many German missionaries came from similar backgrounds as the musicologists discussed in the previous chapter, that is, the *Wandervogel* and *Jugendbewegung*: they were motivated by a dislike for modernity and civilization. They much preferred "primitive" life in Africa and were convinced that only in Africa could a true church be created—that only among Africans could one still find the deep spirituality that was absent from the hectic, modern life of the West.

And yet, as interested as the missionaries and the societies behind them (Herrnhut, Leipzig, Bethel, and St. Ottilien) were in documenting African languages, culture, and music, and as great their love was for the local population, there is no doubt that they were there because German East Africa was a colony. In 1884 the Society for German Colonization (Gesellschaft für Deutsche Kolonisation) was founded with the help of the infamous colonial explorer Carl Peters (1856–1918); in 1885 five German warships had convinced the sultan of Zanzibar that he had no chance of resistance. That same year the German East Africa Society (Deutsch-Ostafrikanische Gesellschaft) was founded, and by 1 April 1891 the area had become a German colony.

A number of British mission societies had been active in East Africa since the 1880s, but once East Africa became a German colony, the German chancellor, Otto von Bismarck, was adamant that German missionaries should be in charge. In fact, as a result of the new colonial acquisition there was a palpable euphoria for missionizing the population in the new territories. Germans throughout the country prayed for the missionaries, collected money for them, and read their letters and articles. Missionaries were among the most admired members of German society.[8]

The majority of mission societies tried to keep their distance from colonial administrators. They settled as far as possible from military posts so that the local population did not see them as part of the German government. For example, Leipzig missionaries purposely chose not to move to Moshi, because the German military was there; rather, they went to Machame. Wherever possible, I have followed what traces I could discover of the connection between colonial authorities and the mission societies (fig. 9.1). Yet, as we will see, their association with imperial Germany was complicated. While a few were very much in the service of the German empire, many questioned the power politics of colonial policies and were instrumental in documenting local customs and music for posterity.[9] Similarly, the behavior of missionaries during the Nazi period varied widely.

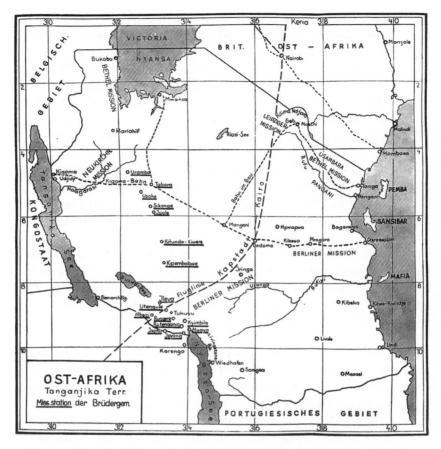

Figure 9.1. Map of mission stations in German East Africa. From Müller and Schulze, *200 Jahre Brüdermission*, 2:464.

German missionary activities were different from those in England or the United States for three reasons. First, they were directly dependent on Nikolaus Ludwig Graf von Zinzendorf and the Moravian Church.[10] Second, they were also strongly influenced by Johann Gottfried Herder in that they promoted *Wissenschaft*, "including a new look at Africa, by redefining the parameters of research," and a study of languages and cultures;[11] as a result, they did fundamental research in both areas. And third, many came directly out of the *Wandervogel* or the *Jugendbewegung* and longed for a return to a simpler life. They hoped to recover something akin to medieval culture in "primitive" societies. In what follows I will first give a short overview of missionary activity in Germany (which was started by the Moravians) and then discuss four different mission societies and some of their missionaries, three Protestant, one Catholic.

CHAPTER NINE

A History of the Missions

THE MORAVIANS

In 1722 Nikolaus Ludwig Graf von Zinzendorf gave permission to religious refugees from Bohemia and Moravia to settle on his estate in Saxony. They founded the village of Herrnhut. While the Bohemian Brethren go back to Johann Hus and received important guidance from Jan Comenius, it was Zinzendorf who newly inspired this religious community. They differed from other religious groups in four respects:

- they had an international outlook with congregations all over the world (among other places, in England, the Netherlands, Switzerland, and the United States);
- they lived in utopian settlements where everyone was supposed to be equal, whether they were craftsmen or aristocrats;
- they considered missionary activity their main responsibility in life; and
- most crucially for our purposes, they considered the singing of chorales to be the most important way to communicate with God both as individuals and as a group.

Even though they were a small community, they exerted a significant influence on many European intellectuals: Johann Wolfgang von Goethe was an admirer, the poet Novalis and the philosopher Søren Kirkegaard came from Moravian families, and the philosopher Friedrich Schleiermacher's education in a Moravian boarding school had a strong impact on his thinking.

Zinzendorf's theology was a mixture of Lutheran orthodoxy, pietism, and mysticism. The congregation took daily guidance from the Holy Spirit through extensive use of lots that determined virtually every aspect of daily

life. For example, lots decided who would be sent to Suriname as a missionary and who would be a good marriage partner for the missionary. Music
played a central role in Moravian communities from the very beginning.
The Moravian brother Michael Weisse edited a German Moravian hymnal
as early as 1531, and these hymns became important sources for Lutheran
chorales.[1]

A remarkable quality of Moravians in the diaspora is that they adapted
to whatever the dominant Protestant denomination was where they lived:
in the Netherlands they were close to Calvinists, in Germany to Lutherans,
and in England to Methodists and Presbyterians. Similarly, their missionaries tried to share the life of the local populations in every possible way.[2] The
first missionaries went in 1732 to St. Thomas in the Virgin Islands, where
they lived with the African slaves; later missionaries went to Greenland
in 1733 and to the Berbice region of Suriname in 1735–38.[3] Other places of
activity in the eighteenth and nineteenth centuries include North America
among Native Americans, Africa, Labrador, Jamaica, Australia, and the
Himalayas.

Zinzendorf did not want to convert an entire people to Christianity;
rather, he concentrated on "individual souls," whom he called "first fruits"
(Erstlinge). The term derives from Revelation 14:4: "These were redeemed
from among men, being the first fruits unto God and to the Lamb."[4] Thus,
Moravians were not interested in power or nation building, but in creating
and developing personal beliefs—in the salvation of individual souls. In the
beginning missionaries were not supported by mission societies but had to
survive by their own skills, such as carpentry, farming, and welding. Remarkably, Moravian missionaries were instructed to respect local cultures
and warned against judging the local populace by comparing them to Europeans. The Moravian theologian Theodor Bechler describes the Moravian
missionary attitude in 1906: "One of the main objectives of the messenger
to the heathens was to keep humans unchanged in the state with which
God has connected them with the systems of the world, yes, to keep it faith-
fully and functionally in it."[5] This went so far, that in the early years, even
polygamy was tolerated. Similarly, they were instructed not to work for
colonial societies. Yet in practice this was not always realized, since they
were also instructed never to disobey local governments.

What is perhaps not well-known is that missionaries did important scholarly work. Johann Gottfried Herder was an admirer of Zinzendorf because he
was free of the usual prejudices found in the Church.[6] Wilhelm von Humboldt
was in touch with numerous Moravian missionaries who made grammars for
him. The Greenland missionary Samuel Kleinschmidt (1814–1886) finished

his grammar of Greenlandic, an Inuit language, in 1845, and it was published in Berlin by Friedrich Wilhelm University in 1851; David Zeisberger (1721–1808) compiled Iroquoian and Algonquian dictionaries; and August Hermann Francke (1870–1930) was a missionary in the Himalayas and in 1925 became professor of Tibetan languages at Friedrich Wilhelm University.

The relationship between the missionaries and their home congregation was close. Before they left, there was a special *Singstunde* (a service that consisted primarily of singing chorales) at which they took their leave by singing "missionary hymns."[7] None of these missionary hymns is great poetry, but they show a wild determination to let people even in the remotest area of the world know about Jesus, undeterred by danger.[8]

Missionaries regularly wrote letters describing their daily life; most of them are preserved in the archives in Herrnhut and in Bethlehem, Pennsylvania.[9] When a letter from a missionary arrived, a bell was rung, and everyone gathered for a *Singstunde* to read the letter out loud and pray for the missionary and the souls to be converted. It is clear from these letters that the fact that Moravians all over the world were supporting them and praying for them was a tremendous help for the missionaries in their daily life.[10] For example, this hymn by Zinzendorf references the prayers for the missionaries:

We walk into distant countries and return
And each one of us tries, as well as we can, to make our fortune
But you, you sacred congregation of God,
Remember the witnesses and light their fire and shine on them.[11]

The days when excerpts from the missionaries' diaries were read by the home congregation were special ones for which Zinzendorf and others wrote new hymns. Meetings could easily last for four hours.[12] Missionaries were also remembered in the liturgical prayers for the Sunday service of 1742.[13]

After Zinzendorf's death in 1760, August Gottlieb Spangenberg (1704–1792) became the leader of the church. A relatively moderate theologian, he got rid of some of Zinzendorf's radical ideas;[14] for instance, rather than concentrating on the "first fruits," he promoted the idea of a popular or state church. Nevertheless, until the mid-nineteenth century all German mission societies more or less imitated the Moravians.

GUSTAV WARNECK AND THE *VOLKSKIRCHE*

The next important reformer was Gustav Warneck (1834–1910), who is generally considered the founder of the field of missiology as an academic discipline.

He served as the first professor of missiology at the University of Halle from 1897 to 1908, even though he was never active as a missionary.[15] In 1874 he founded the journal *Allgemeine Missions-Zeitschrift*.[16] Warneck can be credited with considering the *Volkskirche*, a difficult-to-translate term (some possibilities are "folk church" or "territorial church"), as the main goal of missionary activity. This constitutes a radical departure from the Moravian "first fruits."[17] It was at this point that German missionaries started to differ significantly from Anglo-Saxon ones in that they began to fall under the influence of Johann Gottfried Herder.

Herder argued that every *Volk* had its own history, heritage, and identity. Two new academic disciplines grew out of this idea: linguistics and anthropology. And this, in turn, had a tremendous impact on German mission societies: from the middle of the nineteenth century, at the latest, German missionaries were driven by an agenda they would call *völkisch* (perhaps the closest English equivalent is "ethnicist" or "nationalist"). Missionaries were taught to preserve as much as possible of the local traditions when converting the indigenous population. The local languages were to be preserved, the Bible was to be translated as fast as possible, and hymns were to be similarly translated. (Herder was a strong advocate of local languages, opposing the Church's use not only of Latin, but of any foreign language, such as, for example, French in Germany.)

When applied to missionary practice, the term *völkisch* referred, on the one hand, to a missionary theory "according to which local culture and race would shape the inculturation" of Christianity";[18] on the other, Christianity defined in this way would completely conquer the *Volk* and would not tolerate divergent views. These strongly anti-Western and antiegalitarian *völkisch* traditions remained firmly in place until the middle of the twentieth century.[19] As a result, many of the nineteenth- and twentieth-century missionaries of all denominations did fundamental ethnographic and linguistic work.[20] They usually had little education beyond the mission seminary. Yet, in order to convert the local population to Christianity, they had to learn local languages and in the process compiled dictionaries and grammars. Thus, when Tanganyika became a British mandate after World War I, German missionaries came into conflict with English authorities because the Germans wanted to preserve local languages, while the British were in favor of Swahili, a language that was spoken in most of East Africa.

From there it was but a small step to the ideals of those Christian groups in Germany who opposed modernity and pluralistic thought.[21] These groups were completely alienated by churches in their home country and sought an escape in Africa. The most important, and most eloquent, proponent of this ideology was the Leipzig missionary Bruno Gutmann, who became a role model for a whole series of younger missionaries from other societies in the 1930s (see chap. 11). To quote the Church historian Werner Ustorf: "Was there a unique chance of establishing a new form of symbiosis of Christian faith, Church, 'Volk' or nation, culture, and territory? A resurrection of medieval Christendom in an industrial age?"[22] The question now is: how were these ambitious and idealistic goals translated into action by the mission societies and their missionaries? We will start with the Moravians.

CHAPTER TEN

The Moravians

The main reason for the current reverse colonization is the self-interest of the white race. I see horrors descending upon Europe.
—Traugott Bachmann, *Ich gab so manchen Anstoss* (1957), 138–39

I believe that our old songs are really an excellent fit for the Negro. And not only this: I get more and more convinced that the only fruitful way of serving these congregations on our part is by introducing our old reformation chorales.
—Franz Rietzsch, letter to Samuel Baudert, 10 August–12 September 1932

TRAUGOTT BACHMANN

One of the main reasons that the Moravians decided to start their mission activities in German East Africa was a donation of 800,000 marks by the Breslau (now Wrocław, Poland) businessman Johann Daniel Crakau for the specific purpose of freeing slaves. The first Moravian mission station was opened in German East Africa in 1891 by Theodor Meyer in Rungwe among the Wanyakyusa (also called Konde) in the Southern Highlands of Tanzania (see again fig. 9.1).[1] Four years later additional stations were founded among the Ndali (in the Bandali Mountains), the Safwa (in Utengule), and the Nyiha (in Mbozi). Even though Traugott Bachmann (1865–1948; fig. 10.1) was one of the first generation of missionaries there, he is the most progressive, and the only one who spoke out publicly and early on against colonialism.[2] He made major contributions to documenting Nyiha language, culture, and music. His attitude was apparent in every part of his work: his religious beliefs and practices, his interactions with the local

Figure 10.1. Traugott Bachmann,
1913. Courtesy of UA.

population, and his attitude to music and dancing. He was a true follower of
Herder (whom he had almost certainly never read) in that he knew local languages and cultures better than any of the other missionaries, and he translated the Bible into Nyiha. With respect to music, not only did he make
recordings for Hornbostel that were transcribed, published, and analyzed by
comparative musicologists throughout the first half of the twentieth century, but he was also the first missionary who tried to introduce African
music and dance into the service. Who was this man, and how did he come
to be so different from everyone else?

LIFE

The fact that Bachmann was a Moravian (though he was not born into a
Moravian family) probably had a lot to do with his approach. Any other
mission society probably would have called him back or reprimanded him.[3]
His parents owned a small farm in Saxony close to the Moravian settle-
ment of Niesky. After his confirmation and only eight years of education,
he left school to work on the family farm and as an agricultural laborer

in surrounding farms.[4] In his memoirs, he describes in detail the poverty and simplicity of his childhood and his early fascination with the Moravian Church. When he was accepted in the Moravian Mission Seminary in Niesky, he finally felt at home. In contrast to Leipzig missionaries, who studied for a minimum of four years and also took classes at Leipzig University, the Moravian students studied only for two. The education was mainly concerned with theological and practical matters, such as bookkeeping, but there was one area in which Moravian students had a huge advantage: they read the memoirs of earlier Moravian missionaries. Every Moravian had to write a *Lebenslauf* (a description of their life) that was read loud at his or her funeral. These made for fascinating reading and served as an example for future missionaries. Bachmann was deeply influenced by these early missionaries' biographies. As we have seen, Moravians had a rich history of missionary activities all over the world beginning in the 1720s. From these accounts the students learned how the missionaries gradually got to know the local people and languages, and how they started their linguistic work by making grammars, dictionaries, and Bible translations, always finding images that the local people could identify with. Bachmann repeatedly stressed how inspired he was by his predecessors.[5] Notably, the future missionaries not only received religious education, but they also had to learn various crafts that would be useful to them in the mission stations, such as agriculture, carpentry, bookbinding, shoemaking, and so on. From the very beginning, Bachmann's great passion was gardening.

Bachmann arrived in Rungwe, in German East Africa, in 1892. His first few years were spent learning Kinyakyusa, and he mentioned that a basic grammar of the language had already been written by the Berlin missionary Carl Nauhaus.[6] Bachmann was not yet married when he came to Africa and wrote "that he could think of no one with whom he could go through his life."[7] He thus asked the church leaders to find a wife for him, in those days a common way of arranging marriages. Elisabeth Künzel, whom he had never met, agreed to marry him and arrived in 1895. They had nine children, two of whom died young in Africa.

In 1899 Bachmann was asked to found another mission station in nearby Mbozi. For that he had to learn a new although related language, Nyiha. From the very beginning his work in the mission field was characterized by thoughtful and respectful interaction with the Nyiha. He realized that in order to have good a relationship with the local population he needed the chiefs on his side, so his first step was to visit the twelve chiefs. His attitude was always that he was there to learn from the Nyiha, not they from him. In his first years he spent all his evenings learning the language and trying to understand Nyiha customs. His autobiography is full of fascinating ethnographic information, always presented with utmost respect. Gradually and with great caution, he introduced the Nyiha to nonnative fruits, vegetables, and plants, such as coffee, which to this day is a major source of income in the area.[8]

In 1911–13 Bachmann returned to Germany for a sabbatical. When it came time to go back to Africa, he and his wife decided to leave their children in Germany so that they could be educated.[9] The Bachmanns returned to Mbozi and remained there until 1916, when he was interned by the British and placed in several concentration camps. He was severely mistreated before being sent back to Germany, and it took him years to recover even to the limited extent that he did.[10] Bachmann never returned to Africa and spent the last years of his life as an itinerant preacher for the Moravian Church in Germany, with frequent interruptions caused by depression as a result of his stay in the concentration camps. He died in Niesky in 1948 at the age of eighty-three.

PUBLICATIONS

Bachmann's contributions are in three different areas: he translated the Bible into Nyiha and did some basic work on Nyiha grammar (he was a close collaborator of the Africanist Carl Meinhof);[11] he made many recordings for Hornbostel; and he wrote extensively about his conviction that local customs need to be preserved, and that Christian values could not simply be transferred to Africa. His respect for local customs applied to all areas of life, including the organization of Christian rituals. Thus, he was the first to introduce local melodies with new texts into the service as well as to encourage antiphonal singing and congregational dancing.

As discussed in chapter 1, Wilhelm von Humboldt was in regular contact with missionaries, especially Moravians, who compiled grammars for his linguistic work. Similarly, there is a long correspondence in the Herrnhut Archive between Meinhof and Bachmann. Meinhof's letters are full of encouragement for Bachmann in his later years when he was often depressed, telling him how impressive his work is.[12] Bachmann's first contributions were a Nyiha primer and a translation of the Gospel of Matthew, translations that occupied him for most of his sabbatical. There is a description of the local people's reaction to this first written document in Nyiha: "It is touching to see the enthusiasm with which the people in Mbozi devote themselves to the art of reading. Brother Bachmann cannot create enough reading material. . . . Everyone who can write attempts to make a copy, and weekdays and Sundays one saw people who are usually working with

hoe and ax trying to make a copy and laboring over the letters."[13] Meinhof
checked the entire translation to make sure it was correct.[14] This was followed by a translation of the complete New Testament in 1913, as well
as stories from the Old and New Testament, again thoroughly checked
by Meinhof.[15] It is quite remarkable that a man with so little education
managed to complete these translations.[16] Note, though, that he translated
not from Greek, as Otto Hagena did only a few years later with his Bible
translation into Haya, but from German (chap. 12, p. 189). Concerning Bachmann's recordings for Hornbostel, it seems that it was Meinhof who alerted
the Berlin Phonogramm-Archiv to Bachmann because of the planned Bible
translations.[17] During his years in Africa, Bachmann made some 140 recordings that are kept in the archive and are now digitalized.[18] He sent detailed
annotations on many of these recordings, for example: "This song does not
come from this area, and it was reinterpreted during the performance by the
Nyiha." Frequently he designated the occasion, such as "hunting song," "war
song," and the like.[19] These recordings became an important part of Hornbostel's and Schneider's research; both include transcriptions from Bachmann's
recordings in their publications.[20] Wilhelm Heinitz discussed them in his
lectures on African music in Hamburg University, thus probably alerting
another Moravian missionary, Franz Rietzsch, to the use of phonographs.
Bachmann had no musical background, and to my knowledge he did not
analyze any of these recordings.

As for the use of local music in the service: because Bachmann did not
publish much during his lifetime, there are few firsthand sources. His earliest article was published in 1912 and is entitled "Praktische Lösungen
missionarischer Probleme auf einem jungen Arbeitsfelde (Nyassagebiet,
Deutsch-Ostafrika)" (Practical Solutions of the Missionary Problem in a
New Area). It is remarkable that the Moravian Church would publish such
an article, since it contradicts much of missionary practice at the time. The
second account is his autobiography, *Ich gab so manchen Anstoss* (I Stirred
Up a Few Things).

Bachmann is both important to us and different from his fellow missionaries for one particular reason. A central point of Hornbostel's critique
of missionary practice is that missionaries' practice of introducing Western
music contributes greatly to the loss of "authentic" music. Bachmann almost certainly never read Hornbostel, and yet, he was one of the first to try
to preserve local culture by adapting it for use in Christian rituals.

In order to understand how Bachmann arrived at his decision to allow
dance and local music in church, we need to discuss his general attitude to

colonization and missionary practice. He writes in his memoirs, which he intended for his grandchildren and never expected to be published, "The correct way to colonize has not yet been found" and quotes a 1924 newspaper article about a black South African journalist: "If only the white race would realize that Africa is *our* fatherland. If only they would realize that they should be our staff and not we theirs. As a result they see themselves as masters of the country and treat us as slaves."[21] Bachmann concludes with his own words: "The main reason for the present reversed colonization is the self-interest of the white race. I see horrors descending upon Europe."[22]

His basic principle was always that he was a student who should learn from the local population.[23] While most missionaries felt that the local population did not have the appropriate values and laws to govern their daily life, Bachmann argued the opposite: "The Nyiha are not lawless, but have been guided by unwritten commandments. . . . Since time immemorial they have reflected on what is honest, etc., . . . but all this is conditioned by their social situation and by their climate. This should be taken into account in the moral demands of the mission."[24] In general, he was cautious about applying the term *sinful* and realized early on that what was considered a sin in Europe would not be thought of in the same way in Africa. The most divisive example was polygamy, which no Christian churches allowed. If a man had several wives, he was expected to keep only one if he wished to be baptized or take communion. As a result, there was mass exodus of men before communion. Bachmann argued early on that it was not right to forbid polygamy in Africa, but he could not go against church regulations; he was close to breaking all contact with the Moravians over this issue.[25] In the end, he tried to find compromises.

Local music and dance were regarded by church authorities with similar suspicion. Bachmann describes in fascinating detail how he gradually tried to preserve them and incorporate them into the service. When he arrived in Mbozi in 1899, he remarked that the Nyiha preferred to sing hymns with local melodies.[26] Even though he did not have the background to do musical analyses of the Nyiha songs, he did notice that they were antiphonal and adopted several for the service.[27] He adapted a song welcoming a chief with the original text, "Thou chief of Ihava, slaughter a cow! Then we will greet our chief with great joy!" into a hymn with the text, "Let us rejoice in the Lord Jesus! Our Savior in Heaven!" Another Nyiha song originally went, "Mother, I am going to the chief to pay my debt"; this became, "Mother, I am going to the Lord. I want to leave what I owe behind."[28] Since the Nyiha frequently use colorful images, he tried to find dramatic metaphors for his hymns: he wrote a hymn with the words "Jesus devoured evil," which in the eighth verse says, "Jesus, don't preserve our evil in your throat" (asking Jesus to forgive the evil).

Bachmann got to work on a now-lost hymnbook as soon as he moved to Mbozi. The manuscript was ready for publication in 1916 when he was interned, and he had to leave it behind.[29] The first Nyiha hymnbook appeared in 1932 under the title *Inimbo zya shivanza sha Cilisiti* (Songs of a Christian Congregation). This hymnbook has also been lost, but a 1910 hymnbook from Mbozi edited by Bachmann mentions that four songs with seventeen verses (out of fifty altogether) are Nhiha songs.[30] No other mission societies had chorales by local composers at this point, and when they did introduce them, the melodies were Western; so Bachmann's approach was remarkable.

While Bachmann was quick to adapt local melodies for the service, his embrace of local dance took considerably longer. He describes in detail how his views evolved:

> When the Nyiha celebrate, they never only dance or only sing. When people sing while working or traveling, they always move their arms and legs. Nyihas simply do not sing without moving the body. Our church and school singing is alien to the Nyiha. When in 1905 the mission director Hennig came to inspect the station, the people sang a song that I had adapted from a local melody. I am sure the text was fitting—"You, who came from Europe"—but the way in which I had instructed the people to move did not correspond to the way the Nyiha move. I made them walk in steps. How little did I then understand the spirit of African rhythm! The words and melody were African, but the movement was European. How very different was our return to Mbozi on 30 June 1913 [after his sabbatical]. Dancing had been also prohibited in Mbozi, because from a European perspective dancing is considered "sinful." But once I understood that the Nhiha had harmless dances and songs that went with them, dances were permitted. When I came home from a trip, I was received with drums, songs, and circular dancing. After they had accompanied me to our house and I had sat down, the drum became silent, the singing stopped, and they stopped dancing. Everyone knelt down, tilted their upper body to the side, clapped their hands, and cried, "Father, we greet you!"[31]

Bachmann explains here how he gradually understood that in Africa music and dance cannot be separated. Through careful observation of Nyiha rituals, he came to distinguish between dances for funerals, dances that really have a thoroughly "indecent character" (*unsittlichen Charakter*), folk dances, and circle dances.[32] He did not recommend the "thoroughly indecent" dances for the service, but the others were fully integrated into religious rituals.

So why did missionaries consider dance sinful? First of all, most deeply religious people in Germany around 1900 would have considered any kind of dancing sinful. It was not an activity that Moravians and Lutherans would pursue. Second, in Africa dancing was associated with many rituals, such as male and female circumcision, of which the missionaries usually disapproved, especially with respect to women (I will discuss this topic more fully in connection with Gutmann in chap. 11).[33] Third, dancers would usually combine the drinking of beer with dancing, yet another activity condemned by the church.

Unlike most other missionaries, Bachmann was not concerned that the use of Nyiha melodies and dances would bring up "sinful" associations. He wrote in his memoirs that the Nyiha told him, "We only sing what we can also sing and dance in front of our in-laws," and further, "We fear God, as we fear our in-laws."[34] He also did not forbid the drinking of beer, as Presbyterian missionaries did, because he noticed that when beer drinking was forbidden the Nyiha drank secretly, and he thought that drinking in secret was a much greater sin than drinking in public.[35]

So we have in Bachmann an unconventional missionary, one who was far ahead of his time. Not only did he approach the local culture with deep respect and admiration, but he created the written Nyiha language by translating the Bible, and he introduced local music and dance into the church service. He was a deeply religious man of great modesty who basically followed his Moravian predecessors by trying fully to understand the local culture, even if this led to frequent conflicts with church authorities.

The Moravians were remarkably tolerant, even publishing Bachmann's truly revolutionary guidelines in 1912. But other congregations were not as open. In his last years as an itinerant preacher, he talked about his missionary work in German East Africa all over Germany in order to raise money for the Moravian mission. A letter by the mission director Samuel Baudert dated 16 September 1926 begs him not to get carried away when giving his presentations. Baudert writes that he has received numerous letters criticizing Bachmann's approach to missionary activities: "You know that I trust you entirely and that I also have full understanding of your thoughts, which at present occupy you very fully and move you: freedom from laws and other things. I also understand the reasons you constantly think about these things. . . . But I would like you to consider seriously whether you're not throwing out the baby with the bathwater."[36] Baudert does not specify in his letter which statements of Bachmann upset the conservative congregations. It could have been anything: tolerance of polygamy, different views of property, his belief that Africans do not need to dress in Western clothes and can walk around in the nude, his advocacy of local music and dance. Bachmann's answer is not preserved, but he traveled and talked about his convictions for many more years. And in missionary circles he was considered a mover and shaker who inspired subsequent generations of missionaries.

FRANZ FERDINAND RIETZSCH

The Moravians had another remarkable missionary active in the same area as Bachmann in the 1930s. Franz Ferdinand Rietzsch was much better educated than Bachmann: he was a Lutheran theologian with great musical abilities who was profoundly affected by Hornbostel's article and tried to put his suggestions into practice.[37] His story is worth telling because East African multipart singing was described for the first time in the late 1960s by the Austrian ethnomusicologist Gerhard Kubik. Rietzsch had anticipated some of Kubik's most important findings as early as the 1930s. Moreover, even though he ultimately was unsuccessful in his attempt to bring African music into religious services, the way he failed is most revealing and allows us to understand German cultural history from the 1920s and '30s in a new way. In particular, it shows how closely the early-music revival of the *Singbewegung* (of which Rietzsch was a member) was linked to the history of comparative musicology. Both looked for a long-lost *Ur-Musik* and admired medieval music.

Rietzsch was active among the Wanyakyusa (also called Konde) in the Southern Highlands, mentioned earlier (see again fig. 9.1). The first Konde hymnbook was published in 1905 and falls squarely into Hornbostel's first option for missionary musical practice: the missionaries translated German hymns into Konde.[38] When German missionaries were interned during World War I, the Free Church of Scotland took over, and Sankey hymns and the tonic *sol-fa* system were introduced.[39] (The tonic *sol-fa* system is an English method of sight-singing and notation based on movable *do* that has been extraordinarily successful in Africa.[40]) As a result, when the Germans returned in the late 1920s, both Sankey hymns and Lutheran chorales in Konde translations were sung in church. The 1930 hymnbook *Inimbo sya kiponga ky a kilisiti*, published jointly by the Moravians, the Berlin Mission Society, and the Free Church of Scotland, includes 151 German hymns

Figure 10.2. Photograph of
Franz Rietzsch and
his wife, Hanna, with
their daughter Elisabeth.
Courtesy of UA.

as well as 109 hymns from the Livingstonia Hymnbook.[41] This was the hymnbook in use when Rietzsch arrived in Africa and was a source of great concern to him. But before we discuss the problems he encountered, we have to understand where Rietzsch came from.

RIETZSCH AND THE *SINGBEWEGUNG*

Franz Ferdinand Rietzsch (fig. 10.2) was born in 1902 in Falkenstein, Saxony, the son of a Lutheran pastor. He passed the examinations to become a schoolteacher in Bautzen in 1924 and the first and second theological examinations at Herrnhut in 1928 and 1930, respectively.[42] Two points are of fundamental importance concerning Rietzsch's missionary activities in Tanganyika and their musical focus: first, he was a passionate member of the German movement of the *Singbewegung* as well as a great admirer of Berneuchen;[43] and second, he had a background in comparative musicology.

Rietzsch's articles, letters, and notes are full of enthusiastic references to the *Singbewegung* and Berneuchen. The education of all teachers, including those in elementary school, was shaped by the leaders of the movement, especially after 1926. Many of the leaders (Konrad Ameln among them) taught in the *pädagogische Akademien*, where music education made up a large part of the curriculum;[44] we can assume that Rietzsch learned harmony and counterpoint there. In addition, part of Rietzsch's library is preserved in the archive at Rungwe, Tanzania, the headquarters of the Moravian Church in the Southern Highlands: during a visit in July 2011 I found an old copy of *Zupfgeigenhansl*, in addition to copies of edited choir books of sixteenth- and seventeenth-century music for choir and trombone. He stated in his letters to his sister that he took these books along in the hope of performing sixteenth- and seventeenth-century polyphony with local choirs. We also know from his correspondence that he subscribed to *Musik und Kirche*, and it was only natural for him to publish one of his articles there.[45] He owned several books and articles on Gregorian chant.[46] And finally, because the *Singbewegung* was instrumental in the early-music revival, it makes perfect sense that he traveled to Africa with a clavichord, a French horn, a violin, and three recorders in the hope of teaching the local musicians to play them.[47]

RIETZSCH'S BACKGROUND IN COMPARATIVE MUSICOLOGY

Rietzsch's studies in comparative musicology began when the Moravian Mission director Samuel Baudert sent him to Hamburg to study African languages with Carl Meinhof. In Hamburg he heard about the comparative musicologist Wilhelm Heinitz and attended his lectures.[48] Heinitz, whose main field of research was phonetics, never became a full professor at Hamburg and remained associated with the Institute of Comparative Musicology and the Colonial Institute until his retirement in 1949. Heinitz may have failed to advance in his career during the Nazi period because of an altercation he had with Friedrich Blume. When the latter was criticized for his double-edged views on Nazi ideology in his 1939 book *Das Rasseproblem in der Musik* by Heinitz's student, the SS Unterscharführer Max Singelmann, Blume hit right back by attacking Singelmann's dissertation adviser, the staunch party member Heinitz, who was duly reprimanded.[49] In his lectures,

Heinitz discussed and analyzed phonogram recordings of music from all over the world, including those made by Traugott Bachmann. When Rietzsch informed Baudert about the important role phonographs were playing in ethnographic research, the latter asked him to purchase one for his work in Tanganyika, which would eventually lead to the recordings made by him in the 1930s, now in the Berlin Phonogramm-Archiv.[50]

What articles and books would Rietzsch have read? He owned Robert Lach's *Die vergleichende Musikwissenschaft*, Robert Lachmann's *Musik des Orients*, and Curt Sachs's *Musik des Altertums*. The only one of these that he mentions several times in his correspondence is Lachmann's. He might have also heard from Heinitz about an early and influential article by Hornbostel from 1905–6 entitled "Die Probleme der vergleichenden Musikwissenschaft," and about a major study by Stumpf on the songs of the Bellakula Indians[51]—both articles address Eurocentric listening—but Rietzsch mentions neither in his correspondence. It is possible that he read Hornbostel's article on Wanyamwezi songs: for one thing, it was one of the few scholarly discussions of African music to have been published by this time; second, the Wanyamwezi live in an area where his parents-in-law were missionaries, so he probably heard their music; and third, the journal was available in the university library in Hamburg.[52]

Beside phonetics, Heinitz's research was concerned with what he called "physiological resonance," the relationship between movement and music. In his lectures, he would analyze recordings and arrive at conclusions about the kind of body motions made by the performer.[53] After 1933 he adjusted his research to find favor with the new regime and would measure skulls, faces, and noses in order to try to determine the performer's or composer's race.[54] While his research undoubtedly played into the nineteenth-century racial stereotyping that Nazi *Rassenkunde* had revived for its own nefarious purposes, it also revealed an interest in body language in music and dance that fit into broader trends of the 1920s and '30s. It is therefore somewhat surprising that Rietzsch had so little interest in Heinitz's publications, considering that he knew how central dance was to African music.[55]

After his studies in Hamburg, Rietzsch was sent to the Moravian community of Fairfield, near Manchester (UK), to improve his English. An English colleague there alerted him to Hornbostel's article in the journal *Africa*.[56] "African Negro Music" had a defining influence on Rietzsch, in particular the role Hornbostel ascribed to phonographs and his discussion of "African rhythm."[57]

Indeed, before launching into questions of transcription and analysis, Hornbostel first lays out the importance of phonographs as an ethnographic tool. He warns that it is poor practice to transfer a Western understanding of melody, harmony, and rhythm to African music. With respect to pitch, for example, what European listeners consider out of tune may be in tune by African criteria.[58] Nor are Western music's scales the same as those in African cultures.[59] He goes on to describe various kinds of pentatonic scales, both with and without half steps. Hornbostel offers detailed descriptions of antiphonal singing as well as a discussion of a piece recorded by Traugott Bachmann, in which the Luvembe seem to "caricature . . . European sacred music."[60] (It is possible that the mention of a fellow Moravian missionary's recording was the reason that Rietzsch was alerted to this article in the first place.) Hornbostel describes African rhythm as much more complicated than European—evoking rhythmic heterophony through the term "cross rhythm"—and concludes that it is impossible for Western scholars to place bar lines in transcriptions of African music.[61] Additionally, he argues that individual songs and dances are ephemeral unless they are tied to a specific ritual.[62]

Hornbostel sees music and dance in Africa as intimately linked and attributes to both greater social importance than in cosmopolitan Western culture: "Music is neither reproduction (of a 'piece of music' as an existing object) nor production (of a new object): *it is the life of a living spirit working within those who dance and sing* [my italics]. Of this they are conscious, and the feeling of being possessed (or inspired) gives their singing and dancing a superhuman character, connecting it with the sphere of religion."[63] He relates this to his observation that African languages have melodic speech without stable pitches: rather, they glide, whereas "in singing every sound is fixed at a certain level."[64] Furthermore, the pitches of the speaking voice inflect the outline of the melody. Therefore, Hornbostel warns strongly against underlaying European melodies with African texts (and he must have hymns in mind here): "To translate the words of a European song even into a kindred (Indo-European) language is a most difficult thing to undertake. While this is true of art songs, the difficulty increases still more in the case of folk songs, where words and tune are conceived in one."[65]

There are a number of aspects of Hornbostel's work that had an impact on Rietzsch but that ethnomusicologists have since completely discarded. The most important of these is the idea, discussed in chapter 2, that music of "primitive cultures" exhibits some of the same characteristics as medieval music.[66] Hornbostel's discussion of mode may also have had an impact on Rietzsch's thinking: he calls his first publication "Diesseits und jenseits von Dur und Moll: Unterschiede zwischen europäischer und afrikanischer

Musik" (Beyond Major and Minor: Differences between European and African Music; 1935), a title that seems to refer to Hornbostel's ideas.

For Hornbostel, this parallelism between medieval and African music had practical implications for missionary musical practice if a merging of European and African music was sought (as described in his second option; see above, chap. 9, pp. 123–24): this approach, albeit problematical, might succeed if the Europeans would use old polyphony or Gregorian chant:

> The process would perhaps take a somewhat different course if the Negroes were given as models, instead of modern harmonic forms, old melodic-polyphonic forms, which are less alien to the character of their own music. This attempt at hybridizing would, at any rate, be an interesting experiment; but only great experts could succeed in growing an improved and fruitful variety of *musica africana*.[67]

In a footnote Hornbostel refers respectfully to an article by the Catholic missionary Theodor Rühl entitled "Die missionarische Akkommodation im gottesdienstlichen Volksgesang" (The Missionary Accommodation of Local Music in the Church). Like Father Wilhelm Schmidt, Rühl came from the monastery St. Gabriel, a center of the *Kulturkreislehre*.[68] He suggested that one should perform Gregorian chant in Africa because most of the Gregorian melodies are pentatonic to begin with, and even if they are not, they can easily be adjusted.[69]

Even before he arrived in Africa, then, Rietzsch had learned to question some aspects of the Eurocentric thinking so common among other missionaries. Influenced in particular by Hornbostel's "African Negro Music," he was confronted with, on the one hand, the recommendation that Africans should sing and dance their own "authentic" music in services and, on the other, the theory that African music was closely related to medieval polyphony. Taken together with the ideas about early music and folk song that Rietzsch had absorbed through the *Singbewegung*, Hornbostel's concepts provided a theoretical bridge to integrating East African music into 1930s German constructions of "authentic" music. The question now is, how did Rietzsch realize Hornbostel's suggestions in the mission field?

ETHNOMUSICOLOGICAL OBSERVATIONS

Rietzsch arrived in Tanganyika on 3 November 1931, and after a visit to his parents-in-law, also Moravian missionaries, in Unyamwezi, he settled in Kyimbila, a small village in Nyasa close to Tukuyu and Mbeya among the Wanyakyusa or Konde in early 1932.[70] His colleague was the seasoned missionary Ferdinand Jansa. In the forty-four pages of his first letter (all of Rietzsch's letters are long), written between 10 August and 2 September 1932, he is already able to provide a detailed description of the tonal system and music of the Wanyakyusa.[71] Furthermore, Rietzsch published two short articles during his lifetime, the first in the Moravian journal *Wochenblatt der Brüdergemeine* in 1935 and the second a year later in *Musik und Kirche*, the *Singbewegung's* most important journal.[72] A third article, "Afrikanische Klänge," written in 1935, was published posthumously in 1993.[73] Rietzsch's Nachlass, donated to the Dresden Museum of Anthropology in 1978, contains a number of relevant documents, in particular the settings he wrote for his choir in Kyimbila. In addition, there are many noteworthy remarks about music in Rietzsch's correspondence: the most revealing information is found in his letters to his sister Marianne, nicknamed "Schnicke," a professional violinist with an excellent knowledge of music history and theory.[74] He regularly used her as a sounding board for his research and asked her to provide him with secondary literature. There are also some letters to his father that contain interesting remarks. And finally, the Herrnhut Archive owns the extensive correspondence of the director of the Moravian Mission, Samuel Baudert. This remarkable man looked after his missionaries in every possible way: he constantly supplied Rietzsch with ethnomusicological periodicals and books, wrote encouraging letters, and saw Rietzsch's first article through publication.

As his first letter after his arrival in Tanganyika shows, Rietzsch recognized right away that the Wanyakyusa use two different pentatonic scales, one for instrumental and the other for vocal music. From his reading of Hornbostel and his lectures with Heinitz he was familiar with pentatonic systems, so this by itself was not a particularly striking observation.[75] More crucial is that he was able to find—entirely on his own and without the use of measuring instruments—that the Nyakyusa tonal system used for lamellophones was derived from overtones over one fundamental.[76] His article "Afrikanische Klänge" begins with a vivid description of the *irimba* (which corresponds to the Gogo *ilimba*), the most popular lamellophone among the Wanyakyusa.[77] He tells us how the irimba is made,[78] and then goes on to compare the different kinds:

> There are three kinds of marimba here (marimba is the plural of irimba): the seven-tone and the nine-tone irimba, the nine-tone in two different tunings. I believe the seven-tone is characteristic for this area, because the other folk music is also based on this tuning. What we have here [with

Figure 10.3. Anhemitonic pentatonic scale with two minor thirds in irimba music, also called the "Gogo scale." Adapted from Kubik, *Theory of African Music*, 1:179.

these tones] is a series of natural harmonics, as for example in a horn, or the so-called overtone series. If we start with C′ as the fundamental, the following tone distances will result: C′–G′–C″–E″–G″–B-flat″–C‴–D‴–E‴. The seven-tone irimba shows the following scale (of course relative only with C′ as an assumed fundamental): C′–E′–G′–B-flat′–C″–D″–E″.[79]

The result is a pentatonic scale with two minor thirds, often called the "Gogo scale" (fig. 10.3).

Rietzsch continues with a brief discussion of the harmonies that can result from this scale:

With the European ear one is always looking out for changes of harmony. This does not do justice to this music, however, because harmonically speaking, in the case of the seven-tone irimba the result is of course always an unresolved ninth chord.[80]

What does Rietzsch mean by "unresolved ninth chord?" He is fully aware that this term is not appropriate for Nyakyusa music, but he does not seem to have a better way to describe what he hears.[81] Indeed, in order to communicate his musical observations to his less attuned German readers, Rietzsch had to resort to rhetorical conventions rooted in nineteenth-century ethnography.[82] But he uses this observation as a launching pad to describe in fascinating detail that the beauty of Nyakyusa music is, in effect, found not in the harmonic language, but in the melodic interplay of the two polyphonic parts.

Rietzsch does not offer any explanation as to how he became convinced that the Nyakyusa system is based on overtones. The South African ethnomusicologist Percival Kirby published an article in 1932 in the journal *Bantu Studies* in which he describes tone systems over two fundamentals,[83] but it seems unlikely that Rietzsch was familiar with it. First, in his correspondence with his sister and Baudert he always described in great detail which articles and authors he read, and there is not a single reference to either the journal *Bantu Studies* or to Kirby; and second, Kirby describes overtones over not one fundamental, but two. We can therefore assume that Rietzsch came up with this observation all on his own. Rietzsch was well educated: he must have read Helmholtz and been aware of his discussion of partials. We also know from various remarks by his colleagues and his children that he had an exceptionally good ear, and this, in combination with the tones on the irimba, must have suggested to him that the system was based on overtones over one fundamental.[84]

Thus far, ethnomusicologists had not studied the Nyakyusa tonal system in great detail. But Rietzsch's observations anticipated the more thorough explanation that Gerhard Kubik offered in 1968 of how the tone system of the Gogo, an ethnic group in Central Tanzania in the Dodoma area, is related to the overtone series: "Even in the 1950s the Gogo multipart singing system was still one of the riddles of East African ethnomusicology. . . . Only after the copious documentation of Gogo music by our team (Hillegeist, Kubik, Saprapason) in Dodoma and Mayoni Districts from January 1, 1962, with the support of the now legendary Gogo paramount chief Mazengo at Mvumi, was it possible at last to get to the bottom of the system."[85] Kubik was able to show that the tonal system of the Wagogo is derived from the harmonic series over a single fundamental; specifically, the Wagogo use partials 4 to 9 (see again fig. 10.3) He clarifies that the Wagogo use only tones starting from the fourth partial, because the intervals between the first four partials are the octave, fifth, and fourth, and thus too far apart to be useful.[86]

Kubik's second observation concerns the harmonies associated with this overtone series. He and others have noticed that Wagogo music has a characteristic interval progression (see again fig. 10.3) of a diminished fifth with a third on top, followed by a fourth, another diminished fifth, and a perfect fifth. This is one of the interval progressions that was frequently described as being similar to medieval organum.[87] Kubik explains this progression as a result of the "skipping process," that is, "that harmony is obtained by the simultaneous singing of notes separated by one degree in the scale."[88] In other words, the lower part always sings the tone that the upper part will sing two tones later. The harmonic structure is a direct result of the scale; as Kubik puts it, the "two [are] inseparable aspects of a structural whole."[89] In yet other words, the typical Gogo sound includes two or three tones of the pentatonic scale, which, when all the tones are played simultaneously, becomes what Rietzsch calls an "unresolved ninth chord."

Thanks to the writings of Rietzsch, we now know that the Wanyakyusa and Wagogo had the same tonal system for irimba music. One of the reasons

Kubik gave in support of a Gogo tonal system derived from partials was the presence of yodeling, especially with children. Kubik has observed a similar practice among Wanyakyusa children. Thus it makes perfect sense that both systems are derived from partials.[90]

Might other people have also used this partial-based system? Kubik mentions the tone system of the Wakisi (who live on the northeast bank of Lake Nyasa, now Lake Malawi) as going up to the twelfth partial, although he thinks this practice may be extinct and concludes that "very little has been found out so far about the background of the Gogo multipart system. . . . The central and western parts of Tanzania are too little explored ethnomusicologically to draw up a map of ethnic groups which might share the system."[91]

Rietzsch's observations show that the music in this region is based on partials derived from one fundamental. He also noticed that the vocal music of the Wanyakyusa relied on a different pentatonic scale, although he states that some of the vocal music uses the irimba scale: "The irimba scale mentioned above is also used in folk songs, but nevertheless, it is a separate tonal system, which is not immediately related to the [pentatonic] system that we will be discussing now."[92]

For most of the vocal music, he observes, the Wanyakyusa use a pentatonic scale with the pitches F–D–C–A–G–F (fig. 10.4a): "The scale which results from these melodies has the following structure: F–G–A–C–D–F [Rietzsch lists the pitches in ascending order]. . . . But we should realize that the Banyakyusa are not avoiding the missing tones [B and E] because they don't like them; rather, [it is because] they are completely unable to sing them."[93] He goes on to write that the minor thirds are often connected by a nonspecific gliding pitch, which seems out of tune to European ears because they are used to hearing music in thirds.

Unlike with the irimba music, Rietzsch is vague about the intervals associated with this scale, but he seems to describe some kind of parallel motion:

> To the main melody they add another voice—usually lower—that, when taken on its own, can be considered an independent melody. Sometimes the singers will add another, third, high voice to the other two, which more or less conforms to the main melody but by no means follows the melody in strict parallel. Since the pitch of the tones is often "indeterminate," we occasionally tend to hear thirds in these songs, which probably appear completely by accident and are certainly not intended.[94]

As with Rietzsch's observations on partial-based harmony, Kubik's research corroborates these findings by explaining the multipart singing associated

Figure 10.4a. Anhemitonic pentatonic scale for vocal music of the Nyakyusa.
Adapted from Kubik, *Theory of African Music*, 1:173–74.

Figure 10.4b. Harmonies associated with pentatonic scale. Adapted from Kubik,
Theory of African Music, 1:173.

with this scale and including the Wanyakyusa among the people who use
it. The performance is mainly two-part, and the predominant intervals are
parallel fourths, isolated thirds, unison, and octave (fig. 10.4b).[95]

In view of the fact that Rietzsch has observed that the Wanyakyusa use
both pentatonic scales, it is worth noting that the Spanish ethnomusicologist Polo Vallejo has recently shown that the Wagogo also use both of these
pentatonic scales. The second scale is sung mainly by the elders, and sometimes both pentatonic scales are combined when the elders sing together
with the rest of the ethnic group.[96] Thus, thanks to Rietzsch's research we
can now revise Kubik's observations and conclude that the multipart singing of the Wanyakyusa and Gogo must have been based on the same tonal
systems.

Comparative Musicology and Medieval Music

Unlike modern ethnomusicologists, Rietzsch lacks the terminology to describe precisely what he is hearing; therefore, like many comparative musicologists of his generation, he turned to the Middle Ages for help. In order to
explain the two pentatonic scales he discerned from listening to Nyakyusa
music, he asked his sister to conduct detailed research on medieval improvisation, in particular fauxbourdon. His sister duly sent him summaries of
Heinrich Besseler's discussion of fauxbourdon from his book *Die Musik des
Mittelalters und der Renaissance*.[97]

So what conclusions did Rietzsch draw from his ethnomusicological observations? I mentioned earlier how both comparative musicologists and
early-music specialists saw a parallel between church modes and scales of

"primitive music." As a result, a large part of Rietzsch's article concerns the use of church modes in Nyakyusa polyphony. Numerous remarks throughout his publications and his letters testify to the fact that Nyakyusa multi-part singing made a deep impression on him. He found it in no way inferior to European music, and because early music was closest to his heart and he had learned about church modes in the context of the *Singbewegung*, he set out to discover the same characteristics in Africa. He writes:

> One asks oneself instinctively how it is possible to create such harmonious songs with the limited means of a five-tone system. For it is true that the polyphonic entanglement of the many voices really results in a most wonderful harmony with rather strange and yet also appealing harmonic progressions. Indeed, especially the harmonic aspect of these songs is much richer and more compelling than the few harmonic progressions used in a simple major melody (tonic, dominant, and subdominant, with inversions). This is even more surprising in view of the fact that it is not possible to derive triads from a single pentatonic scale taken on its own; if any, there is only a single one [triad] possible. And this one is of course not enough for harmonic progressions. The key to the harmonic beauty of the local folk songs lies in the fact that the different voices belong to different pentatonic modes. For example, the bass is in a different mode than the melody and the tenor again in a different mode, which are all sung simultaneously, even though every part remains in its own mode.[98]

Rietzsch then presents the modes he discerned in a table (table 10.1).

The first line is the pentatonic scale, followed by five modes. Any of the five tones of the pentatonic scale can become a final, according to Rietzsch. He continues relating the scales to medieval church modes: "Since these are melodic modes, we can, just as with the church modes, derive from these 'authentic' modes five additional 'plagal' modes, wherein the final is not the lowest tone of the melody, but the melody is circulating around the final."[99] He adds that most Nyakyusa songs belong to mode 1 and a few to mode 2.

We have already noted that Rietzsch describes a different pentatonic scale for vocal than for instrumental music. He certainly knew that in pentatonic systems one of the central classification criteria for church modes, the location of the semitones within the scale, is absent. Let us try to put ourselves in his shoes: he is clearly moved by Nyakyusa music and wants to explain its beauty to Western audiences. His reading in comparative musicology has convinced him that African music was similar to medieval and Renaissance music, and so he draws on these parallels to relate his experience of

TABLE 10.1. Rietzsch's pentatonic church modes

Tones	C–D–F–G–A–C D–F–G–A
1. Hauptgeschlecht	C–D–F–G–A–C (Mixolydian)
2. Hauptgeschlecht	D–F–G–A–C–D (Dorian)
3. Hauptgeschlecht	F–G–A–C–D–F (Lydian)
4. Hauptgeschlecht	G–A–C–D–F–G (Aeolian)
5. Hauptgeschlecht	A–C–D–F–G–A (Phrygian)

Source: From his "Afrikanische Klänge," 30.

Nyakyusa music to the repertoire so highly valued in the *Singbewegung*. He writes to his sister, "After all, European music was once on the same level, with monophonic music developing into polyphony. Should we therefore not find some valuable pointers for our work here?"[100] On the other hand, even though his much-admired Hornbostel can be counted among those who subscribed to an evolutionary view of music history, the older scholar was nevertheless cautious in drawing explicit parallels between church modes and African music and never went so far as to apply them to pentatonic music. All Hornbostel offered was a few vague statements that African music is similar to medieval music. There were a number of contemporary scholars, however, who did apply church modes to African music and who believed that Gregorian chant was originally pentatonic. Father Theodor Rühl, from the *Kulturkreistheorie* center in St. Gabriel, Mödling, a scholar who was read by Rietzsch,[101] states clearly in 1927 that Gregorian chant "is based on a natural system common to all cultures" and cites comparative musicologists in support.[102] He lists both of the pentatonic scales described by Rietzsch and relates them to music in antiquity, Asia, America, and Africa.[103] Like Riemann in his *Folkloristische Tonalitätsstudien*, he believes that the seven-note scale grew out of the pentatonic one.[104] The seven-note scale allows triads and is therefore described as harmonic, whereas the pentatonic scale is deemed purely melodic. Rühl concludes that it makes little sense to transfer Western music to Asia or Africa, since minor and major modes are incomprehensible to the local population, and recommends that Christians all over the world be encouraged to compose religious songs in their local style. The last section of the article is devoted to Gregorian chant, which he finds uniquely suited to be sung all over the world for the simple reason that it was originally pentatonic.[105] In support of his theories he cites, among others, Peter Wagner and Curt Sachs as authorities on chant. Then Rühl quotes a private communication from the

TABLE 10.2. Rühl's pentatonic church modes

Pitches	Finalis	Repercussio
1. C–D–F–G–A–C or C–D–E–G–A–C	D	A
2. A–C–D–F–G–A or A–C–D–E–G–A or G–B♭–c–d–f–g	D (D)	F (E)
3. D–E–G–A–C–D or C–A–G–F–D (C) or C–A–G–F–D or D–E–G–A–B–D	E (E)	C (B)
4. Two major thirds: G–A–B and F–G–A	G (E)	E (A)
5. D–F–G–A–C–D–F (F–G–B♭–C)	F	C
6. D–F–G–A–C	F	A
7. D–E–G–A–C–D–E or G–A–B–D–F	F	D
8. F–G–A–C–D–E	G	C

Source: From his "Die missionarische Akkommodation," 128.

Catholic missionary Clemens M. Künster, who was active in the Nyasa area and reports that the local population learned a large number of chant melodies in less than three months (see chap. 13, p. 215). In fact, Rühl believes that all missionaries should be trained to teach chant. He includes a chart (see table 10.2) wherein he transfers all eight church modes to pentatonic steps.[106] But because Rühl was interested only in monophonic music, his work was of limited use to Rietzsch.

The person whom Rietzsch admired above all was Hermann Reichenbach, whose *Formenlehre* appeared in 1929 (see chap. 8). Reichenbach was also well-read in comparative musicology, but, as we have seen, he surpassed others by basing his entire theory of form on church modes and, more specifically, pentatonic modes. A comparison of Reichenbach's pentatonic modes (see again chap. 8, under the heading "The *Jugendmusikbewegung* and the Middle Ages," and fig. 8.2) shows that they are the same as Rietzsch's.

We have seen throughout this book that scholars shared a wish to find the origins of music, a quest that went hand in hand with a desire for authenticity in early-music performance and—for comparative musicologists—a rejection of any hybrid music contaminated by modern civilization. It therefore made perfect sense that Rietzsch would apply the tools he had acquired from his encounters with early music, both before leaving for Tanganyika and supplied by his sister, to try to explain his ethnomusicological observations. In fact, Rietzsch was so convinced of Reichenbach's pentatonic modes that, when he first observed the "Gogo scale" with two minor thirds, he wondered if what he was hearing was indeed correct and considered rejecting it: "Nevertheless, this succession of tones is very suspicious in a song, since Reichenbach correctly rejects those pentatonic scales where we have two minor thirds in a row."[107] When Kubik did his research in the 1960s, these ideas had been dismissed, so he was able to observe African multipart singing free from the biases of comparative musicology.

RIETZSCH'S "AFRICAN" CHURCH MUSIC AND ITS RECEPTION

Even though Rietzsch made important ethnomusicological observations, he was primarily interested in creating church music that would correspond to the tonal system of the Wanyakyusa along the lines suggested in Hornbostel's article "African Negro Music." In his first letter to Baudert, he makes this point explicit: "I already wrote to you that people here are not able to sing melodies in their present European forms, since they are unable to distinguish half steps, let alone sing them. Therefore, the usual melodies are not an option for congregational singing here."[108] In a letter dated 8 September 1935, Rietzsch writes to his former teacher Heinitz, again emphasizing the absorption of triadic harmonies into pentatonicism: "For the Negro here our major-minor harmony is absolutely impossible to sing, especially here where the Wanyakyusa can sing only explicitly 'pentatonic' melodies. They gradually transform every non-pentatonic melody into a pentatonic one. . . . Sound catastrophes are impossible to avoid."[109] As a result, local singers gradually adjusted the melodies to their scale and tuning. Missionaries before Rietzsch usually did not notice the different tonal system, and especially in the earlier part of the twentieth century some described Africans simply as "unmusical."[110] Rietzsch himself was told by a member of his choir that a previous European choir director had accused the Wanyakyusa of being unmusical, and as a result, the best singers in Kyimbila decided to boycott the choir.[111]

What choices did Rietzsch have? As we have seen earlier in this chapter, when he arrived in Kyimbila, the choir sang Lutheran, Moravian, and Sankey hymns. While Rietzsch loved the old chorales and, as we will see, tried to remodel them to fit the Nyakyusa tonal system, he disliked the Sankey hymns intensely. For the most part, Rietzsch mounts reasonable arguments against their usage. They are constantly combined with the tonic *sol-fa* system, which relies on the Western tonal system; as a result, the music sounds terribly out of tune when sung by the Wanyakyusa. In addition, Sankey hymns are seen as ruining Africans' pentatonic tonal system. And the harmonization with tonic *sol-fa* results, according to Rietzsch, "in the most miserable and meager European harmonies (there are really only two of them, and those are the ones which are present on any accordion)."[112] He describes the common practice of starting every choir rehearsal with the singing of a major scale, "which the people here are unable to sing, it always sounds out of tune."[113] When Rietzsch then tried to have them sing a pentatonic scale, he reports, he earned only laughter. Sankey hymns constantly modulate, and these modulations are completely foreign to the Wanyakyusa.[114] Rietzsch further criticizes the simple rhythms, sentimental melodies, and bad text. The last, he writes, is always centered on one's personal salvation and never corresponds to the rhythm and intonation of the Nyakyusa language.[115] Again, he might have been sensitized on this point by Hornbostel, who criticized missionaries for disregarding the rhythm and intonation of African languages in their translations. Rietzsch's dislike of Sankey hymns is so intense that he claims they lead to moral failings: "In Rutenganio, where the Sankey songs are most popular, two choir directors lapsed morally, and in one case I know that it happened immediately after the rehearsal."[116] Unfortunately, he does not go into detail as to the nature of the moral lapses, but he does stress that even those hymns composed by local singers, rather than drawing on Nyakyusa folk music, are simply poor copies (Abklatsch) of Sankey hymns.

Rietzsch's loathing for the Sankey hymns goes hand in hand with his aversion for kitsch and popular culture, especially anything American, just as his fellow travelers in the Singbewegung had rejected these influences on German folk and church music. He writes to his sister on 11 May 1932 that "England is intentionally introducing American kitsch here. And why? Because it is practical, that is how you catch the Negroes."[117] He frequently refers to Sankey hymns as amerikanischer Kitsch or leichtfertige Melodien (lightweight, popular street-song melodies) and belonging to the Großstadtproletariat (big-city proletariat).[118]

Rietzsch made it his mission to introduce what he considered a more congenial musical alternative to this compromised "American kitsch." As we saw earlier, a number of scholars felt there was strong evidence that African and medieval music were both pentatonic and governed by church modes. Thus, it made perfect sense for Rietzsch, with his passionate devotion to the Singbewegung and early music, to rearrange Reformation chorales in a pentatonic system. He immediately realized that it was impossible to write for three parts without parallel fifths and asked his sister to look at early polyphony for help: "Examples of early polyphony might lead me in the right direction."[119] He wrote, "I believe that our old songs are really an excellent fit for the Negro. And not only this: I am becoming more and more convinced that the only fruitful way of serving these congregations on our part is by introducing our old Reformation chorales."[120]

In Rietzsch's papers, I found several settings of these Luther chorales, including his setting of "Nun bitten wir den heilgen Geist" (fig. 10.5). He

uses the pentatonic scale he observed in Nyakyusa vocal music. The chorale melody corresponds to Rietzsch's mode 3 (Lydian), and the pentatonic
scale is F''–D''–C''–A'–G'–F'. The setting is similar to one encountered in the
fifteenth-century *Glogauer Liederbuch*, very likely a collection Rietzsch was
familiar with from the *Singbewegung*, although the Glogau setting is more
difficult.[121]

It was only in 1959 that a composer succeeded in replicating the harmonic language of the Wanyakyusa. A comparison with Stephan Mbunga's
setting of the *Missa Baba Yetu* (fig. 10.6) makes the difference between Tanzanian approaches to pentatonicism and Rietzsch's European one clearer.[122]

As Kubik points out, Mbunga's composition follows very closely the
traditional harmonic patterns of the Lake Nyasa area. To quote Kubik, the
"'*Misa Baba Yetu*,' published in 1959, is perhaps one of the most beautiful African masses ever composed. The *Gloria* ('*Utukufu kwa Baba mbin-
guni . . .*') is an especially lucid illustration of the harmonic pattern we
have discussed."[123] Even though Mbunga's Mass uses the same pentatonic
pitches as Rietzsch, Mbunga's sounds entirely different. Mbunga's voices
move in strict parallel fourths with thirds in between. By contrast, Rietzsch's bass avoids parallel motion with the soprano wherever possible and
follows modal patterns. In other words, he either did not understand that
parallelism is one of the defining features of Nyakyusa music or consciously
ignored the fact; rather, his aim was to persuade the local population that
late medieval polyphony was particularly suited to their tonal system.

Rietzsch's enthusiasm for his "African" music was not shared by his
singers. The choir members took an intense dislike to the music as well
as to Rietzsch and refused to participate in the choir rehearsals and performances. The tension escalated into a veritable choir rebellion that centered
around three points:

- Several local singers claimed that Rietzsch had prohibited the singing of Sankey hymns. (While it is true that Rietzsch loathed Sankey
  hymns, he is adamant that he never forbade them.)
- Rietzsch was accused by some choir members of depriving them of
  "white music and white notation." He only wanted them to sing
  "black music."
- Some of the older singers associated Nyakyusa music with pagan dance and customs, which they felt was threatening to their
  Christianity.[124]

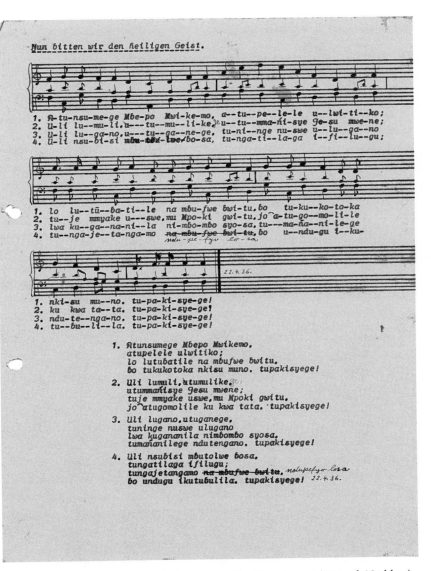

Figure 10.5. "Nun bitten wir den heiligen Geist." In "Kinyakyusa" (Rietzsch Nachlass), owned by the author.

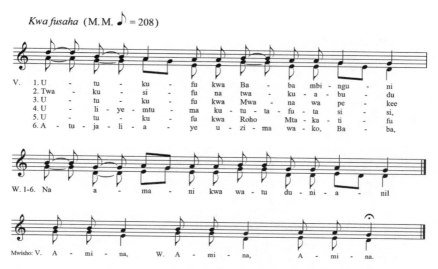

Figure 10.6. Stephan Mbunga, Gloria from *Missa Baba Yetu*. Published by and courtesy of the Benedictine Mission in Peramiho.

Nor did Rietzsch receive strong support for his church-music reforms from most other missionaries. His colleague Ferdinand Jansa later wrote an account of the affair. He admitted that no one had noticed before Rietzsch's arrival that the Wanyakyusa had a different tonal system, and he pointed out that other missionaries were not bothered by the singing that Rietzsch considered to be out of tune. He did not share Rietzsch's distaste for Sankey hymns and in fact was clearly uncomfortable with allowing Africans to sing their own folk music because it was associated with pagan rituals.[125]

However, what is most surprising about the reaction of both Africans and Europeans is that Rietzsch essentially managed to convince himself and everyone else that what he was introducing was real Nyakyusa music. Not a single white or black person commented on the fact that his settings sound very different from the indigenous music of the region. He wrote to Baudert about the choir's refusal to sing his settings: "For the Negro, and even more the Christian, despises particularly his own music. The educated Christian considers his own folk music uneducated and therefore reprehensible. I find this quite frightening. This is particularly sad, because valuable folk treasures are being destroyed."[126] The church elders echo the opinion of white missionaries when they reject these hymns. Rietzsch explains that the members of the choir "were unsure about these hymns mainly because Europeans have more or less rejected them from the very beginning."[127]

Why did the choir members react so passionately against Rietzsch's chorale settings? Of course, they might have felt that this music did not sound like their music. We saw in part II that the first performances of medieval polyphony did not take place until the 1920s, so no one alive really knew what medieval music sounded like. And, no less consequential, most of the other missionaries had little music training.[128] But Rietzsch and other missionaries believed that the choristers' passion for Sankey hymns, with their simple harmonic language, played a significant role.[129]

As a result of the choir revolt, Rietzsch had to give up his church-music activities and was moved to a neighborhood congregation, Rutenganio, where he was mainly active as a missionary. This decision was very likely made by Baudert in consultation with the local bishop, Oskar Gemuseus. Baudert encouraged Rietzsch to concentrate on his scholarship and sent him various books that could further his research. But this did not stop Rietzsch from pursuing his quest to introduce the Wanyakyusa to pentatonic chorale settings.

In a letter to his sister dated 23 September 1935, Rietzsch writes that Bärenreiter had a special sale on recorders and asks her to purchase an entire set for him. He taught his servants how to play the recorder and read staff notation and proudly reports that they learned both in no time at all.[130] Of course, at first they only wanted to play Sankey hymns, but when he refused they were happy to play his three-part pentatonic settings of Reformation-style chorales on the recorder and—so he claims—could not get enough of playing together.

Rietzsch tells his sister that one of the Swahili teachers at the local school, a great lover of Sankey and tonic sol-fa, came by Rietzsch's house, wondering what kind of noises he was hearing. Rietzsch showed him that all of the servants had learned to read staff notation. The teacher expressed surprise, because he thought staff notation was too difficult for Africans to learn.[131] He begged Rietzsch to teach staff notation to his son and perhaps even in the school, but Rietzsch declined. He did, however, take his recorder trio on tour and played to great acclaim all over the Nyasa area. Next the Wanyakyusa elders wrote a letter to Rietzsch apologizing for their past behavior, and Bishop Gemuseus asked him to start his choir work again. But Rietzsch, doubtless wounded by the experience, no longer saw any future in his earlier work. Since it was difficult to disobey a bishop, he did not directly decline, but made excuses every time he was asked to schedule a rehearsal.

Rietzsch was not the only missionary to become disillusioned with his service on the Moravian Mission station in the late 1930s. The chair of the

Moravian Church in the Southern Highlands, Walter Marx, asked to be sent
home early and made it clear that he was no longer convinced they should
continue their work there.[132] It seems that Rietzsch spoke for many of the
younger missionaries when he wrote in a bitter and somewhat sarcastically
formulated letter from 19 January 1936:

> And now we were no longer happy with the singing in our church. There-
> fore we jump at the Negroes and tell them that they have to sing better.
> We practice with them, even place new notational systems in front of
> them, as I did. And he has no idea why we suddenly demand from him,
> what—as he feels instinctively—we do not practice ourselves. . . . In
> many areas, but especially in our church-music work, we in the mission
> resemble some kind of charity association. . . . From a superior position
> we are teaching the "poor" Negroes all sorts of things that are supposed
> to be good for them and that they also want to have and accept. And as
> the pauper at home who has received alms uses the offerings nonsensi-
> cally or squanders them, to the annoyance of his benefactor, so does the
> Negro.[133]

Although in his last years in Tanganyika Rietzsch no longer conducted
his choir, he continued to make recordings of local vocal and instrumental
music. He had pursued this activity from the beginning of his stay, but now
his efforts intensified, and he tried to transcribe and analyze the music.
The recordings are now in the Berlin Phonogramm-Archiv, where I have
managed to track them down.[134] They consist of religious songs created by
the local population and some irimba pieces, and they seem to be among
the earliest surviving recordings of Nyakyusa music. In his letters he describes these performances with great enthusiasm.[135] He writes to his sister
in a letter dated 27 April 1936 that he contacted his old teacher from Hamburg University, Heinitz, and asked for help in publishing some of these
recordings. Heinitz answered that he found them uninteresting, because
they showed European influence.[136] Rietzsch disagrees with Heinitz's judgment and, in an astonishing display of ignorance of the political situation in
Germany, considered sending them to Hornbostel and Lachmann instead—
both of whom had been forced to leave their positions in Berlin in 1933 and
1935, respectively, and emigrate.

The question, of course, is why he never considered introducing these
religious songs into the service. There are two possible answers: first, Rietzsch,
with his *Singbewegung* background, may have felt that a service demanded
the formal chorales linked with the history of the Protestant Church. This

position was held, for example, by Bruno Gutmann, from the Leipzig Mission, who worked with the Wachagga at the foot of Mount Kilimanjaro (chap. 11) and was greatly admired by Rietzsch. Gutmann started out in the early twentieth century favoring local rituals, even though he did not quite know how to incorporate them into the service. When he too fell under the spell of the *Singbewegung* after World War I, he changed his mind: he now argued repeatedly that the Gospel and the Lutheran chorale were inextricably connected. He translated most Lutheran chorales into Chagga, translations that are still sung today.[137]

But it is also possible that Rietzsch never attempted to introduce the popular songs because the church elders and white missionaries would have objected. He writes in one of his last letters from 1938 to his sister: "It is a fact that missions reject the presence of folk songs in the service—and with their enlightened pietistic point of view will always do so."[138]

Encouraged by Baudert, Rietzsch concentrated on his scholarship. In order to get help with his efforts to write pentatonic polyphony, he wrote to Bärenreiter describing his situation in Tanganyika and asked if they could send him some early polyphony. He announced with great pride that Konrad Ameln, whom he knew as one of the most important leaders of *Singbewegung* (see chap. 8, pp. 110–11 and 117), had written him a long letter showing great interest in the tonal system of the Wanyakyusa. Ameln seems to have hoped that Rietzsch's research would benefit his own projected book on pentatonicism. (To my knowledge, the book was never written.) According to Rietzsch, Ameln felt that "the music of the natives has to be researched in great detail for us to understand its relationship to our own music."[139] In addition, Rietzsch considered submitting his own three-part pentatonic settings to Bärenreiter, expecting that such a collection of chorales would sell well.

Baudert also asked Rietzsch to work on a new hymnbook with the support of Wanyakyusa church leaders.[140] This book was supposed to include hymns by local composers, hymns that were typical of Nyakyusa music. Rietzsch consulted with various other Protestant missions in Tanganyika, but the hymnbook was never completed.[141]

Rietzsch was due to return to Germany in 1939, but before he and his family could board the boat, the war started, and he was interned by the British. They confiscated his substantial instrument collection; it is not clear where it is now.[142] He and the other Moravian missionaries were allowed to return to Germany in late 1939.

Back in Germany, he was too old to be drafted into the army, so he had to find employment as a Lutheran pastor. The Moravian Church felt unable to employ him further, even though he repeatedly asked if they could find him a position. The reasons for their refusal are difficult to determine. It might be connected with the fact that he had joined the NSDAP in 1936, against the wishes of Baudert.[143] But then, several of his colleagues did too, and their employment was continued.[144] In 1942, after Rietzsch had again asked to be reinstated by the Moravians, three of his old colleagues from Africa were asked to evaluate him: Theodor Tietzen, Bishop Oskar Gemuseus, and Walter Marx.[145] All three described him as absolutely honest and decent, though lacking in social skills. Marx stresses that, deep down, Rietzsch was not a Moravian, but more of a Lutheran—and hence an outsider to the community.[146] Combined with the fact that Rietzsch did not come from an old Moravian family, as did most of his colleagues, his theological differences with the Moravians might have been the reason for his termination. He spent the war in Spremberg, in Saxony, as a Lutheran pastor; after the war he led congregations in two other small Saxon towns, Tschirla and Rochlitz. Rietzsch died in 1979.[147]

It is perhaps not surprising that Rietzsch did not remain in close contact with his Moravian colleagues. On the other hand, his friendship with various members of the *Singbewegung*, in particular Ameln but also Christhard Mahrenholz and the Swiss theologian and church-music historian Markus Jenny, continued to flourish during and after the war. They regularly sent food and scholarly books to East Germany and also visited him. However, he never returned to his scholarly work.

CHAPTER ELEVEN

The Leipzig Mission

We would have loved to join them in singing their own music. But that is extremely difficult for us who are white. They have a completely different tonal system. Their scales would sound entirely different than ours. We have always listened to them singing their own songs. With some of them we could roughly sing along. But when we wanted to play them on the harmonium, it became impossible. And I should add that even today most of us are unable to sing their songs. Thus we had no choice but to translate our German songs and teach them our melodies. And they did this with great enthusiasm. So they ended up singing our dear old German folk songs.
—Paul Rother, *Mein afrikanischen Jungen* (1935), 12

Our chorales are incomparably valuable for bringing crowds into the mood of collective emotion to have all souls resonate toward one goal.
—Bruno Gutmann, *Gemeindeaufbau aus dem Evangelium* (1925), 92

There is no doubt that the Leipzig Mission was founded as a result of Prussian colonialism.[1] They were invited to work in German East Africa because the country had become a German colony and the foreign office no longer tolerated foreign missionaries. Yet, this is not a simple story of colonial exploitation: the Leipzig Mission employed a number of missionaries, the most important of whom was Bruno Gutmann, a member of the *Singbewegung*, who, believing that German society was corrupt, idealized the Chagga way of life (the Wachagga live in Tanzania at the foot of Mount Kilimanjaro).[2] Gutmann did fundamental work on the Chagga language and culture and attempted to document and preserve their rituals; he was never a supporter of the colonial government.

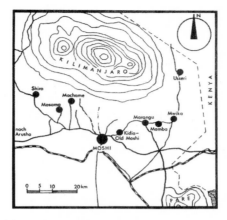

Figure 11.1. Map of the Leipzig Mission stations in the Kilimanjaro Area. Courtesy of
Althaus, *Mamba-Anfang* (1968), 103.

    The history of colonial activities extends back nearly eight years before
the arrival of German missionaries. The Leipzig Mission was founded in
Dresden in 1836 and then moved to Leipzig twelve years later. Their missionaries were active in Australia (1838–49), southern India (from 1840),
German East Africa (from 1892), and also Papua New Guinea (after 1953).
The first missionaries to appear in the Kilimanjaro area were Anglicans,
who established a station there in 1885 (fig. 11.1).[3] Even before the arrival of
Carl Peters in the Kilimanjaro area in 1891, the Wachagga had been attacked
by the German Reichskommissar Hermann von Wissmann, who, with the
support of a rival Chagga chief, had two hundred Kibosho warriors killed
and another sixty injured.[4] As the historian Horst Gründer has shown, the
Chagga chiefs regularly used the German presence to strengthen their own
position in their fight against other chiefs.[5]
    Circumstances for the Wachagga became worse when Peters followed
von Wissmann as Reichskommissar in late August 1891. Peters had hoped
to attract mission societies to the region because he thought it would help
him procure cheap labor from Africans.[6] Within a few months of Peters's
arrival, Anglican missionaries reported that he wanted to turn the fertile
countryside into a German plantation. The English missionaries were
alarmed: not only had they baptized the Wachagga, but they also had established hospitals and schools and encouraged the people to plant crops, fruit,
and timber,[7] and they felt that they could not continue their work with Peters in charge. In 1891 the Anglican missionary Alfred Stegall described the
violence of Peters's activities: "Dr. Peters is there, and the barbarity which

he seems to delight in showing towards the natives, and the immorality of almost all of the Germans would furnish, I think, material for a report which could hardly be credited in Europe."[8] Although Peters was ordered back to the coast in February 1892, atrocities continued under his successor, Albert von Bülow.[9]

In 1893 the German government forbade "behavior hostile to the Reich" (*reichsfeindliches Verhalten*), and the Anglicans were replaced by missionaries from Leipzig.[10] The local population and their chiefs now lived in fear of the German military. In general, the sympathies of the Leipzig missionaries were with the Wachagga.[11] The mission director Karl von Schwarz was concerned about becoming a tool of the government; he admonished his missionaries repeatedly that they were servants of God, not the Kaiser.[12] There are, perhaps as a result, numerous examples of Leipzig missionaries intervening with racist settlers on behalf of exploited local workers. Bruno Gutmann, in particular, did not shy away from confronting the colonial administration and was opposed to Chagga working on any nonmissionary plantations, so much so that the Leipzig mission director repeatedly asked him to restrain himself.[13] There is no doubt that the Leipzig Mission profited considerably from their own plantations and defended their existence.[14]

BRUNO GUTMANN AND THE LEIPZIG MISSIONARIES

The central figure among Leipzig missionaries—both at the time and now for us—was Bruno Gutmann (1876–1966; fig. 11.2). Even though he came from a modest background and never attended a university, he became one of the great Africanists of the first half of the twentieth century. He was a superb linguist, who made Chagga a written language, compiled a grammar, and translated the New Testament into Chagga. Furthermore, to this day the Wachagga also consider him a great Chagga poet for having translated the New Testament and many German hymns into their language, and because he employs specifically Chagga imagery in his texts. The year 1926 saw the publication of a large, three-volume study of Chagga law, which the British anthropologist J. H. Driberg reviewed at length in the ethnographic journal *Africa* in 1929 and called "the best monograph which we have read on an East African tribe."[15] Other anthropologists followed suit: Sir E. E. Evans-Pritchard called Gutmann "the German social anthropologist,"[16] and Franz Steiner and Lucien Levy-Brühl were profoundly affected by his ideas. More recently, the Harvard anthropologist Sally Falk Moore relied heavily on his work in her study of Chagga law.[17] Even though his writing style suffers from "affected ponderous prose" and his approach to ethnography is

Figure 11.2. Bruno Gutmann with his teachers (1912). Courtesy of Leipzig Mission.

dated,[18] his work on Chagga culture remains to this day the most detailed and important we have. In addition to the work on Chagga law, in the 1930s he published three compendiums of Chagga initiation lessons. Finally, he produced more than a dozen theological and mission studies and numerous articles and letters.

His research into music is also of interest to us, although it is markedly different from Rietzsch's. He lacked the background to analyze local music or introduce it into the service. Thus, when in 1913 Hornbostel asked him to make recordings for the Berlin Phonogramm-Archiv, Gutmann delegated the task to the remarkable missionary Elisabeth Seesemann.[19] Nonetheless, he is responsible for the documentation and preservation of numerous Chagga rituals that include music. His training in Germany had prepared him well for the challenges he faced.

All of the Leipzig missionaries sent to Africa or India attended the six-year mission seminary located in Leipzig at the Mission House, but they could also attend lectures at Leipzig University. As a result, Gutmann was able to sit in on lectures by Wilhelm Wundt, which had a profound influence on him.[20] Leipzig missionaries were taught to walk a fine line between *völkisch* and Christian values. The mission director Karl von

Schwartz recommended in 1893 that missionaries apply the same methods that had already been successfully developed in Indian mission stations: "If at all possible preserve local customs, distinguish sinful from purely human, and make patient use of sacred local customs through the teaching of God's word and the entire elevating influence of the Christian model."[21]

But the music education the Leipzig students received was more narrowly focused and less open to working with local traditions. Music in Leipzig, a conservative city, was still taught in a Mendelssohnian tradition.[22] The mission had hired Albin Bickrodt to prepare the missionaries musically for their service, and he focused primarily on Lutheran music.[23] Particularly favored were chorales by the seventeenth-century Lutheran pastor Paul Gerhardt. Bickrodt gave his students little encouragement to import local music into the service.

After completing his training, Gutmann was sent to German East Africa in 1902, first to Mamba, where he worked with the older missionary Gerhard Althaus, then in 1904 to Machame, where he started his ethnographic work. It is here that he had his first run-ins with colonial officials, defending the local population who were taxed by the German administration and forced to work under miserable conditions on German plantations.[24] Two years later he established a new mission station in nearby Masama. In 1908 he had to return to Germany because of health problems. He married Elisabeth Förster in 1909, and in 1910 he returned to Africa, this time to the small town of Old Moshi. Here he stayed, with several interruptions, until 1938. All German missionaries were expelled in 1920 because German East Africa had come under British rule and was now "Tanganyika Territory," but he was able to return to Old Moshi in 1926.[25]

During his lifetime, Gutmann was widely admired by Africans, other missionaries, and German academics. He received two honorary doctorates: one in theology in 1924 from the University of Erlangen, and another in 1926 from the law faculty at the University of Würzburg—a remarkable achievement for someone who was essentially self-taught.

CHAGGA CHURCH MUSIC IN THE FIRST YEARS

Even though Gutmann considered the documentation and preservation of Chagga rituals and culture one of his primary goals, he made no attempt to preserve local music except when it was associated with rituals. From the very beginning of missionization, several of the Leipzig missionaries offered explanations of why Chagga music could not be used in church. By far the most common was the close association of African music with dance, which many considered morally suspect. Gutmann's missionary colleague and brother-in-law, Paul Rother (1878–1956), provides a detailed description of male circumcision rituals that can be summarized in one sentence: The dancers are naked, sexually aroused, and drunk.[26] Clearly, missionaries— and this was true of all denominations—did not consider this an appropriate source of music for a Christian service.

The Wachagga also practiced female genital mutilation. The German military doctor A. Widenmann described in 1899 how the girls undressed and danced around, naked save for a few shells, until they collapsed of exhaustion and the excision of the genitalia was performed.[27] Elisabeth Seesemann wrote an article in the missionary journal about Chagga women in which, the Leipzig Mission Society having forbidden her to state in direct and precise language what was happening to the women, she concluded: "All the songs and ugly, disgusting dances, performed by naked girls rubbed with ointment, wearing only clasps, necklaces and pearls—all this is inexpressibly sad. . . . The ceremony is accompanied by dances and songs, songs which are almost impossible to write down because of their filthy content and others that breathe an unimaginable sadness and melancholy."[28] Thus, for some of the missionaries in areas where female circumcision was practiced, it was impossible for them to think of these dances and their music as something positive. Other music was not mentioned.

And yet, in 1935, thirty years after his negative experience with dance, Rother published a memoir called *Meine afrikanischen Jungen* (My African Boys). A lot had happened: numerous scholars in Germany and abroad were now treating African music seriously, and Rother, who was musically much more up-to-date than Gutmann, might well have read Hornbostel's articles on African music in the ethnographic journal *Africa*. He provided a different rationale for not introducing local music when he described his experiences at the Teachers Training College in Marangu:

> At the end came the singing. Every day we sang for half an hour. And they were always participating fully. We would have loved to sing with them in their way. But to do so is really very difficult for us white people. They have a completely different tonal system. Their scales would sound completely different than ours. We always heard them sing their own songs. Sometimes we sort of were able to sing with them to some degree. But when we tried to play them on the harmonium, it was a different matter. And I have to add that even today most of us are unable to sing their songs. Thus, we had no choice other than to translate German

songs and teach them our melodies. And they participated in this with great pleasure. Therefore, they sang our old German folk songs.[29]

The Leipzig missionary Georg Fritze (1889–1944), who was responsible for the 1931 hymnbook, in that year also explained why the missionaries were unable to use local music. His is an astonishing view for this date, especially when compared to statements by Rietzsch (chap. 10) and Hagena (chap. 12):

> Even though the Wachagga have always been singing, they don't have songs such as we do. It is similar with the birds in Africa. The African birds sing, but they don't have songs like our birds at home. The singing of the Negroes is more a purely melodic and rhythmically strong speech [*stark bewegtes Sprechen*], mainly antiphonal, and it could possibly be used for epic material, also of a biblical nature.[30]

In short, we have seen that Lutheran chorales were introduced by the Leipzig missionaries for three reasons: first, and most important, this is what the Mission Society had trained them and expected them to do, and they needed real songs in the Western style, which the Wachagga did not have. Second, there were too many distasteful (in Europeans' view) rituals associated with local music and dance for them to merit seriously consideration of use in the church. And third, they did not understand the African tonal system and were unable to sing the African songs.

THE CHAGGA HYMNBOOKS

The first handwritten hymnbook in Chagga dates from 1897; the last printed hymnbook under Leipzig supervision is from 1955. All of them are essentially translations of German chorales.[31] The 1929 hymnbook includes most of Gutmann's translations as well as newly created texts appropriate for the Wachagga. Of the 256 hymns, almost all the melodies are German, and only a few of the texts are by local poets. This hymnbook was reissued by Leipzig missionaries in 1967, and the chorales were still being sung in 2011 when I visited Marangu. I was told by Athanasius Mphuru, the son of the Lutheran pastor in Marangu, that he much prefers Gutmann's translations into Chagga to the Swahili texts. He is very upset that Chagga is dying out, because the language is so much richer than Swahili. In 1933 Rother published a four-part version of this hymnbook. Most are translations of

Figure 11.3. Leipzig missionaries were also active among the nearby Maasai and introduced Lutheran chorales to them as well. Here they are listening to the Leipzig Thomaner Choir on a phonograph. Photograph by Leipzig missionary Wilhelm Guth, between 1927 and 1938. Courtesy of Leipzig Mission.

German chorales, none are trying to imitate Chagga music, and all are typical of Western music settings.

Early on in the missionizing project, there was general consensus among the missionaries who taught the German chorales that the Chagga were simply unmusical because they could not sing the German songs in tune (fig. 11.3). Gutmann wrote in 1907:

> On two afternoons each week I practiced singing with my twenty-four choirboys, to gradually get the church singing to a more elevated level. For their efforts they are getting 1 rupee for Christmas and also clothing. But even though I selected the best singers, thus far I have not been able

to teach them how to sing in tune. . . . It is completely incomprehensible to me that especially our people from Machame are such terrible singers, but this is the fact. . . . In their own songs this is not so apparent, because they are mainly sung in falsetto. Nevertheless, no matter whether it sounds good or bad, if the singing of sacred songs becomes for our people an important inner need and joy, then it is always sung well for our Lord.[32]

Similarly, the missionary Karl Knittel wrote in 1913 that the Chagga people's singing was very "primitive." Students had asked him if they could sing four-part chorales, which they did with great enthusiasm. He also gave them regular violin and harmonium lessons, which he found desperately challenging: "I really want to run away. They don't have any ear whatsoever."[33]

How would the Lutheran chorales have sounded? Even though the Leipzig missionaries had no training in comparative musicology, some of them realized that the Chagga tonal system was differed from their own, because it relied on a pentatonic scale with the relative pitches F–D–C–A–G–F. (See chap. 10, pp. 148–52, for more on pentatonic scales.) Just as missionaries observed with the Wanyakyusa, they found the Wachagga unable to sing half steps; also, they gradually adjusted all Western melodies to their tonal system.

GUTMANN, FOLKLORE, AND *GEMEINSCHAFT*

Even though Gutmann did not use Chagga music in the service, he felt strongly that their traditions needed to be documented. To this end, and in accordance with what the Grimm brothers and members of the *Wandervogel* had done, he documented every one of their fairy tales, proverbs, and sayings that he heard; he was just as concerned as Hornbostel that Chagga culture not die out. Gutmann also observed Chagga rituals and attempted to adapt them to Christian usage. And, most originally, after years of ethnographic observation, he concluded that only among the Wachagga could one find true participatory music making as had been described by the leaders of the *Jugendmusik-* and *Singbewegung*.

All three of these subjects are so intricately intertwined that it is impossible to discuss them separately. Gutmann started in 1905 with a publication entitled *Neun Dschagga Märchen* (Nine Chagga Fairy Tales) and ended in 1961 with the article "'Stammenentfremdete Massen' unter den Bantu" (Masses Alienated from Their Tribes among the Bantu). In between he wrote a total of 148 articles and books.[34] Throughout his life Gutmann

Figure 11.4. Harvest dance of male youths with drums by missionary Wilhelm Guth, taken probably after 1924. Courtesy of Leipzig Mission.

consistently argued that only in Africa are the original extended-family ties still present, and that they needed to be preserved and protected against modern society. The concept of *Gemeinschaft* was central to his work. Like members of the *Jugendmusik-* and *Singbewegung*, he was hostile to popular and American culture, writing in a letter to his daughter: "Robberies and thefts now occur all the time. . . . The cinema, with all of its bad pictures, teaches the blacks properly how they should go about stealing and robbing. And it is so sad that all of these temptations come from Europe and America, where no one is concerned when people do bad things which ruin other people."[35]

The sources of Gutmann's ideas are not hard to trace. As the anthropologist J. C. Winter has demonstrated, Gutmann's early work is firmly rooted in the publications of the German sociologist Ferdinand Tönnies (1855–1936),[36] but they use slightly different terminology. The terms *Gemeinschaft* and *Gesellschaft* are central to Tönnies's view: *Gemeinschaft* refers to groupings based on feelings of togetherness, that is, family and neighborhood, *Gesellschaft* to groups that are sustained by them being instrumental for their members' individual aims and goals, that is, the state or a corporation. Gutmann adapts these concepts to his description of Chagga society. The individual is still organically bound to the community, which he organized into what he calls "primal ties," of which there are three: the clan, the neighborhood, and the age group. Clanship is the most important of these because it is based on blood. He quickly realized that folklore played a crucial role in maintaining the primal ties in each group.

Two examples: In contrast to other missionaries, he never opposed either male circumcision or female genital mutilation and argued that every family should decide for themselves whether they wanted this for their children or not. Instead, he studied circumcision rituals and published their texts. (This is by no means common; most ethnographers give a description of the rituals, but few knew the languages well enough to transcribe all of the texts.) He then adapted the rituals to Christian confirmation classes, because both represent coming-of-age rites. And these adapted rituals, minus the circumcision aspect, are still practiced today. Similarly, he helped revive an old Chagga harvest festival with local instruments (long narrow drums) that he had made according to instructions from local musicians (fig. 11.4).[37] This festival, too, is still held every year.

GUTMANN AND *SINGBEWEGUNG*

In 1920 all the German missionaries were interned by the British and then sent home. Once they got there, they found that musical life in Germany had been fundamentally transformed by the *Jugendmusik-* and *Singbewegung*, which, as we saw in part II, also are centered on *Gemeinschaft*. For members of the movement, the old folk songs and chorales that they believed went back to the Middle Ages exemplified the spirit of community at its best. This feeling of *Gemeinschaft* went hand in hand with a passionate interest in folk music from all over the world. African folk songs were particularly welcome, because in Africa there were no concerts; everyone participated in the performance of music and dance. And then, there was the general belief that music in "primitive" cultures was similar to medieval music.

When Gutmann and his fellow missionaries returned to Germany in 1920, they were warmly welcomed by leaders of the *Singbewegung*. They were invited to music retreats not only to talk about African music, but also to describe the reception of the Lutheran chorale in Africa.[38] Gutmann published three books with the *Singbewegung* publisher Bärenreiter and two articles in the journal *Die Singgemeinde*.[39] Numerous other publications reflect the new spirit of the 1920s.

Gutmann's publications for *Singbewegung* audiences address two areas. First of all, he describes African music and folklore. His account of the musical instrument called the *Brummbogen* (the English term is "musical bow") and its usage are invaluable.[40] Similarly, in his article for *Die Singgemeinde* he transcribes and explains the greeting songs of the Wachagga, which teach children how to interact with adults and with each other in a respectful manner; but he ends pessimistically: "The greeting songs of the Wachagga are doomed. And with them goes a part of the inner control from which the African acquired the pleasant demeanor that characterizes him. Now he is increasingly attacked and crushed by the formlessness of the modern European, from which he can only degenerate."[41]

The second area of interest to the *Singbewegung* concerns the manifestation of *Gemeinschaft* among the Wachagga. According to Gutmann, only in Africa can you find real *Gemeinschaft*; moreover, participatory music making is at its best when the Wachagga sing Lutheran chorales. The earlier education of sayings, greetings, and didactic songs that the Wachagga received from their mothers and grandmothers—customs Gutmann documented in fascinating detail—had laid the groundwork for communal chorale singing: "They already knew the elements, and now they found them again in a higher and more pure order."[42] He continues, "Our chorales are incomparably valuable for bringing crowds into the mood of collective emotion to have all souls resonate toward one goal. They have been accepted by our people gladly and willingly."[43] In contrast to the Moravians and the Bethel and St. Ottilien missionaries of the 1920s and '30s, Gutmann made no attempt to incorporate local music into the service; local music and sayings were valuable only insofar as they prepared the Wachagga for what he considered to be the supreme expression of music, religion, and community: the Lutheran chorale.

Thus, it is not surprising that the Chagga hymnbooks include predominantly German melodies alongside a few English and Sankey hymns.[44] However, Gutmann created new poetry for these melodies in order to incorporate Chagga events and daily life. There is, for example, the so-called Kibo song, which refers to the highest peak of the Kilimanjaro massif. Here is the first verse in Gutmann's German translation:

There towers a chief beautiful and light	Es ragt ein Häuptling schön und licht
High above our heights:	hoch über unsre Höhen:
It is the Kibo, it is he whose face	der Kibo ist's, das Angesicht,
Everyone in the country sees.	das alle Lande sehen.

High above the sea of clouds	Hoch übers Wolkenmeer
He is striving for heaven.	Strebt in den Himmel er.
The last evening light	Der letzte Abendschein
Sends us greetings from him so pure	Grüßt von ihm her so rein
And will become home up there.	Und wird zur Heimat droben.[45]

In his publications he laments the loss of communal singing in Germany and asks, "Where are the shepherd and crèche songs of the German Middle Ages?"[46] The answer is clear: in Africa, among the Wachagga. To stress his point, Gutmann published another article in *Die Singgemeinde* on German Christmas customs and carols in Africa;[47] needless to say, only in Africa can one experience a true Christmas spirit.

From these years onward, Gutmann (and his colleagues from Leipzig) no longer offered apologies for not using local music in church services, instead affirming that "the chorale is the strongest missionary power of the Lutheran Church."[48] In his book *Das Dschaggaland und seine Christen* (The Country of the Wachagga and the Christians among Them; 1925), Gutmann also includes a chapter on the chorale in Chagga congregations. He begins by criticizing young Indian Christians who want to sing local music in church. Fortunately, according to Gutmann, the church elders did not approve, announcing: "We feel that by singing the German chorales the voices of our [departed] missionaries are still with us." Gutmann concludes: "In this way the chorale is inextricably linked to the Gospel."[49] In other words, the Gospel and the Lutheran chorale belong together; one cannot stand without the other. And according to Gutmann, African Christians understood this link and have made it their own. They used chorales as chorales had been used in the Middle Ages in Germany.

Gutmann gives numerous illustrations of how he adapted Lutheran chorales to Chagga rituals. For example, he used the melody of "Werde munter, mein Gemüte" for the ritual associated with preparing the canal to run again after the rainy season. After a short devotion, they all sing:

Again the water is flowing in the canal. Accompany it!
Our songs are supposed to say: Accept it, get ready!
The source of our fathers which they dug with patience.
Watch out that it doesn't get dirty! Everyone fill your cans and use it.[50]

Gutmann himself comments on the fact that his contrafacta are right in line with Luther's, who turned Latin sequences and hymns into German chorales. He regularly describes the enthusiasm with which the Wachagga sing his chorales. And indeed, to this day there are annual choral competitions in Tanzania for which the choirs spend years preparing. These competitions usually include three pieces, and one is always a Lutheran chorale selected by the church leaders.[51] There can be no doubt that these chorales have become part of Chagga culture.

Gutmann's story is worth telling for a number of reasons. Most broadly, his letters and articles give a snapshot of Chagga culture in an earlier time. Furthermore, Gutmann's accounts of the Wachagga are important because of the ways in which his ideas were intertwined with his involvement in other contemporary movements, the *Jugendmusik-* and *Singbewegung*, dedicated to the revival of participatory music making of folk music and early music. Untangling these strands in Gutmann's missionary activities sheds fascinating new light on German cultural history during the 1920s and '30s. In particular, it shows how the spirit of *Gemeinschaftskultur* was closely associated with music and dance in "primitive" cultures. The ideas of the *Jugendmusik-* and *Singbewegung* provide a context for understanding Gutmann's work in Tanganyika.

CHAPTER TWELVE

The Bethel Mission

I have already thought for some time about Negro music. I agree with what the Negro Ballanta said at the conference in Le Zoute: "A people can only sing from their heart when it sings its own songs." We must also introduce African melodies into our church service. Perhaps American Negro songs can be of some help here.
—Letter from Walther Trittelvitz to Martha Hosbach, 17 January? 1927, VEM Archiv

Every missionary finds it difficult to use European melodies, and feels at the same time that it would be desirable to use gradually more and more local melodies. The reason for the difficulty with using European melodies is that African music is completely different.
—Otto Hagena, "Musik in der Evangelischen Heidenmission," VEM, 1

The Bethel Mission is one of the smaller Lutheran Mission Societies, yet it had a great effect on German religious life of the late nineteenth and twentieth centuries. The Bodelschwingh family, who were the main figures of the Bethel Mission, had an almost saintly reputation in Germany because they were intimately associated with helping the mentally handicapped and homeless in Germany and underprivileged Africans. The facts that no Bethel patient was killed in the Nazi euthanasia program during the war and that Fritz von Bodelschwingh (1877–1946), son of the founder Friedrich von Bodelschwingh (1831–1910), was one of the leaders of the Confessing Church, the Lutheran Church that stood in opposition to Hitler, further contributed to Bethel's reputation. The musical life in the town of Bethel was extraordinary lively and completely dominated by members of the *Singbewegung*. Even though none of the missionaries had any training in ethnomusicology, they shared a strong background in the *Singbewegung* and did important research on African music. Again, we will concentrate on two questions: (1) what scholarly contributions the missionaries made, and (2) what kind of music was performed in the mission stations.

BEGINNINGS

In 1889 Prussia took possession of Dar es Salaam and called the mainland "Deutsch Ost Afrika" (German East Africa). As we have seen in previous chapters, the person behind this takeover was the German colonial explorer Carl Peters, founder of the German East Africa Company.[1] It is no accident that in the same year both Protestant and Catholic Mission Societies were established in Germany. Peters, who was a close friend of the Berlin pastor Ludwig Diestelkamp and his son-in-law Fritz Berlin, also a pastor, had advocated the founding of the Deutsch-Ostafrikanische Missionsgesellschaft as early as 1886, mainly in order to build a strong German presence in this area: what better way was there to spread German culture than through the establishment of German mission societies?[2] The following year Peters left the society after some disagreements; it is not quite clear what the quarrel was about, but it seems that it had something to do with the fact that Peters had also gotten in touch with the Benedictines—something that would have been hard for Protestants to swallow.[3] The organization changed its name to Deutsche Missionsgesellschaft für Deutsch-Ostafrika and set up a mission station in Dar es Salaam and a hospital in Zanzibar. The main points of the by-laws were:

1. to spread the Gospel to the "heathens,"
2. to give the local population the benefit of German counseling,
3. to help the sick, and
4. to build Christian schools.[4]

In 1890 the Lutheran pastor and founder of the "von Bodelschwingh-sche Anstalten, Bethel," Friedrich von Bodelschwingh, was asked to join the Mission Society. He was an old friend of Diestelkamp, who knew that Bodelschwingh had originally wanted to become a missionary during his theological studies in Basel, where he had developed close personal friendships with Africans and African missionaries.[5] In addition, the mission society desperately needed nurses and deacons to work in African mission stations, something that Bodelschwingh could provide. A member of the Westphalian nobility with close links to the Hohenzollern family, he had established Bethel, close to Bielefeld, in 1872, originally to care for epileptic patients. Very soon the institution began taking in mental patients and handicapped people, as well as the homeless, with the goal of rehabilitating them. In order to care for Bethel's many patients, he designated a house for deaconesses, Sarepta, and a house for deacons, Nazareth, from which most of the nurses and helpers came.[6]

Bodelschwingh was a highly charismatic man who was so successful in fundraising and lobbying for his institution that other mission societies felt threatened by his activities.[7] He arranged benefit concerts and lotteries, established mission fundraising societies all over Germany, and built a special fund-raising office in Bethel called Dankort (place of thanks), which acknowledged the donors and kept them informed about the activities of the missionaries.

He quickly became the most influential board member of the Mission Society, allowing him to set the agenda for the coming years. In 1906 he moved the Society to Bethel and became its director. Shortly afterward the Society came to be called Bethel Mission, a name that it kept until 1970–71, when it merged with the Rheinische Mission in Wuppertal; the combined mission was named the Vereinigte Evangelische Mission (United Protestant Mission).

From the very beginning, Bodelschwingh put his personal stamp on the mission. While Herrnhut and Leipzig had their own mission seminaries, Bodelschwingh decided against this course of action because it would be too expensive. Instead, he selected his missionaries personally and with great care. They were usually theologians rather than simple missionaries, and their family background was also taken into consideration: he preferred sons of theologians, academics, and landowners. Often several generations of a family worked for the Bethel Mission. In addition, Bodelschwingh liked to recruit members of Wingolf.[8]

After their examinations the prospective missionaries entered the *Kandidatenkonvikt*, where they received basic nursing and technical training. The *Kandidatenkonvikt* became a theological school (*theologische Schule*) in 1905. It is a sign of Bodelschingh's fundraising abilities that Kaiser Wilhelm II and his wife, Auguste Viktoria, were both strong financial supporters of the project.[9]

In contrast to other mission societies, for Friedrich von Bodelschwingh and his successor, Friedrich ("Fritz") von Bodelschwingh Jr., the work in the inner mission (*innere Mission*; the term refers to taking care of disadvantaged people within Germany) was intimately connected to that of outer mission (*äußere Mission*, referring to the population in non-Western countries that missionaries intended to convert to Christianity). Pastor

Fritz even referred to the outer mission as the "heart of the congregation" in Bethel.[10] Most missionaries were expected to work for a certain length of time in Bethel with the patients or the homeless before they went to Africa; Bodelschwingh was convinced that the work with mental patients would make them better missionaries. In the 1890s the Bethel missionary Paul Döring wrote about how well the work in Bethel with the mental patients prepared him for the service among the heathens.[11] As we will see, the next generation of missionaries would no longer make such comparisons. But Bethel was also the first mission society in Tanganyika that established homes for patients with mental problems.[12]

In addition, both Friedrich and Fritz von Bodelschwingh made sure that the patients in Germany were kept up to date about the missionary activities. After the mission moved to Bethel, the patients were present when the missionaries were sent out from Bethel's Zionskirche (where everyone worshipped on Sundays) in a special service. They read the missionaries' letters and prayed together for the missionaries and the African Christians. Pastor Fritz was convinced that this would be beneficial for the patients, distracting them from their ailments, and that through their prayers they would really help the new Christian communities as well as the missionaries in Africa. We know from numerous letters from the missionaries that it was a great help for them to be aware that so many people in Bethel were remembering them in their prayers.[13] And as we will see, this connection to Bethel attracted a specific kind of missionary.

MISSIONARY ACTIVITIES

Even before Bodelschwingh became the director of Bethel, he argued that German missionaries should not remain at the coast around Dar es Salaam but explore other places. He concentrated on three areas: northwest of the Usambara Mountains, among the Shambaa; Rwanda; and the area around Bukoba, west of Lake Victoria, among the Haya. Ernst Johanssen and Karl Wohlrab arrived in the town of Mlalo (Usambara) in 1891 and started their missionary work with the consent of the chief Sikinyassi (see again fig. 9.1).[14] Very soon another eight stations were established. The first years were very slow, but by 1914 the mission had baptized two thousand Christians. A printing press in Vuga was established that printed religious literature in Kishambaa and Swahili.

In 1907 Johanssen was sent to found a mission station in Rwanda, a kingdom informally ruled by Prussia since 1897; he was joined by Karl Roehl, who had translated the Bible into Swahili, and a number of other missionaries. They were all forced to leave in 1916 when the Belgians occupied the country.[15] Rwanda had not proved to be a good area for Protestant conversion: in 1914 there were still only a hundred members of the congregation, while the Catholics could count almost fifteen thousand.[16]

The Bukoba area west of Lake Victoria, originally thought of mainly as a transit point for the trip to Rwanda, became a full-fledged mission station in 1910.[17] The agricultural scientist Wilhelm Rascher and his wife, the remarkable Anna Rascher,[18] were joined by the African pastor Andrea Kajerero,[19] and from 1912 on by the missionary Paul Döring. By 1914 the congregation included thirty-three members.

After World War I Bethel continued to work only in Usambara and in Bukoba.[20] In the rest of this chapter I will concentrate on the musical life in these areas, which were markedly different. The Shambaa were highly receptive to Western music, and from the very beginning the missionaries called them "musical." The Swedish missionary and scholar Bengt Sundkler, who spent many years in Tanzania, wrote in 2000 about the singing at the beginning of the twentienth century that "the Shambaa are among the great musicians of East Africa, and their choirs sang chorales and spiritual songs in harmony. The effect of vibrating responses from one hill to another, sometimes on moonlit nights, was unforgettable."[21]

The Haya, on the other hand, were considered completely unmusical by the missionaries, at least until the missionary Otto Hagena came to live with them. But before I give an account of the musical activities, we need to turn our attention to the mission inspector Walter Trittelvitz, himself a passionate musician who made a strong impact on the musical activities of the mission stations in Tanganyika.

MISSION INSPECTOR WALTHER TRITTELVITZ

Walther Trittelvitz (1870–1958; fig. 12.1) was responsible for the Bethel Mission stations for forty-two years, from 1897 until 1939 (in 1934 he stepped down of his own free will to become the assistant mission inspector).[22] Trittelvitz was a typical Bodelschwingh appointment in that he was the son of a Lutheran pastor, and like Bodelschwingh a member of Wingolf. The fact that he was a superb fundraiser was of primary importance, since the fundraising office for all of Bethel was directed by the Bethel Mission until 1959. He wrote numerous books and articles and even edited the *Kinderbote*, in which he told many thousands of German children about the work being done in Africa. (The importance of the Bethel Mission can be illustrated by the fact that *Der Kinderbote* was the most popular German children's

Figure 12.1. Mission inspector Walther Trittelvitz. Courtesy of VEM.

magazine in the first half of the twentieth century with approximately eighty thousand copies printed.[23]) All of these activities contributed significantly to the mission's financial success. When the mission ran into serious financial difficulties in 1922, Trittelvitz was sent to the United States to conduct a fundraising campaign, which turned out to be highly successful.

Trittelvitz had two qualities that distinguished him from other mission directors and inspectors. First of all, he had no preconceived notion as to how mission activities should take place; he rarely gave his missionaries specific tasks but instead let them decide on their own how to deal with situations in the mission field. To quote his successor Curt Ronicke, "Trittelvitz gave comfort and calmed down, he explained and admonished, he asked and learned, he criticized (but only rarely), and he praised. He never commanded anyone. For him it was important, to find a new way to the common work by discussing the pros and cons of the different points of view."[24] Rather than directing their activities, he would simply send articles and books that he felt might be of use.

Second, Trittelvitz had a passionate love of music. He can definitely be counted among those who profited enormously from the musical life of Wingolf as described by Paul Tillich in his letter to Thomas Mann.[25] In numerous letters to his missionaries, he mentions participating in string quartets, and he also demonstrates an excellent knowledge of music theory.[26] So we can assume that he understood East African music better than the average missionary.[27]

Trittelvitz expressed a wish to combine anthropological research with mission activities as early as 1910; like Rietzsch, he argued that it was the job of missionaries to preserve local customs.[28] Nevertheless, until 1926 his musical agenda was conventional: he oversees the publication of hymnbooks in Shambaa and Haya of German chorales and folk songs, with translations into the local languages. The first Kishambaa hymnbook, entitled *Mbuli za Mviko*, was published in 1902, and an expanded edition was issued in 1907. It includes 102 songs, all translations of German chorales and religious folk songs.[29] The first Buhaya hymnbook was mentioned by Paul Döring in a letter to the board of directors dated 11 June 1913, where thirty-two German chorales appeared in translation.[30] Trittelvitz translated thirty-two German chorales. The Haya in particular had trouble singing the German melodies in tune; even so, Trittelvitz was the only missionary who did not believe that the Haya were simply "unmusical."

Trittelvitz is particularly interesting to us because after 1926 we can observe a radical shift in his attitude toward music in the mission stations. While his earlier letters and publications show his thinking to be in line with what one would expect from a Lutheran pastor, all this changed in 1926 after he met the Sierra Leonean music scholar and composer Nicholas G. J. Ballanta at the International Missionary Conference in Le Zoute, Belgium.[31] Ballanta had been sent by his patron George Foster Peabody to speak in Le Zoute. Neither Peabody nor Ballanta could have expected that his presentation would have such a profound effect on a mission society.

BALLANTA'S INFLUENCE ON THE MUSIC IN THE MISSION STATIONS

Nicholas Ballanta, as we have seen, was adamant that there was no similarity between medieval music and African music. Moreover, he strongly recommended that African music be performed in churches all over Africa.

The question is, of course, what could Ballanta have talked about at Le Zoute that made such an impact? It seems likely that his paper expressed many of the ideas found in his surviving publications. And we have to ask ourselves how much of this material his audience would have been able to take in. Even though his presentation in Le Zoute has not been published, we do have a short account by Edwin Smith, superintendent of the British and Foreign Bible Society, on the conference and Ballanta's performance:

> Members showed out of varied experience how in the proverbs, folk tales, legends and religious rites pegs are to be found upon which to hang Christian truth. Reference was made particularly to African music. Mr Ballanta, a Negro who has devoted himself to a study of this subject, said: "The African loves music intensely. I believe that one way of approaching him is to get him to sing about the love of God in his own way. The songs you hear in Africa may not be suitable for use, but substitute other words and adopt the tunes. Take short stories and put them to African music. Fit words to his tunes telling the truth of the Gospel and you will do a great deal towards getting that truth into his mind."[32]

In other words, Ballanta wants missionaries to use local music with Christian texts in the local language. This idea had already occurred to the Moravian missionary Traugott Bachmann in the 1910s, but for other mission societies it must have been a radical suggestion.[33] It is likely that Ballanta warned of the mistakes described above of setting tonal languages to Western melodies.

Trittelvitz also seems not to have given a written account of the lecture, but we know from letters to his missionaries that Ballanta's presentation made a great impression on him. He wrote in a letter to Martha Hosbach (1927), wife of the Usambara missionary Wilhelm Hosbach: "I have already thought for some time about Negro music. I agree with what the Negro Ballanta said at the conference in Le Zoute: 'A people can sing from their heart only when it sings its own songs.' We must also introduce African melodies into our church service. Perhaps American Negro songs can be of some help here."[34] Trittelvitz also understood that much of African music is pentatonic, that it is antiphonal, and that the rhythmic language is complex, because he mentions it later in his correspondence.

Several changes happened as a result of Ballanta's lecture. Trittelvitz must have realized that he could not alter liturgical music overnight, so his first idea was to introduce American Negro spirituals in Africa. In a letter addressed to both Martha Hosbach and Marie Müller,[35] wife of Samuel Müller, director of the Usambara hospital in Bumbuli, he mentions a choir (it is unclear whether it is African American or African) that sang spirituals at Le Zoute. (This choir seems not to have been connected with Ballanta.) Trittelvitz writes that spirituals would be attractive to Africans because they have antiphonal singing and they lack half steps—that is, their songs are pentatonic. He seems to be aware that there are several pentatonic scales, and recommends that one first find out which one is used by the Shambaa or Haya. He continues: "Even though our congregations have gotten used to singing half steps we can still learn something from the booklets [of spirituals], that is their way of delivery. Solo and choir always alternate. As far as I know, also in the African songs antiphonal singing plays a big role."[36] He urges the missionaries to introduce these spirituals into their congregations. Martha Hosbach's response was not encouraging: she was not convinced that these songs were "authentic Negro songs; moreover we like neither the songs nor the text. We really find it dreadful."[37] She is equally critical of local music: it is so much simpler (*eintönig*) than Western music, and she cannot imagine that people would want to return to that kind of music after having been exposed to Bach. And then, many of the local songs have indecent contents (*unsittlichen Inhalt*), so the local population would reject them. She does include two Shambaa melodies that might be turned into chorales.

Trittelvitz gets a similar reaction from Samuel and Marie Müller. Neither likes the spirituals: they sound like the sacred songs people are singing in England (probably a reference to Sankey hymns).[38] Trittelvitz responds that local music will probably work better with the Haya, who have been very resistant to European music.[39]

Spirituals come up again in Trittelvitz's correspondence with Otto Hagena. In a letter dated 20 January 1930 he quotes extensively from a letter by Elisabeth von der Heyden, stationed in Rwanda. Frau von der Heyden writes:

> I still have not expressed my thanks for the American spirituals. Frau Wohlrab was kind enough to pass on to me one of the three copies that have been sent to Usambara, and they have been received here with enthusiasm. In no time at all the singers had learned the melody, and they belted them out from the balcony with great enthusiasm and from the deepest heart. The listeners were equally receptive to them downstairs. I was told that the old Bakehuru [women] wanted me to know that it was the first time they had really sung.[40]

This letter must have felt to Trittelvitz like a major triumph.

In October 1930 the Third Lutheran Mission Conference took place in Dar es Salaam, and much to the surprise of Bethel missionaries, other mission societies had also started to incorporate African music into the service. The Usambara missionary Paul Wohlrab published an account of the event:

We felt this especially strongly when we visited the mission station Maneromango.[41] When the missionaries from the different areas greeted the congregation, they answered with a variety of songs. First they sang chorales, then local songs. There was a surprising difference. The chorales where slow and pale, but with the first local songs the whole crowd became extremely animated and lively. Men, women, and children sang with renewed enthusiasm. One could observe all their musical emotions sprang to life in these songs.[42]

Wohlrab closes by saying that all musical missionaries will need a phonograph to record the songs, because "a rendition of these songs in our notational system—if at all possible—will be very difficult, because we cannot express the unusual sound color through notes."[43] As a result of this conference, a decision was reached that all mission societies should try, with the help of Africans, to identify local melodies and use them in the service.

By 1933 Trittelvitz felt comfortable enough to write about the use of local music in the service in the Bethel mission magazine. In an article entitled "Geiger von Bumbuli" ("The Violinist from Bumbuli," a town in the Usambara Mountains), he wrote:

But is it really right that we bring the local population our own music? This question is being asked all over the mission field now, aren't we making the Africans too European? Why don't we let them use their old African music? For a long time the missionary thought African music was inappropriate for the Christian service. And for many years I have begged them again and again: collect the songs of the local population and write the local melodies down. . . . Now this thought is coming up everywhere in Africa.[44]

In 1936 a new church was dedicated in Bukoba in which Haya music was performed alongside the typical Bethel brass ensembles. The missionary Heinrich Scholten writes that first the brass ensembles played the hymn "Tut mir auf die schöne Pforte." Then he asked all eight chiefs to bring their drums inside the church:

A few months ago we asked every chiefdom for a drum. All eight of them arrived. . . . Shortly before the beginning of the service the Europeans and chiefs came. On the square in front of the church a vast mass of people assembled. We had to arrange for a second service under the trees. . . . The seminary students from Kigarama sat with their trombones on the balcony. Two stands for the eight beautifully decorated Buhaya drums were standing in front of the pulpit. Around these were standing eight chosen representatives from the congregations. . . . After the sermon the drums were consecrated. Every drummer recited a Bible passage, then he hit his drum with a few strong beats.[45]

We see, then, that Ballanta's presentation had at least as great an effect on the music performed in Bethel mission stations as Hornbostel's article had on Moravian music stations. (It is possible that also the director of the Berlin and Leipzig Missions heard him at Le Zoute and changed direction as a result.) Let us now turn to one missionary, Otto Hagena, who was chosen to implement Trittelvitz's vision of African music among the Haya.

OTTO HAGENA

Otto Hagena fits the typical profile of the missionaries chosen by Trittelvitz and Bodelschwingh. He became a close friend of the former, and their corre-spondence is particularly illuminating because both shared a great interest in music. He provides one of the earliest attempts at analyzing Haya music and did much to preserve local songs. His work in Africa is characterized by a deep respect for the Haya people and their culture. Finally, his personal biography and letters, especially during the war, give a glimpse of his moral character, as can be seen from his interactions with the Haya during the Nazi period and afterward, when he had to serve as a courier in the German air force (fig. 12.2).

Hagena was born on 4 February 1902 in Stolpe/Oder, in eastern Ger-many, the son and fourth child of a Lutheran pastor.[46] His mother died when he was sixteen. In 1912 his father moved the family to Eisleben, where Martin Luther was born and died. From 1916 to 1921 Hagena attended the famous boarding school Schulpforta, close to Naumburg, where many of Germany's greatest classicists and theologians were educated. Its most famous alumnus was Friedrich Nietzsche; others include Friedrich Gott-fried Klopstock, Johann Gottlieb Fichte, Leopold von Ranke, Ulrich von Wilamowitz-Moellendorff, and Carl Richard Lepsius. As a result of this stellar instruction, Hagena's Latin and Greek were outstanding, which was very useful to him in Africa when he worked on the Haya translation of the Bible. He also learned to play the violin and brass instruments and received an excellent background in music theory.[47] He writes that when he left the school in 1921 he took with him "respect and understanding for scholarly truth and thoroughness."[48] Because he was one of ten children, his father

Figure 12.2. Otto Hagena.
Courtesy of VEM.

was only able to pay for one semester of his theology studies, so he spent all his vacations working in mines or factories, and during the semester he also tutored high school students privately. He studied theology at Tübingen and Halle, where he joined the fraternity Wingolf. After a stint with Graf Bassewitz as a house tutor, he came to Bethel to study at the *Kandidatenkonvikt*, where he also worked with epileptic and mental patients and the homeless. In Bethel he became engaged to Adelheid Johanssen, the daughter of the great Haya missionary Ernst Johanssen. The introduction to the Johanssen family and the stay at Bethel were crucial in his decision to become a missionary. He writes that originally he had planned to work as a pastor with his old friends from the mines or the factory at Mansfeld, but his stay in Bethel led him to change his mind.[49] He was duly sent to London for three months to improve his English, and in 1928 he studied general phonology (*allgemeine Lautlehre*) and the grammar of African languages with Diedrich Westermann at the Institute for Oriental Studies at Friedrich Wilhelm University in Berlin while simultaneously serving as an assistant pastor in the Himmelfahrtskirche of Pastor Berlin, mentioned above. (He was originally supposed to study with Meinhof in Hamburg, but the arrangement fell through.) Even though Westermann and Hornbostel were in regular contact, Hagena seems not to have met the later. Given his interest in music, however, it is surprising that neither Westermann nor Hornbostel supplied him with a phonograph. There is also no mention in his letters of any studies in comparative musicology.

He married Adelheid in 1929 and arrived in Buhaya the same year. His immediate task was to found a so-called central school in Kigarama where young people would be educated as teachers. In addition, he served as a pastor for the local congregation and was responsible for erecting school buildings.

So how did Hagena fare in the mission field, and what are our sources for his achievements? A lot of information is provided in his correspondence with Trittelvitz and with his family and friends.[50] He also published a paper entitled "Lieder der Haja" (Songs of the Haya) in 1939,[51] and he responded in the 1930s to a questionnaire sent out by the Heidelberg theology professor Gerhard Rosenkranz for his 1951 book *Das Lied der Kirche in der Welt: Eine missionshymnologische Studie* (The Song of the Church Throughout the World: A Study of Mission Hymns).[52] Both of these works provide much important information on Haya music.

Any discussion of Hagena's teaching activities at Kigarama has to start with some background. While it was normal for missionaries to comment on the inability of the Africans to sing in tune in the first years of their work, the musical abilities of the Haya were generally considered beyond hope. The first Haya missionary, Ernst Johanssen, wrote in his fundamental book *Führung und Erfahrung im 40jährigen Missionsdienst* (Leadership and Experience in Forty Years of Mission Service) that the Haya were simply "unmusical": "The Haya have only the small hymnbook by Döring in their language, and the songs sound really terrible wherever you have a service." He concludes a little later: "The people here, in any case the adults, have no ear at all for our melodies."[53]

A colorful account written either in 1913 or, at the latest, 1916 is given by the Bukoba missionary Paul Döring, who was responsible for the hymnbook mentioned above and worked, with the help of Haya Christians, on the translation of the Bible into Haya. He describes how the missionaries were received by the local teacher and assistant pastor Josua, from Uganda:

Suddenly a festively dressed group of people arrive singing loudly. My first thought was: what bizarre songs the Catholics have. Gradually I understand the text and I suddenly realized that they have exactly the same text as we do. And at the same time, I also understood whom I had in front of me [namely, the local Lutheran congregation]. Now, as they continued singing happily, I had time to reflect how these bizarre melodies might have come into existence—how much could be credited to the local population, how much to the English, and how much to us. I was unable to sing along, but my companions were soon able to join in the new melodies. Often it sounded as if they were singing a second voice. The Baganda cannot be great singers; even melodies which they knew earlier, such as "Kommet zum Heiland" and "Sicher in Jesu Armen," they sing in a totally distorted manner.[54]

It is clear that Döring believes that there is one correct version of the hymn tune he heard and that the congregation sang something quite different. Since this area had a strong local Christian tradition, this might have been a case where the Haya and Baganda congregation had created their own melody, only distantly related to the German one.[55]

As mentioned earlier, after Trittelvitz met Ballanta he wanted to introduce Haya music into the church, so in his last letter to Hagena before he left for Buhaya he wrote:

Only a real folk-like missionary activity will get through to the soul of the people. In recent times the name Gutmann has been mentioned frequently when this issue comes up. Your kind father-in-law has studied the issue from the very beginning with similar interest. I would be happy if you would receive my thoughts favorably, and if you could do this with respect to African music, I would be especially glad, because I always had the wish that this area should be worked on in a thorough way. You will always have an open ear if you have something to tell me on this subject. . . . The only problem is that not all of our colleagues in Usambara share this openness.[56]

As we can see from Trittelvitz's next letter to Hagena on 3 August 1929, his suggestion was immediately implemented. Trittelvitz encourages Hagena to look for local music and even suggests that the reason the Shambaa in Usambara are so receptive to Western music is that they have little interest in preserving their own music. He believes that with the Haya it might be the other way around.[57]

Hagena describes in a letter dated 26 September 1929 what kind of possibilities he sees:

Concerning music, I am trying to take in African melodies or, more accurately, African ways of singing, so that I can also sing them. But that is
not so easy. And I also often don't have time. But even if I am not able to
do it at this point, I don't see yet consequences and possibilities of usage
in church. One will also need to do serious scholarly research to investigate the *possible* connections between the musical tone when speaking
and the pitches of the melody. What literature do we have on this?[58]

We have here for the first time a missionary who tries to join the Haya in
their singing and acknowledges that it is difficult. Moreover, like Ballanta
and Hornbostel, he knows that problems will arise when trying to fit texts
in tonal languages to Western melodies.

Since he did not know how to introduce local music, he started to teach
them typical sixteenth- to eighteenth-century settings of Lutheran chorales.
The results were immediate. In a letter dated 22 September 1930 he writes
to one of his friends, "It is a great pleasure to sing with these boys who were
supposedly so unmusical. You will not be able to assemble in every school
of forty kids a choir that can sing so much in tune. Approximately eight
students of the upper class are able to write down the notes of a slowly sung
melody. We have even sung Bach chorales."[59] This passage shows that he is
still teaching the Haya students Western chorales, as well as staff notation,
and that they have no trouble learning it, probably because they are young.
Similarly, he writes to Trittelvitz on 17 December 1931: "By the way, your
assumption that the Haya have no talent for music is wrong. I never believed it and can only tell you that our choir here is not any worse than the
choir of the Gymnasium in Eisleben."[60]

In an unpublished paper entitled "Aus dem Wachsen und Werden einer
Hayagemeinde" (About the Growth and Development of a Haya Congregation), Hagena describes how the members of the congregation bring their
hymnbooks to every service, where they are inspired by the singing of the
school choir. As a result, the congregation now wants to sing four-part chorales. He uses solfège (but not the English tonic *sol-fa*) to teach them and
concludes:

From my own experience I also believe that the report that is constantly
repeated [that the Haya are unmusical] has to be revised; all we can say is
that they are not trained to sing in the European way. But as a whole they
are entirely capable of taking in European art and reproducing it. A few
days after I sang the four-part chorale "Ach bleib mit deiner Gnade" with
my choir for the first time, I received a letter from our teacher Petelo—the

natives prefer to do these things in writing—begging me to have the boys sing every Sunday. When he hears them, he gets so warm inside his heart. But our real task is to cultivate their own music, fertilized by a certain depth of expression, to a tool of praising God in a Haya way.[61]

All of these letters show that Hagena would really like to introduce local music into the service but doesn't know how to go about it.

How does he describe Haya music? In a letter he describes his first impressions of the Haya tonal system. Their music is so different that he is unable to write it down in staff notation or even repeat a simple melody:

> By the way, there is no correct notation (insofar as our staff system would permit it altogether), and we are far from a correct tonal reproduction of musical reality. The strange falling of the voices, the seeming or real sliding of the voices from the pitch one is on, though they are never pulled down, is unimaginably foreign to us. I have to ask them to sing a succession of eight tones to me at least ten times before I can sing it myself. It is clear that it will not be easy for me to study this music.[62]

He realizes that the Haya have a different tonal system, for which our notational system is inadequate. Trittelvitz had enclosed an Uha melody (the Uhas of southern Tanganyika were also considered "unmusical") and suggested to Hagena that their tonal system was pentatonic.[63] Hagena doubts that the melody is really pentatonic because there is a half step on the fourth tone. Both Trittelvitz and Hagena seem to be aware of current musicological thinking when they discuss the possibility that the pentatonic scale is the original scale of all humanity. A more detailed explanation of the tonal system is given in his answer to Rosenkranz, who had asked to what extent it was possible to use local music in the Haya church:

> Every missionary finds it difficult to use European melodies, and feels at the same time that it would be desirable to use gradually more and more local melodies. The reason for the difficulty with using European melodies is that African music is completely different.
>
> The first reason for the difference is the tonal system by itself. Even though our local population does use half steps in contrast to other Bantu tribes, their tonal system does not correspond in any way to ours.[64]

The second reason he gives is that "local people seldom use longer strophes that would allow a closed train of thought. The rule is rather an alternating couplet which is repeated again and again."[65] Third, the song of the local population is generally antiphonal, and, of course, most chorales are not antiphonal. Hagena's fourth point resonates with Hornbostel and Ballanta, who were opposed to translating European texts into local languages. Hagena explains in detail why this will not work: "The completely different language rhythm of Bantu languages can almost never be translated without violation of the melodies which were created for our German language rhythm."[66] Fifth, the local people do not use melismas in their melodies. There are cases where this seems to happen, but in reality the tone glides down and continues on the new tone with the same syllable.[67] Sixth, the singing tone is produced in a completely different way. The sound does not resonate in the head or chest; rather, the tone is "somehow nasal, which results in a restrained and suspended sound."[68] Seventh, the Haya melodies often end on the third, which increases the suspended character of their singing. "We Europeans" somehow feel that the melody is left hanging in the air. Eighth, the range of the local melodies is small, usually not more than five tones. Ninth, the Haya does not like to make big leaps: he rarely goes over a third. And tenth, "I have the impression, even though I cannot prove it yet, that local singers prefer a falling melody, rather than an ascending one."[69] Again, this last remark is in agreement with ethnomusicological research, in which African scales are usually notated in descending order.

How do Hagena's observations relate to those of ethnomusicologists? Unfortunately, to this day no detailed study of Haya music or the tonal system(s) exists.[70] And again, there seem to be very few musicians left who still can play the music as it was done in Hagena's time.

Several Bethel missionaries have given accounts of some of the characteristic Haya instruments: they describe the Haya drums, the enanga (an African zither used to recite Haya epics,[71] and the amakondele (antelope horn) orchestras,[72] but none of them talk about tonal systems.[73] The tonal system of the Haya is not mentioned in any of the known African music histories, nor is it included in Hugh Tracey's article on African scales, because Tracey mainly included xylophones and mbiras in his study, for the simple reason that their tunings are most reliable.[74] There is a remarkable account of Kiziba music (an area not too far from the Haya, on the border with Burundi) from 1910 by Hermann Rehse, in which he says that the octave is divided into thirty intervals; he claims furthermore that instrument makers are not concerned about tunings when they make their instrument but are nevertheless able to adjust it in performances.[75]

Fortunately, we have quite a number of recordings: Tracey recorded Haya music in 1950 that is now digitalized and available online.[76] And the

same is true of recordings made by Bethel missionary Werner Both, who was
in Buhaya in the 1960s and established a music school in Ruhija.[77] Upon repeated listening I found that Hagena's description of the Haya tonal system
is accurate: if you transcribe the enanga and endigini pieces you get roughly
(and it really is very rough) the following descending scale: D–C-sharp–B–
A–G-sharp, with A and G-sharp as the main tones.[78] Note, though, that this
is by no means the only tonal system used by the Haya; there are lots of
pentatonic pieces. The missionary Martin Brose, who took over the Ruhija
School of Music in 1967, found that the tuning of the enanga is changed
according to which song is being performed.[79] When Hagena says he cannot
repeat a Haya melody before he has heard it at least eight times, the most
likely reason is that the Haya have what Ballanta called "inflections." And
this is one of the main reasons both argue that the Western notational system is inadequate to represent what is going on in the music. In addition,
Hagena puts his finger on a phenomenon that is particularly disturbing for
Western musicians: that there is not necessarily one correct tuning.[80] Kubik
has shown in fascinating detail how the tunings differ from musician to musician.[81] Again, this accords with Rehse's early descriptions of Kiziba music.

We have then in Hagena a well-educated missionary who observed that
even though the majority of African tribes have pentatonic or heptatonic
systems, "his" people have a system that includes half steps; who was aware
of the problems of translating German hymns into Haya, a tonal language;
and who similarly did not believe that the rhythm of the Haya language
could be brought in line with translations of German poetry. In short, he
brought forth ten strong arguments against translating German chorales into
Haya and advocated local music instead.[82] Most important, he gave what
amounts to one of the earliest descriptions of Haya music. Like Ballanta, he
never claims that Haya music is like medieval music. Unfortunately, Hagena did not have any ethnomusicological training and never published his
findings on Haya music.

What other options did a missionary with scholarly interests have, aside
from recording and analyzing music? First, Hagena played a major role in
the New Testament translation into Haya in that he revised the existing
New Testament translation by comparing it with the Greek original.[83] (The
earlier missionaries probably did not know Greek very well.) This is where
his formidable training from Schulpforta in Greek came in handy.[84]

Second, Hagena directed his ethnographic ambitions elsewhere, namely
toward the collecting of folk songs, sayings, and literature. His only publication, "Lieder der Buhaya," was published at the urging of Trittelvitz, who

repeatedly asked him to collect local songs. Clearly, Trittelvitz must have had in mind something along the lines of Achim von Arnim and Clemens Brentano's *Des Knaben Wunderhorn*, a collection of German folk songs and poems published in 1805 (vol. 1) and 1808 (vols. 2 and 3). Brentano says that the songs were collected in order to preserve them, and this is also Hagena's prime motivation. Every German grew up with the *Wunderhorn* collection, so it seems natural that Hagena would have wanted to compile something similar in Haya. The collection exists in Haya and in German.[85] Similarly, he must have been aware of Bruno Gutmann's collections of Chagga folk songs, which probably served a similar purpose (see part III, chap. 11).

Hagena's remarkable sensitivity to other cultures can already be seen in the introduction. He writes that any study of foreign music, sayings, and tales involves discoveries of things that are familiar and things that seem alien to us. One is overjoyed in finding that there are common emotions to all peoples, even people who are geographically very distant. And there is just as much to be discovered that will continue to seem different and enigmatic to one, even after many years. While he is aware that some people believe that Africans are on a lower cultural level, he does not share this feeling and has collected these songs in order to prove to the world what cultural treasures can be found in Africa:

> How great is your surprise when you work with the cultural treasures of a people that is generally considered arrested on an animal-like step of the evolutionary scale, whose people are generally thought to live by animal instincts, and live out their life half asleep, only as a collective whole, with minimal individual inner life. I don't think that anyone who works in the mission field would think along those lines. But for that reason, the joy is enormous when you can prove through contact with the people and their souls how uninformed the judgments I just mentioned are. The following lines are an attempt to let you participate in my joy and amazement of discovering this culture. I am reproducing a few songs of our native population, the Haya, at the West Shore of Lake Victoria, which they sing during their *amayaga*.[86]

He goes on to explain that *amayaga* are dances that are used for all kinds of festive occasions: there are love songs, songs intended to keep up the laws, songs that accompany the building of a house, and many more. All songs are sung frequently and for many years. Many mention German colonial administrators who left the country almost twenty years earlier. So these songs are not like the ones described and recorded by Rietzsch, who only stayed a few months. Unlike many scholars, he acknowledges the help of an African colleague, in this case Petelo Nschekela. "Since they have all been written down by our informant, the teacher Petelo Nschekela, . . . we can assume that they are songs that were really sung often and that there are many more songs like this transmitted by the people."[87] Even though Hagena hoped that by writing these songs down they would be preserved, this is not what happened. By the 1960s, when the church musician and missionary Werner Both came to Buhaya, they had been completely forgotten. Both knew Hagena's collection through the Bethel Mission but told me that none of the songs were sung any more.[88] Gutmann managed to preserve these songs by reinterpreting and repurposing them as part of Christian rites; it seems, then, that Hagena would have had to combine his songs with rites, as Gutmann did, in order to preserve them.

As we have seen from his letters, Hagena's work in the mission field was remarkably successful, but after three years his wife developed major depression, and the entire family, which now included three children, had to return to Germany. As in the other chapters, it is of interest how our missionary fared in Nazi Germany. Back in Germany he took a congregation in Dortmund in 1932. In 1933 he joined the Confessing Church. His letters to his wife make clear how much he disapproved of the Nazi regime.[89] In early 1937 he was sent to Buhaya again, this time without his family, to take care of some six thousand Christians and nineteen congregations run by local pastors, whom he supported in their work. He returned to Germany in 1939 and was drafted into the army, where his career advanced rapidly: he was a private in January 1940, a corporal by April, a sergeant by December, a lieutenant by June 1941, and by August 1943 a lieutenant colonel.

Hagena was close to the Bekennende Kirche leaders Ernst Wilm and Fritz von Bodelschwingh, the latter also a close friend of Trittelvitz.[90] As a result, there was never any doubt in his mind where he stood with respect to the Nazi regime. When his wife writes him that their son Hermann is being considered a candidate for an elite Nazi boarding school (also called *Napola* or *Nationalpolitische Erziehungsanstalt*), he is adamant that he will not give permission, even though his old school, Schulpforta, has been turned into one.[91]

In a letter dated 1 April 1941 he writes:

> This evening I heard the news that Bethel has again been bombed, with sad results. But do our people even have the right to get upset about this, when the life of the patients in Bethel is not considered "worthy of liv-

ing" ["*lebenswert*"]? The enemy is just doing a job for them that they really want to do themselves.[92]

In August 1941 he was assigned as a courier to the Luftwaffenfüh-rungsstab, and as a result he flew all over Europe. His letters to his wife are remarkably open and could have posed a serious threat to his life had they been read by the Nazis. As early as 1940 he writes to her about the war:

> There is much that would point to the end. But it seems to me that the world is not yet ready for the judgment. It is possible that the insanity of this war will still become larger and God's judgment will appear in every-thing? But above all it is the lie which grows into enormous dimensions.[93]

Once he was made a courier, he became fully aware of what the Ger-mans were doing on the Eastern Front. He writes to his wife in March 1942:

> You know how much I have always tried to act in deep agreement with you. I would love to go back to Africa, because service in Russia would be hard for me for many reasons. I would dutifully do my service there, if I had to, but to go voluntarily there, when the war is also moving into the civilian population, and is really a war of extinction, that I do not want to do.[94]

In one of his last letters he writes:

> It is so horrible what is happening now. It almost seems like when a body is heavily wounded it becomes numb, and then the soul too can no longer take in the horrendous extent of suffering and pain.[95]

He died in a plane crash on 8 August 1943 in the area of St. Jakob in Austria, on a flight from Vicenza, Italy, to Munich. All the passengers died with him, but his courier's map survived intact.[96]

One would like to think that Hagena's political attitudes went hand-in-hand with his wish to help underprivileged people, his respectful treatment of the Haya in Tanganyika; but of course, things are never this simple.[97]

POSTLUDE

So what happened to Lutheran church music in Buhaya after the war? Un-fortunately, the legacy of Trittelvitz and Hagena was quickly forgotten

after the latter's departure. The Swedish church took over from the Germans, and even though they were sympathetic to local music, not much
changed.[98] In the 1960s and 1970s there were two well-educated musicians
from Germany working in Ruhija, a music school in the northern diocese
that educated church musicians from all over Africa: first, Werner Both,
born in 1928 in East Prussia and a deacon from Bethel's institute Nazareth;
then Martin Brose, a well-educated music teacher.[99] Both was educated by
one of the leaders of the *Singbewegung*, Wilhelm Ehmann, who was director
of the Church Music School in Herford.[100] Ehmann was supportive of Both's
African work—so much so that he wanted Bärenreiter to publish a recording made by Both of African music in the 1960s.[101] Neither Ehmann nor
anyone in the Bethel Mission thought it was necessary to give him any ethnomusicological training before he left. His church music duties in Tanzania were vaguely defined and mainly involved taking care of church music
activities, especially brass bands. He arrived at the Bible School of Ruhija in
1961 and at first did exactly what was expected of him: conduct brass choirs
and sing chorales. But he quickly understood that there was great music to
be found among the Haya. With the strong support of Bishop Josiah Kibira
(1925–1988), he established a music school in Ruhija in 1964. Two African
students, Joas Kijugo and Blasio Mulyowa, would regularly go with him to
visit the surrounding villages and look for local musicians who would then
give them lessons on the various instruments or teach them how to build
them. Mulyowa was put in charge of the instrument-building workshop
at Ruhija. All three of them went to the court of the Kabaka in Kampala
and learned from Evaristo Muyinda how to play and build amadindas and
akadindas.[102] Both was essentially self-taught and left to his own devices
until his sabbatical in 1965 when he participated in inspiring seminars in
Cologne with Marius Schneider. Back in Africa, Both and his students did
numerous radio programs on East African music in Swahili on Deutsche
Welle that were recorded in Moshi and Mwika, all to make sure that Africans appreciated their own music. He advocated the use of the enanga
to accompany the reading of the Gospel and the Epistle, drums were used
instead of church bells to call the congregation to the service, and when
Bukoba Cathedral was consecrated he had an amadinda ensemble perform.
Most important, he made hundreds of recordings between 1961 and 1968,
mainly from Tanzania but also from Uganda and Kenya. Now in the Berlin
Phonogramm-Archiv, most of this material remains to be analyzed.[103]

The reaction of African church leaders to Both's work is complicated.
On the one hand, they supported his music school and his efforts. On the
other, Bishop Josiah Kibira (fig. 12.3) belonged to the first generation of Af-

Figure 12.3. Bishop Josiah
Kibira, who became the first
black president of the
Lutheran World Federation
in 1977. Courtesy of VEM.

rican Christians who appreciated Lutheran music. Kibira was a great but
also controversial African church leader. Fluent in German after his studies
at Hamburg University, he became the first black president of the Lutheran
World Federation in 1977.

Educated by Otto Hagena in the 1930s, Kibira loved singing Bach chorales in his choir, and he composed and conducted Lutheran hymns himself
with the choir.[104] So it is understandable that he did not want only Haya
music in his churches. For him the Gospel was intimately associated with
European hymns, and African music had heathen associations.[105] In addition, he did not feel it was right that Both constantly traveled around recording music; he wanted him to stay at the music school and teach.[106] So
in 1968 he fired Both from his job and had him replaced with Martin Brose,
who also supported local music but was perhaps more diplomatic in his
dealings with Kibira.[107]

Both's student Joas Kijugo was sent to Ehmann's Herford School of
Church Music in 1971, where he studied until 1974.[108] Again, the school

reflects Kibira's preferences for the Lutheran church music he had grown to love. In addition, he might have felt that a degree from a German conservatory would count for more than an American or African degree.[109] It did not occur to him or the mission administrators to have him study in Cologne with Marius Schneider, as Stephan Mbunga did.[110] After he graduated from Herford, Kijugo spent four years in Ghana before returning to Ruhija to teach there.

Martin Brose studied church music at Union Theological Seminary in New York and was director of the Ruhija School of Music from 1968 to 1972. He did not run into problems with Kibira, who was supportive of his efforts to introduce Haya music into the service. But throughout his tenure Kibira was adamant that Lutheran chorales be sung as well. Similarly, both Western and African music continues to be taught at the Ruhija music school. This combination of traditional German hymns and African music in the churches in the Buhaya and Kagera region continues to this day, as confirmed by Sylvia A. Nannyonga-Tamusza's and Thomas Solomon's recent study.[111] In fact, as Kofi Agawu writes, "What sense does it make, after a century and a half of regular, continuous, and imaginative use, to describe the guitar as a 'foreign' instrument in Africa, or a church hymn as representing an alien musical language, or a perfect cadence as extrinsic?"[112]

In this chapter we have been able to trace a clear evolution of the mission administrators and missionaries from the view of the "unmusical" African to a serious study and appreciation of their music. Most striking is the influence of the little-known African music scholar and composer Nicholas Ballanta, whose presentation so profoundly affected the agenda of mission administrators and missionaries. Indeed, he might have achieved more for the Haya with his presentation than Hornbostel did with "African Negro Music." His lecture encouraged missionaries to include local music in the service. And no Bethel missionary or administrator ever mentioned that African music was similar to medieval music. Last but not least, thanks to the notes and recordings of the missionaries, we have been able to reconstruct some of the Haya's music. At the same time, we have also seen that an African bishop educated in Lutheran music by a missionary grew to love this repertoire so much that he wanted it sung in his churches.

CHAPTER THIRTEEN

The Catholic Missionsbenediktiner St. Ottilien

They have essentially remained children among the different peoples of humankind. Their music is on the same level as the music of the civilized people was in their infancy. . . . Music of the Negro shows great poverty with respect to notes, and the culture that is shown in their music stands on a relatively low step.
—Ludwig Berg, *Die katholische Heidenmission als Kulturträger* (1923–28), part 7, 172

The reaction of the Bantu to this music in general is quite satisfactory. For it is a fact that the Bantu can sing Gregorian chant fairly well, and, if properly trained, as is required anywhere, they sing it very well. . . . Why is Gregorian chant so familiar to the Bantu? The affinity between African music and Gregorian chant is remarkable. It is mostly the affinity of mode, and it is indeed considerable.
—Stephan Mbunga, *Church Law and Bantu Music* (1963), 19

In terms of the number of missionaries and the scope of their program, the most important Catholic order working in East Africa was that of the Benedictines of St. Ottilien.[1] Previously there had been German-speaking Catholic missionaries in East Africa: the Holy Ghost Fathers (also called the Congregation of the Holy Spirit, founded in France in 1703)[2], who were active in Zanzibar from the 1860s, and the White Fathers, founded in 1868 by Cardinal Lavigerie, who worked in the area around Lake Victoria. The Benedictines were quick to establish mission stations in German East Africa and ultimately had a considerable number of scholars and musicians who left behind important documents about their work.

A few words about their background: the Missionsbenediktiner, as they were called, were founded in 1884 by the Swiss monk Andreas Amrhein with the specific purpose of sending out missionaries.[3] The explorer and political agitator Carl Peters was instrumental in establishing the St. Ottilien mission in East Africa. Peters, who had the support of Bavarian bishops in Munich and Augsburg and of Prince Ludwig of Bavaria, got in touch with Amrhein at the suggestion of his Bavarian agent, Freiherr von Gravenreuth, in 1887. Amrhein was portrayed by German officials as a "German-minded man," someone who would make sure that the German influence rather than French would dominate in East Africa.[4] But as the historian Horst Gründer has shown, the Benedictines were more or less dependent on the German East Africa Society, who were often dictatorial in their dealings with the local population, and also the Benedictines were very close to Dar es Salaam.[5] As a result of their close relationship with the colonial authorities, they suffered severely from the Maji Maji Rebellion of 1905–7, and several of their missionaries were killed. The main reason for the rebellion was the suppression of blacks by the colonial government, but the missionaries were hardly blameless: they supported the colonial government and demanded radical changes from the local population in their way of life.[6] On the positive side, missionaries were constantly trying to buy slaves to liberate them, and they established several schools for them. Stations were established in Dar es Salaam (1894), Peramiho (1898; made an abbey in 1931), Lindi (1913), Ndanda (1906; made an abbey in 1927), and more recently, the all-African monastery Hanga Abbey, founded in 1957 by Peramiho (fig. 13.1). To this day Hanga Abbey promotes the singing of Gregorian chant.[7]

MOTU PROPRIO

Before we turn to a description of Catholic mission activities, a few general remarks on Catholic Church history are in order. A central event for the Benedictines in the first half of the twentieth century was the 1903 *motu proprio* of Pope Pius X, which resulted in a document entitled *Tra le sollecitudini*. Certainly all missionaries were aware of it, and many comment on the implications of this text in their letters and articles.[8] Among the provisions: Pope Pius X repeated his prohibition of singing the Mass in any language other than Latin, he once again banned women from church choirs, and he forbade the use of the piano and "all noisy and irreverent instruments," such as drums, for example, which would be relevant for Africa. Gregorian chant training was strongly encouraged, as was the singing of Renaissance polyphony.

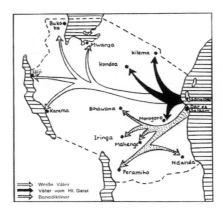

Figure 13.1. Catholic Mission stations in German East Africa. Hertlein, *Die Kirche in Tanzania*, 41.

The document complicated missionary activities for the priests and brothers: if they were to convert any Africans to Catholicism, they needed to translate religious songs into local languages so that people would understand what the new message was all about. But they also wanted to adhere to the pope's guidelines, and as a result most walked a fine line, using Latin texts for the Sunday Mass and Swahili for the liturgical hours. Thus, even though there were cautious attempts to introduce local music in the 1940s, these were not widely publicized. Nevertheless, they were significant.

Everything changed with the Second Vatican Council of 1962–65, which permitted the use of local languages and music. The effect on the liturgy was immediate and profound.

CATHOLIC PERCEPTIONS OF THE EVOLUTION OF AFRICAN MUSIC

Perhaps unsurprisingly, the views and approaches of the Catholic missionaries mirror those of the Protestants in almost every respect. The earliest Catholic priests were convinced that Africans were on the same evolutionary level as Europeans in the Middle Ages or even earlier. However, as two statements will demonstrate, they held these paternalistic views considerably longer than the Protestants. The first is from the Benedictine missionary Beatus Iter (1891–1961), from an article he wrote for the St. Ottilien Mission journal of 1933: "There I see the Wangoni and other tribes of the mission area of Peramiho in front of me, and much, much later going the same paths, which our own ancestors had taken long ago. I see them receiving not only faith from the Church, but goods of superior culture, among them song and music, working through them, internalizing them, and bringing forth individual creations from them."[9] There is not the slightest doubt for Beatus Iter that Western music (and culture) is superior and much more highly evolved, and that therefore it must replace local music.

Similarly, the Catholic scholar Ludwig Berg (1874–1939), who had a tremendous impact on Catholic mission societies, wrote in 1928 that the music of the Africans is simplistic (see the epigraph at the beginning of this chapter).[10] Berg had no doubt that Africans would eventually come to appreciate Western music and instruments. He cited approvingly his contemporary, the theologian Julius Richter, who saw the violin as an indispensable tool for teaching Africans how to sing Western hymns and chant, even though, as he reported, "the Negro first called it the thing which screams."[11] And Catholics also turned to medieval music, specifically to Gregorian chant, as most appropriate for Africans, since they believed the medieval church modes corresponded to African tonal systems.[12] The year 1928 was also the year that Eberhard Drinkwerder, a theologian from St. Ottilien who was influential in forming the agenda for the Benedictine missionaries, wrote that a missionary could not simply transplant German customs to the mission stations; rather, he should always ask himself how a local priest would feel about something. Yet, that is not what happened.[13] Missionaries stuck mainly to Catholic rites and liturgy, with the exception that they translated the texts into Swahili.

COELESTIN VIVELL

The earliest presentation of African music associated with St. Ottilien is, unexpectedly, not by a missionary, but by the distinguished Gregorian chant scholar Coelestin Vivell,[14] who lived far from Africa in St. Ottilien but spent most of his life in the Benedictine Abbey of Seckau in Styria, Austria. It is unclear how he came to write his article on music in South Zanzibar in the inaugural journal of *Missionsblätter* of St. Ottilien, since he seems never to have set foot in Africa.[15] In seeking an explanation—this was his only publication on African music—I think it likely that this is yet one more occasion in which medieval and "primitive" music are equated with each other. That is, since the Benedictines seem not to have had a specialist on African music, they looked for the next best thing, a medievalist, and asked him to write the article because he was an eminent scholar of Gregorian chant, which was generally placed in the same category as non-Western music at this time. He must have gotten his material from other publications or from oral communications by missionaries.

As might be expected from someone writing in 1897—particularly from someone writing about something he had not personally experienced—his view is full of the usual prejudices: he stresses that even though the Mag-wangwara are at a low cultural stage, they have a strong ability to imitate people and sounds through "melodious changes of pitch. . . . Even their everyday speech is full of poetic images. Thus, the Negro in South-Zanzibar does not say 'The sun is going down,' but 'The sun is saying good-bye to the trees.'"[16] He goes on to report that although they are talented public speakers, they have not had any success thus far in the musical arts; their musical instruments are of the simplest construction. He admits that they demonstrate astonishing abilities on these instruments, and make "such a hellish spectacle" (Höllenspektakel) that a European cannot bear it.[17] We learn that the Wahehe, who drink blood and milk exclusively, only sing rather than playing instruments in their war games: "They form three battle rows, which you can identify through the white, red, and black shields, and they manage to form beautiful pictures through their constantly changing groupings. . . . All this takes place with singing." Vivell stresses that they accompany every part of their life with songs. He reserves his particular condescension for their religious belief, arguing that even though they have "some kind of God they believe in," this God is not concerned with their daily life. Their entire religious belief is taken over by magic and fortune-telling. He finds very little poetic content in their songs.[18]

There is only very vague information about their tonal systems. In an attempt to classify the music, Vivell says that the melodies are either minor or major. Curiously, even though he was a chant scholar, he does not draw a parallel to church modes. He describes the intervals of the Wahehe's music as not very precise, comparable to a spoken tone or the song of birds, seemingly implying that in their singing they are closer to birds than to humans. Nevertheless, he must have heard about Wanyamwezi polyphony, because he mentions it. The African voices are loud, reedy (näselnd), or screechy (kreischend).[19] He concludes: "The tropical heat has given the Negroes a hot temperament, and they make music, sing, and dance with passion."[20]

The reason I have discussed Vivell's article in such detail is that it accurately encapsulates how most missionaries at the end of the nineteenth century viewed Africans and their music. The Africans are intellectually, religiously, and also musically on a low level: they are "all emotion," and their utterances do not really rise to the level of music. This one-sided view is somewhat surprising considering that Vivell was an excellent chant scholar and was one of the earliest to talk about the oral transmission of Gregorian chant. I find it hard to believe that he would have written this article if he had actually visited Africa himself.

CASSIAN SPIESS

Cassian Spiess (1866–1905), also spelled Spiss, is interesting for us for three reasons: he was killed in the Maji Maji Rebellion; he was a good musician and made the first Swahili hymnbooks; and he was a gifted linguist who published a number of dictionaries with the Oriental Institute at Friedrich Wilhelm University.

Born in St. Jakob, Austria, in 1866, and schooled in the diocesian seminary in Brixen (now Bressanone),[21] he arrived in Zanzibar in 1893. He developed a serious case of malaria and returned to Europe in 1895, but two years later he went back to East Africa, to a station called Tosamaganga in an area inhabited by the Wahehe. In 1898 he was asked to take charge of the Wangoni area. He became friends with the son of the ruling family, Mputa Gama, who became chief of the Wangoni a year after Spiess's arrival and gave him the property on which Peramiho, the first mission station in the inland, was erected.[22] By all accounts he was a wise and gentle person, and as long as he was the superior of Peramiho, "relations between the mission and the Wangoni leadership were exceptionally good. This was largely due to the general approach of Fr. Cassian in his mission work, but also to his affable and generous personality."[23]

Unfortunately, Spiess was appointed vicar apostolic of South Zanzibar in 1902, and his successor, Father Franziskus Leuthner, lacked Spiess's personal skills. He alienated the local population to such an extent that his behavior eventually contributed to the Wangonis' participating in the Maji Maji Rebellion and the killing of both Leuthner and Spiess. Not only did he criticize Chief Mputa in public, but, even worse, he destroyed the Ng'anda ya Nyasele, a place of sacred worship for the royal family. Chief Mputa, after complaining to the German authorities in Songea, demanded compensation from Leuthner, who was ordered to pay fifteen rupees. Leuthner refused.[24] Mputa thereupon rescinded his permission to operate the school on Wangoni territory, the parents withdrew their children, and the school had to close. Spiess returned to Peramiho in 1903, concerned about Leuthner's behavior, and gave three rupees to Mputa to try to appease him. Nevertheless, the damage was done, and relationships become increasingly hostile. So when the Maji Maji uprising started in 1905, the Wangoni decided to participate.

Spiess was killed along with two brothers and two sisters on a visitation tour in 1905 and was buried in the cathedral at Dar es Salaam. The uprising was directed against the colonial regime, the mission, and also the converts, so even though Spiess may not have been a personal target, the fact that he was a cleric was enough to put his life in danger.[25] The Wagoni were thoroughly defeated in the uprising, and the colonial administrators conducted reprisals.[26] In the end, many chiefs simply gave up and converted to Christianity, often right before they were executed. The number of Catholic converts grew exponentially after the uprising. While in 1907 there were only 484 Christians, by 1916 there were 4,372. Peramiho grew into an important center of Catholicism.[27]

Spiess did not work long in Tanganyika, yet his contributions were substantial. A gifted linguist, he translated prayers and hymns into Wangoni, and in 1901 he wrote the first hymnbook for the Benedictines.[28] Subsequently, the 1923 hymnbook from Lindi, entitled *Chuo cha Sala Catoliki*, includes many of his translations, a bilingual Mass (in Kiswahili and Latin), and hymns in liturgical order for the church year. Thirty-eight of the 106 songs were translated by Cassian Spiess into Swahili. In fact, his Swahili translations were so important to him that when he was ordained a bishop in St. Ottilien in Bavaria, the congregation sang a Swahili song.[29] His translated hymns are for the most part popular German hymns; it did not occur to him to use local melodies. But the fact that he translated a mass into Swahili in spite of the pope's clear preference for Latin masses indicates that he understood that a mass in Latin would have limited appeal for his local population. In fact, since most of the hymns translated by Spiess into Swahili became nationally known, he contributed in an important way to making Swahili a national language.[30]

Like many missionaries of his generation, Spiess felt that in order to communicate effectively with the local population he needed a thorough knowledge of their language and culture.[31] In 1900 he published the first Kihehe dictionary with the Institute of Oriental Studies of Friedrich Wilhelm University.[32] This was followed by a Kingoni and Kisutu dictionary in 1904.[33] He was the first of several Benedictine missionaries in Tanganyika to have made substantial contributions to scholarship.

CLEMENS KÜNSTER

The missionary Clemens Künster (1861–1935; fig. 13.2), from Lendersdorf (Aachen), was born too early to have had any exposure to comparative musicologists. He attended the conservatory in Cologne from 1885 to 1888, where

Figure 13.2. P. Clemens Künster.
Courtesy St. O.

he graduated and passed an "examination to become a piano teacher" (*Reifezeugnis als Klavierlehrer*);[34] he then taught piano in Cologne until he was thirty years old. He entered St. Ottilien in 1893; his ordination followed in 1901.[35]

Since Künster was the first missionary with real musical training, it is not surprising that he was also the earliest Catholic missionary in Tanganyika who made an attempt to analyze African music and African instruments, concentrating especially on the irimba. He also set the course for Catholic Church music in German East Africa by successfully advocating for the use of Gregorian chant.

Künster was posted to Tanganyika in 1902, first to Nyangao and after the Maji Maji Rebellion in 1906 to Ndanda, then Dar es Salaam, and finally Lake Nyasa (now Lake Malawi), where he founded the mission station Lituhi. In 1913 he upset the German district commissioner Freiherr von Nordeck zu Rabenau when he accused the commissioner of mistreating the local people;[36] St. Ottilien evidently had no desire to stand up to the German authorities and decided to recall their missionary instead.[37] The year 1918 found him in Diessen, Germany, and from 1922 to 1925 he was at the Benedictine Abbey of St. Joseph in Louisiana; he returned to Ndanda in 1928, then moved a year later to Nyangao. From 1930 on, then about sixty-nine years old and having relocated three times in the preceding decade, he wrote numerous letters to St. Ottilien begging for permission to retire. His wish was finally granted in 1932. He died in Diessen in 1935.

Künster published two works of interest: an article on African music instruments and a small book entitled *Harmonisches System zur Begleitung der gregorianischen Choralmelodien* (A Harmonic System to Accompany Gregorian Chant Melodies).[38] In addition, he was an important informant for Theodor Rühl's article "Die missionarische Akkommodation."[39] His article and book were written at roughly the same time in 1905 and 1906, very soon after he arrived in Africa. In the article he begins by describing African instruments. The fact that he considers them at all worthy of description, and that he had them placed, as cultural treasures that deserve to be looked at, in a museum in Dar es Salaam established by the Benedictines is significant, especially when compared to the attitude of Vivell, only a few years earlier.[40] He immediately focused on the irimba, probably because it is so easy to derive the tonal system from the keys of this instrument. Throughout his article he talks about African music in general without specifying any particular tribe, but he does indicate that the irimba comes from the mission station in Nyangao in the southern part of German East Africa. His description deals more with the tonal system than with the actual instrument:

> The longest tongue stands, as is shown in the picture, in the center, and gives according to nature the lowest tone of the instrument, that is, the fundamental tone. The three shorter tongues to the right side of this fundamental tone add to the fundamental tone the minor third, pure fifth, and pure octave, and the ones standing on the left side the remaining tones of the diatonic scale built up from this fundamental tone, except for the sixth tone. Note also that the second tone of this scale exists only in the octave, which is indicated by the shortest tongue of the left side. . . . If we sum up all tones from a musical point of view, taking D as the fundamental tone we could say that we have here a scale known in the Middle Ages as a Dorian mode, considered the first of the church modes, except that it does not have a B-natural or a B-flat.[41]

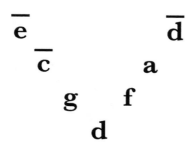

Figure 13.3. Künster's African tonal systems.
From his "Etwas über afrikanische
Musikinstrumente," 86.

Künster continues to explain that the irimba comes from "uncultivated
heathens" (*unkultivierte Heiden*) from the center of Africa. It is clear that
he is searching for *Ur-Musik*. He repeatedly uses the term "natural man"
(*Naturmensch*) when describing African musicians and the tonal system
they use; in his view, the arrangement of the tones has been "invented by
natural man all on his own," since it could not possibly derive from either
Greek music or Gregorian chant, the latter of which was, until recently,
unknown to the Africans. He concludes therefore that the tonal system
must "be based on the natural, unspoiled musical feeling, uninfluenced by
all things conventional and habitual."[42] According to Künster, the pitches
B-natural and B-flat were simply left out by the "savages" (*Wilde*), because
these were invented only with the transition from diatonicism to chromaticism, which he considers "the beginning of all modulation," "the transition
from nature to art."

Three observations conclude his short article:

1. The Dorian scale and all other ancient scales are not the result of
    theoretical reasoning.
2. The ancient scales correspond to the elemental, unspoiled musical
    human emotions, much more so than our major and minor scales,
    which suffer from "overcivilization" (*Überkultur*) and "effeminacy"
    (*Verweichlichung*).
3. We have in our ancient melodies (that is, Gregorian chant), an inex-
    haustible fountain of "untouched and unspoiled" (*urwüchsiger und
    urkräftiger*) melodies and thus also harmonies; and it must therefore
    be not just the duty of the sons of the Holy Church—but also to the
    advantage of the whole musical world—to listen to the words of the
    Vicar of Christ, who calls out to us, *recedite ad fontes*, go back to
    the sources.[43]

These ideas are further elaborated in his book *Harmonisches System zur Begleitung der gregorianischen Choralmelodien*.[44] Künster's immediate reason for having written this book is the *motu proprio*, which reintroduced Gregorian chant to Catholic churches all over the world. Lamenting that performers no longer appreciate and understand monophonic music, Künster's goal was to develop a system of chant singing that employed what he considered to be a harmonically appropriate accompaniment.[45] (When I attended vespers in St. Ottilien in September 2015, the antiphons were still accompanied by the organ very much in Künster's "style.")

The most relevant chapter of Künster's book is entitled "The Chorale Corresponds to the Natural Taste of the People, Because It Is Natural Song."[46] He believes that Gregorian chant is "natural song" (*Naturgesang*) because it is "adapted to human nature, yes, even more, it is and always will be part of human nature. It is not a passing artistic invention, whether by the [ancient] Greeks or some other people or even by the Catholic Church; and its scales (even though they might sometimes sound strange to the uninitiated) are based on human nature and from it have sprung."[47]

According to Künster, most people believe that the major scale is the original scale and that the church modes can only be found in highly cultivated people. Obviously, he disagrees. In order to find an answer to the question of which scale was the original, Künster turns to African music and finds that the local songs prove that church modes are considerably older than anything else. Because he has spent a long time in the center of German East Africa and has listened to these melodies and then transcribed them, he feels he can say without a doubt that they correspond to church modes. He is critical of a number of amateur travelers without a music background who have simply notated African songs in minor, because minor is significantly different from the church modes. Künster then includes transcriptions of nine songs that he assigns to one of the modes (fig. 13.4). (One song is in mode 8, two in mode 7, three in mode 4, two in mode 1, and one in mode 2). He summarizes his findings: "We see [that] all these melodies of the uncultivated and also partly cultivated people are almost exclusively written in our old modes."[48] This is followed by a list of Gregorian chant pieces and old hymns, which are naturally also in church modes. The chapter concludes with the by now familiar description of the irimba and its tonal system. He then proceeds to the remainder of the book: the simple instruction, clearly meant for the general reader, of how to accompany Gregorian chant on the organ.

In short, Künster set out to prove that medieval modes are natural,

Figure 13.4. Künster's African church modes. From his *Harmonisches System*, 14–15.
Courtesy St. O.

already found among the most "primitive" humans, a kind of *Ur-Musik*, by analyzing the songs he found in Africa; these songs are in neither major nor minor, but in one of the church modes, mostly Mixolydian, Phrygian, and Dorian. He is not interested in doing scholarly research, only in showing the similarity between Gregorian chant and African music. Thus, we often find notes saying something like "This formula also appears in the chorales in the 3rd and 4th tone."[49] There is no attempt at describing the harmonic or rhythmic language; he gives us only references to humming, yodeling, clapping and stomping of the feet. His agenda is clear: to prove that Gregorian chant is the one true and original musical language and as such should be revived and sung all over the world.

The musical language was to him far more important than the language of the words it expressed. As he indicated in a letter dated 26 April 1929, there should be time on weekdays for a "quiet Mass" (*stille Messe*), in which the use of Swahili will be fine: "One should also leave time for the people to pray in their own heart in their own way, and should encourage them to think on their own, that they don't just sing and pray without thoughts; then it would just be a mechanical rote prayer."[50]

When the Catholic priest and missionary Theodor Rühl recommended in his 1927 article "Die missionarische Akkomodation" that Gregorian chant was particularly suited for African tonal systems, he had first consulted with Clemens Künster. In this influential article, read by many missionaries (for example, Rietzsch) and also by Hornbostel, not only does he repeat Künster's claim that Gregorian chant is based on a foundation that would be natural to all people, but now adds that this has been confirmed by comparative musicologists,[51] quoting a letter from Künster at length:

> I would like to add to what I already wrote about the naturalness of chant in my book. From my own personal experience in German East Africa (now English) during my last stay at Lake Nyasa, I was able to introduce Gregorian chant at my station in three to four months by using only my Gradual. After three months the entire congregation (one hundred Christians and one thousand catechumens and heathens) was able to sing the simple Commune (Kyrie, Gloria, Credo, Sanctus, and Agnus Dei). Twenty to thirty boys first sang it alone, then the entire congregation of boys, girls, men, and women sang antiphonally with them. The church was built only from bamboo. In addition, I gave a fifteen-minute singing lesson to the entire congregation after the mass every Sunday. After three or four months I told my African head teacher that I now wanted to stop with the singing lessons after the mass, because it could be too much for the people, especially the older ones. . . . Whereupon the teacher told me, "No, you cannot do that; because the people are coming so eagerly to mass because they love to sing the chant." The people, in any case, the majority, had to cross a river full of crocodiles in a log boat, which was not without danger.[52]

In sum, we have in Clemens Künster a missionary who was a well-trained musician but not a scholar, and who was the first one to be able to give an explanation of the tonal system he encountered, and who was able to listen to and notate the melodies he heard. What he encountered reminded him of what he knew best: the medieval church modes. He argued that precisely because the church modes are found in Africa among "natural men," they are the true and original tonal system. As a result, he introduced Gregorian chant with great success in Tanganyika. He was not interested in ethnomusicological or ethnographic work, and he did not try to describe African rhythm or multipart singing. His main agenda was to follow the pope's direction from the *motu proprio* and have everyone sing chant, while also allowing the use of Swahili and tribal languages as well as Latin.

MEINULF KÜSTERS

Meinulf Küsters, baptized Johann Wilhelm Küsters, was the most important scholar among the St. Ottilien Benedictines and the only one with a thorough education in anthropology.[53] Born in 1880 in the famous Rhineland pilgrimage site Kevelaer, he decided early on to become a missionary. In 1910 he entered St. Ottilien, and in 1914 he became a priest, taking the name Meinulf.[54] What distinguishes him from his missionary colleagues is that his order enabled him to do serious anthropological and linguistic studies before he ever set foot in Africa. Usually missionaries become interested in anthropology through their missionary activities, but with Küsters it was the other way around. His first missionary contacts occurred in 1913–14, when he was with Father Wilhelm Schmidt in St. Gabriel.[55] During World War I he served as a chaplain and paramedic. He then studied anthropology between 1916 and 1920 (with some interruptions) in Leipzig with Karl Weule and African languages with Hans Stumme; he also sat in on lectures in philosophy and social psychology with Wilhelm Wundt.[56] The St. Ottilien Archive preserves a booklet of the lectures he attended in Leipzig: he participated in Turkish, Berber, and, of course, African language classes, in addition to lectures and seminars in ethnography. In between he had internships in various anthropology museums (especially in Munich and Berlin, but he also knew the collections in Cologne, Frankfurt, Leiden, and Tervüren). His doctoral dissertation, "Das Grab der Afrikaner" (The African Grave, 1920), was passed *magna cum laude* at Leipzig University and then published at Leipzig University in a number of issues of *Anthropos* (1919–20 and 1921–22). The years 1920–22 found him back in St. Ottilien teaching anthropology and religion at the Gymnasium and working for the anthropology collection in the Munich Museum. The next three years (1923–26) he spent as a missionary in South Africa among the Zulu (Inkamana). In 1926 he returned to Munich to be curator of the museum's Africa collection until 1932, again with some interruptions. He had planned to write his *Habilitation* in Munich, but his work at the museum was interrupted in 1927 when he was asked to inspect mission schools in southwestern Tanganyika. Keeping these schools running was a time-consuming task, so it is remarkable that Küsters managed simultaneously to do fieldwork among the Mwera, Ngoni, Ndendeule, Pangwa, and Matengo. He left not only detailed notes, but also films and photographs, and made recordings for Hornbostel and Schneider. Returning to Munich in 1928, he brought with him a substantial collection of African art (approximately eight hundred pieces) that was displayed in a special exhibition in 1929.[57] From 1928 to 1932 he was back in Munich. In 1932 he resigned his job at the museum and returned to Africa to work among the Ngoni (Peramiho), the Uwemba (Bena), the Lugarawa (Pangwa), and again with the Bena in Kifanya. He died in St. Ottilien in 1947.[58]

Küsters's ethnographic writings appear objective, as we will see below. However, one cannot help but notice a patronizing—if affectionate—condescension for his students in his descriptions of African students in the non-scholarly missionary journals.[59]

Küsters had no special background in music, yet he wrote numerous ethnographic and linguistic studies, and in some of the former music is discussed. Moreover, he was in touch with both Hornbostel and Schneider and made recordings that were evaluated and transcribed by Schneider in the first volume of his *Geschichte der Mehrstimmigkeit*. Hornbostel's and Schneider's correspondence with Küsters is preserved in the Berlin Phonogramm-Archiv and includes a number of interesting remarks.

First, an overview of Küsters's publications: he published three books, beginning with his dissertation *Das Grab der Afrikaner*; then came a prayer book for women about to marry (1922) and a co-authored *Elementary Kiswahili Grammar or Introduction into the East African Negro Language and Life* (1926).[60] Additionally, he published thirty-nine articles, of which thirteen are in scholarly journals or books; the others are for the most part in the mission journal *Missionsblätter* of St. Ottilien. Finally, he left a large number of unpublished papers, both in St. Ottilien and in private possession. The most important of these is his manuscript on the Wamwera, which he finished in 1931–32 and planned to submit as a *Habilitation*, but failed to publish because of lack of funds. The book was finally published in a revised version by Maria Kecskési in 2012.[61]

The correspondence between Hornbostel, Küsters, and Schneider, preserved in the Berlin Phonogramm-Archiv, documents the scholarly interests of both Hornbostel and Schneider; on the whole, they ask specific questions, which Küsters tries to answer. (I am only including the letters that include relevant information relevant to our topic.) They are less interested in the social circumstances and rituals of the songs and dances, so there is little on this topic in Küsters's letters. A recurring theme throughout the correspondence is that Hornbostel wants only those recordings of African music that show no Western influence. Küsters writes to Hornbostel in a letter dated 7 May 1927 that the highlands of Matengo and the Nyasa area show practically no European influence, since people there don't even know Swahili: "I managed to find the ancient songs that are used for circumcision rituals or more precisely, initiation rituals of girls. Modern influences are noticed here only coming from the Congo, from where also the marimba has been introduced and a few of the dances."[62] Hornbostel frequently asks Küsters about musical instruments, in particular the panpipe, clearly in the hope of finding proof for his theory of the cycle of blown fifths. In the 7 May letter Küsters describes the marimba, tells him that he was unable to record string instruments because they are so soft, and regrets once more that he has not encountered panpipes in this area.

Nearly a year later, in a letter dated 4 March 1928, Hornbostel returned to his question about wind instruments, in particular panpipes:

> Most important for us would be the observation, whether with wind instruments with finger holes (flutes, clarinets, etc.) the arrangement of the holes happens arbitrarily or is copied from older models, or according to certain transmitted rules of measuring (spans, finger span, etc.), and in the latter case to investigate the rules accurately. I don't even need to mention that panpipes are of the greatest interest to us. Even the fact that they are not there is important.[63]

Küsters's letter of 14 February 1929 to Hornbostel contains two interesting observations: first, he describes the Africans' enthusiasm for singing into the phonograph: "After some initial shyness the blacks really enjoyed the phonograph so much that they would walk for days from their home just to see the instrument and speak into it."[64] Then he discusses the "trills" (i.e., ululation) the women do (they are generally sung by women, but men can perform them very well too). He believes that for the women the trill is an expression of their joy over the achievement of a task: "I have, for example, observed that in all dances the dancers perform with renewed vigor after hearing the trill."[65] A little later he continues:

> The way of making the trill is not connected to the lip plug, as far as I can judge, because I have recorded the trilling with the Wamwera, as well as the Wangoni and Wanyassa, and the latter two don't use the lip plug. The tip of the tongue vibrates the front palate. In order to create a different tone, they sometimes cover the mouth with the right hand.

Figure 13.5. P. Meinulf Küsters at the Munich Oktoberfest making recordings with Mwera women, 1930. Courtesy St. O.

The tone is always very piercing, and for this reason a single woman can drown out an entire crowd with her trills. This happens in several songs that I recorded at Lake Nyasa. In these recordings the main singers were standing directly in front of the phonograph, while the trilling woman was far away.[66]

Remarkably, there is a photographic record of Küsters's recording of several Sara-Kaba women who had traveled to Munich for the Oktoberfest in 1930; Küsters used this opportunity to make a recording (fig. 13.5).[67] As Kesckési has shown, the Sara-Kaba women were among four hundred people of color from countries considered to be exotic that were exhibited as a tourist attraction at the Oktoberfest.

After Hornbostel emigrated in 1933, Marius Schneider took over the Phonogramm-Archiv and the correspondence. In a letter dated 16 July 1934, Küsters gives Schneider permission to use transcriptions of the phonograms he has sent to Berlin in his forthcoming book *Geschichte der Mehrstimmigkeit* (fig. 13.6; the first volume of Schneider's book deals with polyphonic music of *Naturvölker*, the second with medieval polyphony). On 11 December

Figures 13.6a and 13.6b. Küster's examples as transcribed in Schneider, *Geschichte der Mehrstimmigkeit*, 1:30–31.

Figures 13.6a and 13.6b. (*continued*)

1934 Küsters writes to say that he has received a copy of the book, thanks Schneider, and asks him whether scholars still believe, as he has heard earlier, that the tonal system of *Naturvölker* is the same as that of the ancient Greeks. Schneider answers on 28 January 1935 that the question regarding the similarity of the Greek tonal system to that of the *Naturvölker* is an old one that he believes should now be addressed differently. He relates it all to the concept of tonality (*Tonalität*) to be discussed in his forthcoming book, of which the church modes were only a part.[68] Küsters replies on 8 March 1935 that "among the old recordings recorded some time ago there is one of a Wangoni fairy tale. . . . The melody is so reminiscent of a choral melody [he must mean chant] that I would like to call your attention to it."[69]

In sum, we see that the correspondence between Küsters and Hornbostel on the one hand, and Küsters and Schneider on the other, reflects their particular interests: in Hornbostel's case, the measuring of the panpipes (which could result in possible universals) and the wish to find music uncontaminated by European influences; in Schneider's, interest in the different tonalities in polyphony and how they relate to medieval modes. Schneider analyzed and classified in his book a large number of polyphonic compositions from all over the world. His main interest was in seeing where the African pieces collected by Küsters in his volume—three from the Mwera, thirteen from the Angoni, four from the Nyassa, two from the Suto, one from the Tengo, and seven from the Zulu—fit in his tonality circles. In all of his transcriptions he gives only the pitches, with an occasional mention of whether a soloist or a choir is singing and metronome markings.[70] There are no texts (which we know were provided by Küsters, along with translations); nor is there any information on the instruments or singers or about the specific occasion on which this piece was performed. This is in a way a pity, since Küsters was the only trained anthropologist who could have provided information on the cultural context. On the other hand, Schneider had a clearly defined agenda of comparing polyphony from all over the world, so he could have never written the kind of book he did he did had he taken the other items into consideration.

There is, however, a lot more material on music and dance in Küsters's publications and Nachlass that still can provide the cultural contexts for these recordings. In the book on the Mwera edited by Kecskési, Küsters states clearly that music and dance cannot be separated.[71] Kecskési included only a sampling of Küsters's descriptions of dances. The typescripts in St. Ottilien have far more detailed material on such matters as how the invitation for the dance is issued, who does what, at what time the dance takes place, how the people are dressed, what kinds of formations are made, who participates, and, of course, what its purpose is. Küsters carefully lists the various occasions at which the dances are performed, yet even though the Mwera are among the tribes that practice female genital mutilation, Küsters completely ignores this topic when he describes the female initiation dances. Drums play a major role, and since different types are needed, they often have to be borrowed from neighboring villages. All of the drums are listed by name and their physical appearance described.

Küsters avoided liturgical discussions. Perhaps he felt that since the singing of Gregorian chant was decreed by the pope, it required no further discussion. And as we have seen, he also commented on the similarity of an African song to Gregorian chant, so it is likely that he felt chant would work well in Africa.

There is only circumstantial evidence that the Benedictines were also influenced by the *Jugendmusik-* and *Singbewegung*. Although a large number of Catholics were involved in the movement, especially in Juventus and Quickborn,[72] I have found no information in Küster's biography that he was a member. And yet, there is an unpublished paper by Küsters entitled "Neger feiern Ostern" (Negroes Celebrate Easter) in which he strongly recommends participatory music and rituals.[73] He describes how their *Volksgemeinschaft* makes them all into a close-knit community, a community that not only sticks together but gives strength to the individual—a view close to the ideas of Bruno Gutmann. Küsters writes: "It is important for the missionary to get to know this social sense of the people and to use it for religious purposes. Christianity can only become strong when it does not enclose the individual but the entire community, where it can give congregational life its character. The liturgy of our church provides a great help for the missionary here. Catholicism is by nature communal."[74] He then provides numerous examples of Catholic rites that he has introduced in Africa (without specifying where he did this)—for example, noting that as many as three thousand people would pray before the Stations of the Cross during Lent. When he asked people to come to the school and mission on Palm Sunday with lots of palm branches, seven hundred people did so, making the church as green as a forest: "When I sprinkled the holy water over the palms, people were no longer quiet; the hands with the palm branches went up, and a murmur went through the church, inspiring, uniting, bestowing the right expression on the communal spirit. I could well imagine how the Jews once pulled branches from the trees and spread their clothes on the path. Christ would today find a similar reception here."[75] Küsters realized that rituals were crucial for attracting people to church, but it does not even occur to him to use local ones or to adapt them for religious purposes, as Gutmann did with the Chagga. Both understood that there was a rare sense of communal spirit in Africa, but Küsters wanted to transplant Catholic customs there, while Gutmann wanted to save local culture by giving the rituals a religious reinterpretation. It fell to the next generation to combine Catholic liturgy with African musical elements.

JOHANN BAPTIST WOLF

Johann Baptist Wolf (1908–1986) was not a trained musician or musicologist, but as the first Catholic priest to introduce local melodies into the Catholic Mass and Hours he nevertheless had a major impact on Catholic liturgy in Tanzania. Born and raised in Paderborn, he joined the abbey of Münsterschwarzach in 1927. After his studies at S. Anselmo in Rome, in 1932 he was sent to Peramiho, where he taught at the Teacher Training College and became the founding editor of the monthly paper *Katoliki*. From 1936 on he also taught at the seminary for priests in Peramiho, advancing to rector in 1940. He held this position until 1968, when the African priest Stephan Mbunga, a student of his, took over. The next several years saw Wolf back in Germany, but in 1982 he returned to the newly founded Benedictine monastery in Nairobi, where he remained until his death.

We have observed throughout this book that in comparison with the Protestants, the missionaries of St. Ottilien were slow to introduce local music into the service. The remarkable story of how this finally happened begins with Schneider's sending the first volume of his *Geschichte der Mehrstimmigkeit* to Peramiho as a gift to Küsters because he had included so many transcriptions from Küsters's phonogram recordings. This very book was studied by Wolf in the years before World War II, according to Mbunga:

> P. Dr. Johannes Baptist Wolf OSB even made new melodies for a new "Ordinary" in Swahili (that is, for the Kyrie, Gloria, Sanctus, and Agnus Dei). The occasion was the book by Marius Schneider (1934/1969: 81–87, 90–91, 100), where P. Dr. Wolf had found many melodies of the Wangoni, the Wanyasa, and the Wamanda that had been collected by P. Dr. Meinulf Küsters. In the Kingoni songs he found above all the intervals of the prime and the second, and in the Wanyasa songs also the fifth. Then he looked for chant melodies with these intervals and noted that the word and melodic accents were the same. People really liked this "Ordinary," and we children also sang it at home and everywhere else.[76]

Figure 13.7. Johann Baptist Wolf's chant as influenced by Schneider, *Geschichte der Mehrstimmigkeit*. In Mbunga, "Afrikanische Musik in Gottesdienst," 58. Courtesy St. O.

Several points are striking about this incident: first, here is a conscious effort by a missionary to imitate local music from a study of transcriptions of this same local music made a few years earlier by a comparative musicologist in Berlin (who had never been to the area) of the very music he is surrounded by. The striking point is that Wolf did not compose these Mass ordinaries from pieces he had *heard*, as Traugott Bachmann had done at the beginning of the twentieth century, but only from pieces he had *seen* written down. He then studied Gregorian chant in order to find pieces that used the same tonal patterns, much as Rietzsch had done in his adaptations of Lutheran chorales. Second, he composed new pieces that fitted these interval patterns (fig. 13.7). And third, the fact that Schneider was both a medievalist and a comparative musicologist trying to show analogies between these two repertoires shows yet again how the most important musicologists of the first half of the twentieth century continued to lump both repertoires into the same group. And now the medieval repertoire included not only Gregorian chant, but also medieval polyphony.

7. Wimbo wa Wapagazi Wangoni

Figure 13.8. Wangoni song. In Gerold, *Chiriku*, 6. Courtesy St. O.

Similarly, the hymnbook edited by Wolf and P. Gerold in 1933–34 has
Wangoni songs in it, also modeled on the transcriptions of Schneider.[77] The
example reproduced in figure 13.8 is pentatonic and has the characteristic
parallel fourths typical of Wangoni music, as can be seen by Schneider's transcriptions. (The majority of the songs in Wolf's hymnbook, though, are Swahili translations of some of the most popular German folk songs. Thus, one
finds a religious retexting of the popular German canon "I fahr, i fahr, i fahr
mit der Post" next to such English hymns as "Nearer My God to Thee." In
1944 Wolf published an Angoni travel song in the Tanzania journal *Katoliki*.[78]
According to the historian Wolfgang Kornder, songs by Wolf were still being
sung in Tanzania in the late 1980s when he did the research for his book.[79]

The question is, of course, why Wolf started to introduce Angoni music
only after he was introduced to Schneider's transcriptions. Why hadn't he
listened to the melodies all around him? We can only speculate, but I sus-

pect that Schneider's authority as a scholar was such that only after he confronted Wolf with written versions of some of these songs did the latter dare to have his parishioners sing them. But it is also possible that his musical training was not sufficient to allow him to make his own transcriptions.

STEPHAN MBUNGA

After the Second Vatican Council, summoned by Pope John XXIII and held between 1962 and 1965, it became possible to let go of much of the Latin liturgy.[80] It was Wolf's student Stephan Mbunga (1927–1982; his first name is sometimes spelled Stefan or Stephen) who seized the opportunity to help local music in East Africa assume a prominent role in celebrations of the Catholic Mass.[81]

Mbunga studied theology at the seminary of Peramiho, was ordained a priest in 1957 (fig. 13.9), and had his first congregation in Nkoma/Lituhi in the Ruvuma region. From 1959 to 1962 he studied canon law in Rome, earning a Ph.D. with a dissertation entitled "Church Law and Bantu Music." From Rome he went to Cologne, where in 1962–63 he studied ethnomusicology for a semester with Marius Schneider. Schneider, a deeply religious Catholic with close connections to the Benedictines in Africa, was considered the most important ethnomusicologist in Germany in the 1960s (see chap. 3, pp. 39–58). Mbunga became the director of the Peramiho Theological School in 1968, a position he held until 1972, and from 1965 to 1972 he was also director of the Music Conservatory in Dar es Salaam. He also periodically taught anthropology and ethnomusicology in Basel and served as a priest for Catholic students in Dar es Salaam from 1979 until his death.

Mbunga's most important scholarly studies are his published dissertation, *Church Law and Bantu Music*, and the article "Afrikanische Musik im Gottesdienst" (African Church Music in the Service; 1975). In his dissertation, written in the years immediately before Vatican II, Mbunga still strongly advocates the singing of Gregorian chant in Africa. He stresses that in contrast to many other countries in Europe, where only a choir or a schola cantorum sings the chant, in Africa the entire congregation was able to participate.[82] He continues:

> The reaction of the Bantu to this music in general is quite satisfactory. For it is a fact that the Bantu can sing Gregorian chant fairly well, and, if properly trained as it is required anywhere, they sing it very well. . . . Why is Gregorian chant so familiar to the Bantu? The affinity between African music and Gregorian chant is remarkable. It is mostly the affinity of mode, and it is already considerable.[83]

Figure 13.9. Ordination of Stephan Mbunga on 9 October 1957. Mbunga is the second person from the right; the others are Andreas Mlowe, Daniel Mbunda, and Urban Luambano. Courtesy St. O.

He cites numerous authorities who believe that Gregorian chant has the same characteristics as African folklore, and for that matter, universal folklore.[84]

By the time he published his 1975 article, his position on Gregorian chant and African music had evolved. His paper came out of an ethnomusicological symposium arranged by the Consociatio internationalis musicae sacrae (CIMS) in Rome in 1975, which was attended by many distinguished ethnomusicologists, including Bruno Nettl, who later became perhaps the most influential American ethnomusicologist; Klaus Wachsmann, who started out as a chant specialist and became a pioneer of African music studies;[85] Josef Kuckertz, a former student of Marius Schneider and the main ethnomusicologist at the Free University of Berlin; Andrew McCredie, the eminent Australian scholar; and Karl Gustav Fellerer, a specialist on Catholic Church music who contributed a paper on Palestrina.[86] In his article Mbunga begins with an overview of biblical missionary activities, concentrating especially on St. Paul, who argued that early Christians should not be bound by Jewish laws. He gives numerous examples of heathen melodies and customs being appropriated by Christians, then quotes from the *Sacra*

Congregatio de Propaganda Fide of Pope Gregory XV (1622; adapted 1659), which had recommended against the transplantation of European customs to the people to be missionized, arguing, for example, that nothing is more absurd than to transfer what one does in France, Spain, or Italy to China.[87]

Next Mbunga summarized the missionary activities among the Wangoni in Africa, which included the introduction of Gregorian chant; but by this point he no longer supported singing chant in Africa:

> One can easily imagine that [the singing of Gregorian chant] was generally rather unsatisfactory with the exception of the seminaries and monasteries; music remained a foreign element and the text was incomprehensible. The foreignness remained of a basic nature, even though both Gregorian chant and local music share a certain simplicity. But it would be wrong to deduce from this similarity that Gregorian chant has a universal character.[88]

He concludes by citing the missionary Father Paul Jans (1886–1962), who believed that the introduction of European music in Africa was a grievous mistake: "We have introduced European music, but for a few exceptions, it has been a fiasco. The result has been that these people, who in their own songs do not drag [the tempo], nor lose the sense of rhythm, in our churches drag and have no sense of rhythm."[89]

Vatican II paved the way to introducing local elements. In the 1960s Mbunga worked with a group of colleagues and students who together brought about changes: they first introduced drums into the service, then other Wangoni instruments, and finally dances. The songs Mbunga wrote became increasingly popular, and his *Missa Baba Yetu* was played every day in the transmissions from Radio Vatican for East and Central Africa.[90] In his article, Mbunga included musical examples of some of his compositions; however, he provided only melodies, with the expectation that these would be accompanied by instrumental improvisations.[91]

At first Mbunga's reforms were not easily accepted.

> Some missionaries and catechists reacted negatively; they reproached the composer that the introduction of local melodies into the church would create a heathen atmosphere. . . . This attitude of the catechists is based on the conviction that European culture is a desirable status symbol per se, and in addition they equate the European intellectual world with modern life. Thus we grappled in the liturgical commission in contentious meetings with the questionable attitude of earlier mission

periods, with a time period where one was generally so afraid of heathen influences that one was unable to recognize the value of original,
authentic music elements; and one allowed the indigenous local music
with its instruments and dances to go to waste in favor of inauthentic
imports.[92]

And yet, this is not the end of the story. By no means did the singing of
Gregorian chant disappear. Sister Barbara Ruckert of the Missionsbenediktiner informed me in 2015 that she had just finished editing two antipho-
nals in Swahili, one for feast days and one for daily usage. They are currently
being sung at the Tanzanian monasteries of Hanga, Ndanda, and at Peramiho
for vespers. After having taught there for years, she was struck by how easy
it was for the local population to learn this chant.[93] Similarly, the Abbey of
Songea is regularly singing Gregorian chant for the liturgical hours. Just as
Gutmann's translations of Lutheran chorales into Chagga have become part
of Chagga literature, so too has Gregorian chant in Swahili translation.

In sum, the first Catholic missionaries saw the Africans whom they were
trying to convert as simple people "of nature." Their music was not considered worthy of preservation; quite the contrary, it was found threatening because it was associated with rituals, dance, and superstition not approved of
by the Church. At the beginning of the twentieth century, Clemens Künster
tried to understand the tonal system of the people he was trying to convert and found it similar to medieval church modes. Thus, there was no
doubt for him that Gregorian chant should be sung all over Africa. And he
seems to have been highly successful. Erich Moritz von Hornbostel and Marius
Schneider collaborated with a missionary from the next generation from
St. Ottilien, Meinulf Küsters, a well-educated anthropologist, who made recordings for them. These recordings were especially useful for Schneider, a medievalist, who wrote two books on the relationship between the music in "primitive" cultures and Western polyphony. When he sent this book to Tanganyika,
it fell into the hands of Küsters's successor, Johann Baptist Wolf, who studied
Schneider's transcriptions of Angoni music and wrote a Mass and various liturgical pieces in the style of Schneider's transcriptions. Thus, the medieval anal-
ogy was by no means eliminated, since Schneider was convinced that medieval
and African polyphony share some of the same tonal principles. Only after Vatican II, with Stephen Mbunga, was genuine Angoni music performed in Catholic
churches.

At the same time, Catholic missionaries also came into contact with
comparative musicologists, who had a decisive influence on the music performed in the mission stations. They too were contacted by Hornbostel and,

more important, by Schneider, Hornbostel's successor and a devout Catholic. And they too made phonogram recordings that were duly evaluated by Hornbostel and Schneider. The significant point about Schneider is that he started out as a scholar of medieval music who set out to prove that early-medieval polyphony was constructed along more or less the same lines as African polyphony. His publications and transcriptions of African music went on to have a great impact on the music practiced in the Benedictine mission fields. Ultimately, Schneider's work helped introduce local music to the Catholic service.

Conclusions

In this book we can observe an interaction between three seemingly distinct but surprisingly connected worlds in the first half of the twentieth century: that of the founders of comparative and historical musicology in Germany; that of the scholars and musicians—for the most part members of the German youth movements, the *Jugendmusik-* and *Singbewegung*—who were studying, discussing, and performing early European music; and that of Protestant and Catholic missionaries in German East Africa. The result of studying these three interconnected worlds in one volume is an alternative music history of Germany, a history concerned not with high culture and the repertoire of the concert hall, but with scholars, musicians, and missionaries who shared a passionate interest in music of the Middle Ages, folk music, and participatory music making (*Gemeinschaftsmusik*).

I have pursued my inquiry in three areas. The first one concerns the history of our discipline, upon which this study throws new light. A hundred years ago no one really knew what medieval music sounded like or had a clear overview of its sources, let alone the ability to decipher them. One of my findings is that both historical and comparative musicologists set out to reconstruct early music, but they did it using fundamentally different methods than scholars of the past two or three generations have employed. Comparative musicologists searched for the origins of music and were convinced that medieval music must have been similar to the music they encountered and recorded in "primitive" societies. They compared musics from different countries and cultures, just as comparative linguists, whose example they followed, compared languages. Classicists, anthropologists, and literary historians all know about the fieldwork undertaken by Milman Parry and Albert Lord among Bosnian *guslars* between 1933 and 1935 in order to reconstruct how Homeric epics were memorized and performed. But no one seems to have noticed that comparative musicologists anticipated their methods when they attempted to learn what medieval music sounded like as early as 1920 through a comparison with "primitive" music. Comparative musicologists believed that medieval and African music shared similar tonal systems and modes, and they regularly compared African and Icelandic polyphony to medieval organum. Some comparatists were even convinced that much of medieval polyphony was largely improvised.

Historical musicologists, meanwhile, produced catalogs of medieval music sources, deciphered the notation (modal rhythm), identified isorhythm, and organized the first performances of medieval and Renaissance polyphony in Karlsruhe and in Hamburg in the 1920s. The singers who participated in these performances were students of the most important historical musicologists of the period, Friedrich Ludwig and Wilibald Gurlitt; and Ludwig's and Gurlitt's student Heinrich Besseler organized these events. A collegium musicum was established in many universities where historical musicologists strived for historically informed performances.

While comparative musicologists paid attention to the research done by music historians, their interest was rarely reciprocated. As a result, few historians were much interested in improvisation; they concentrated exclusively on written sources and documents. The exceptional historians who did pay attention to the research done by comparatists were Jacques Handschin and his student Manfred Bukofzer. It has been almost entirely overlooked that these two contributed in a major way to the demise of comparative musicology by proving that Hornbostel's theory of the blown fifth relied on faulty measurements and by criticizing the evolutionary underpinnings of the discipline.

The second focus of this book is on the fact that almost all of the historical musicologists who participated in the performances in Karlsruhe and Hamburg were members of youth movements, the closely related *Wandervogel* and *Jugendmusik-* and *Singbewegung*. Distrustful of modern individualism, they worshiped community (*Gemeinschaft*), which is the very reason none of their names are listed in the programs of these early concerts: what mattered to them were not the achievements of individuals, but those of the group as a whole. They abhorred modernity, technology, and the bourgeois concert life, prizing instead hiking and communal singing, either in nature or in city parks where thousands from all political parties would participate. Their center was the reconstructed medieval castle Burg Ludwigstein. Most students of Ludwig and Gurlitt were followers of the movement, and Besseler, Friedrich Blume, and Konrad Ameln were among the leaders. Again, medieval and folk music from all over the world took center stage. Folk-music archives were established in Freiburg and Berlin,

and two publishing houses, Bärenreiter and Möseler, were founded to provide printed music. One of the leaders of the youth movement, Herman
Reichenbach, who was forced into emigration in 1933 and has been entirely forgotten, wrote an influential book read by most members entitled
Musikalische Formenlehre in which Gregorian chant is represented as the
foundation of all music.

Third, in order fully to understand and describe the work of the missionaries in German East Africa, it is crucial to know their cultural and musical
backgrounds. It would be a gross simplification simply to call them tools of
colonialism, although some of them certainly were. Most of them had read
articles and books in comparative musicology or attended lectures by academics in related fields. Even before the Phonogramm-Archiv was founded in
Berlin to collect music from all over the world, Protestant missionaries were
inspired by the ideas of Johann Gottfried Herder; that is, they did serious
ethnographic and linguistic research and tried to preserve local languages,
sayings, fairy tales, and even rituals wherever possible. After 1905 Hornbostel, the director of the archive, contacted many missionaries, providing them
with free phonographs on the condition that they send back their recordings,
which they invariably did in due course. Moreover, some missionaries absorbed Hornbostel's research and did serious ethnographic work on music
that is now largely extinct. Their notes and the recordings provide our only
access to a lost music. Moreover, they tried whenever and wherever possible
to preserve the local music and introduce it into the service.

No less than music scholars, most missionaries were closely linked with
the youth movements that swept through Germany in the first half of the
twentieth century. They published articles and books with Bärenreiter, arguing that only in Africa was the true community spirit still present. Surprisingly, this worked both ways: members of the youth movements were
also attracted by the "African way of life," and African polyphony was
studied in an attempt to reconstruct European medieval polyphony. Missionaries were invited to sing-alongs to report how African people perform
rituals together and sing Lutheran chorales that had been translated and
fully assimilated into local languages. For missionaries and many people
in Germany, the tribal society was the ultimate realization of the medieval
Gemeinschaft, a fulfillment of the romantic longing for a lost past where
everyone looked out for one another and there was no distinction between
performer and audience.

The three overlapping circles—music scholars, members of the youth
movements, and missionaries—together introduced a new strand into the
musical culture of early twentieth-century Germany, one that favored com-

munal music making and emphasized the proximity of the European early music to the "primitive" music in Africa. Interestingly, this strand transformed music making in Africa itself. Lutheran chorales, Gregorian chant, and Sankey hymns were so completely assimilated by local populations that in due course they made this music their own. Today Lutheran chorales are a regular requirement in Tanzanian choral competitions, and Catholic Christians in Tanzania ask German music directors to compose liturgical hours in Swahili.

ACKNOWLEDGMENTS

A t various stages of my work I have received advice and support from my family, friends, colleagues, students, and informants. It is my great pleasure to thank them here.

This is without a doubt my most personal book. From 1932 to 1939 my parents lived in Rungwe, Tanganyika, where my father, Joseph Busse, served as a Moravian missionary; from 1959 to 1961 he was the principal of the All African Theological Seminary of the Lutheran World Federation in Marangu at the foot of the Kilimanjaro massif, where he taught many future Lutheran church leaders from all over Africa. My older siblings were all born in the Southern Highlands in Tanganyika before the war, while my younger sister, Dorothea, and I, born after the war in Hamburg, accompanied my parents to Marangu from 1959 to 1961. From 1962 to 1971 my father was in charge of the Bethel Mission, from 1967 on as director. Like many of the missionaries I am discussing in this book, my father was sent by the Moravian Church to study with the Africanist Carl Meinhof and the anthropologist Georg Thilenius at the University of Hamburg, both before and after his time in Tanganyika, and he published extensively on African languages and on the rituals and myths of the Wanyakyusa. He must have known many of the missionaries I discuss, even though I have a strong feeling that he and one of my subjects, Franz Rietzsch, were not close. (Rietzsch referred to my father in one of his letters as "one of the unmusical ones.") Even though I was only twenty-two when my father died, I remember our numerous conversations about Traugott Bachmann and Bruno Gutmann, both of whom he admired enormously. In addition, my older sisters were able to supply me with much anecdotal information on some of the missionaries and scholars discussed here. For example, Katharina, my oldest sister, twelve years my senior, remembers visiting Meinhof with my father and being greeted by a lion skin with a mounted head.

The second part of this book also has a personal dimension. My god-father, Gerhard Günther (1889–1976), nephew of the German orientalist and missionary to Armenia Johannes Lepsius, was a member of the Stefan George circle in Heidelberg and a leader of the *Jugendbewegung* in Hamburg. He knew most important intellectuals in postwar Germany and was a close friend of Ernst Jünger. Only when I began writing this book did I understand why my father and godfather were such close friends, even though my father had no ear for poetry. Günther was passionately interested in the Middle Ages (he wrote a book on the liturgical drama *Der Antichrist*) as well as in East African culture, a topic on which he published several books. Like other members of the *Jugendbewegung*, he was convinced that only in Africa would one still find authentic, inspired Christianity.

My most moving experiences involve the families of two missionaries discussed at length. In April 2012 I read a paper on Franz Rietzsch at a conference at the Archive in Herrnhut. My sister Katharina, by profession a therapist, insisted that I contact his children. To my great surprise, all eight of Rietzsch's children appeared with their families; in fact, there were altogether more than twenty-five relatives of Rietzsch in the room. And they provided me with many additional letters and information. Similarly, when I read a paper on Otto Hagena at the Universität der Künste in Berlin in June 2016, three of his surviving children came, as well as many grandchildren. The Hagena children were very small when their father was killed in the war, and for them it was clearly important to learn more about his missionary activities. Again, I was provided with lots of additional letters. Two missionaries from the Bethel mission, Werner Both and Martin Brose, both music specialists, were similarly helpful and supplied me with numerous documents, publications, and recordings.

I have read several papers related to the material presented in this book. An earlier version of chapter 3 was read in September 2016 in Mainz at the Annual Meeting of Gesellschaft für Musikforschung and on 15 May 2018 at a conference I organized with Sebastian Klotz and Lars-Christian Koch at the Humboldt Forum, Berlin. Versions of chapter 10 were read at the University of Vienna (April 2012), Zurich (May 2012), Peabody Conservatory (November 2012), Trondheim (April 2016), Graz (January 2013), Salzburg (June 2012), the Wissenschaftskolleg zu Berlin (October 2015), and the Institute of Advanced Studies in Bucharest (May 2016). I presented material from chapter 11 at the University of Chicago (February 2014) and at the Bauhaus Universität Weimar (June 2019); chapter 12 at a conference in London at the British Academy (July 2016), at Weimar-Jena (October 2016) and at the Universität der Künste in Berlin (June 2016); and chapter 5 at the Academy of Music in

St. Petersburg, Russia (November 2016). In April 2016 I was invited by Barbara Rocksloh-Papendieck to talk about my project to a large group of interested people, among them several who had spent their life working for the Gesellschaft für internationale Zusammenarbeit. It was a most stimulating experience, and I could not help thinking of the Berlin salons of the nineteenth century. In all those places I received valuable feedback. In 2015 I was awarded the Faculty Research Lectureship at the University of California, Davis, and I read a public lecture on material from chapter 10 in May 2015. Sections of chapter 10 appeared in the *Journal of the American Musicological Society* 66 (2013): 475–522. I would like to thank the University of California Press for permission to publish the material.

I have received generous support for this project: in 2011–12 I held a Lise-Meitner Fellowship of the Austrian Science Fund: M 1200 G17 at the University of Vienna and simultaneously a Presidential Fellowship of the University of California. The Vienna Institute of Musicology was a singularly stimulating place for this project. I was extremely fortunate that Gerhard Kubik took an interest in my project and allowed me to attend his lectures during my year in Vienna. It was an eye-opening experience. I would especially like to thank my dear friend Birgit Lodes, who was my host for this year and who shared my interest in this project from the very beginning. August Schmidhofer was a constant source of advice on anything relating to Africa and comparative musicology. I am also grateful to Michele Calella and Wolfgang Fuhrmann for their reactions to my project. I was fortunate to spend a week in the archive of the Moravian headquarters in Herrnhut with a group of students from Vienna. One of them, Johanna Herbst, has become a close friend.

At Herrnhut I was welcomed with great warmth by the late Marianne Küchler and her children, Heinz and Sabine. Küchler was a Moravian missionary in Tanganyika at the same time as my parents and Rietzsch. And thanks to the late Bishop Theo Gill for steering me to the Küchlers and giving me much other information. Peter and Jill Vogt were a great source of information on Moravian music.

I spent a year in 2015–16 at the Wissenschaftskolleg zu Berlin. I cannot imagine a more stimulating environment for this project. Most of the book was written there. The help I received from the librarians was invaluable, and I would like to thank Stefan Gellner and Sonja Grundt in particular. They not only delivered the books I asked for but found many additional sources I did not even know existed. I was also surrounded by a remarkable group of fellows. Among them I would especially like to thank the linguist Holger Diessel, who helped me with chapter 1; the art historian Finbarr

Barry Flood, who made me appreciate some of the questions addressed by comparative musicologists; Lorraine Daston, who made me realize that most of my work is in the history of science; the historians Michael Gordin, Erika Milam, and Jonathan Sheehan, who knew how to ask the right questions; Ina Hartwig and Barbara Stollberg-Rilinger, who shared my interest in biographies; Ralph Ubl, who regularly enlightened me about relevant art-historical work; and Katharina Biegger, Fred Cooper, Ibrahima Diop, Luca Giuliani, Daniel Jütte, Wolf Lepenies, Reinhart Meyer-Kalkus, Daniel Schönpflug, Dylan Joseph Montanari, Luc Steels, Michael Steinberg, Constanta Vintila-Ghitulescu, and Torsten Wilhelmy.

In 2011 I traveled to Tanzania and was warmly received wherever I went. I am particularly grateful to Claudia Zeising for her hospitality in Rungwe and to Pastor Clement Mwaitebele, the Reverends Amoni Mwambande and Joakim Mwasungwa in Rungwe, and Athanasius Mphuru in Marangu. And special thanks to Melania Mrema, a woman of great integrity. Nico Calvin was a great help in transcribing the Nyakyusa texts.

Much of my research was done in archives, and I would like to thank Rüdiger Kröger, Olaf Nippe, and Dietrich Meyer at the Unitätsarchiv, Herrnhut; Wolfgang Apelt at the Archiv der Vereinigten Evangelischen Mission; Elke Boormann at the archive of the Leipzig Mission; Bruder David Gantner at the archive in St. Ottilien; Susanne Rappe-Weber from the Archiv der Jugendbewegung in Burg Ludwigstein; Dietmar Schenk at the archive of the Universität der Künste in Berlin; Joakim Mwasungwa at the Moravian archive in Rungwe, Tanzania; and Clemens Gütl from the Vienna Phonogramm-Archiv. Many of these archivists made valuable suggestions, and most contributed images to the book. My thanks go to Lars-Christian Koch, Susanne Ziegler, Ricarda Kopai, and Albrecht Wiedmann for their hospitality at the Berlin Phonogramm-Archiv, which became a second home for me, and for having generously shared information, papers, and recordings with me. John Shepard, of the Jean Hargrove Music Library at the University of California, Berkeley, was similarly helpful, giving me access to the Bukofzer papers and photographs. André Bernard, from the Guggenheim Foundation, was kind enough to let me see all the Ballanta papers. And Dyke Kiel sent me a manuscript of Nicholas Ballanta's book, as well as his opera.

My editor, Marta Tonegutti, was enthusiastic about the project from the very beginning, and she, Tristan Bates, Caterina MacLean, and Meredith Nini helped me get the manuscript ready for publication. I am extremely grateful to Barbara Norton for her expert copyediting. Thanks to Torbjørn Rødland for help in selecting the cover photograph and to Ryan Li for designing the cover.

Thanks to James Q. Davies and Nicholas Matthew for reading and commenting on the entire manuscript and including it in their series. I might add that the fact that James comes from South Africa and shared many of my interests in the history of African music was a big help to me.

My colleagues and students at the University of California, Davis have supported the book in many ways. My former student Sarah Eyerly, now at Florida State, wrote a dissertation on eighteenth-century Moravian improvisation with me and was helpful when I started to explore the Moravian archives. There is no doubt that she was one of the main reasons I started this project in the first place. My colleagues invited me to give several presentations, which were invariably stimulating. I would like to thank all of them, in particular Juan Diego Diaz and Beth Levy. Special thanks to Bryce Cannell for setting the musical examples and to Stephen Bingen, Philip E. Daley, and Rudy Garibay for helping with the images.

Various scholars provided me with valuable advice. I have to begin by thanking the historians James Sheehan and Margaret Lavinia Anderson, who were excited about the project from the very beginning and steered me toward Suzanne Marchand's book *German Orientalism in the Age of Empire*. After reading it I knew I was on the right track. Special thanks should also go to Kofi Agawu, Paul Berliner, Bernhard Bleibinger, Philip Bohlman, Magnar Breivik, the late Reinhold Brinkmann, Philippe Canguilhem, Thomas Christensen, Hermann Danuser, Valentina Sandu-Dediu, Andreas Dorschel, Anselm Gerhard, Thomas Grey, Ulrich van der Heyden, Ralph Hexter, Yves Häberli, Hans-Joachim Hinrichsen, Stephen Hinton, Adam Jones, Sebastian Klotz, Dorothea Kolland, Janna Kniazeva, Lars-Christian Koch, Andrea Lindmayr-Brandl, Lewis Lockwood, Laurenz Lütteken, Franz Michael Maier, the late Anthony Newcomb, Jann Pasler, Ava Bry Penman, Klaus Pietschmann, Jesse Rodin, Dörte Schmidt, Monika Schwarz-Danuser, Julia Simon, the late Rudolf Stephan, Richard Taruskin, Barbara Titus, and Christiane Wiesenfeldt. Herman Reichenbach Jr. was similarly helpful in personal conversations and telephone calls.

Portions of the manuscript were read by Bonnie Blackburn, Annegret Fauser, Tobias Robert Klein, Katherine Lee, Daniel Leech-Wilkinson, Stefan Menzel, Peter Revers, Henry Spiller, Kay Shelemay, Renata Tanczuk, Christian Utz, and Josh Walden. All of them made valuable contributions, for which I thank them. I cannot express sufficient gratitude to the late Bruno Nettl, who read chapter 10 in an earlier version and helped and advised me throughout the project. His knowledge of comparative musicology was immense, and he told me about many personal meetings he had with the scholars in part I and II. He took particular interest in Herman Reichenbach and even tried to locate additional papers in the college where Reichenbach last taught. I am only sorry that he did not live to see the book come out.

I have been most fortunate with the readers, Stephen Blum and Reinhard Strohm, who saved me from many mistakes and frequently steered me in the right direction. Reinhard is a very old friend, who told me back in 1993 that Besseler's intellectual background was the *Zupfgeigenhansl*. At that point I did not fully understand what he meant. Further, there are two close friends and colleagues at University of California, Davis, to whom I am particularly grateful: Pablo Ortiz is a composer, yet he immediately understood the implications of my work and was one of the first to point out the fact that Thomas Binkley's recordings come straight out of the "oriental" hypothesis. And Christopher Reynolds read through the entire manuscript, making improvements on virtually every page. I feel extremely fortunate to have a friend who would do something like this for me.

I have received strong support from my husband, Karol Berger, and our children, Anna Katharina (Kasey), Matthew, and Susanna. Initially Karol was not all that enthusiastic about the project. This changed once I discovered the importance of comparative musicology and the *Jugendmusikbewegung* for the missionaries, began to trace the interaction of medievalists with comparative musicologists and missionaries, and found that my project suggested an alternative history of music scholarship in Germany. As always, he made major contributions to the book, not only reading the entire manuscript but also steering my work in new directions. It would have been a very different book without him. In fact, he and our close friends Rebecca Berlow and Andrzej Rapaczynski came with us to Tanzania, a country none of them would have ever visited without this project. Rebecca accompanied me to churches and made valuable recordings. It was an important experience for all of us, and I am so grateful for their support and companionship.

I can honestly say that without all of this generous support I would have never been able to complete this book. I am very fortunate, indeed, to be able to draw on the assistance of so many exceptional people and so many generous institutions.

Konrad Ameln (1899–1994), German musicologist and leader of the *Singbewegung*. He was a specialist in the Lutheran chorale, editor of the journal *Die Singgemeinde*, and closely associated with Bärenreiter. Ameln also was interested in "primitive" music.

Traugott Bachmann (1865–1948), Moravian missionary active in Rungwe and Mbozi. He translated the New Testament into Nhiya and was one of the first missionaries to introduce local music into the service. His recordings for Hornbostel were transcribed and analyzed by comparative musicologists.

Nicholas G. J. Ballanta (1893–1962), Sierra Leonean music scholar, first winner of a Guggenheim Fellowship in music. He tried to describe African music from an African perspective and was adamant that African music had nothing in common with medieval music. After his talk in 1926 at the International Mission Conference in Le Zoute, Belgium, the Bethel Mission changed course and tried to introduce African music into the service.

Samuel Baudert (1879–1956), mission director of the Moravian Church, a major supporter of the scholarly work done by Bachmann and Rietzsch.

Heinrich Besseler (1900–1969), German musicologist, leader of the *Jugendbewegung*, and a strong proponent of *Gemeinschaftsmusik*. He published extensively on music of the Middle Ages and helped organize the first concerts of medieval music in Karlsruhe and Hamburg. He was a supporter of the Nazi regime but made sure that all of his Jewish students received their doctoral degrees. After the war, he was a professor in Leipzig.

Friedrich Blume (1893–1975), musicologist and leader of the *Singbewegung*. He worked closely with Bärenreiter, served as the editor of *MGG* I, and was a supporter of the Nazi regime, which did not prevent him from making a career in postwar West Germany.

Franz Boas (1858–1942), German-born American anthropologist and linguist, who educated most leading American anthropologists. He was a friend of Erich Moritz von Hornbostel.

Friedrich von Bodelschwingh (father; 1831–1910), Lutheran theologian and founder of the von Bodelschwinghsche Stiftung, Bethel, for mental patients. He was the director of the Bethel Mission **and the father of Friedrich von Bodelschwingh**, also called Fritz (son; 1877–1946), also a theologian, who became his father's successor and was a member of the anti-Nazi Confessing Church (*Bekennende Kirche*) under Hitler.

Manfred Bukofzer (1910–1955), German-born American musicologist and a student of Besseler, Handschin, and Hornbostel. Most of his publications are in medieval studies. He did experiments in Basel proving that Hornbostel's theory of the blown fifth was based on incorrect measurements. He was a professor at the University of California, Berkeley.

Wilibald Gurlitt (1889–1963), musicologist and leader of the *Jugendbewegung*. He was a professor at Freiburg and with his students organized the first performances of medieval music in Karlsruhe and Hamburg. He was concerned with authentic performances of early music.

Bruno Gutmann (1876–1966), German missionary of the Leipzig mission. He carried out fundamental linguistic and anthropological studies of the Wachagga and reinterpreted Chagga rituals as Christian rites. He fell under the influence of the *Singbewegung*, translated Lutheran hymns into Chagga, and argued that only in Chagga culture was the community spirit present as it was in Luther's time.

Otto Hagena (1902–1943), missionary for the Bethel Mission. He did fundamental work on the translation of the Bible from Greek into Haya and gave the earliest description of Haya music. His student Josiah Kibira became the president of the Lutheran World Federation.

Jacques Handschin (1886–1955), Swiss musicologist and close friend of Hornbostel. He specialized in music of the Middle Ages and wrote two fundamental books, *Musikgeschichte im Überblick* (1948) and *Der Toncharakter* (1948), that undermined the evolutionary view of music history.

Wilhelm Heinitz (1883–1963), comparative musicologist at Hamburg University (though he never became a full professor) who taught Franz Rietzsch. He was an early supporter of Hitler.

Walther Hensel (1887–1956), music educator and one of the leaders of the *Singbewegung* who longed for the Middle Ages. He was a Nazi sympathizer but eventually ran into problems with the regime.

George Herzog (1901–1983), Hungarian-born comparative musicologist and a student of Hornbostel and Boas. He published on African and Native American music. He taught at University of Indiana, Bloomington, where Bruno Nettl was one of his students.

Erich Moritz von Hornbostel (1877–1935), director of the Berlin Phonogramm-Archiv. He wrote a series of highly original articles that helped establish the new discipline of comparative musicology. He was forced to emigrate in 1933 and died in Cambridge in 1935. He learned shortly before his death that his much-touted theory of the blown fifth was proven wrong by Bukofzer.

Kurt Huber (1893–1943), Swiss-born folk-music specialist and music psychologist. He taught at Munich, where he joined the opposition group Weisse Rose. He was executed in 1943.

Fritz Jöde (1887–1970), elementary school teacher and one of the leaders of the *Jugendmusikbewegung*. He conducted sing-alongs attended by thousands of people and founded music schools all over Germany. After 1933 he collaborated with the Nazis in the hope of saving the youth movement. After the war he taught in Hamburg and Trossingen.

Josiah Kibira (1925–1988), bishop of the Northwestern Diocese in Tanzania and first black president of the Lutheran World Federation (1977–84). He attended a school run by Hagena and came to advocate the use of both German and African music in the service.

P. Clemens Künster (1861–1935), missionary for the Missionsbenediktiner, St. Ottilien. He was instrumental in introducing Gregorian chant in Tanganyika because he believed it to be close to African music.

P. Meinulf Küsters (1890–1947), missionary for the Missionsbenediktiner, St. Ottilien, anthropologist, and curator at the Munich Museum of Anthropology. He made extensive recordings for Hornbostel and Schneider, which were transcribed in Schneider's *Geschichte der Mehrstimmigkeit*.

Robert Lachmann (1892–1939), comparative musicologist, student of Hornbostel and Johannes Wolf. He became an important orientalist and emigrated to Palestine in 1935.

Friedrich Ludwig (1872–1930), German musicologist who published fundamental catalogs, books, and articles on medieval polyphony. He introduced the highest standards into manuscript studies. Besseler, Ameln, and many other leaders of the *Jugendmusik- and Singbewegung* were among his students.

P. Stephan Mbunga (1927–1982), Tanzanian priest, scholar, and composer who wrote the *Missa Baba Yetu*. He was instrumental in introducing African music into the Catholic service.

Carl Meinhof (1857–1944), German linguist who developed a comparative grammar of Bantu languages. He was in close touch with missionaries, many of whom he taught African languages and then used as informants. He taught in Berlin and Hamburg and joined the Nazi Party in 1933.

Hans Paasche (1881–1920), German Imperial Navy officer during World War I. He participated in putting down the Maji Maji Rebellion, but it was such a traumatic experience that he became a lifelong pacifist. He was a member of the *Wandervogel* and glorified the African way of life in his fictional bestseller *Die Forschungsreise des Afrikaners Lukanga Mukara* (1912–13). He made many recordings for Hornbostel. He was murdered by a right-wing death squad.

George Foster Peabody (1852–1938), American banker and philanthropist, who supported Hampton University and many other civic and humanitarian efforts. He was a great supporter of Ballanta.

Carl Peters (1856–1918) colonial explorer who played a large role in establishing the colony of German East Africa. He was in close contact with several mission societies. He was extremely cruel to the local population, so much so that he was brought to justice in Germany, dishonorably deprived of his commission, and deprived of all his pension benefits.

Herman Reichenbach (1898–1958), intellectual leader of the *Jugendmusikbewegung*. He studied with Gurlitt and helped introduce medieval music into the movement. He wrote an influential textbook, *Formenlehre* (1929), in which he argues that medieval music and music theory are central to all musical forms. He was forced to emigrate in 1933 and died in the United States, where he had taught physics because he was unable to find a position in music.

Franz Ferdinand Rietzsch (1902–1978), Moravian missionary in Tanganyika. He carried out fundamental research on Nyakyusa music and tried to introduce Lutheran pentatonic chorales into the service. Rietzsch joined the Nazi Party in Africa after attending a big party organized by a German plantation owner specifically to recruit new members.

Paul Rother (1878–1956), Leipzig missionary and brother-in-law of Bruno Gutmann. He was in charge of musical education in Marangu and frequently spoke at gatherings of the *Singbewegung* about the Wachagga and the Lutheran chorale there.

Theodor Rühl (1903–1959), Catholic priest from St. Gabriel. Active as a missionary in China and Japan, he wrote an article read by Hornbostel and missionaries in Africa advocating the singing of Gregorian chant.

Curt Sachs (1881–1959), comparative musicologist and close collaborator of Hornbostel, is best known for his instrument classification system. He had to emigrate in 1933 and taught at New York University from 1937 to 1953.

Marius Schneider (1903–1982) began as a medievalist, then became a comparative musicologist. A student of Hornbostel, he attempted to understand medieval polyphony through a study of polyphony in "primitive" cultures. From 1955 to 1968 he was the chair of ethnomusicology in Cologne, where he educated many prominent German ethnomusicologists.

Georg Schünemann (1885–1945), historical and comparative musicologist. He was the vice rector and then rector of the Berlin Musikhochschule, where he fundamentally reformed music education. He published in comparative musicology because he believed it would be possible to reconstruct medieval music through a study of non-Western music.

Cassian Spiess (1866–1905), missionary and bishop of St. Ottilien. He did important work in linguistics and was killed as a result of the Maji Maji Rebellion.

Carl Stumpf (1848–1936), German philosopher and psychologist and a close collaborator of Hornbostel. He was a professor in Berlin, where he established the Berlin Phonogramm-Archiv.

Walther Trittelvitz (1970–1958), close collaborator with Hagena. He was responsible for the activities of the Bethel Mission for forty-two years. He heard Ballanta in Le Zoute in 1926 and advocated the singing of African music in church.

Johann Baptist Wolf (1908–85), active as a missionary in Peramiho, Tanganyika, where, in the library, he found Schneider's *Geschichte der Mehrstimmigkeit*, which included transcriptions of local music from recordings made by Küsters. He then compared them to Gregorian chant and introduced the chant most similar to Schneider's transcriptions into the service.

Johannes Wolf (1869–1947), historical musicologist in Berlin, specialist in medieval notation and theory. He was close to comparative musicologists and resigned from the German Musicological Society in 1933 to protest the dismissal of Alfred Einstein.

NOTES

INTRODUCTION

1. The Berlin Phonogramm-Archiv was founded in 1906 by Carl Stumpf and Erich Moritz von Hornbostel for the purpose of collecting and classifying recordings from all over the world.

2. Comparative musicology is the precursor to ethnomusicology and is based on the cross-cultural study of music.

3. See my *Medieval Music and the Art of Memory*, chap. 1.

4. Note that Dahlhaus noticed the close connection between medieval music and comparative musicology as early as 1989. Dahlhaus, *Die Musiktheorie im 18. und 19. Jahrhundert*, 2–3.

5. Lord, *The Singer of Tales*.

6. The only difference is that Parry and Lord did the fieldwork themselves, while most comparative musicologists relied on fieldwork done by others.

7. See esp. Simon, *Das Berliner Phonogramm-Archiv*, and Ziegler, "Erich M. von Hornbostel," 146–68.

8. Adler was the first scholar to us the term "vergleichende Musikwissenschaft" in "Umfang, Methode und Ziel der Musikwissenschaft."

9. Hornbostel, "African Negro Music," 20–62.

PART ONE

1. See Koch, "Images of Sound," 476–78. The Vienna Phonogramm-Archiv was founded a year earlier, in 1899. Hornbostel gave his first important lecture, "Die Probleme der vergleichenden Musikwissenschaft," in 1905 in Vienna.

2. "Das vornehmste Mittel wissenschaftlicher Erkenntnis ist die Vergleichung." Hornbostel, "Die Probleme der vergleichenden Musikwissenschaft, " 40. Unless otherwise indicated, translations are my own.

3. See also A. Schneider, "Northern and Western Europe," 80; he was the first to call attention to this point.

4. "Erst studierte die Philologie die einzelnen Sprachen gesondert, bis die *verglei-chende* Sprachwissenschaft die verknüpfenden Fäden spann. Auch hier mußte sich der Entwicklungsgedanke sozusagen von selber einstellen, als Pfadfinder dienen und zu neuen Gruppierungen führen. Die bis dahin wenig beachteten Sprachen der sogenannten *Naturvölker* gewannen mit einemal ein besonderes Interesse; innerhalb der bekannten Sprachgebiete der Kulturländer wurden die Dialekte sorgfältiger studiert und so der Vergleichung ein immer reicheres Material zugeführt." Hornbostel, "Die Probleme der vergleichenden Musikwissenschaft," 41.

5. "Wie die Philologie zuerst die einzelnen Sprachen in ihrem Wortschaftz, ihren Flexionsgesetzen und ihrer Syntax jede für sich getrennt erforschte, so hat sich die Mw. bis in die jüngste Zeit aussschliesslich mit der Geschichte unseres europäischen Tonsystems und den europäischen Kompositionsformen beschäftigt. Während aber die vergleichende Sprachwissenschaft binnen kurzem vollständig eroberte, hat die Muskwissenschaft auf dem neuen Wege erst ein paar schüchterne Schritte gewagt, und es wäre verfrüht, von einer vergleichenden Musikwissenschaft als einem gesicherten Kulturbesitz zu sprechen. Zwar findet sich in den Gesamtdarstellungen der Musikgeschichte wohl meist auch eine flüchtige Skizzierung exotischer Musikverhältnisse; doch stellt sich die Betrachtung vorwiegend auf einen künstlerischen, subjektiv-ästhetischen Standpunkt und das Streben nach wissenschaftlicher Objektivität gehört der allerjüngsten Zeit an." Hornbostel, "Über die Verbreitung des Phonographen," 185.

6. Viennese comparative musicologists also modeled themselves on comparative linguistics. See in particular Lach, "Die Musik der turk-tartarischen, finnisch-ugrischen und Kaukasus-Völker," 23. Similarly, as we will see in part III, Hornbostel was in close contact with Carl Meinhof, the main specialist in African languages. Meinhof, who had himself originally been a Lutheran pastor, worked closely with missionaries, who helped him develop grammars. For Meinhof, see Sara Pugach, *Africa in Translation*. He also advised Hornbostel on the missionaries who could make recordings for him, such as Traugott Bachmann (see chap. 10, p. 138).

CHAPTER ONE

1. Arens, *Sprachwissenschaft*, 102–11. For a short English history of linguistics, see Robins, *A Short History of Linguistics*.

2. Partial translation in Moran and Gode, *On the Origins of Language*.

3. Herder, *Abhandlung über den Ursprung der Sprache*, 1–156. For Herder and music, see Bohlman, *Song Loves the Masses*.

4. Arens, *Sprachwissenschaft*, 105.

5. This conclusion of Herder's also influenced all German Protestant missionary work. This is why missionaries made such efforts not only to learn the languages of the people they were trying to convert, but also tried to understand their thinking patterns (see part III).

6. Berlin, *Three Critics of the Enlightenment*, 238.

7. Particularly Wilhelm von Humboldt and later Franz Boas were very much influenced by his ideas. Forster, "Herder's Role." On Herder's influence on Humboldt, see Sapir, "Herder's 'Ursprung der Sprache.'"

8. Arens, *Sprachwissenschaft*, 58, 127.

9. Sandys, *History of Classical Scholarship*, 2:438–39.

10. Schlegel, *Über die Sprache und Weisheit der Indier*.

11. Ibid., 28.

12. Schlegel also wrote a book on Greek poetry: *Über das Studium der griechischen Poesie*, 1797.

13. Bakker, *A Companion to the Ancient Greek Language*, 1.

14. Robins, *A Short History of Linguistics*, 191.

15. Rask, *Undersøgelse om det gamle nordiske*; Engl. trans. of parts in *A Reader in Nineteenth-Century Indoeuropean Linguistics*, 29–37.

16. Arens, *Sprachwissenschaft*, 169–72.

17. Ibid., 171.

18. Old Norse sagas and the Eddas can be easily read by modern Icelandic-speakers. See Vikør, *The Nordic Languages*.

19. See, in particular, chap. 4 on Georg Schünemann.

20. Bopp, *Über das Conjugationssystem der Sanskritsprache*, 10.

21. Bopp, *Vergleichende Grammatik des Sanskrit*.

22. Arens, *Sprachwissenschaft*, 196.

23. Bopp, *Vocalismus, oder sprachvergleichende Kritiken*, 152.

24. Robins, *A Short History of Linguistics*, 196–201.

25. Hoenigswald, "On the History of the Comparative Method," 5.

26. Schleicher, *Compendium der vergleichenden Grammatik*.

27. Robins, *A Short History of Linguistics*, 200.

28. "Die Sprache ist gleichsam die äußerliche Erscheinung des Geistes der Völker; ihre Sprache ist ihr Geist, und ihr Geist ihre Sprache, man kann sich beide nie genug identisch denken." Humboldt, *Ueber die Verschiedenheit des menschlichen Sprachbaus*, 6.7:38; trans. Losonsky, *The Heterogeneity of Language*, 50.

29. Humboldt, ed. Di Cesare, *Ueber die Verschiedenheit des menschlichen Sprachbaus*, 214.

30. Cited from Mueller-Vollmer, "Wilhelm von Humboldt," part 4. Mueller-Vollmer has provided an excellent analysis of Humboldt's language philosophy.

31. Humboldt's notes on the Basque language were edited in Hurch, *Die baskischen Materialien*, and Mueller-Vollmer, *Wilhelm von Humboldt*.

32. Mueller-Vollmer, "Wilhelm von Humboldt."

33. Humboldt, *Prüfung der Untersuchungen über die Urbewohner Hispaniens*.

34. Schumann (1719–1760) made a grammar of the Arawak language which somehow ended up in the Jena library. Humboldt asked Goethe for help in getting access to the grammar; Christlieb Quandt (1740–1824) compiled an Arawak dictionary and grammar and translated St. Paul's Epistle to the Romans into Arawak.

35. Zeisberger, *Delaware Grammatik*.

36. Mueller-Vollmer, *Wilhelm von Humboldts Sprachwissenschaft*, 63.

37. Mueller-Vollmer, "Wilhelm von Humboldts sprachwissenschaftlicher Nachlaß," 181–204.

38. Humboldt, *Gesammelte Schriften* (1903–36), 3:300–341.

39. Mueller-Vollmer, "Wilhelm von Humboldt," part 7.

40. Mueller-Vollmer, "Mutter Sanskrit und die Nacktheit der Südseesprachen," 117. The quarrel between Bopp and Buschmann was published in *Jahrbücher für wissen-schaftliche Kritik* in 1842, so it is entirely possible that some comparative musicologists read it there. See ibid., 127, and Mueller-Vollmer, "Wilhelm von Humboldt," part 7.

41. Mueller-Vollmer, "Mutter Sanskrit," 127.

42. Trabant, *Apeliotes oder der Sinn der Sprache*, 189.

43. Mueller-Vollmer, "Mutter Sanskrit," 131.

44. Trabant, *Traditionen Humboldts*, 95, 61.

45. There is no good English term for this word, but I suggest "psychology of people"; eventually the field became known as social psychology.

46. Bunzl, "Franz Boas and the Humboldtian Tradition," 17–78.

47. Klautke, *The Mind of the Nation*, 61–62.

48. See below, chaps. 11 and 13.

49. Wundt, *Völkerpsychologie*, 3:230.

50. Bunzl, "Franz Boas and the Humboldtian Tradition," 63.

51. As a result, Boas wrote *The Central Eskimo*, 399–670.

52. Bunzl, "Franz Boas and the Humboldtian Tradition," 66.

53. Ibid., 70. Bunzl has an extensive discussion of Humboldt's influence on Boas.

54. Ibid., 73.

55. Nettl, *Becoming an Ethnomusicologist*, 38. On Herzog, see also Ballanta, chap. 6.

56. The best book on the topic in music is Schneider, *Musikwissenschaft und Kulturkreislehre*, 88.

57. See also Rice, "Comparative Musicology."

58. Curt Sachs would apply the theory to musical instruments, Schneider adjusted it to discuss polyphony (see chap. 3, p. 50).

CHAPTER TWO

1. For example, his paper "Die Probleme der vergleichenden Musikwissenschaft," and his article with Otto Abraham, "Vorschläge für die Transkription." *Kulturkreislehre* is thoroughly investigated in A. Schneider, *Musikwissenschaft und Kulturkreislehre*. For his writings, see Hornbostel, *Opera Omnia*; see also Kaden and Stockmann, *Tonart und Ethos*; and Simon, *Das Berliner Phonogramm-Archiv*. For an excellent recent study of Hornbostel, see Klotz, *"Vom tönenden Wirbel menschlichen Tuns."*

2. See also Stockmann and Kaden, introductions to *Tonart und Ethos*, 1999, 5–21, 21–39.

3. Part I, pp. 12–13.

4. For a detailed biography of Hornbostel, see van Roon, "Ein Zauberkünstler," 44–77.

5. Letter from Hornbostel to Aby Warburg, 16 November 1906. GC/2170, Warburg Institute Archive (hereinafter WIA).

6. In 1925 he told Warburg that it was because of him that he switched from chemistry to comparative musicology. The letter also includes a detailed discussion of rituals (GC/16146, WIA). In later letters there are numerous exchanges on alphabets, zodiac signs, and hieroglyphs. The relationship deserves a separate study. Stephen Blum read a

paper on Hornbostel and Warburg at a conference at the Humboldt Forum in June 2019; see Blum, "E. M. von Hornbostel as Listener and Scientist."

7. Letter from Hornbostel to Aby Warburg, 16 November 1906, GC/2170, WIA. The entire correspondence in the Warburg Institute has been digitalized.

8. Aby Warburg visited the Pueblo Indians of northern New Mexico between December 1895 and May 1896. He lectured on the topic in 1923. For a detailed discussion of the issue, see Freedberg, "Warburg's Mask," and Bredekamp, *Aby Warburg*.

9. A *Habilitation* is a second dissertation.

10. Klotz, "Hornbostel, Erich Moritz, Ritter von."

11. Hornbostel, *Opera Omnia*, 189–90. Penny, *Objects of Culture*, has shown how prevalent this collecting was in imperial Prussia.

12. The anthropologist Felix von Luschan "saw to it from then on that no German travelling researcher set out without taking a set of phonographic equipment with him and without being instructed in the scientific use of the phonograph of the Psychological Institute of Berlin." Simon, *Das Berliner Phonogramm-Archiv*, 26.

13. Hornbostel, "African Negro Music," 31.

14. On Stumpf, see chap. 1, p. 28.

15. "Daß das Studium der Melodien wenig kultivierter Völker der musikgeschichtlichen Forschung wertvolle Anhaltspunkte gewähren kann, ist von den Vertreters der letzteren allezeit anerkannt worden. Aber auch psychologisch-ästhetische Untersuchungen können sich solcher Betrachtung ohne Nachteil nicht entschlagen. Denn die Grundlagen des Musikgefühls sind nicht abgesondert von dessen historischer Entwicklung zu verstehen, auch erleichtert die Gegenüberstellung jener und unserer Musik die Erkenntnis der gemeinsamen Wirkungsmittel und damit die Analyse. Außer ihrer musiktheoretischen Bedeutung werden diese Studien übrigens mit der Zeit auch eine anthropologische gewinnen, indem sie neue Kennzeichen für Verwandschaft oder früheren Verkehr getrennter Stämme liefern." Stumpf, "Lieder der Bellakula-Indianer, " 405.

16. "Hier ergibt sich die Berechtigung, an die Kulturgeschichte der Völker anzuspinnen, auch, wenn man die kulturärmeren nicht für geschichtslose Spätgebornene halten mag, die eben anfangen, die Entwicklung zu wiederholen; sondern lieber für die Nachkommen von früh Versprengten und Abgetrennten, die in ihrer Isolierung den Urbesitz langsam und einseitig vermehrt und um so weniger Altes aufgegeben haben, je weniger Neues ihnen von außen zukam." Hornbostel, "Melodie und Skala," 12.

17. Surprisingly enough, Hornbostel's relative Aby Warburg did not share the evolutionary biases described by Hornbostel. Bredekamp, *Aby Warburg*, 116–19.

18. This is again a point he might have taken from comparative linguists, who were interested in studying languages, such as Icelandic, that were not influenced by other languages. See also Hornbostel, "Phonogrammierte isländische Zwiegesänge."

19. Ludwig is also concerned with authenticity. He tries to finding the original version of early polyphony, whether in Notre Dame organa, troubadour and trouvère music, or in early motets. See my *Medieval Music and the Art of Memory*, chap. 1, and below, chap. 7.

20. Hornbostel, "Über vergleichende akustische und musikpsychologische Untersuchungen," 167. He adds that in Africa you can see the gradual development from melody to polyphony.

21. Hornbostel, "African Negro Music," 34–35.

22. This matter is discussed in Blum, "European Music Terminology and the Music of Africa." Blum also comments on the fact that Hornbostel connects melody with movement. See also Christensen, *Stories of Tonality in the Age of François-Joseph Fétis.*

23. I am not including here a detailed discussion of Abraham and Hornbostel, "Studien über das Tonsystem und die Musik der Japaner," and "Phonographierte indische Melodien," or of Hornbostel and Lachmann, "Das indische Tonsystem bei Bharata und sein Ursprung." Hornbostel and Lachmann talk about Indian melodies "that are based on modes like our church modes." The authors describe an originally pentatonic scale that later developed into a modal system. And yet they are too careful as scholars to state that medieval modes and ragas are the same thing.

24. Hornbostel, "Wanyamwezi-Gesänge," 1033–34.

25. Hornbostel, "African Negro Music," 37.

26. Hornbostel, "Phonogrammierte isländische Zwiegesänge," 319n16.

27. The letter from Handschin to Hornbostel was finished on 18 July and is in the Berlin Phonogramm-Archiv.

28. See Ziegler, "Polyphony in Historical Sound Recordings." There is little doubt that Hornbostel's student Marius Schneider's 1933 book *Geschichte der Mehrstimmigkeit,* generally thought to be the first systematic discussion of the issue, continues very much the kind of research started by Hornbostel. See also Agnew, "The Colonialist Beginnings," on Hornbostel's discussion of polyphony.

29. S. Blum correctly describes Hornbostel's outline of the evolution as "a kind of museum or laboratory in which these and other 'transitions' might be observed or studied." Yet, precisely for this reason his remarks are worth studying. Blum, "European Musical Terminology," 18.

30. "Durch den Phonographen erst ist uns ein wirklich ursprüngliches Material zugänglich geworden, an dem wir lernen können, wie schriftlose Völker unter verschiedenen Bedingungen der materiellen und geistigen Kultur ganz allmählich aus einfachsten Anfängen kompliziertere Formen der Mehrstimmigkeit entwickeln. Die Analogien dieser Formen mit den uns aus dem frühen Mittelalter überlieferten sind so frappant, daß wir wohl berechtigt sind, trotz gewisser, namentlich durch die verschiedene melodische Tradition bedingte Unterschiede, die alteuropäische Entwicklungsreihe mit den exotischen in Parallele zu setzen. Man gewinnt dadurch die Möglichkeit, die exotische Formen der Mehrstimmigkeit nach ihrer zeitlichen Aufeinanderfolge zu ordnen, andererseits die Lücken der europäischen Überlieferung zu ergänzen." Hornbostel, "Über die Mehrstimmigkeit in der aussereuropäischen Musik," 298–99.

31. "Das frühmittelalterliche *Organum* aber wird man nicht mehr als eine durch die gräzisierende Musiktheorie verschuldete Verirrung interpretieren dürfen." Ibid., 299.

32. Ibid., 302–3.

33. "Hiermit sind wir bei den höchst entwickelten Formen angelangt, die sich unter den bisher untersuchten Beispielen exotischer Mehrstimmigkeit finden. Nach unserer heutigen Kenntnis bricht also bei den noch schriftlosen Völkern, deren ganze musikalische Kultur mit der Improvisation verwachsen ist, die Entwicklung der Mehrstimmigkeit auf einer Stufe ab, die in Europa etwa zu der Zeit erreicht war, als die Notierung in der Mensuralnotation festere Formen anzunehmen began und dadurch weiterer Krei-

sen von schöpferisch begabten Musikern eine Gedächtnishilfe zugänglich wurde, ohne die auch wir schwerlich über ein musiklisches Mittelalter hinausgekommen wären." Ibid., 303. Blum has pointed out that Hornbostel assumed that "non-European music shows characteristics which are the natural outcome of pure melody"; Blum, "European Musical Terminology," 25. As a result there was "a desire to reinforce certain points of a melody 'with greater fullness of sound.'" Blum suggests to "extend the European concept of 'harmonic relations' to whatever sounds occur simulatenously."

34. See my *Medieval Music and the Art of Memory*, chap. 5.

35. See ibid., chap. 1.

36. He also mentions East India, Japan, Sumatra, and New Guinea. Hornbostel, "Wanyamwezi-Gesänge," 1040.

37. Ibid., 1041.

38. See chap. 1, pp. 17–18.

39. For more recent information on Jón Leifs, see Ross, "The Life of Leifs." See also Ingólfsson, *John Leifs and the Musical Invention of Iceland*. Leifs was educated in Germany and was a member of the *Singbewegung*. His compositions include "medieval sounding chants with parallel fifths, inspired by the oral practice of *tvísöngur*." During the war he advocated an Aryan-Icelandic supremacist philosophy.

40. "Wer die Phonogramme, deren Bearbeitung hier vorgelegt wird, hört, wird sich dem Eindruck kaum entziehn können, dass da frühmittelalterliche Gesänge erklingen." Hornbostel, "Phonogrammierte isländische Zwiegesänge," 300.

41. Ibid., 301.

42. Ibid., 308.

43. "Aber wir wissen heute, dass das Singen in Quintenparallelen keine ausgeklügelte Sache ist, sondern ganz im Gegenteil so natürlich, dass es überall und schon bei den primitivsten Völkern, wie den Adamanesen oder den Feuerländern, vorkommt. Zu diesem führt ein weiterer Schritt: man bemerkt die grössere Fülle des Quintenklanges gegenüber dem Einklang und der Oktave und spart ihn wegen dieser schätzenswerten Eigenschaft als Schlusseffekt auf. Auch diese Entdeckung ist von 'Naturvölkern' gemacht worden, ostafrikanischen Negern, die teils, wie die *rimur*-Sänger, bloss den Schlusston durch eine Quinte auszeichnen (z.B. Wanicha), teils am Strophenende vom Einklang oder Oktaven zu Quinten- (oder Quarten-) Parallelen übergehen (Wanyamwezi oder Wasukuma). Da an einen historischen Zusammenhang mit dem europäischen Organum schwerlich gedacht werden kann, beweisen diese Fälle mindestens die Möglichkeit seiner natürlichen Entstehung im Volksgesang." Ibid., 309.

44. Ibid., 311.

45. "Wie mir scheint, entgehe ich den Schwierigkeiten, die Sie am Schluss erwähnen, indem ich meine Basis verschiebe beziehungsweise erweitere: bereits die Spätantike hat auch mehrstimmigen Gesang gekannt, obgleich für sie die Mehrstimmigkeit vorwiegend instrumental beziehungsweise instrumentalbegleitet und speziell für die Orgel charakteristisch war." Letter from Handschin to Hornbostel, 18 July 1930, Berlin Phonogramm-Archiv.

46. For a summary, see Nettl, *The Study of Ethnomusicology*, 46.

47. Nettl, "Contemplating Ethnomusicology," 177.

48. Stumpf, *Die Anfänge der Musik*, 31–34, 112.

49. Hornbostel, "Melodie und Skala," 16; see also Stumpf, *Die Anfänge der Musik*, 109ff.

50. A longer discussion of pentatonicism is found in Hornbostel, "African Negro Music," 37–38.

51. Reichenbach, *Formenlehre*, 27; see also this book, chaps. 8 and 10.

52. "Ich habe immer, so weit es anging, die Platten in einer Gegend aufgenommen, wo keine Europäer sich dauernd aufhielten. Es war übrigens nach der ersten Scheu die Freude der Schwarzen an dem Grammophon so gross, dass sie tageweit aus der Heimat kamen, um auch einmal dieses Instrument sehen und hineinsprechen zu können." Letter from Küsters to Hornbostel, 14 February 1929, Berlin Phonogramm-Archiv.

53. See, for example, Hornbostel, "Die Probleme der vergleichenden Musikwissenschaft," 96–97. See also Nettl's thoughtful insights on this question in "Contemplating Ethnomusicology," 178–81.

54. Hornbostel, "African Negro Music," 42.

55. Ibid., 47.

56. Nettl, "Contemplating Ethnomusicology," 179.

57. Ibid., 185.

58. See my *Medieval Music and the Art of Memory*, chap. 1.

59. Taruskin, "On Letting the Music Speak for Itself."

60. See esp. Hornbostel and Lachmann, "Asiatische Parallelen." See also Schneider, "Northern and Western Europe," 89.

61. See in particular my discussion of Rietzsch in chap. 10, pp. 145–47.

CHAPTER THREE

1. Bernhard Bleibinger has written an excellent dissertation on Marius Schneider. I will be relying extensively on his research. Bleibinger, *Marius Schneider und der Simbolismo*.

2. I would especially like to thank Rudolf Stephan for illuminating information on Schneider and his background.

3. The first to publicly accuse him was Herzog, who in 1951 wrote a devastating review of Schneider's book *El origen musical*. To quote Nettl, he criticized him "for adhering to views supported by Nazi ideology. In his review the reader also senses sorrow, as Herzog takes Schneider, his old friend and associate in the 1930s whose early work he regarded as solid, severely to task for having lost his way in political orthodoxy." Nettl, *Becoming an Ethnomusicologist*, 58.

4. To quote Nettl, "My own meeting with Schneider, in 1957, suggested that he continued to maintain these intellectually and politically no longer tenable views." *Ibid.*, 58. However, Nettl wrote to me in an email on 11 May 2016 that upon meeting Schneider he might have been prejudiced by Herzog's negative opinion.

5. Zimmermann, *Tonart ohne Ethos*. Zimmermann visited numerous archives. The book reads well but is not always reliable from a scholarly point of view.

6. I would like to thank Ric Trimillos for telling me about his experiences as a Fulbright student with Schneider in 1964–65. When Schneider was "challenged" by some of his students about his belief in the efficacy of *Kulturkreislehre*, his classic reply was, "I

pose the questions; I leave it to you gentlemen to provide the answers." Trimillos found Schneider a brilliant person and a polyglot. I would like to thank Bruno Nettl for directing me to Trimillos as a former student of Schneider. Similarly, Professor Emeritus Dieter Gutknecht found his lectures and seminars among the most stimulating he ever attended (private communication, 17 January 2013).

7. He also thanks Georg Schünemann and Curt Sachs for help in his early article. Schneider, "Der Hochetus."

8. See also Ziegler, "Erich M. von Hornbostel."

9. The archive of UdK contains detailed correspondence about the Berlin Phonogramm-Archiv.

10. Bleibinger, *Marius Schneider und der Simbolismo*, 27–28.

11. Letter from Stumpf to Stein, 11 July 1933, 1.2620, Archiv der UdK, Berlin.

12. Letter from Schneider to Stein, 19 July 1933. He adds that he would like this letter to be kept private because he does not want to harm Hornbostel. For a detailed account of the issue, see also Schneider, "Bericht des Phonogrammarchivs," 17 February 1934, Archiv der UdK, Berlin. No answer from Hornbostel is preserved, so we have only one side of the story.

13. Bleibinger, *Marius Schneider und der Simbolismo*, 27.

14. Schneider writes in his "Bericht": "Since Hornbostel received a clear message about the new organization of the circumstances in the Phonogramm Archiv, he made peace with the situation. I have the impression from the negotiations that there is a basis for peaceful collaboration" (2). We have no letters from Hornbostel on this issue after 1933.

15. See E 486/36 and E 1196/36, Berlin Phonogramm-Archiv. Bleibinger has investigated the matter in detail and also consulted with the Polish ethnomusicologist Jan Steszewski about it.

16. All documents are found in Bleibinger, *Marius Schneider und der Simbolismo*, 32–33.

17. See Prieberg, *Handbuch deutscher Musiker*.

18. Handschin, though, wrote to Schneider's friend Higini Anglès: "Schneider's *Mehrstimmigkeit* is a terrible book; but Besseler asked me to wait a little with my review, so that Schünemann is not preventing the Habilitation of Schneider." Letter from Handschin to Anglès, 14–15 September 1936, Caja G-H, Handschin, Epistolari Higini Anglès, Biblioteca de Catalunya, Barcelona. See also Bleibinger, *Marius Schneider und der Simbolismo*, 33. It is not entirely clear why Schünemann was not supportive of Schneider's *Habilitation*.

19. "Es gibt kein Institut, das wie das unsere Musik und Rassenforschung so eng miteinander verbindet und dadurch mehr der kulturellen Problemstellung Adolf Hitlers entspräche. . . . Nachdem uns nun eine große einmalige Hilfe zur Rettung unserer alten indogermanischen Bestände gewährt worden ist, wird die Indogermanenfrage in den nächsten zwei Jahren eine gründliche Untersuchung erfahren. . . . Wollen wir den Gedanken Adolf Hitlers auf jedem Gebiet zum Durchbruch verhelfen, so müssen unsere Mittel unbedingt erhöht werden." Letter from Marius Schneider to the Generaldirektor, 9 May 1938, E 487/38, Berlin Phonogramm-Archiv.

20. "Wir benötigen dringend eine weltanschauliche und kulturpolitische Beurteilung des Musikwissenschaftlers Marius Schneider. . . . Dr. Schneider steht in dem Verdacht,

streng konfessionell katholisch gebunden zu sein und entsprechende Tendenzen auch in seine wissenschaftliche Arbeit hineinzutragen. Es wäre wertvoll, Feststellungen darüber zu erhalten, wie weit sich eine solche Haltung im Privatleben von Schneider dokumentiert, der unseren Informationen zufolge weder Parteigenosse ist noch einer Gliederung angehört. Das von ihm geleitete Phonogramm-Archiv soll bezeichnenderweise von 'christlichen Missionen,' besonders katholischen Forschungsreisenden Unterstützung erfahren. Es ist anzunehmen, dass diese Querverbindung nur aufgrund der romkirchlichen Bindungen Schneiders zustande gekommen sind." Letter from Herbert Gerigk quoted in Bleibinger, *Marius Schneider und der Simbolismo*, 58.

21. See chaps. 10, 11, and 13 and introduction.

22. Bleibinger, *Marius Schneider und der Simbolismo*, 59–73.

23. Ibid., 67–73. See also Potter, *Most German of the Arts*, 159.

24. See Maurer Zenck and Peterson, *Lexikon verfolgter Musiker und Musikerinnen der NS Zeit.* De Van (1906–1949) was a French musicologist of American birth. He collaborated closely with the Vichy regime and was suspended from all musical duties after the war; de Vries, *Sonderstab Musik.* De Van criticizes Schneider for not "being willing to condemn Jews" and was unwilling to help advertise a publication by de Van on Jewish musicians. Prieberg, *Handbuch*, 6261.

25. Bleibinger, *Marius Schneider und der Simbolismo*, 72–73.

26. There is little doubt concerning Fellerer's Nazi sympathies. See especially the article by his former student Dieter Gutknecht, "Universitäre Musikwissenschaft," 215.

27. Bleibinger, *Marius Schneider und der Simbolismo*, 72.

28. Schneider, *Die Ars nova.*

29. When Wolf's book appeared, the historical musicologist Friedrich Ludwig wrote a devastating forty-four-page review, concentrating mainly on small inaccuracies in the description of the sources. Ludwig, "Review of Johannes Wolf," 597–641. The review became legendary among medievalists and did so much damage to Wolf's reputation that he never became a full professor. For a more detailed discussion of the review, see my *Medieval Music and the Art of Memory*, 10–12; see also chap. 7, pp. 93–94.

30. Einstein was Jewish. Potter, *Most German of the Arts*, 66–67.

31. Leech-Wilkinson, *The Modern Invention of Medieval Music*, 64–87. Similarly, Bleibinger recognizes the importance of comparative musicology for Schneider's medieval work, but he does not seem to be aware of Leech-Wilkinson's book; Bleibinger, *Marius Schneider und der Simbolismo*, 14–16. See also Haines, "The Arabic Style," 369–78. On the relationship between Gregorian chant and Sephardic music, see Idelsohn, "Parallelen zwischen gregorianischen und hebräisch-orientalischen Gesangsweisen," 515–24.

32. "Erst im XV. Jahrhundert ringt man sich von der Kultur des Mittelalters, von dieser Kreuzung hellenistischer und orientalischer Geistesart los, um das eigentliche europäische Kulturleben zu begründen. Wie stark im XIV. Jahrhundert neben dem hellenistischen gerade der orientalische Einfluß noch war, läßt sich überall im gesellschaftlichen Leben, in der Staatsform, Philosophie, Literatur und Kunst erkennen. Im Laufe dieser Arbeit werden wir des öfteren auf die Zusammenhänge mit der orientalischen Musikpraxis hinweisen müssen." Schneider, *Die Ars nova*, 14.

33. Leech-Wilkinson, *The Modern Invention of Medieval Music*, 64.

34. Ibid., 85–86.

35. Ibid., 74.

36. Schneider, *Die Ars nova*, 77.

37. "Denn in dieser Zeit, wo die freie Improvisation in so hoher Blüte stand, war eine niedergeschrieben Komposition beinahe nur das Gerüst, auf dem sich das Musikstück aufbaute. Bald komponierte man eine Stimme dazu, bald ließ man eine weg, man brachte hoqueti an, wo gar keine vorgeschrieben waren. Wir wissen mit Sicherheit, daß die Bordunpraxis sehr verbreitet war; aber wir besitzen kein Denkmal, in dem eine Bordunstelle aufgezeichnet wäre. Man notierte eben noch bis zum XVII. Jahrhundert bei weitem nicht alles so bis ins einzelne, wie wir das heute gewöhnt sind." Ibid., 18.

38. "Es ist wohl nicht abzuleugnen, daß die Notationstechnik einen großen Einfluß auf die Musik selbst ausübte." Ibid., 18.

39. See my *Medieval Music and the Art of Memory*.

40. Ernest Ferand, who wrote the first detailed study of improvisation, is similarly at a loss to explain exactly how it was done. See Ferand, *Die Improvisation*.

41. "Aus dem unpersönlichen Charakter dieser Werke erklärt sich auch die sonderbare Art, mit der das Mittelalter mit seinen Kompositionen umgeht. Je nachdem man Stimmen oder Instrumente zur Verfügung hat, läßt man eine Stimme weg oder komponiert—oder improvisiert gar—eine andere Stimme dazu. . . . Der mittelalterliche Musiker komponiert keine Motette etwa so, wie das der moderne Künstler tut, der seinen Genius auf Grund eines sicheren technischen Könnens frei walten lässt. Eine Motette der Ars nova wird 'zurechtgebaut' im primitivsten Sinne des Wortes. Dafür gibt uns die nur für den Intellekt faßbare Technik der Isorhythmik und der bei Coussemaker abgedruckte Traktat über Motettenkomposition des Aegidius de Murino ein klares Bild." Schneider, *Die Ars nova*, 78.

42. See Wolf, "Ein Beitrag zur Diskantlehre," 504–34.

43. See my *Medieval Music and the Art of Memory*, chap. 4.

44. Ludwig, "Review of Johannes Wolf." See also this chapter, p. 258n29.

45. Schneider, "Marius Schneider," 133–34.

46. Ibid.

47. Schneider, *Geschichte der Mehrstimmigkeit*, 1:9.

48. "Die einzige Möglichkeit, diese Vorgeschichte auf indirektem Wege zu erkennen, besteht in der Erforschung der heute noch bei den verschiedensten Naturvölkern erkennbaren Entwicklungsreihe *analoger*, rezenter Musikformen." Ibid.

49. Lord, *The Singer of Tales*.

50. "Die Tatsache, daß der Verfasser die Musik der Naturvölker zur Erklärung der Frühgeschichte europäisch-mittelalterlicher Musikkultur heranzieht, dürfte vom Gesichtspunkt der Methode von vielen Lesern nur mit großer Zurückhaltung angenommen werden. Deswegen sei gleich zu Anfang bemerkt, daß hier keineswegs irgendwelche direkte kulturhistorische Beziehungen zwischen den exotischen und mittelalterlichen Musikkreisen gesucht werden sollen. Das wäre ein unsinniges und zugleich aussichtsloses Unternehmen." Schneider, *Geschichte der Mehrstimmigkeit*, 1:10.

51. Stumpf, *Die Anfänge der Musik*, 97–101.

52. "It is not possible to observe an original version of polyphony with one group of people and then consider this the beginning of polyphony altogether, for the simple reason that there are many kinds of polyphony" (Man kann auch nicht bei einem Volke

irgendeine Urform der Entstehung der Mehrstimmigkeit feststellen und diese dann ohne weiteres als den Anfang aller Mehrstimmigkeitsformen bezeichnen, denn es gibt viele Formen der Mehrklangsbildung). Schneider, *Geschichte der Mehrstimmigkeit*, 1:10.

53. He talked about "musikalisches Unterbewusstsein."

54. Hornbostel, "Melodie und Skala," 11–23.

55. Schneider, *Geschichte der Mehrstimmigkeit*, 1:16, 18, 104; see also Schneider, "Diskussionen: Zur außereuropäischen Mehrstimmigkeit," 34–38.

56. See a complete list in Schneider, *Geschichte der Mehrstimmigkeit*, 1:28. All of these circles can be further enlarged.

57. Ibid., 2:8–9.

58. Ibid., 2:98.

59. "Die Verbreitung zeigt, dass sich das Mittelalter hier eine kaukasische Technik zu eigen gemacht hat. Es hat natürlich nicht alles wörtlich übernommen, denn es musste diese neue Kunstform den liturgischen Forderungen anpassen. So allein erklärt es sich auch, wie man zu der so wunderlichen Zerstückelung eines durchgehenden liturgischen cantus firmus kam. . . . Diese Technik wurde dann auf die vorhandenen liturgische Vorlagen übertragen." Schneider, "Kaukasische Parallelen," 53.

60. "Solche Ähnlichkeiten technischer Merkmale sind bislang ebenfalls noch nirgendwo sonst bekannt geworden." Ibid.

61. For other scholars who have argued that there was a relationship between Georgian and medieval polyphony, see Siegfried Nadel and Susanne Ziegler.

62. Schneider, "Wurzeln und Anfänge der abendländischen Mehrstimmigket," 166.

63. "In der ars antiqua überwiegt das kaukasische, in der ars nova (insbesondere in Italien) das neumediterrane." Ibid., 167.

64. Handschin, "Marius Schneider," 150.

65. Schneider, *Geschichte der Mehrstimmigkeit*, 1:106f.

66. Schneider, *Musikwissenschaft und Kulturkreislehre*, 181. See also Schneider's discussion of the relationship between *Tonalitätskreis* and *Kulturkreis*, 177–84.

67. Fleischer, *Neumen-Studien*; and Riemann, *Folkloristische Tonalitätsstudien*, esp. 34. Schneider's analysis of Gregorian chant, which he believed to have been originally pentatonic, is in agreement with that of Reichenbach; see chap. 8, pp. 113–15.

68. See chap. 13 on how Johann Baptist Wolf adapted these melodies for church use.

69. For an overview of all studies dealing with the relationship of medieval polyphony to non-Western polyphony, see the excellent article by Traub and Ziegler, "Mittelalterliche und kaukasische Mehrstimmigkeit." The authors discuss publications by Robert Lach, Siegfried Nadel, and Marius Schneider. Since Traub is a medievalist, they go systematically through all the medieval examples in Schneider's volume and conclude that his theories can no longer be supported.

70. For a summary, see Nettl, *The Study of Ethnomusicology*, 16.

71. "Der gemeinhin ganz unreflektiert gebrauchte Begriff 'Mehrstimmigkeit' ist gleichwohl—auch wenn kein anderes Wort zur Verfügung zu stehen scheint—oft problematisch als Bezeichnung außereuropäischer und archaischer Klanggestaltung, die weithin nicht von der Vorstellung einer Gleichzeitigkeit mehrerer Stimmen ausgeht." Eggebrecht, "Polyphonie."

72. Handschin, "Marius Schneider," 2:150–51.

73. Ibid., 151. Bleibinger has a summary of all reviews: *Marius Schneider und der Simbolismo*, 165–70.

74. See Traub and Ziegler, "Mittelalterliche und kaukasische Mehrstimmigkeit," which comes to a similar conclusion.

75. Parry, "Studies in the Epic Technique."

76. Berliner, *The Soul of Mbira* and *Thinking in Jazz*. See also Blum's fundamental article "Composition." It is characteristic that Blum, an ethnomusicologist who is equally at home in historical musicology, recognized the importance of improvisation and composition in the mind early on.

77. Brenner, *Die kombinatorisch strukturierten Harfen- und Xylophonpattern*.

78. "Ars organi," Ottoboni lat. 3025, Biblioteca Apostoloca Vaticana.

79. See my *Medieval Music and the Art of Memory*, chap. 5. See also Stephen C. Immel, "The Vatican Organum Treatise." Strangely enough, Schneider does not mention the Vatican Organum Treatise. It was well-known by the time Schneider wrote his book. Rudolf von Ficker wrote an article in 1932 that should definitely have been consulted by Schneider: Ficker argues that the Vatican organum treatise was written before Notre Dame polyphony. Ficker, "Das Organumtraktat."

80. See chap. 13, pp. 224–27, on the extraordinary effect his *Geschichte der Mehrstimmigkeit* had on music in the Benedictine African congregations.

81. "Musikalische Rassekriterien lassen sich nur in geringem Maße durch die Analyse des formalen Aufbaus (Tonleiter, Intervallfolgen, Satzbau usw.), sondern wesentlich durch die Beschreibung von Stimmklang und Vortragsweise gewinnen. Die formalen Elemente sind übertragbar. Stimmklang und Vortragsweise hingegen scheinen sich nur zu vererben." Schneider, "Ethnologische Musikforschung," 139.

82. See esp. Potter, *Most German of the Arts*, 134, 179, and 216. The main proponent of the theory that the *lur* provided proof of the Germanic origins of the major triad was Oskar Fleischer; it continued to be promulgated by the amateur musicologist Richard Eichenauer.

83. Schneider, *Geschichte der Mehrstimmigkeit*, 2:16–17. According to Blume, Schneider reiterated this point at the Indogermanenkongress. Bleibinger, *Marius Schneider und der Simbolismo*, 44–45.

84. Nettl, *Becoming an Ethnomusicologist*, 80.

85. See also Bleibinger, *Marius Schneider und der Simbolismo*, 62–63.

86. Hornbostel, "Fuegian Songs," 361–62.

87. See especially Trippett's perceptive discussion of the issue in *Wagner's Melodies*, 342–45. See also Meyer-Kalkus's discussion of the amateur scholar Ottmar Rutz in *Stimme und Sprechkünste*, 88–94. More recently, David F. Garcia has unearthed the correspondence between Melville J. Herskovits and Hornbostel. There can be no doubt from Hornbostel's letters that he believed that such things as musical style, gesture, and voice production to be hereditary. Herskovits was one of the earliest to advocate that these traits are cultural. Garcia, *Listening for Africa*, chap. 2; see also Hornbostel, "Fuegian Songs," 752.

88. Blume, *Das Rasseproblem in der Musik*.

89. Herzog, *A propósito*, 43.

90. Schneider, review, "*A propósito* [and] *El origen musical*," 32–33.

91. Retzius, "Über die Schädelformen der Nordbewohner."

92. Ryback, *Hitler's Private Library*, 110.

93. See also Schneider, *Kulturkreislehre*, 75–76.

94. Wallaschek, *Anfänge der Tonkunst*, 163.

95. Lach, *Die vergleichende Musikwissenschaft*, 90f.

96. Hornbostel, "Fuegian Songs," 361–62.

97. Ibid., 361.

98. Ibid., 364–65n26.

99. Trippett, *Wagner's Melodies*, 342.

100. "Musikpsychologische Bemerkungen über Vogelgesang," in Grimm, *Über den Ursprung der Sprache*, 21; trans. in Trippett, *Wagner's Melodies*, 433. Trippett has an excellent discussion of the issue.

101. See also Schneider's 1939 article, "Ethnologische Musikforschung," where he wrote that *Stimmklang* and *Vortragsweise* are always based on the European point of view. He repeated again and again that one therefore has to be very cautious in one's judgment (139–40).

102. Kunst, *Ethnomusicology*, 12–13.

103. See esp. Heinitz, "Musikwissenschaft und Völkerkunde," 43–54; see also Schneider, *Kulturkreislehre*, 76, and https://institutsgeschichte-muwi.blogs.uni-hamburg .de/die-etablierung-eines-neuen-forschungszweiges-wilhelm-heinitz-biomusikologie-in-der -disziplinaeren-oeffentlichkeit/ for more on the subject.

104. Boas, "Changes in the Bodily Form of Descendants of Immigrants."

105. Herzog, *A propósito*, 47.

CHAPTER FOUR

1. The offer from Heidelberg came in 1920. Schünemann also declined an offer to become director of the Salzburg Mozarteum in 1939. See Elftmann, *Georg Schünemann (1884–1945)*.

2. Schünemann, "Zur Geschichte des Taktschlagens." Schünemann was strongly influenced not only by Wolf and Kretzschmar, but also by Max Friedländer, who specialized in the German lied. For more information on Wolf, see above, p. 258n29.

3. Schünemann, *Das Lied der deutschen Kolonisten in Russland*.

4. Kestenberg (1882–1962), a student of Busoni, became Musikreferent für Wissenschaft, Kunst und Volksbildung in 1918. He instituted the Akademie für Kirchen- und Schulmusik, where teachers for Gymnasiums were educated not only practically, but also academically. Fritz Jöde and Herman Reichenbach, whom we will meet in part II, were teachers there. Kestenberg was Jewish; he was fired in 1933 and emigrated via Prague and Paris to Israel, where he became general manager of the Palestine Orchestra. For a fascinating account of the relationship between Kestenberg and Schünemann, see the letters from Kestenberg to Schünemann published in Schenk and Mahlert, *Leo Kestenberg: Gesammelte Schriften*, vol. 3.2.

5. Schünemann was also a passionate choir director who conducted two men's choirs, the Siemens Chor and the Liedertafel Westend. Elftmann, *Georg Schünemann*, 18.

6. Some of the early-music concert programs are kept in the Archiv der UdK. They include medieval and Renaissance polyphony, Gregorian chant, and music of the seven-

teenth century. See, for example, an announcement of 17 November 1933 of a concert on which Paul Hindemith and Günther Ramin, among others, performed on viola d'amore, various gambas, and Bach's own harpsichord. Akte Schünemann, Archiv der UdK, Berlin.

7. "Ich bitte für einen Vortrag im Chor-Dirigenten-Kursus um einige Walzen über Mehrstimmigkeit und Tonsysteme (Java, Siam, Wanyamwezi, Russen, Mingrelia usw.). Ausserdem erbitte ich das Metallophon mit Java und Siamesischen Tonleitern." Schünemann to the Phonogramm-Archiv, 15 October 1929, Akte Schünemann, Archiv der UdK, Berlin.

8. The performers are Mahebook Khan and Mushraff Khan. Akte Schünemann, Archiv der UdK, Berlin.

9. Raden Mas Jodjana and Raden Ayon Jodjana were accompanied by a gamelan group. Akte Schünemann, Archiv der UdK, Berlin. There is a colorful account of the event in the *12 Uhr Blatt* of 26 February 1935.

10. Letter from Hornbostel to Schünemann, 7 July 1931, and from Schünemann to Hornbostel, 18 July 1931. Akte Schünemann, Archiv der UdK, Berlin.

11. Akte Schünemann. Archiv der UdK, Berlin. I was not able to find any information on him.

12. Schenk, *Die Hochschule für Musik zu Berlin*, 103–48.

13. Schünemann, "Beziehungen neuer Musik zu exotischer und frühmittelalterlicher Tonkunst," on the relationship between contemporary, exotic, and medieval music, was one of the first to realize the importance of this topic. He discusses Debussy, Stravinsky, Busoni, Alois Haba, Hindemith, Krenek, and Schoenberg as having been influenced by folk music or non-Western and medieval music, in particular medieval polyphony.

14. See Schenk, introduction to Kestenberg's letters to Schünemann, in *Leo Kestenberg*, vol. 3.2, 94–95.

15. For more information on Schünemann's activities at the Amt Rosenberg, see von Haken, "Der Einsatzstab Rosenberg und die Erfassung musikalischer Kulturgüter." Schünemann mainly made catalogs of items in French libraries intending that they be sent to Germany. There is no evidence that he was involved in the removal of musical instruments from Wanda Landowska (115).

16. Schünemann, "Zur Geschichte des Taktschlagens." He begins with a summary of mensuration signs encountered between 1300 and 1600. For some theorists he relies on Coussemaker, but in many cases he has read the original manuscript or a printed edition.

17. The study shows clearly the influence of one of his professors, Johannes Wolf.

18. A watered-down version of this research was published by another member of the *Jugendmusikbewegung*, Guido Waldmann (1900–1990), born in St. Petersburg of German parents; Waldmann, "Die deutschen Kolonisten," 98–107. Waldmann became editor of the journal *Hitlerjugend* in 1935 and from 1935 on also served as the editor of *Musik und Volk*. As we have seen throughout, not all Nazis had trouble getting jobs after the war. Waldmann, for example, became rector of the Musikhochschule Trossingen.

19. See https://www.lautarchiv.hu-berlin.de/einfuehrung/chronologie/. The recordings are now held at Humboldt University but will be transferred to the new Humboldt Forum in Berlin.

20. Schünemann dealt only with the music; the dialects were evaluated in von Unwerth and Schirmunski, "Sprachgeschichte und Siedlungsmundarten."

21. Even though his study received overall very good evaluations, his attempt to formulate laws was criticized by his mentor, Max Friedländer. Elftmann, *Georg Schünemann*, 29.

22. "Sie haben ihr Deutschtum rein erhalten und sind zum größten Teil noch nicht durch Industrie und Großstadtkultur in ihrer Lebensart bedroht. Viele von ihnen, so die Wolgakolonisten, blieben von jedem Verkehr mit der früheren Heimat so gut wie abgeschlossen. Sie sprechen noch ihren alten Dialekt und singen ihre deutschen Lieder, die sich von einem Geschlecht zum anderen forterben. Das Lied erinnert sie an die deutsche Heimat und an ihre eigene Geschichte, es ist ihr unvergänglicher Besitz, der anderthalb Jahrhunderte überdauert hat und noch heute trotz russischer Umgebung und Beeinflussung von allen erhalten und neu erworben wird. Diesen Kolonisten von der Wolga, aus Südrussland, Sibirien und von den Ansiedlungen bei Petersburg ist die vorliegende Sammlung zu verdanken. Sie umfaßt volks- und volkstümliche Lieder, Kunstlieder, geistliche und Brüderlieder." Schünemann, *Das Lied der deutschen Kolonisten*, X.

23. Ibid., 83.

24. Ibid. On Stumpf's evaluation, see Elftmann, *Georg Schünemann*, 31.

25. Schünemann, "Über die Beziehungen."

26. The other was the Viennese comparative musicologist Robert Lach, who commented on the similarities between Georgian and medieval polyphony in "Vorläufiger Bericht."

27. "Es können aber an die Stelle sagenhafter Berichte die Ergebnisse der vergleichenden Musikwissenschaft treten, und sie *müssen* es, wenn die Probleme der griechischen und mittelalterlichen Musik wie die Fragen nach dem Zusammenhang von Kunstlehre und Volksmusik nicht ganz in der Luft schweben sollen. Es ist nicht nötig, die Musik unzivilisierter Völker oder die Kunst asiatischer Kulturvölker so, wie wir sie seit Aufnahme der phonographischen Methode studieren können, den Vorstufen der musikalischen Entwcklung gleich zu stellen, aber es kann aus einer systematischen Zusammenfassung der Einzeluntersuchungen ein Vorbau für die Musikgeschichte geschaffen werden, der sich nicht an Beschreibunben und mühsame, wenig verlässliche Konstruktionen, sondern an die *lebendige, praktische* Musik hält." Schünemann, "Über die Beziehungen," 175.

28. Ibid., 178.

29. Ibid., 179.

30. "Wenn irgendwo, so läßt sich auf deutschem Boden im Volkslied das Schöpferische und Eigene der freien Melodievariierung aus den verschiedenen Aufzeichnungen bis in unsere Tage hinein erkennen. Es ist im Grunde das gleiche produktive Moment, das in der Musik der Naturvölker zu immer neuen Variantenbildungen treibt." Ibid., 182.

31. Ibid., 183.

32. Another important study on Georgian polyphony, which is related to medieval polyphony, is by Siegfried Nadel. See the excellent discussion on Nadel's work in Ziegler, "Siegfried F. Nadel and His Contribution to Georgian Polyphony." Nadler's book *Georgische Gesänge* was published in 1933.

CHAPTER FIVE

1. See, for example, Charles, "Bukofzer, Manfred," in which his ethnomusicological work is summarized in a single sentence: "and he also did research in ethnomusicology."

2. There are numerous anecdotes about Handschin. According to one, he regularly took off his trousers during his organ performances in Basel churches and hung them over the railing of the balcony, much to the amusement of the Basel congregation. Martin Staehelin, private communication.

3. For a fuller account of Handschin's life and scholarship, see my *Medieval Music and the Art of Memory*, 31–39.

4. There are several newspaper clippings of his choir concerts in the Nachlass, Elizabeth Hargrove Music Library, University of California, Berkeley.

5. The dissertation was published in Strasbourg in 1936. On the relationship to Besseler, see esp. Schipperges, *Die Akte Heinrich Besseler*, 310–11, and *Kommentierte Edition des Briefwechsels Heinrich Besseler-Jacques Handschin (1925–54)*. https:// www.uni-tuebingen.de/fakultaeten/philosophische-fakultaet/fachbereiche/altertums -und-kunstwissenschaften/mwi/forschung/drittmittelprojekte/kommentierte-edition -briefwechsel-besseler-handschin-dfg.html. There is an extensive correspondence with Besseler in Bukofzer's Nachlass at the Elizabeth Hargrove Music Library, University of California, Berkeley. Besseler wrote to Bukofzer on 11 September 1946, shortly after the end of the war, trying to make the case that after 1937 he lost all support in the ministry, when a person sympathetic to serious scholarship was replaced by an SS member who made it impossible for Besseler to continue his work and to stay in touch with his students abroad (he mentions Edith Gerson-Kiwi and Edward Lowinsky). Then Besseler insinuates that he and his friend Kurt Huber (who was executed in 1943) were both victims of the same SS member. Publications in which he wanted to include Jewish scholars (Alfred Einstein and Bukofzer) were not allowed. He complains about the horrible war years, writing that he was not able to work as a scholar, but even worse was mistreated as a simple soldier from 1943 on. The letter ends with praise for Bukofzer's publication and his wish to hear from him. In a letter to Blume of 27 November 1955, Bukofzer writes about Besseler: "Now first to your 'major question' concerning Besseler. It was a big relief for me to hear from you that you are not blind to his weaknesses, since I had more or less given up hope of convincing anyone in Germany that he [Besseler] distorts facts with the false brilliance of new linguistic creations" (Nun zunächst zu Ihrer "grossen Frage" bezüglich Besselers. Es war mir eine Erleichterung von Ihnen zu hören, dass Sie nicht blind gegen seine Schwächen sind, da ich schon mehr oder weniger die Hoffnung aufgegeben hatte, auch nur irgendjemand in Deutschland davon zu überzeugen, wie er mit falschem Glanz sprachlicher Neubildungen die Tatsachen verzerrt). Letter from Bukofzer to Blume, 27 November 1955, Elizabeth Hargrove Library, University of California, Berkeley. The letters from Bukofzer to Besseler that are preserved in his Nachlass only discuss medieval music. Concerning Friedrich Blume, he kept at the beginning of his Nachlass a newspaper clipping from Blume's article "Deutsche Musikwissenschaft," in *Deutsche Wissenschaft, Arbeit und Aufgabe* (Leipzig: Hirzel, 1939), a book dedicated to Hitler for his fiftieth birthday, where Blume writes: "Das deutsche Volk hat sich und seinem Schicksal in der Musik seit Jahrhunderten eine 'Siegesallee' grossartigster Denkmale gesetzt" (For centuries the German nation has set for itself and its musical destiny a "victory avenue" of the grandest monuments in music). He continues that a nationalistic musicology can only take its point of departure from the center of German life (16). However, Bukofzer's subsequent letters show that eventually he was able to establish a

warm relationship with Blume and was happy to serve as the editor of the groundbreaking and magisterial work *Die Musik in Geschichte und Gegenwart* (cited herein as *MGG*, ed. Blume).

6. His Warburg years allowed him to become interdisciplinary; hence his collaboration on Kantorowicz, *Laudes regiae*, in which he wrote the sections dealing with the music of the *laudes*.

7. Kniazeva, *Jacques Handschin in Russland*.

8. Mazo, "Russia, the USSR and the Baltic States."

9. Handschin, *Musikgeschichte im Überblick*, 31.

10. Ibid., 98.

11. "Dabei müssen wir uns vorstellen, dass die Mehrstimmigkeit in der Hauptsache eine Angelegenheit der Sänger, d.h. der 'Aufführungspraxis' war: aufgezeichnet wurde die zur gegebenen Melodie hinzuzufügende Stimme nur selten, meist wurde sie von den Sängern, die nur die Melodie vor sich hatten, improvisiert." Ibid., 153.

12. Sight is a simple improvisational technique. See my *Medieval Music and the Art of Memory*, chap. 6.

13. See Trowell, "Fauxbourdon," and my *Medieval Music and the Art of Memory*, chap. 6.

14. "Die NW.-brasilianischen Panpfeifen lassen auf ein bestimmtes System der Abstimmung schließen: man nimmt ein Rohr so, daß sein erster Überblaston (Duodez) mit dem Grundton der Modellpfeife übereinstimmt: so fährt man fort, die neu gewonnenen Töne in andere Oktavlagen bringend, wo nötig, eventuell sie in Oktaven verdoppelnd. Der Überblaston is nicht die reine, sondern aus physikalischen Gründen eine etwas vertiefte Quinte (Duodez) des Grundtones. Der Grad der Vertiefung ist mit der Rohrweite variable, also von zufälligen (botanischen) Faktoren abhängig. Diese Abhängigkeit kann indes, da sie auch praktisch gering ist, vernachlässigt werden. Als theoretisches System ergibt sich dann ein absteigender Zirkel von zu kleinen Quinten, der Blasquintenzirkel. . . . Führt man den Zirkel mit Quinten von 678 Cents (= Hundertstel des temperierten Halbtons, reine Quinte = 702 Cents) durch, so gelangt man nach 23 Schritten wieder zum Anfangston: 678 x 23 = 15.594; 1200 x 13 = 15.600 = 13 Oktaven; Differenz = 6 Cents = ¼ pythagor. Komma, also unmerklich)." Hornbostel, quoted Schmidt, "La généalogie des instruments de musique et les cycles de civilisation," 569–70. Hornbostel's description can be found in "Musikalische Tonsysteme."

15. For a longer explanation, see Kunst, *Music in Java*, 25, and "Around von Hornbostel's Theory of the Cycle of Blown Fifths."

16. Thus it is not surprising that Hornbostel asks Meinulf Küsters (see chap. 13, p. 218, 220), a Benedictine missionary and anthropologist active in Tanganyika, whether he has found any panpipes among the tribes he recorded for Hornbostel.

17. "Da dieser uns zu früh entrissene Forscher [Hornbostel] mir verbunden war und ich ihn in mancher Hinsicht bewunderte, fiel es mir schwer, an diesem seinem Liebling, der Blasquinten Theorie, zu zweifeln. Und doch: die Verworrenheit seiner Darlegung, in der Tatbestand und Erklärungsversuch nicht klar geschieden sind, . . . dies alles musste mir Zweifel eingeben. Ich regte daher einen Mitarbeiter unseres Seminars, Dr. M. Bukofzer, zur Nachprüfung der akkustischen Behauptung an, von der die Theorie aussgeht: dass die Quinte, welche man beim Überblasen auf gedeckten Rohren (nach Abzug der

Oktave) erhält, verkleinert ist und sich mit ungefähr 678 Cents (statt 702) bemisst. Die Nachprüfung, die im Physikalischen Institut der Universität Basel durchgeführt wurde, ergab ein negatives Resultat: die 'Streuung', das heisst die Mannigfaltigkeit der akustischen Resultate sei so gross, dass von einer konstanten Vertiefung, und gar von einer Vertiefung um 24 Cents, nicht gesprochen werden könne." Handschin, *Der Toncharakter*, 80.

18. He calls them "absolute Tonhöhen."

19. "Ihre größte Schwäche ist vielmehr ihr hochspekulativer Charakter. Sie hat einer alten Hochkultur unwahrscheinliche Wunderwerke von Feinabstimmung zugemutet, die selbst mit unseren technischen Hilfsmitteln nicht genau erzeugt werden können und die sich nur rechnerisch durchführen lassen." Ibid., 81. See also A. Schneider's review of the theory of the blown fifths in *Musikwissenschaft und Kulturkreislehre*, 112–45, and Kaden, "Hornbostels akustische Kriterien für Kulturzusammenhänge."

20. Bukofzer, "Blasquinte," in *MGG*, ed. Blume.

21. Ibid., 1919–23.

22. Bukofzer, "Präzisionsmessungen an primitive Musikinstrumenten," and "Kann die 'Blasquintentheorie' zur Erklärung exotischer Ton-Systeme beitragen?"

23. "O Sie böser Mann! In das leichtsinnige Paris fahren Sie immerzu und nach dem bürgerlichen wohlanständigen Cambridge kommen Sie nicht! Wir haben sogar hier im Fitzwilliam Museum (wie Sachs neulich sagte—sehen Sie, er hat uns besucht) eine schöne Musikhandschrift. . . . Die Versuche von Ihrem Bukofzer erschüttern mich gar-nicht. Erstens weiß ich nicht wie er's gemacht hat, weiß aber aus Erfahrung, dass wenn man es drauf anlegt, man beim Aufblasen von Rohren eine ungeheure Schwankungsbreite erhalten kann. . . . Wenn man nun sieht, dass [sich] die südostasiatische temperierte 7stufige Leiter und ihre indonesischen Vorläufer, und ebenso die verschiedenen Slendroleitern mit ihren absoluten Tonhöhen *ganz systematisch* aus dem einen System von 23 Tönen ablei-ten lassen (ich habe noch eben eine, wahrscheinlich sehr alte, Leiter gefunden, die das Rätsel einer ganzen Gruppe von indonesischen Leitern—die bisher unerklärlich waren—löst), dann kann man schwer das 23-Tonsystem für 'nicht-existent im Eigensinne' halten, und es kommt einem (mir wenigstens) nicht so wichtig vor, ob für seinen Ursprung die eine oder andre Hypothese angenommen wird." Letter from Hornbostel to Handschin, 16 September 1935. The letter is owned privately; I would like to thank Franz Michael Maier for kindly providing me with a copy.

24. See esp. A. Schneider, *Musikwissenschaft und Kulturkreislehre*, 168–72.

25. Husmann, *Grundlagen der antiken und orientalischen Musikkultur*, 183–84; and Kunst, *Around von Hornbostel's Theory of the Cycle of Blown Fifths*. Ernst Heins writes: "After 1950 Jaap Kunst himself gradually abandoned the theory of blown fifths and its cultural-historical implications, as his students can testify, although he never did so pub-licly." Heins, "On Jaap Kunst's Music in Java," 97.

26. For more recent discussions of musical universals, see Nettl, "An Ethnomusi-cologist Contemplates Universals."

27. Rudolf Stephan, who together with Carl Dahlhaus, Ludwig Finscher, and Joachim Kaiser was a musicology student in the late 1940s in Göttingen, said that Handschin's two books "hit them like a bomb" when they first appeared. Private communication, 20 October 2016.

28. Handschin, *Musikgeschichte im Überblick*, 28.

29. A detailed discussion of Stumpf's research can be found in Simon, *Das Berliner Phonogramm-Archiv, 1900–2000.*

30. Handschin, *Musikgeschichte im Überblick,* 61. Scholars are still discussing the question of whether Greek music was polyphonic. Andrew Barker and Richard Crocker certainly believe it was; Crocker, "No Polyphony before AD 900!"; and Barker, "*Heterophonia* and *Poikilia.*"

31. The topic has most recently been discussed by Kenneth Levy and Leo Treitler. While Levy argues for stable transmission of chant, Treitler believes it was recreated every time. Levy, *Gregorian Chant and the Carolingians;* Treitler, "Homer and Gregory."

32. Lachmann, "Musiksysteme und Musikauffassung," 1.

33. "Letzteres hat, wie ich an anderer Stelle ausführte, Vertreter der modernen 'vergleichenden Musikwissenschaft' zu der grotesken Annahme veranlasst, dass, wie diese Neumen die Melodiebewegung nur ungefähr angaben, so auch die Sänger des heiligen Gregor mehr oder weniger nur das Auf und Ab der Melodie reproduzierten, d.h. kein genaues Tonbewusstsein hatten—während sie im Gegenteil Tonsystem und Tonleitern viel besser präsent haben mussten als jemand, der nach präzisen Tonzeichen singt." Handschin, *Musikgeschichte im Überblick,* 32. Another passage where he directly refers to Lachmann is Handschin, "Aus der alten Musiktheorie," 22.

34. See, for example, the discussion of Marius Schneider in chap. 3.

35. "Was das historische Verhältnis zwischen Heptatonik und Pentatonik betrifft, so glaubt man im allgemeinen—es ist ja so herrlich 'einleuchtend'—, dass die Pentatonik, weil das einfachere, auch das ältere System sei und die Heptatonik sich daraus 'entwickelt' habe. Ich sehe eigentlich nicht, was dafür zeugen würde, und insbesondere sehe ich keinen Grund für die von leichtgläubigen Musikwissenschaftlern aufgestellte Behauptung, die Musik der Babylonier oder Sumerer müsse 5tönig gewesen sein." Handschin, *Der Toncharakter,* 47.

36. Handschin, *Musikgeschichte im Überblick,* 42. He advocates exactly the same position with regard to medieval polyphony and disagrees with Ludwig, who had argued that simple organa must be earlier, while more complicated ones should be later. See my *Medieval Music and the Art of Memory,* chap. 1.

37. Nettl, *Theory and Method in Ethnomusicology;* and Merriam, *The Anthropology of Music;* and Hood, *The Ethnomusicologist.*

CHAPTER SIX

1. I am mainly concerned with his scholarly writings. He also wrote an opera, *Afiwa* (first performed in Keta, Gold Coast, and Lome, Togo, in 1936, and in Freetown, Liberia, in 1937). The first U.S. performance took place at Cottey College, Nevada, Missouri, on 16–17 April 2010, conducted by Dyke Kiel. The opera combines folk elements from Africa with Western music. Thanks to Dyke Kiel for sending me a DVD. See also Beckley, *African and Western Aspects.*

2. The best article on Ballanta is by Klein, "'Proud Possessions of the African'"; see also Nketia, "The Scholarly Study of African Music: A Historical Review"; Wright, "Ballanta (Taylor)"; Wright, "*Shine like de Mornin' Star*"; and Klein, "Ballanta, Nicholas George Julius"; Klein, Nketia and Wright were not able to look at the substantial file on Ballanta at the Guggenheim Foundation.

3. I am grateful to Dyke Kiel and the Logie Wright Foundation in Freetown, Sierra Leone, for providing me with the copy of Ballanta's manuscript "The Aesthetics of African Music."

4. The review is at the Guggenheim Foundation in the Ballanta Folder. I would like to than André Bernard for allowing me to see all of the Ballanta materials.

5. In his Guggenheim application he lists Liberia as his birthplace; however, in the Wikipedia article by Betty and Dyke Kiel his birthplace is listed as Kissy, Sierra Leone.

6. Ballanta, "An African Scale."

7. He uses the hyphenated name Ballanta-Taylor in his first publications.

8. Peabody supported Ballanta and his mother for many years. The amount for Ballanta is not specified, but he sent $150 per year for the mother. Letter from Peabody to Moe, 10 March 1927, Ballanta Folder, GF. He exchanged many letters with Peabody, as documented in Ware, *George Foster Peabody*. See also Klein, "'Proud Possessions of the African,'" 48.

9. Ballanta, *Saint Helena Spirituals*.

10. He was also a supporter of women's suffrage.

11. He established the Peabody Collection at Hampton University, a collection of rare African American historical materials. Zoka, *Civil Rights and Politics at Hampton Institute*, 16.

12. Damrosch's letter is short but strong. He mentions that Ballanta studied with the composer Percy Goetschius.

13. I was not able to find out anything about him.

14. All of these letters are in the Ballanta Folder at the Guggenheim Foundation.

15. See esp. Hollinger, *Protestants Abroad*: "In 1900 or 1920 a young man or woman thinking of becoming a missionary was contemplating one of the most honorable and widely admired of callings" (3).

16. As cited in Klein, "'Proud Possessions of the African,'" 49n92.

17. Then there comes a somewhat surprising statement, namely that he has observed that the folk songs of Hungary and Poland are similar to those of Africa. To my knowledge he never wrote more about this.

18. Klein, "'Proud Possessions of the African,'" 49–56.

19. Ibid., 50.

20. Letter from Ballanta to Hornbostel, 8 September 1930, Berlin Phonogramm-Archiv.

21. Letter from Hornbostel to Ballanta, 6 October 1930, Berlin Phonogramm-Archiv.

22. Letter from Ballanta to Hornbostel, 29 April 1931, Akte Hornbostel, Berlin Phonogramm-Archiv. Klein gives a list of the lost recordings in "'Proud Possessions of the African,'" 52n102.

23. Berlin Phonogramm-Archiv, 8 October 1931.

24. Ballanta Folder, GF.

25. Ibid.

26. The Phelps-Stokes Fund was established in the United States in 1911 to support African organizations. In the 1920s they embarked on an ambitious program to assess and improve schooling in Africa.

27. Jones was asked by the British and American Missionary Societies, in cooperation with the Colonial Office, to oversee two educational commissions in Africa. He

published reports on West, South, and Equatorial Africa, and later also on East Africa. *The Times* [London], 17 January 1950.

28. The first scholar was Charles Loram, from the University of Witwaterstrand, Johannesburg; the second was Rudyard Boulton, from the University of Chicago, an ornithologist previously at Carnegie Mellon who specialized in Africa and became a spy for the Central Intelligence Agency. I would like to thank Chris Reynolds for this information. See Helms and Hood, *A Look Over My Shoulder*, chap. 6. Boulton's first wife was Laura C. Boulton, an ethnomusicologist, who accompanied him on his expeditions to Africa and made recordings of African music. Laura Boulton (also spelled Bolton) was in regular touch with Herzog. For a detailed discussion of Laura Bo(u)lton, see Geyer, "From the Arctic North to the Desert Southwest."

29. Letter from Thomas Jesse Jones to Peabody, 2 November 1934, Ballanta Folder, GF. In addition, Peabody writes to Moe on 27 October 1934: "My daughter, Mrs. Waite, went to London four years ago where I had arranged to have him come to discuss some of the questions respecting African music but he seemed strangely urgent in his not staying as long as Dr. Thomas Jesse Jones and she both thought he might look for some opportunity to go further into some of the questions, and since then his fewer and briefer letters have been to me disappointing, I am sorry to say." Clearly, Ballanta did not want to meet Jones.

30. Ballanta Folder, GF. It seems never to have occurred to Hornbostel that the recordings may have been lost.

31. Alvin Johnson served for years as treasurer of the American Musicological Society.

32. Both reviews are in the Ballanta Folder, GF.

33. Wright, *"Shine like de Mornin' Star,"* 17.

34. Merriam, "From the Editor."

35. Ibid.

36. Roberts, "The Awkward Squad," 809.

37. George Herzog (1901–1983) received his PhD under both Boas and Ruth Benedict in 1931, won two Guggenheim Fellowships (1935 and 1947), and participated in a University of Chicago anthropological expedition to Liberia (1930–31). Most of his publications are on Native American music, but he also published on West African music. Skoog, "The Life of George Herzog."

38. Even though he has numerous examples from music by specific tribes, he talks about African music in general rather than concentrating on areas. See above.

39. Ballanta, "An African Scale," 6; my italics.

40. Letter from Ballanta to Herzog, 8 September 1930, Akte Hornbostel, Berlin Phonogramm-Archiv.

41. Ballanta, "Music of the African Races," 752.

42. Ibid. See also Klein "'Proud Possessions of the African,'" 58–59.

43. Ballanta, "Gathering Folk Tunes," 3.

44. Jones, "African Drumming," 1–16.

45. Ballanta, "Music of the African Races," 753. All of this is also repeated in chap. 2 of his book manuscript. See also Klein, "'Proud Possessions of the African,'" 60, who was the first to observe that Ballanta uses the term "cross rhythm." Herzog clearly did not try to understand what Ballanta was writing: he simply criticized him for writing that duple time is used in Africa, without going into any detail.

46. Ballanta, "Gathering Folk Tunes," 3, 11, and "Music of the African Races," 752.

47. Ballanta, "Gathering Folk Tunes," 11.

48. Similarly, Joseph Busse told me that a German missionary in Buhaya said, "Go to the swamps," at the end of the service instead of "Go in peace"—for thirty years. Apparently not a single member of the congregation ever laughed about this mistake. However, Kofi Agawu, in a highly original article, casts some doubt on the common interpretation of speech tone and melodies ("Tone and Tune"). For a comprehensive view of the problem, see also Klein, "Lied und musikalische Lyrik in Afrika," 288–89.

49. Herzog accused Ballanta of not realizing that intervals in "primitive" music often do not coincide with the tones of the tempered system (Report 1). Herzog must not have understood Ballanta fully. Ballanta wrote in a 1928 report to the Guggenheim Foundation: "It is thus seen that there is no settled number of sounds within an octave in African instruments. The reason for this is that every musician makes his own instrument according to his own conception, only fixing those tones which he considers necessary; but it should be added that all instruments of the same kind follow strictly the same tuning" (4). Ballanta is also adamant that the European tuning system will not work for Africans (5).

50. For a full analysis of Ballanta's tonal system, see Klein, "'Proud Possessions of the African,'" 61–66.

51. Ballanta, "Music of the African Races," 752.

52. See esp. Kubik, "Sozialisierungsprozeß und Gesänge der Initianden," 352–60. But see also Arom and Voisin, "Theory and Technology in African Music," 258.

53. Letter from Peabody to Moe, 13 November 1928. GF, Folder Ballanta. Ballanta reports that the instrument met with a positive reception from the local population. Klein also noted that Ballanta wrote to Steinway about a seventeen-tone piano. Klein, "'Proud Possessions of the African,'" 55.

54. Ballanta, "Music of the African Races," 752. See also Klein's detailed explanation of the tonal system in "'Proud Possessions of the African,'" 64–65.

55. Ballanta, "Music of the African Races," 753.

56. See also Klein, "'Proud Possessions of the African,'" 64–65.

57. Report by George Herzog, 15 November 1936, Ballanta Folder, GF.

58. Report from 12 February 1939, p. 3, Ballanta Folder, GF. Herzog is, of course, correct in criticizing Ballanta for calling "the African not culturally developed" and writing that "the Negro in his native habitat [is] 'a carefree individual.'" Still, this was a common prejudice at the time.

59. Similarly, his interactions with the Liberian Charles Blooah, who was in a doctoral program at the University of Chicago and went with him on a field trip to Africa, were problematic, to say the least.

60. Titon, *The Oxford Handbook of Applied Ethnomusicology*, 15–16. According to Nettl, the symptoms manifested themselves by 1940 at the latest, but it seems likely that his similarly devastating reviews of Helen Roberts might have also been the result of his mental problems. Nettl, *Encounters in Ethnomusicology*, 90–92.

61. For an excellent discussion of various positions of African rhythm, see Agawu, *Representing African Music*, 55–70.

1. Letter from Konrad Ameln to Heinrich Schumann, 23 June 1979, no. 39.06, AJ. Hilmar Höckner (1891–1968) was a member of *Jugendmusikbewegung* who studied with Gurlitt from 1921 to 1923.

2. Besseler, "Zum Tode Wilibald Gurlitts," 49.

3. Ibid., 48.

4. "Das Freiburger musikwissenschaftliche Seminar, in seiner Pflege älterer Musik ausgehend von der Kammermusik das 17. und 18. Jahrhunderts, die es z.T. auf alten originalen Instrumenten darbieten kann, dem Repertoire seiner 'Praetorius-Orgel,' der Vokalmusik der Barock- und Renaissance-Zeit und der niederländischen Motette und Chansons des 15. Jahrhunderts, fand bald den Weg immer weiter in das Mittelalter zurück, zur italienischen Trecento-Kunst, zum mittelalterlichen instrumentalen Stantipes, zur altfranzösischen Motette, zu Leonin und Perotin und zum Gregorianischen Choral." Ludwig, "Musik des Mittelalters in der Badischen Kunsthalle Karlsruhe," 447.

5. Besseler, "Musik des Mittelalters in der Hamburger Kunsthalle," See also Leech-Wilkinson, *The Modern Invention of Medieval Music*, 49–52.

6. Ludwig, "Musik des Mittelalters in der Badischen Kunsthalle Karlsruhe," 447–57.

7. See also my *Medieval Music and the Art of Memory*, chap. 1.

8. For a more detailed biography of Ludwig, see my *Medieval Music and the Art of Memory*, chap. 1. For a study of Jacobsthal's life and his contributions to scholarship, see Sühring, *Gustav Jacobsthal*.

9. See my *Medieval Music and the Art of Memory*, 15–21.

10. Rudolf Stephan, private communication, October 2015. See also Günther, "Friedrich Ludwig in Göttingen," 169. who writes that Besseler was dissatisfied with his studies with Gurlitt and therefore came to Göttingen.

11. All of those mentioned, aside from Husmann and Anglès, became leaders of the *Singbewegung*. Husmann was not only an important medievalist but also a student of Hornbostel's who published extensively in comparative musicology.

12. See my *Medieval Music and the Art of Memory*, 12.

13. Machaut, *Musikalische Werke*.

14. In *Collected Works of Guillaume de Machaut*, vol. 4.

15. Ludwig, "Die geistliche nichtliturgische/weltliche einstimmige und die mehrstimmige Musik," 1930 edition.

16. Review of Wolf, "Geschichte der Mensuralnotation," 620.

17. For a lively account of the rediscovery of the Middle Ages in the twentieth century, see Cantor, *Inventing the Middle Ages*.

18. There is a vast body of literature on this topic. Most of the controversy is summarized in Wolf, *Stupor Mundi*. See also Lerner, "Ernst Kantorowicz and Theodor E. Mommsen," 189, and Lerner's recent biography, *Ernst Kantorowicz: A Life*.

19. Ludwig, "Perotinus Magnus," 369.

20. "Singbewegung war, als wir uns zeitweise tagtäglich um den Tisch setzten, um irgendetwas miteinander zu singen, etwa Josquins damals noch in keiner praktischen Neuausgabe vorliegende 'Missa pange lingua' (wie es unter Anleitung von Heinrich Besseler um 1925 in Göttingen geschah)." Blankenburg, "Was war die Singbewegung?" 258.

21. "Das Ganze zeigt ein höchst anziehendes Bild echt mittelalterlichen Gemein-schaftssinnes, eines unermüdlichen gemeinsamen Arbeitens im Dienst des heiligen Werkes, eines liebevollen Weiterschafftens an der gemeinsamen Aufgabe ohne radikalen Bruch mit dem Alten trotz dem Ausgehen von immer neuen künstlerischen Vorrausset-zungen . . . , obwohl mindestens Leonins und Perotins Künstlerindividualitäten deut-lich zu unterscheiden sind, das Bild eines harmonischen Zusammenfließens." Ludwig, "Musik des Mittelalters in der Badischen Kunsthalle Karlsruhe," 438.

22. Hildebrand's son, Cornelius (1932–2014), was recently discovered to have owned a major collection of "degenerate art" that his father had amassed during the Nazi years. Cornelius gave the collection to the Bern Museum, where it is currently being evaluated.

23. The instrument was destroyed in World War II but reconstructed after the war. See Schwandt and Gümpel, "Gurlitt, Wilibald."

24. Both Höckner and Pfannenstiel were members of the *Jugendmusikbewegung*.

25. "Und ich schrieb an meinem ersten Buch, dessen Thema mir ebenfalls Gurlitt gegeben hatte (erst sollte ich über die Musik der Naturvölker eine große zusammenfas-sende Arbeit schreiben). Regelmässig trafen wir uns in den Seminarübungen und im besonderen im Collegium musicum an zwei Abenden. (Coll. mus. Vocale et instrumen-tale). Da durfte niemand fehlen. Wir sangen alte Chormusik aus alten Stimmbüchern mit den alten Schlüsseln. Viele Niederländer Josquin, Lasso. Auch Motetten aus dem 13. Jahrhundert." Höckner to Pfannenstiel, 18 June 1967, Akte 39.168, AJ.

26. See my "Wann wurde das Notre-Dame-Repertoire kanonisch," 257–61.

27. See esp. Leech-Wilkinson, *The Modern Invention of Medieval Music*, 56ff., for an excellent discussion. Graetzer also has a good discussion of the issue in "Bearbeitung der Bearbei . . . Zu Rudolf Fickers editorischen Bemühungen."

28. Leech-Wilkinson, *The Modern Invention of Medieval Music*, 1.

29. Orff, *Lehrjahre bei den alten Meistern*, 7, 141f.; and Einstein, "Der musikhisto-rische Kongress in Wien," 498.

30. Ficker, *Musik der Gotik: Perotinus*, 1.

31. Jochum recorded Orff's *Carmina burana* again in 1952 with the Bavarian Radio Symphony Orchestra, now available on Naxos. He also recorded von Ficker's "Sederunt" with the orchestra in 1957.

32. For an excellent biography, see Schipperges, *Die Akte Heinrich Besseler*.

33. Wilibald Gurlitt, "Dissertationsgutachten," 29 May 1923, in Schipperges, *Die Akte Heinrich Besseler*, 387. See also Besseler, "Umgangsmusik und Darbietungsmusik im 16. Jahrhundert"; Hinton, "Alte Musik als Hebamme einer neuen Musikästhetik der zwanziger Jahre"; and Hinton, *The Idea of Gebrauchsmusik*.

34. See also Berger's discussion in *A Theory of Art*, 159–202.

35. See also Hinton, "Alte Musik als Hebamme einer neuen Musikästhetik der zwan-ziger Jahre," 328.

36. See also Schipperges, *Die Akte Heinrich Besseler*, 32.

37. See also ibid., 43–35.

38. "Seine Betrachtung geht von der Gebundenheit des mittelalterlichen Daseins aus. Alles Leben, Schaffen, Empfangen geschieht in der Gemeinschaft, die sich dem Einzelnen darbietet als abgestuftes Reich von Körperschaften und Ständen, vom umfassendsten Kreis der Kirche angefangen. Die auf Überlieferung und Autorität gegründete, letzlich

stets auf die religiose Mitte bezogene Umwelt umfaßt alle Elemente als Glieder *eines* Organismus; damit ist eine selbstherrliche Kunst, die dem Leben von sich aus Sinn zu geben beansprucht, im Mittelalter unmöglich." Besseler, "Musik des Mittelalters in der Hamburger Kunsthalle," 43.

39. "Sie sind nicht zum Zuhören, sondern zum Singen oder inneren Mitmachen bestimmt. Das heißt: sie wollen nicht als einheitliches Klanggebilde von einem Zuhörer hingenommen werden, sondern ihr musikalischer Sinn erfüllt sich in der lebendigen Beziehung zwischen den Ausführenden." Ibid., 46.

40. Similarly, the *Blätter für die Kunst*, where poetry from the Stefan George circle was published, in particular volumes 9–12 (between 1910 and 1919), were not attributed to any specific poets because they were thought to be a product of the whole circle. And yet, everyone knew who the authors were.

41. See esp. Stephan, "Die Musik der Zwanzigerjahre," 10. Leech-Wilkinson also has a penetrating summary of Besseler's thoughts in *The Modern Invention of Medieval Music*, 167–79.

42. Schipperges shows that the entire music department in Heidelberg was involved in the preparation of the volume, in particular Walther Lipphardt and Manfred Bukofzer (sequences and fauxboudon), as well as, among others, Wolfgang Stephan, Hans Eppstein, Edward Lowinsky, Edith Kiwi, and Fritz Dietrich. See Schipperges, *Die Akte Heinrich Besseler*, 72–76.

43. Ibid., 75–76.

44. Ibid., 78–82.

45. For a full list, see ibid., 306–64.

46. Bukofzer, Friedrich, and Lipphardt were involved with the *Jugendmusik-* and *Singbewegung*.

47. Schipperges, *Die Akte Heinrich Besseler*, 307, 306–64.

48. Ibid., 246–27.

49. See Brown, "Sachs, Curt."

50. "Man müßte hier das Fundament der ganzen abendländische Musik schildern, Antike und Orient ebenso wie das nordische Altertum und die europäische Völkerkunde (nicht die exotische). . . . Legt man den Ersatzband 'Musik der Antike' in dieser Form an, so ergibt sich auch eine bessere Verbindung mit meiner Mittelalter-Darstellung. Es fragt sich überhaupt, ob nicht die ganze 'christliche Spätantike' (S. 24–64 meines Bandes) besser in den neuen Einleitungsteil verwiesen und dadurch Platz für die Behandlung des 16. Jahrhundert gewonnen wird, das in meiner Darstellung fühlbar zu kurz gekommen ist." Quoted in Schipperges, *Die Akte Heinrich Besseler*, 247.

51. Ibid., 247.

52. See Bleibinger, *Marius Schneider und der Simbolismo*, 334; and Schipperges, *Die Akte Heinrich Besseler*, 187–88.

53. Schipperges, *Die Akte Heinrich Besseler*, 395–98. Huber's contribution was called the "best of the week." Schneider was already under heavy attack by the Nazis. He writes about the unfairness of academic evaluations concerning Schneider (397) and does not shy away from criticizing other colleagues with sharp words.

54. Ibid., 266–67.

55. For a complete list, see ibid., 433–34.

CHAPTER EIGHT

1. See Laqueur, *Die deutsche Jugendbewegung*; and Kindt, *Dokumentation der Jugendbewegung*.

2. "Steglitz wurde der Mutterboden einer Jugendbewegung . . .; die sich das Ideal des fahrenden Schüler aus dem Mittelalter holte, um daran in der neuen Zeit gesund und selbstherrlich zu werden, die sich dann auf einmal ziemlich plötzlich erhob, als die Sterne günstig standen, und in romantischer Begeisterung in wenigen Jahren sich über ganz Deutschland ergoß, sodaß zu Tausenden und Abertausenden die vom Alter gekränkte Jugend durch die Wälder brauste." Blüher, *Wandervogel*, 50.

3. Donat, "Auf der Flucht erschossen."

4. The German magazine *Der Spiegel* has a video of the meeting online at https://www.youtube.com/watch?v=onjAkYFFHdQ; it includes the numerous circle dances that were to become so important for future meetings of the *Jugendmusik-* and *Singbewegung* in that singers usually assembled in circles.

5. Künkele, "Burg als Symbol." The file is in AJ, entitled "Aufsätze zu inhaltlichen Zielsetzungen der Ludwigsteiner [1920–32]," 1.

6. Ulrich van der Heyden told me a particularly moving story. Since he is a historian of Africa, he was asked a number of years ago by the director of the Berlin Phonogramm-Archiv if he could identify any of the people who made early recordings for Hornbostel. He was able to give them a lot of information on Paasche. A little later he received a phone call from an eighty-year old woman who told him that thanks to these recordings (at the beginning of each of which Paasche always described what he is recording), she was able to hear her father's voice for the first time. Private communication, 21–22 October 2016, Sondershausen, Thüringen.

7. *Die Forschungsreise des Afrikaners Lukanga Mukara*, Letter 2, 2.

8. Ibid., Letter 2, 28–29.

9. Ibid., Letter 9, 99.

10. Letter from Paul Tillich to Thomas Mann, 23 May 1943, in Tillich, *Gesammelte Werke*, 26.

11. Funck, "Alte Musik und Jugendmusikbewegung," 64–65.

12. The best book on the *Jugendmusikbewegung* is Kolland, *Die Jugendmusikbewegung*; see also Antholz, "Jugendmusikbewegung"; and Hodek, *Musikalisch-pädagogische Bewegung*.

13. Weimar Germany had an outstanding music education system instituted by Leo Kestenberg, then in charge of the Zentralinstitut für Erziehung und Unterricht. He was responsible for hiring Jöde and Reichenbach.

14. Prieberg, *Musik im NS Staat*, 244. See also Reinfandt, "Fritz Jödes Schaffen zwischen Idee und Wirklichkeit," 285–88.

15. Reinfandt, "Fritz Jödes Schaffen zwischen Idee und Wirklichkeit," 287. See also his obituary below (p. 108) for his friend Reichenbach on the Nazi period.

16. See esp. Jonas-Corrieri and Scholz, *Die deutsche Jugendmusikbewegung in Dokumenten ihrer Zeit*, 190–96.

17. Jöde, "Alte Madrigale," in Jonas-Corrieri and Scholz, *Die deutsche Jugendmusikbewegung in Dokumenten ihrer Zeit*, 329.

18. For a full list, see Reinfandt, "Jöde, Fritz."

19. A typical program would include two Heinrich Isaac songs, one by Paul Hofhaimer, then a Russian song, followed by an Ukrainian one, and so on. One frequently finds annotations by him in his papers, such as "useful as a final song in singing evenings."

20. I would especially like to thank his son, also called Herman Reichenbach, for information on his father and the family. This account is based on our numerous phone conversations and e-mail exchanges. I am also grateful to the archivist of the UdK, Dietmar Schenk.

21. Reichenbach came from a well-educated family: one of his brothers was the distinguished philosopher of science Hans Reichenbach (1891–1953), a close friend of Albert Einstein and Adorno (he taught at UCLA after his emigration); the other was Bernhard Reichenbach (1888–1975), a prominent journalist, who was the London correspondent for Süddeutscher Rundfunk after World War II. All three brothers were part of the *Jugendbewegung* and to varying degrees communists or socialists in the Weimar years. Their father was of Jewish heritage, while their mother was Lutheran. All three had to leave after 1933.

22. The dissertation exists in manuscript form at the University of Freiburg.

23. Ekkehart Pfannenstiel writes: "Thanks to Gurlitt, Höckner and Reichenbach got to know early music (motets from the thirteenth century, Josquin, Lassus, Schein, Rosenmüller, Händel, etc." N.d., File Gurlitt, AJ. Höckner refers to Hilmar Höckner, another member of the movement. I also found a postcard, dated 11 June 1921, to his friend Willi Siegele (father of the musicologist Ulrich Siegele) in which he announces that he will be visiting Stuttgart, having spent some time with the monks in Kloster Beuron to study Gregorian chant. File Reichenbach, AJ.

24. Jonas-Corrieri and Scholz, *Die deutsche Jugendmusikbewegung in Dokumenten ihrer Zeit*, 1019; and Potter, "German Musicology," 101.

25. From 1921 on he was married to Leni (Helene) Chai, a woman of great wealth whose father was the Chinese owner of a shipping company; her mother was German. In Prague, Leni, a close friend of the journalist Hermann Budzislawski, bought first one-third, then one-half of the political and cultural journal *Die Weltbühne*, made famous by the contributions of Kurt Tucholsky, Carl von Ossietzky, Else Lasker-Schüler, Erich Kästner, Carl Zuckmayr, and many others.

26. The ban on interracial marriages was not ended until 1967, when the case of Richard and Mildred Loving, who sued to have their marriage recognized in their home state of Virginia, went all the way to the Supreme Court. The Court's decision invalidated all laws prohibiting interracial marriage. Thanks to Kathryn Olmstead for information on this matter. Reichenbach's wife stayed in New York, and eventually they divorced. He remarried, this time to a woman from Hamburg with whom he had two sons.

27. Jöde, Nachruf auf Herman Reichenbach, File Reichenbach, 216, in AJ.

28. This was, for example, the case with Hans Reichenbach, who taught at UCLA.

29. "You were not a great administrator and not a fast worker, as one says; but what you started was deeply thought through and was for all of us a great help" (Du warst kein großer Organisator und warst kein schneller Arbeiter, wie man so sagt; aber was von Dir ausging, kam aus der Tiefe und war für uns alle Lehre und Hilfe). Jöde, Nachruf, File Reichenbach, 215.

30. Jöde, Nachruf, File Reichenbach, 26, AJ.

31. There is correspondence on the issue between Pfannenstiel and Friedrich Blume, who advised against publication because it was out of date. File Reichenbach, AJ.

32. Wilhelm Ehmann made the area around Bielefeld (including Bethel) a center of the *Singbewegung*; he grew up in Bethel, where many of our missionaries come from.

33. Blume, "The Period of the Reformation"; and Blankenburg, "The Music of the Bohemian Brethren."

34. His original name was Julius Janiczek.

35. After his dissertation he became first a schoolteacher, and after Czechoslovakia's independence in 1918 he was given responsibility for folk-music education for all of Czechoslovakia. In 1919 he gave up his teaching position to concentrate fully on his research into folk music and the organization of singing retreats. Hensel became director of the *Jugendmusikschule* in Dortmund in 1925, and in 1930 he moved to Stuttgart, where he was responsible for singing at the *Volkshochschule*. After the annexation of the Sudetenland he divorced his wife, remarried, and moved back to the Sudeten area (Teplice). He received the Eichendorff-Preis from the German University in Prague in 1941. Richter, "Walther Hensel."

36. For an excellent discussion of this matter, see Antholz, "Drittes Reich." After the war Hensel lived in Munich, where a position had been created for him as an "advisor on matters of folk songs." By all accounts he became increasingly bitter and in 1956 died of a heart attack. Numerous obituaries refer to his isolation after his divorce from his first wife. File Walther Hensel, AJ.

37. To quote some characteristic statements: "Medieval music is a light that moves in space" (Die mittelalterliche Musik ist ein Licht, das sich im Raume bewegt); "The folk song is the song of a people in a community: in community with God, in community with nature, in community with one another, and in community with tradition" (Das Volkslied ist das Lied vom Menschen in der Gemeinschaft: in der Gemeinschaft mit Gott, in der Gemeinschaft mit der Natur, in der Gemeinschaft mit seinesgleichen und in der Gemeinschaft mit der Überlieferung); "Our people have to drink from cleanest sources if they want to become musically healthy again; they have to dip into the youth fountain of old German art again, so that the view will become free again to recognize heavenly, everlasting beauty in music. Those old melodies are unsurpassed to this day with regard to strength and inner beauty" (Unser Volk muß, wenn es wieder musikalisch gesunden will, aus den lautersten Quellen trinken; es muß in das Jungbrünnlein altdeutscher Kunst hinabtauchen, auf daß der Blick wieder frei werde, wahrhaft himmlische, unvergängliche Schönheit in der Musik zu erkennen. An Kraft und Innerlichkeit stehen jene alten Weisen bis heute unerreicht da.) Hensel in a sing-along in Winnenden, 1954, File Hensel, AJ.

38. He had academic appointments at the University of Münster (1930–39), at the Teacher Training Academy in Elbing, East Prussia (now Elblag in Poland), and in Dortmund. In 1933 he refused to exclude his socialist students from their final examinations and was promptly fired from his job and even imprisoned for a short time. As a result of Nazi intimidation he completely reversed his politics, joined the SS, and composed National Socialist hymns for male choir with such titles as "Wir wollen ein starkes Reich sein" (We Want to Be a Strong Empire) and "Das Lied vom neuen Reich" (The Song of the New Empire); Prieberg, *Musik im NS Staat*, 140–41. In 1937 he joined the NSDAP. Punishment for his Nazi activities came after the war: he was no longer allowed to teach

at the University of Münster; Thamer, Droste, and Happ, *Die Universität Münster im Nationalsozialismus*, 287. He spent the rest of his life in Lüdenscheid, where he organized music festivals; in addition, he taught hymnology at various church music schools. The title "professor" (which he had doubtlessly longed for his entire life) was granted to him by the state of Nordrhein-Westfalen only in 1980.

39. The term *Quempas* derives from the first words of the Christmas carol "Quem pastores laudaveres." Ameln wrote to Heinrich Schumann that he sold more than three million copies. Letter, 23 June 1979, File Ameln, AJ.

40. On Ameln's musical tastes, his former student Andreas Marti wrote: "He liked almost without exception music from the sixteenth and seventeenth centuries, supplemented by some high-level research papers on the Middle Ages. The later periods were treated more or less in passing, mainly through critical remarks on the decadence manifest in them." Marti, "Konrad Ameln," 38.

41. Private communication, Elisabeth Rietzsch, 22 September 2011. There are numerous letters from Rietzsch to Ameln among Ameln's papers in the Universitätsarchiv Augsburg. I would like to thank Werner Lengger for information on the letters. They are all written after World War II.

42. On Berneuchen, see Stählin, *Berneuchen*.

43. Theodor Stelzer was part of Berneuchen as well as the Kreisau Circle around Helmut James Graf von Moltke who was executed in 1945. For more on Berneuchen, see Hering, "Konservative Ökumene," 75. The Confessing Church was the branch of the Lutheran Church that opposed the Nazis.

44. Möckel, *Umkämpfte Volkskirche*, 207–9; and Schlingensiepen, *Dietrich Bonhoeffer, 1906–1945*, 300, 340.

45. For the best overview, see Antholz, "Jugendmusikbewegung," part 2.d., "Verlagswesen."

46. "Die deutsche Jugendmusikbewegung," *Der Drachentöter* (1931), 190.

47. Kallmeyer, *25 Jahre deutscher Verlagsbuchhändler*, 16.

48. File Herbert Just, AJ.

49. "Die historische Fundierung sehe ich in der mittelalterlichen Lehre von den Kirchentonarten. Deren Bedeutung liegt nicht im lediglich tonartlichen Sinne, sondern darin, daß sie Kategorien für formale Traditionen sind; es sind die melodischen Urgestalten, von denen jedes vorkommende Werk nur eine Variante ist. Ich mußte dies mit einiger Ausführlichkeit dartun, da sich diese Auffassung von den üblichen Darstellungen der Kirchentonarten völlig unterscheidet." Reichenbach, *Formenlehre*, 17.

50. Ibid., 19–27.

51. Ibid., 27–34.

52. "Die Theoretiker der mittelalterlichen Kirchenmusik hätten statt des griechischen auch ein pentatonisches System nehmen können." Ibid., 27.

53. Fleischer, *Neumen-Studien*; Riemann, *Folkloristische Tonalitätsstudien*, esp. 34; and Wagner, "Germanisches und Romanisches."

54. Reichenbach, *Formenlehre*, 27n4.

55. Müller-Blattau, "Die Tonkunst in altgermanischer Zeit."

56. "Die musikethnologischen Forschungen der Gegenwart haben zu dem Ergebnis geführt, daß die pentatonische Skala fast allen Musikkulturen zugrunde liegt,

nicht nur den orientalischen, sondern auch den germanischen. Wir haben in der Pentatonik so etwas wie die Urskala der gesamten Musik vor uns." Reichenbach, *Formenlehre*, 27.

57. Both Chailley, *Formation et transformation du langage musical*, 11–28, and Nettl, *Study of Ethnomusicology*, 42–49, include excellent discussions of "Universals of Music." See also Day-O'Connell, "Pentatonic."

58. See Mbunga, *Church Law and Bantu Music*, 19–20; and Hansen, *Grammar of Gregorian Tonality*. I would like to thank Peter Jeffery for this reference.

59. Kurth, *Grundlagen des linearen Kontrapunktes*. Kurth considers the melodic line as a closed unit and maintains that polyphonic pieces are determined by their linear structures. *Finkensteiner Blätter* and *Die Singgemeinde* regularly included articles on Gregorian chant (especially by Walther Lipphardt).

60. See http://www.zpkm.uni-freiburg.de/2014/2014/, accessed 1 February 2020.

61. See Lütteken, "Wiora, Walter."

62. Huber was not a member of the *Jugendmusikbewegung* but a deeply religious Catholic who joined the resistance group Weisse Rose.

63. Becking, "Der Gegenwartswert mittelalterlicher Musik," is very much in the spirit of the *Jugendmusik-* and *Singbewegung*. He also conducted a collegium musicum at Prague University.

64. Becking, "Der musikalische Bau des montenegrinischen Volksepos."

65. For example, Treitler, "Homer and Gregory."

66. AJ, Letter from Jöde to his wife, Hilde, Fall 1937, 1, AJ.

67. Notes of Jöde, 21 July [no year], AJ.

68. Jonas-Corrieri and Scholz, *Die deutsche Jugendmusikbewegung in Dokumenten ihrer Zeit*, 205.

69. All of these quotations come from the File Hensel, AJ, where his sayings are summarized.

70. We will hear more about it in chap. 10 from the missionary Franz Rietzsch.

71. Home, home, home, roaring waves carry me,
   Home, home, home, the angels lead me,
   Home, home, home, to the blessed beach,
   Heavenly crowds take me home.

Reusch, "Erziehungsaufgabe im tiefsten Sinn des Wortes." Reusch was a committed Nazi; see his *Musik und Musikerziehung*, 2–7, where he praises Prussian military marches and mythical *Volksgemeinschaft*.

72. Note by Ekkehart Pfannenstiel in File Jöde, AJ.

73. Handschin, "Die Musik der deutschen Jugendbewegung," 353–54.

74. "Der polyphone Stil ist der wahre Repräsentant der wirkenden Gemeinschaft; und die ältere Musik als Ganzes vertritt die Bindung zwischen Musik und Lebensstil, welche in unserer Zeit des allzusehr dominierenden Konzertbetriebs verloren gegangen ist." Ibid., 353.

75. "Seit einigen Jahren veranstaltet die Volksmusikschule der Musikantengilde.V. Chrlottenburg einmal im Sommer ein Singtreffen für alle musikfreudigen Jugendlichen Berlins. Der Tag, der in einer großen amphitheatralischen Freilichtbühne im Volkspark Jungfernheide begangen wird, hat nun schon seine traditionelle Bedeutung. . . . Man kann

sich dem Erlebnis nicht entziehen, wenn man dabei ist; wenn die Riesenrunde der 4000 festlich gekleideten Menschen zu leben beginnt, wenn Zurufe, Kritik, Anfeuerung und Scherz hin und her geworfen werden und schließlich alles sich vereinigt zum gemeinsamen Singen. . . . Und eine Gelegenheit ist das Singtreffen. Man sehe sich nur die soziologische Struktur der Teilnehmerschaft an, man vergleiche sie mit dem Publikum eines Orchesterkonzertes, mit den Teilnehmern einer politischen Feier, mit den Besuchern einer modernen Theater-, Film- oder Tanzpremiere . . . Der Jugendbewegungstyp überwiegt. Viele kommen in Gruppen geradewegs von der Sonnabend-Sonntags-Fahrt. Die Banner aller Parteien oder Konfessionen vom Hakenkreuz bis zum Sowjetstern sind vertreten, ohne daß die geringste Störung auftritt. Das ist eine Tatsache, die sich nicht wegdiskutieren läßt. . . . Dazwischen sitzen—durch das mitveranstaltende Charlottenburger Volksbildungsamt gerufen—Männer und Frauen aus allen Ständen, nur der Stand fehlt, der sonst in den Witzblättern als der typische Berliner bezeichnet wird: der intellektuelle Snob." Reichenbach, "Singtreffen der Berliner Jugend."

76. Mehl, "Walther Hensel."

77. Quoted in Conrad, *Richard Gölz*, 37.

78. The invitation said clearly: "Every participant agrees (1) to do without alcohol or tobacco during the week [and] (2) to participate in all work activities and celebrations unless he has been allowed to take leave by the Director." *Die Singgemeinde* (1926): 25.

79. Jonas-Corrieri and Scholz, *Die deutsche Jugendmusikbewegung in Dokumenten ihrer Zeit*, 168.

80. The work in Neukölln is described in "Proletarische Musikarbeit in Neukölln," 798.

81. Bukofzer's papers are in the Elizabeth Hargrove Music Library of the University of California, Berkeley, where one can find programs of his collegium performances.

82. "So wird die Verantwortung zur Gemeinschaft nicht aufgefaßt als ein Befehl zur Unterordnung, sondern als das Bewußtsein, Glied eines Ganzen zu sein, das einem Aufgaben stellt." Reichenbach, "Die Musik der Jugendbewegung," 935.

83. Ibid.

84. "An größeren Orten entstehen Musikschulen, in denen im Sinne der gemeinsamen Musikauffassung der Grund zur Musikpflege gelegt wird . . . Es läßt sich nicht mehr leugnen, daß eine Generation herangewachsen ist, die in kein Konzert geht . . . , die kein Konservatorium absolviert hat. . . . Die aber eine Bach'sche Chorfuge vom Blatt singt, ihre Schein'sche Suite im Kopf trägt und ihr Leben in Musik . . . verankert hat." Ibid.

85. For a discussion of the relationship between *Singbewegung* and Nazi ideology, see Bayreuther, "Die Situation der deutschen Kirchenmusik um 1933."

86. "Aber noch etwas anderes kam dazu, was uns mit geheimnisvoller Macht anzog und mitriß. Es waren die kompakten Kolonnen der Jugend mit ihren wehenden Fahnen, den vorwärtsgerichteten Augen und dem Trommelschlag und Gesang. War das nicht etwas Überwältigendes, diese Gemeinschaft? So war es kein Wunder, daß wir alle, Hans und Sophie und wir anderen, uns in die Hitlerjugend einreihten." Scholl, *Die weisse Rose*, 14. Inge Scholl includes a lively account of their hikes and singing together.

87. The concept of *Gemeinschaft* was sharply criticized in Adorno, *Dissonanzen: Musik in der verwalteten Welt*, 62–101. The quotation appears above on p. 89 at the beginning of part II.

PART THREE

1. Hornbostel, "African Negro Music"; Hornbostel, "Die Probleme der vergleichenden Musikwissenschaft," 97.

2. The Africanists Carl Meinhof and Diedrich Westermann and the British ethnomusicologist Arthur M. Jones were also Protestant theologians or missionaries. Jones, *Evangelisation: Report of the General Missionary Conference in Northern Rhodesia Held,* was summarized in the journal *Books for Africa,* 20, with specific suggestions on how to reform the service—only three years after Hornbostel's paper, and very likely under his influence. Meinhof and Westermann also helped missionaries with their Bible translations.

3. The main points of Hornbostel's article will be discussed in connection with Rietzsch's musical observations (see chap. 10, pp. 145–47).

4. Hornbostel, "African Negro Music," 61–62.

5. In 1907 the missionaries felt that the chorales by Gerhardt were "still too intellectually rich and the people intellectually too poor" (noch zu gedankenreich und die Leute zu gedankenarm) and were not convinced that the local population would fully understand them. See "Paul Gerhardt," *MBBG* (1907), 119; and Kornder, *Die Entwicklung der Kirchenmusik,* 62.

6. See esp. McGuire, *Music and Victorian Philanthropy.* Sankey or Gospel hymns are named for Ira D. Sankey, the musical associate of the late nineteenth-century evangelist Dwight L. Moody. A simple way of spreading the Gospel, they are usually in a major key with simple, repetitive rhythmic patterns; see Eskew, "Gospel Music." On Sankey hymns as a "colonizing force," see Agawu, "Tonality as a Colonizing Force in Africa."

7. For Hornbostel and other early comparative musicologists' attitude on "authenticity" and "universals" after 1933, see Nettl, "Contemplating Ethnomusicology," 178–81.

8. Altena, *Ein Häuflein Christen mitten in der Heidenwelt des dunklen Erdenteils,* 15–16, 26.

9. For an excellent recent study on the impact of American missionaries and their children on American society, see Hollinger, *Missionaries Abroad.* Hollinger shows that liberal Protestant missionaries were advocating anticolonialism early on and are responsible for such institutions as Amnesty International and the Peace Corps.

10. The best, if short, description of the Moravians is von Mücke, " 'Entirety of Scripture.' " In English they are also called "Unity of Brethren." In German they call themselves "Herrnhuter," "Brüdergemeine," or "Brüderunität." See also Mettele, *Weltbürgertum oder Gottesreich.*

11. See esp. Ustorf, "*Wissenschaft,* Africa, and the Cultural Process," 124; and Fiedler, *Christentum und afrikanische Kultur,* 25–27.

CHAPTER NINE

1. Singing and improvisation with chorales in the eighteenth century is discussed in Eyerly, " 'Singing from the Heart,' " and *Moravian Soundscapes;* for a recent article on the importance of Moravian hymns, see Strohm, "Michael Weisse." See also Strohm, "Sacred Songs."

2. For a recent book on Moravians, see Mettele, *Weltbürgertum oder Gottesreich.* The most detailed account of Moravian mission activities until 1930 is Müller and

Schulze, *200 Jahre Brüdermission*; see also Baudert, *Advance Guard*; and Beck, *Brüder in vielen Völkern*. Kornder, *Die Entwicklung der Kirchenmusik*, also has a lot on Moravian music in Tanzania; and Rosenkranz, *Das Lied der Kirche in der Welt*, provides some information on early Moravian missions. While it is true that on the whole Moravian missionaries tried to share the life of the local population in every way, the record is not unspotted. A recent book shows that some Moravians supported slavery; Hüsgen, *Mission und Sklaverei*. And by today's standards it is troubling that Zinzendorf urged the slaves to accept slavery on Earth, but God would free them from everything "slavish." See also Peucker, "Aus allen Nationen." Peucker also shows that in the nineteenth century, even though former slaves were officially considered members of the Moravian Church in Winston-Salem, yet they were buried in racially segregated cemeteries.

3. A particularly lively account of Moravian culture in Suriname has been published by the historical anthropologist Richard Price, who juxtaposes oral testimonies of modern Saramakas with documents written by eighteenth-century German Moravian missionaries and Dutch colonial administrators. See Price, *Alabi's World*.

4. See also the numerous paintings by the Moravian painter Johann Valentin Haidt (1700–1780), in which he brings together many of the baptized "first fruits" from all over the world. It is even possible to identify most of the individuals in the painting. Copies of the various versions are in the Moravian settlements of Zeist, Bethlehem, and Herrnhut.

5. "Eins der Hauptaugenmerke der Heidenboten ist gewesen, die Menschen in ihrer Verfassung, darinnen sie Gott mit dem Systema der Welt verknüpft, ungestört zu erhalten, ja wohl in demselben treuer und gebräuchlicher zu machen." Bechler, "Einzelbekehrung," quoted in Hoekendijk, *Kirche und Volk in der deutschen Missionswissenschaft*, 51.

6. "Nikolaus Ludwig, Graf und Herr von Zinzendorf und Pottendorf, geboren 1700, ging im Jahre 1760 als ein Eroberer aus der Welt, desgleichen es wenige und im verflossenen Jahrhundert keinen wie ihn gegeben." Herder, *Adastrea*, 32–37. Herder was fully aware of the fact that without the ethnographic and linguistic work done by Moravian missionaries, he would not have been able to formulate his main ideas. Nevertheless, he also says clearly that he does not believe that the Inuits in Greenland should obey Western laws, which are foreign to them. *Adrastea*, parts 2 and 5, entitled "Unternehmungen des vergangenen Jahrhunderts zur Beförderung eines geistigen Reiches." Lessing was also full of admiration for the Moravians. "Gedanken über die Herrnhuter," 20.

7. Baudert writes that these hymns often did not have literary value but were supposed instead to speak "from the heart." *The Advance Guard*, 58.

8. One sample: "Lamb, accompany us to all corners of the world, and all places that have not yet been set foot to, and make us witnesses to the masses, otherwise we will suffer from the crowds. Make room through all rivers and waters and also go into the caves of the cannibals. And let us go to them with confidence, the world and also the devil should see this, that no door is locked to your messenger, which cannot be opened by the cross, all gates have to open, as soon as the cities know your name." Schulze, *200 Jahre Brüdermission*, 1:348–49.

9. Diaries of missionaries also made it into the archives, so the Moravian archives are an excellent resource for the study of missionary activity. Of course, there is also another side to the many documents assembled in Herrnhut and Bethlehem since the eighteenth

century. As Mettele has shown, Zinzendorf and the Moravian Church were able to carefully control the information that came out. *Weltbürgertum oder Gottesreich*, 33–40.

10. Beginning in 1747, Zinzendorf kept all Moravian congregations informed through a text produced in multiple manuscripts entitled "Diarium des Gemeinhauses, der Hütten, des Jüngerhauses."

11. Schulze, *200 Jahre Brüdermission*, 349–50.

12. Baudert, *The Advance Guard*, 56.

13. Schulze, *200 Jahre Brüdermission*, 1:350–51.

14. See esp. Peucker, "'In Staub und Asche,'" 128; see also Hoekendijk, *Kirche und Volk in der deutschen Missionswissenschaft*, 52–54.

15. Warneck was also one of the first mission specialists to have joined the fraternity Wingolf (see chap. 8, pp. 103–4).

16. Other important works are his three-volume *Evangelische Missionslehre* and his survey of the history of the Protestant Missions, *Abriss einer Geschichte der protestantischen Missionen*, which was translated into English.

17. Johannes Hoekendijk was the first to describe Warneck as a proponent of what he called "ethno-pathos." Hoekendijk, *Kirche und Volk in der deutschen Missionswissenschaft*, 97–103.

18. Ustorf, "Wissenschaft, Africa, and the Cultural Process," 106.

19. Hoekendijk, *Kirche und Volk in der deutschen Missionswissenschaft*, 103.

20. See also Fiedler, *Christianity and African Culture*, 14–22.

21. See esp. Ustorf, "Religion in the Colonial Twilight," in *Robinson Crusoe Tries Again*, 59–114.

22. Ustorf, "'Survival of the Fittest': German Protestant Missions, Nazism and Neocolonialism, 1933–1845," 93–114.

CHAPTER TEN

1. The Nyakyusa people are called Wanyakyusa, the definite plural form; the indefinite plural is Banyakyusa, and the language is Kinyakyusa. By all accounts, the Moravians had little contact with the colonial administrators. They were there because German East Africa was a German colony, but the archival documents contain almost no mention of interaction between them and the officers. The most exhaustive treatment of the relationship between the Moravians and both German and British colonial adminstrators is Wright, *German Missions in Tanganyika 1891–1941*. Wright, a historian, concentrates particularly on the Moravian and Berlin Mission Societies.

2. On Herrnhut's unwillingness to collaborate with colonial authorities, see Gründer, *Christliche Mission und deutscher Imperialismus*, 218–20.

3. See the letter below (pp. 141–42) by the mission director Samuel Baudert, reprimanding him for talking so openly about his convictions.

4. Bachmann wrote an autobiographical essay that was published after his death with an introduction by E. Förster and Hans-Windekilde Jannasch: Bachmann, *Ich gab so manchen Anstoss*. Jannasch was the son of a Moravian missionary born in Labrador. He was an educator and a member of the *Jugendbewegung* who taught for years at the *Jugendbewegung* boarding school Wickersdorf. It is perhaps no accident that Jannasch

wrote so much on missionaries, as we have seen in part II of this book; Jannasch, *Unter Hottentotten und Eskimos.* The best discussion of Bachmann is Fiedler, *Christentum und afrikanische Kultur.*

5. Bachmann, *Ich gab so manchen Anstoss,* 60–61.

6. Merensky, *Deutsche Arbeit am Njaßa,* 360–68.

7. Bachmann, *Ich gab so manchen Anstoss,* 88. In the eighteenth century Moravians used lotteries to settle on the best marriage partner for their missionaries because they believed that the Holy Spirit would guide them thereby to the right choice; see Eyerly, "Der Wille Gottes," and *Moravian Soundscapes,* chaps. 2 and 3. This custom was abandoned in the late eighteenth century.

8. Bachmann, *Ich gab so manchen Anstoss,* 64–65.

9. The Moravians had special boarding schools for missionary children. This was accepted procedure for virtually all missionaries until 1940; the motto was: missionary activity comes first, family second. The resulting damage to children was horrific, a subject that has only recently caught the attention of historians. By all accounts, Bachmann's children never grew close to their parents even though they were placed with relatives and not in boarding schools; the youngest daughter was only eighteen months old when she was so placed. One of his sons hated Africa so much that he refused to ever set foot there. For a fascinating book on the topic, see Motel, *"Mama, mein Herz geht kaput": Das Schicksal der Herrnhuter Missionskinder.* Bachmann and his wife also suffered horribly from the separation and were not at all sure that this was a correct decision. See Bachmann, *Ich gab so manchen Anstoss,* 155–56; and Petersen, "Darum," 18.

10. Bachmann, *Ich gab so manchen Anstoss,* 165–81; see esp. 180–81 for a moving account of his inability to recover after his release in 1919.

11. The first study of Nyiha was done by another Moravian missionary, Joseph Busse, who consulted with Bachmann; Busse, *Die Sprache der Nyiha in Ostafrika.* Nyiha is a Bantu Niger-Congo language and is closely related to Safwa, but much less so to Nyakyusa.

12. File Traugott Bachmann, UA.

13. "Es ist rührend, mit welchen Eifer die Mbozi-Leute sich der Kunst des Lesens widmen. Bruder Bachmann kann ihnen nicht genug Lesestoff . . . herstellen. Jeder, der schreiben kann, sucht sich eine Abschrift anzufertigen, und wochentags und sonntags sah man in jeder freien Zeit die sonst nur an die Arbeit mit Hacke und Axt gewöhnten Hände sich an den Buchstaben abmühen." JB 1903, 33–34, UA Herrnhut. See also JB 1904, 27.

14. Unitätsarchiv, MD, 15, pp. 157, 167, 325, and 371. It is published under the title *Ilivangeli lya ku Mataji. Xinyiha.*

15. *Testamenti Umupwa wa mwene witu Yesu Cilisiti umuposhi wa nsi;* the first printing was two thousand copies. See also *Inongwa izya mwa Tesitamenti mukali Shiniha* (Stories from the Old and New Testaments), which includes some 118 pictures by Schnorr von Carolsfeld, selected by Bachmann.

16. He also published Nyiha fairy tales: see Bachmann, "Nyiha-Märchen: Gesammelt und übersetzt von Missionar Tr. Bachmann."

17. Letters from Bachmann, Berlin Phonogramm-Archiv. The letters are dated 4 April 1907, 9 June 1907, and 15 June 1907.

18. The Bachmann recordings are digitalized and available on demand from the Berlin Phonogramm-Archiv.

19. Letter from Bachmann, 21 December 1908, Berlin Phonogramm-Archiv.

20. Hornbostel, "African Negro Music," 43; Hornbostel mentions the help of a local speaker who helped Bachmann transcribe the text. For Schneider, see *Geschichte der Mehrstimmigkeit*, vol. 1, nos. 182–200.

21. Traugott Bachmann, *Ich gab so manchen Anstoss*, 138–39.

22. Ibid.

23. Bachmann was a modest man and reluctant to publish his thoughts. See his "Praktische Lösung missionarischer Probleme auf einem jungen Arbeitsfelde, Nyaßagebiet, Deutsch-Ostafrika."

24. Cited from Bachmann's unpublished autobiography; and Fiedler, *Christianity and African Culture*, 56.

25. Bachmann, *Ich gab so manchen Anstoss*, 133–37; see also Fiedler, *Christentum und afrikanische Kultur*, 75.

26. See Rosenkranz, *Das Lied der Kirche in der Welt*, 104–05.

27. The missionary Tietzen made a translation of Bachman's antiphonal song:

"Laßt uns binden an unsere Arbeit! Laßt uns arbeiten für Gott!
Ja, laßt uns an die Arbeit binden!
Laßt uns Kraft anwenden, an ihn zu glauben! Laßt uns arbeiten für Gott im Himmel!
Ja, laßt uns Kraft anwenden."

The first line of each strophe is used as a refrain. Rosenkranz, *Das Lied der Kirche in der Welt*, 106.

28. Rosenkranz, *Das Lied der Kirche in der Welt*, 105.

29. Kornder, *Die Entwicklung der Kirchenmusik*, 156.

30. Adolf Schulze, *200 Jahre Brüdermission*, 2:483 n. 9; I think the numbers mentioned by Rosenkranz cannot be correct: forty Nyiha songs; Rosenkranz, *Das Lied der Kirche in der Welt*, 105.

31. "Bei den Festlichkeiten der Nyika wird niemals nur gesungen oder nur getanzt. Wenn bei der Arbeit oder auf Reisen die Leute viel singen, dann vertritt die Bewegung der Arme und Beine die des Tanzes. Ohne Bewegung des Körpers singt der Nyika nicht. Unser Kirchen- und Schulgesang ist dem Nyika fremd. Als wir im Jahre 1905 Missionsdirektor Hennig zur Visitation einholten, sangen die Leute ein Lied, das ich nach einer einheimischen Melodie gemacht hatte. Der Text war sicher passend: 'Du von Europa Gekommener,' aber die Art und Weise, wie sich die Leute nach meinem Willen bewegen sollten, paßte nicht zu der Eingeborenen. Sie sollten im Schritt gehen! Wie wenig war mir der Geist des afrikanischen Rhythmus aufgegangen! Wort und Melodie afrikanisch und die Haltung europäisch. Wie so ganz anders war dann unsere Einholung am 30. Juni 1913. Das Tanzen war die ersten Jahre auch in Mbozi verboten, weil von Europa aus gesehen tanzen 'Sünde' ist. Als mir klar wurde, daß die Nyika harmlose Arten von Tänzen und zu ihnen gehörende Lieder hatten, wurden diese erlaubt. Wenn ich von einer Reise nach Hause kam, wurde ich mit Trommeln, Gesang und Reigentanz eingeholt. Nachdem man

mich bis zu unserem Hause begleitet, und ich mich gesetzt hatte, schwieg die Trommel und der Gesang, und man hörte auf zu tanzen. Alle knieten nieder, neigten sich mit dem Oberkörper nach der Seite, klatschten mit den Händen und riefen, 'Vater, wir grüßen dich!' " Bachmann, *Ich gab so manchen Anstoss*, 128–29. I believe that the fact that Bachmann talks about "permitting" songs does not mean that he as a European knows better; rather, as their pastor he feels responsible for their spiritual welfare and encourages or discourages certain behavior.

32. Bachmann, "Praktische Lösungen," 9–10.

33. This must be what Bachmann considered "thoroughly indecent dances." What the missionaries called "female circumcision" is now commonly referred to as "female genital mutilation," which can be anything from removal of the clitoris (making sexual satisfaction for the female impossible) to removal of the labia majora and/or the labia minora, and/or infibulation.

34. Rosenkranz, *Das Lied der Kirche in der Welt*, 105.

35. Bachmann, "Praktische Lösungen," 13.

36. "Du weißt, daß ich Dir volles Vertrauen schenke und daß ich auch Verständnis für die Gedankengänge habe in denen Du Dich jetzt sehr stark beschäftigst und die Dich bewegen. Freiheit vom Gesetz und anderes. Ich verstehe auch die Ursachen, die immer wieder die Gedanken in Dir aufregen . . . Aber ich möchte Dir doch ernstlich zu bedenken geben, ob Du da nicht manchmal das Kind mit dem Bade ausschüttest." Letter from Samuel Baudert to Bachmann, 16 September 1926, Personalakte Bachmann, UA.

37. Letter from Rietzsch to Baudert, 1 November 1934, Personalakte Franz Ferdinand Rietzsch, UA.

38. Kornder, *Die Entwicklung der Kirchenmusik*, 61.

39. See esp. McGuire, *Music and Victorian Philanthropy*, chap. 3, where he describes the use of the tonic *sol-fa* in Madagascar; for another study on Madagascar, see Schmidhofer, "Zur Inkulturation liturgischer Musik in Madagaskar im 19. Jahrhundert"; for South Africa, see Olwage, "Scriptions of the Choral: The Historiography of Black South African Choralism" and "Singing in the Victorian World: Tonic Sol-fa and Discourses of Religion, Science, and Empire in the Cape Colony."

40. See also my "Tonic Sol-fa in Africa."

41. "Inimbo sya kiponga kya kilisiti basitendekisye na baputi." For the Sankey songs, see *London Sacred Songs and Solos*.

42. Missionsdirektion, Personalakte Rietzsch, UA.

43. For Berneuchen, see chap. 8, p. 111.

44. Antholz, "Jugendmusikbewegung."

45. He mentions in his letter to Baudert (written between 10 August 1932 and 2 September 1932), p. 12, that he subscribed to *Musik und Kirche*. Rietzsch's own publication is entitled "Kirchenmusikalische Fragen in der Missionsarbeit."

46. In his letter to his sister Marianne ("Schnicke"), written between 11 and 19 May 1932, he includes a full list of the contents of his library. The chant books are Peter Wagner, *Elemente des gregorianischen Gesangs*; Dominicus Johner, *Cantus ecclesiastici*; Hermann Halbig, *Kleine gregorianische Formenlehre*; Peter Piel, Paul Manderscheid, *Har-*

monielehre (mit Kirchentönen); and P. Basilius Ebel, *Das älteste alemannische Hymnar mit Noten: Kodex 386.*

47. Letter, 10 September 1931, Personalakte Rietzsch, UA.

48. Bruno Nettl informed me that Heinitz told him in the late 1950s that he was "nicht Musik*ethnologe*, sondern Musik*biologe.*"

49. See Petersen, "Musikwissenschaften in Hamburg 1933 bis 1945." See also Gerhard, "Musikwissenschaft," 172.

50. On 24 February 1931 Rietzsch received permission to buy a phonograph, which was then sent to Africa (letter from Baudert to Rietzsch, Personalakte Rietzsch, UA). In a letter dated 4 February Baudert asks Rietzsch to seek advice in the matter from Heinitz. Before his death Rietzsch gave the recordings to the Museum für Musikinstrumente der Universität Leipzig, whence they were then sent to Berlin. I have published the recordings in *Walzenaufnahmen von Franz Rietzsch.*

51. Stumpf, "Lieder der Bellakula-Indianer."

52. Hornbostel, "Wanyamwezi-Gesänge." In his letters and publications he often compares the music of the Wanyamwezi to that of the Wanyakyusa.

53. Heinitz, *Strukturprobleme in primitiver Musik.*

54. For an entertaining account about Heinitz's research and Nazi ideology right after World War II, see "Die Brust aufgeschlitzt."

55. See Allgayer, "Wilhelm Heinitz." The Hamburg ethnomusicologist Albrecht Schneider, who has made a detailed study of Heinitz's Nachlass in the Hamburg Staatsbibliothek, describes, for example, how Heinitz studied the amount of rubato in seven renditions of "Am stillen Herd," from Wagner's *Meistersinger*; Schneider, "Music and Gestures," 93. Even though I could not detect any influence of Heinitz's work on Rietzsch, I did find a copy of Heinitz's *Habilitation* in the archive in Rungwe, Tanzania. The book is also mentioned in the list of his books in the letter to his sister.

56. letter from Rietzsch to Samuel Baudert, 2 April 1931, 2, Personalakte Rietzsch, UA; and Hornbostel, "African Negro Music." For more on Hornbostel's article, see above, pp. 123–24.

57. See also Carl, *Was bedeutet uns Afrika?*, 139–45. For a recent article on Hornbostel's contribution, see also Grupe, "E. M. von Hornbostel und die Erforschung afrikanischer Musik." Kubik, *Theory of African Music*, 3:87–91, provides a typically thoughtful explanation of how Hornbostel might have arrived at his theory of "African rhythm." See also Nettl, "Contemplating Ethnomusicology," on Hornbostel's view of "authentic music."

58. Grupe, "E. M. von Hornbostel und die Erforschung afrikanischer Musik," 108. even argues that Hornbostel anticipates the *emics/etics* debate.

59. See also my discussion of Hornbostel in chap. 2, p. 32.

60. Hornbostel, "African Negro Music," 43. Grupe, "E. M. von Hornbostel und die Erforschung afrikanischer Musik," discusses in some detail how ethnomusicologists since Hornbostel have challenged his ideas on rhythm. What he described as a caricature of the Luvembe seems to be an example of intentional adoption of European customs by colonial subjects. See also Ranger, *Dance and Society in Eastern Africa.*

61. Hornbostel's discussion of rhythm, while perceptive for its time, has been challenged by a number of ethnomusicologists, including Blacking, "Some Notes on a Theory

of African Rhythm"; Grupe, "E. M. von Hornbostel und die Erforschung afrikanischer Musik," 109–12; and Waterman, "The Uneven Development of Africanist Ethnomusicology." See esp. the discussion of Hornbostel's "African rhythm" in Kubik, *Theory of African Music*, 2:87–89.

62. Hornbostel, "African Negro Music," 40.

63. Ibid., 59. He continues: "Music exorcises evil powers (disease and the dead) and attracts the benignant ones (rain, fertility, good luck in hunting, and in war, etc.)," 59–60.

64. Ibid., 56.

65. Ibid., 61.

66. Nettl summarizes recent views best when he writes, "But the thought of establishing a set of musical areas for the world in the belief that this rather specialized concept would provide a key to prehistory and its laws is no longer taken seriously." *The Study of Ethnomusicology*, 334.

67. Hornbostel, "African Negro Music," 62.

68. For a detailed discussion on *Kulturkreislehre*, see Nettl, *The Study of Ethnomusicology*, 320–38, and chap. 1 above.

69. For a more detailed discussion of Rühl, see this chapter, below, and chap. 13.

70. For more information on the Moravian missions in the Nyasa area, see Müller and Schulze, *200 Jahre Brüdermission*, 461–502. As in all Moravian communities, there was an elected chair, Walter Marx, and a bishop, Oskar Gemuseus. In addition, we find missionaries with a variety of backgrounds: theologians, carpenters, nurses, teachers, merchants, tailors, famers, etc. Nyakyusa Christians were very quickly educated as evangelists and took over numerous congregations. In 1926 there were 4,964 baptized Christians and another 1,778 who wished to be baptized. Today the Moravian Church in Tanzania is one of the largest in the country, with more than 400,000 members.

71. Letter from Rietzsch to Baudert, written between 10 August and 2 September 1932, Personalakte Rietzsch, UA.

72. Rietzsch, "Dieseits und jenseits von Dur und Moll," and "Kirchenmusikalische Fragen in der Missionsarbeit." Rietzsch's work was discussed earlier in Kornder, *Zur Entwicklung der Kirchenmusik*, 114–25; and Fiedler, *Christentum und afrikanische Kultur*, 117–22 (*Christianity and African Culture*, 138–41). My discussion of Rietzsch is indebted to Kornder's and disagrees with that put forth by Fiedler, who seems not to have the musical background to understand what Rietzsch was trying to achieve.

73. Rietzsch, "Afrikanische Klänge." The essay was edited by the anthropologist Bernd Arnold, who was employed at the Dresden Museum of Anthropology. He became interested in Rietzsch when he noticed two carved African sculptures of Rietzsch, one in the Herrnhut Museum für Völkerkunde and the other in the Herrnhut Archive. Rietzsch's papers were passed on to him by Rietzsch's oldest daughter, Elisabeth Rietzsch. Arnold, in turn, gave the papers to Martin Brose, who was kind enough to give them to me. They are now privately owned and used with permission of the owner.

74. The letters are in the possession of the Rietzsch family, and I would like to thank them for having allowed me to read them.

75. As we saw in chap. 8, members of *Singbewegung* were familiar with pentatonic scales and had learned that medieval music was originally pentatonic.

76. On the use of the term *tone systems*, especially in Hornbostel's writings, see Blum, "European Musical Terminology and the Music of Africa." As we will see, Rietzsch's description parallels that of Kubik's explanation of the Gogo system.

77. The now generally accepted term *lamellophone* was first used in Kubik, "Probleme der Tonaufnahme afrikanischer Musiker." He defines it as "a musical instrument whose sound is generated essentially by the vibration of thin lamellae or tongues of metal, wood or other material." Kubik, "Lamellophone"; see also Tracey, "Mbira Music of Jege a Tapera," in *Handbook for Librarians*.

78. It is "a small flat wooden box that is held by both hands so that the fingers lie at the bottom while the thumbs pluck the old umbrella ribs [or stretchers], which are attached more or less radially on top of the box" (ein kleines Holzkästchen, das mit beiden Händen gehalten wird, so daß die Finger unten liegen, währen die Daumen oben die Töne aus Stücken von alten Regenschirmspeichen herauszupfen, welche ein wenig strahlenförmig auf das Kästchen gespannt wird). Rietzsch, "Afrikanische Klänge," 25.

79. "Es gibt drei Arten von Marimba (marimba ist die Mehrzahl von Irimba) nämlich die siebentönige und die neuntönige Irimba (letztere in zwei verschiedenen Stimmungen). Mir scheint die siebentönige Irimba für hier die typische zu sein, denn ihre Stimmung liegt auch anderer hiesiger Volksmusik zu Grunde. Und zwar handelt es sich [bei diesen Tönen] um die Naturtonreihe etwa eines Hornes bzw. um die sog[enannte] Obertonreihe. Von C' als Grundton ausgegangen, ergibt [sic] sich folgende Tonabstandverhältnisse: C' G' C" E" G" B" C"' D"' E"' usw. Die siebentönige Irimba weist folgende Skala auf: (natürlich nur verhältnismäßig von C' als angenommenen Grundton aus): C' E' G' B' C" D" E"." Ibid., 26. The German note name B indicates B-flat.

80. "Mit dem Europäerohr sucht man zunächst immer viel zu sehr nach Harmoniewechsel. Damit aber wird man dieser Musik nicht gerecht, denn harmonisch betrachtet, kann es sich bei der siebentönigen Irimba natürlich immer nur um einen nichtaufgelösten Nonenakkord handeln." Ibid., 27.

81. Rietzsch often mentions in his letters that Western terminology cannot be transferred to Nyakyusa music. The only words they have are "song" (*Lied*) and "sound" (*Klang*). The English have introduced English terms, but they do not really describe what is going on in African music; "Thus, we really have to find words from the local culture and transfer them to music" (Da heißts eben aus dem hiesigen Volksleben Worte zu suchen, die man aufs musikalische überträgt). Letter from Rietzsch to his father, 27 February 1932, 5. For example, he calls a fermata a roof.

82. Similarly, Julien Tiersot, a French ethnomusicologist, described the tuning of the Indonesian angklung as producing a "ninth chord" and saw African music as related to both plainchant and an *Ur-Musik*. See Fauser, *Musical Encounters*, 250–52.

83. Kirby, "The Recognition and Practical Use of the Harmonics of Stretched Strings by the Bantu of South Africa."

84. Indeed, the entire Rietzsch family is very musical. Each of his four sons worked as an organ tuner, for which you need an excellent ear.

85. Kubik first described his findings in "The Traditional Music of Tanzania," and in greater detail in his *Mehrstimmigkeit und Tonsysteme in Zentral- und Ostafrika* and also his "Multipart Singing in Sub-Saharan Africa: Remote and Recent Histories Unravelled," 196.

86. Kubik, *Theory of African Music*, 1:177.

87. For example, as late as 1951 Marius Schneider described the origins of these "tonal gebundene Parallelismen," as mysterious. *Geschichte der Mehrstimmigkeit*, vol. 1, and "Ist die vokale Mehrstimmigkeit eine Schöpfung der Altrassen?," 45.

88. Kubik, *Theory of African Music*, 1:174.

89. Ibid., 1:179.

90. Kubik, *Mehrstimmigkeit und Tonsysteme*, 15–16. Kubik has made a recording, now in the Vienna Phonogrammarchiv, no. 7367, of three Wanyakyusa boys singing polyphony with yodeling phrases in between, which now needs to be reevaluated in light of Rietzsch's descriptions of the overtone series. See Kubik, *Musikgeschichte in Bildern, Ostafrika*, 137.

91. Kubik, "Multipart Singing in Sub-Saharan Africa," 197.

92. "Die oben angeführte Irimbaskala wird zwar auch beim Volksgesang angewandt, ist aber ein System für sich, das mit dem jetzt zu behandelnden System unmittelbar nichts zu tun hat." Rietzsch, "Afrikanische Klänge," 29.

93. "Die aus seiner solchen Melodie herausgezogene Tonleiter ergibt folgenden Aufbau: F G A C D F. . . . Es ist nun aber nicht so, daß die Banyakyusa die beiden fehlenden Tonstufen etwa vermieden, weil sie ihnen nicht gefielen, sondern sie können sie überhaupt gar nicht singen." Rietzsch, "Diesseits und jenseits von Dur und Moll," 71.

94. "Zu der eigentlichen Melodie tritt eine—meist tiefere—Gegenstimme, die für sich genommen auch als eine selbstständige Melodie betrachtet werden kann. Zuweilen tritt dann beim Singen noch eine dritte hohe Stimme hinzu, die sich mehr oder weniger dem Lauf der Hauptmelodie anpaßt, ihr aber durchaus nicht streng parallel folgt. Da, wie gesagt, die Tonhöhen oft 'unbestimmt' sind, sind wir zuweilen geneigt, gewisse Terzklänge in diese Gesänge hineinzuhören, die aber wohl nur zufällig erscheinen, sicher jedenfalls nicht bewußt gestaltet sind." Ibid., 72.

95. Kubik, "Mehrstimmigkeit und Tonsysteme in Zentral- und Ostafrika," 15.

96. Polo Vallejo, *Patrimonio musical de los Wagogo de Tanzania: Contexto y sistemática*, 252, 347–55.

97. Letter to his sister Marianne, 27 April 1936, 1. In another letter to Marianne, dated 21 March 1936, he indicates that he had learned about the existence of fauxbourdon from an article by Fritz Dietrich entitled "Zur Kultmusikfrage," published only two months earlier.

98. "Man fragt sich unwillkürlich, wie bei den beschränkten Mitteln eines nur fünftönigen Systems ein so wohlklingender Gesang möglich sei. Denn das polyphone Gewirr der vielen Stimmen ergibt tatsächlich einen ganz wunderbaren Zusammenklang mit ganz eigentümlichen, aber auch für uns sehr wohlklingenden Harmoniefortschreitungen. Ja, gerade die harmonische Seite dieser Gesänge ist viel reicher und überzeugender als etwa die paar Harmonieverbindungen, die man bei einer einfachen Dur-Melodie anwendet (Tonika-, Dominant- und Subdominant-Dreiklang mit Umkehrungen). Das nimmt umso mehr Wunder, als es nicht möglich ist, aus einer einzelnen pentatonischen Tonleiter allein Dreiklänge abzuleiten; es ist da, wenn überhaupt, immer höchstens ein einziger möglich. Der genügt natürlich nicht zu harmonischen Fortschreitungen. Der Schlüssel zu den auch harmonischen Schönheiten der hiesiegen Volkslieder liegt darin, daß die verschiedenen Stimmen eben verschiedenen pentatonischen Geschlechtern

angehören. So beispielsweise der Baß einem anderen Geschlecht als die Melodie, und der Tenor wieder einem anderen Geschlecht, die aber alle gleichzeitig gesungen werden, wobei jedoch jede der einzelnen Stimmen immer in ihrem Geschlechte bleibt." Rietzsch, "Afrikanische Klänge," 33.

99. "Da es sich um melodische Geschlechter handelt, kann man nun entsprechend den Kirchentönen von diesen 'authentischen' fünf weitere 'plagale' Geschlechter ableiten, in denen der Grundton nicht der tiefste Ton der Melodie ist, sondern die Melodie um den Grundton herumschwingt." Ibid., 30.

100. "Schließlich hat doch auch die europ. Musik mal auf der hiesigen Stufe gestanden wo die Einstimmigkeit in Mehrstimmigkeit überging. Sollte es da nicht manchen wertvollen Anhaltspunkt für die hiesige Arbeit geben?" Letter from Rietzsch to his sister Marianne, 11 January 1932, 7.

101. Letter from Rietzsch to his sister Marianne, 11–19 May 1932.

102. "Daß der Choral musikalisch auf einer allen Völkern natürlichen Grundlage beruht, wurde schon gesagt, und dafür wurde das Zeugnis vergleichender Musikforscher angeführt." Rühl, "Die missionarische Akkommodation," 128.

103. Ibid., 116. Rühl includes copious notes referring to works by, among others, Stumpf, Hornbostel, Otto Abraham, and Johannes Wolf. Rühl (1903–1959) was associated with St. Gabriel, teaching at the Catholic University in Bejing from 1935 to 1940, and was found in 1941 in Tokyo. After the war he served as a parish priest in Plauen, East Germany, from 1951 to 1953, when he was denounced by a member of his congregation for having "sexual relations" with his housekeeper. He was dismissed from the order and became an organ builder and close associate of the distinguished organ builder Jehmlich in Dresden. Private communication, Horst Jehmlich, 12 June 2013; and Personalkartei, Generalat, Rome.

104. Gelbart and Rehding, "Riemann and Melodic Analysis: Studies in Folk-Musical Tonality," 141–64. Note that even though Riemann's book was written in opposition to the scientific observations made possible through recordings, Riemann, Hornbostel, and Stumpf all shared a belief in the evolution of the seven-note scale from the pentatonic one.

105. "Es sind nur weniger Völker, denen dies eine Schwierigkeit macht, denn die pentatonische Skala mit den beiden Halbtönen als Nebenstufen oder die siebenstufige Tonleiter findet sich sozusagen überall." Rühl, "Die missionarische Akkommodation," 128–29.

106. Ibid., 128n28.

107. "Trotzdem ist diese Tonfolge in einem gesungenen Liede höchst verdächtig, da Reichenbach wohl mit vollem Recht solche pentatonischen Leitern ablehnt, bei denen die 1½ Tonschritte sich unmittelbar folgen." Letter from Rietzsch to his sister Marianne, 11 January 1932, 12.

108. "Ich hatte Dir schon geschrieben, dass die Melodien in ihren jetzigen europ. Formen von den Leuten hier nicht gesungen werden können, da sie Halbtonschritte weder unterscheiden und noch weniger singen können, so daß also unsere üblichen Melodien für den Gemeindegesang als solchen gar nicht in Frage kommen." Letter from Rietzsch to Baudert, 10 August–12 September 1932, 14, Personalakte Rietzsch, UA; see also pp. 19, 29, and 35.

109. "Dabei ist dem Neger unsre Dur-Moll-Harmonik absolut unsingbar; vollends hier, wo die Banyakyusa [sic] nur ausgesprochen 'pentatonische' Tonfolgen singen können. Sie singen jede nichtpentatonische Melodie nach und nach in eine pentatonische um. . . . Da sind Klangkatastrophen unvermeidbar." Letter from Rietzsch to Heinitz, 8 September 1935, Nachlass, private collection.

110. Kornder, *Die Entwicklung der Kirchenmusik*, 63, 182–84.

111. Letter to his sister Marianne, 11 May 1932, 13.

112. "In den dürftigsten und magersten europäischen Harmonien (eigentlich sind es nur zwei, und zwar gerade die beiden, die auf jeder Ziehharmonika drauf sind)." Letter from Rietzsch to Baudert, 10 August 1932, 19, Personalakte Rietzsch, UA.

113. ". . . die Leute jedoch garnicht singen können, sie muss immer falsch klingen." Ibid., 17.

114. Ibid., 26.

115. Ibid., 22, 24–25.

116. "Denn in Rutenganio, wo die Sankeylieder am meisten in Schwang sind, sind in verhältnismäßig kurzer Zeit 2 Chorleiter in sittlicher Hinsicht gefallen, von einem weiß ich, daß das unmittelbar nach der Chorstunde gewesen ist." Ibid., 25.

117. "England macht bewußt hier draußen in amerikanischem Kitsch. Warum? Weil das praktisch ist. So fängt man Neger!" Letter to his sister Marianne, 11 May 1932, 2. Rietzsch's position is very much in line with Kofi Agawu's accurate analysis of the impact of these hymns on African society, which he considers to be a colonizing force. See Agawu, "Tonality as a Colonizing Force in Africa," 334–55.

118. Letter to his sister Marianne, 11 May 1932, 7; letter to his father, 27 February 1932, 5; and letter to his sister Marianne, 23 September 1935, 7.

119. "Beispiele früher Mehrstimmigkeit könnten da eventuell auf den richtigen Trichter helfen." Letter to his sister Marianne, 23 April 1936, 6.

120. "Ich glaube daß ihm [dem Neger] unser altes Liedgut in hervorragender Weise entspricht. Und nicht nur dies: ich komme immer mehr zur Überzeugung, daß das Reformationslied überhaupt das einzige ist, womit wir unsererseits den Gemeinen allein fruchtbar in dieser Richtung dienen können." Letter from Rietzsch to Baudert, 10 August–12 September 1932, 21, UA. See also Rietzsch, "Diesseits und jenseits von Dur und Moll," 72, where he draws a parallel between early Western and African polyphony. He continues in typical *Singbewegung* spirit: "This is no longer so foreign to us in Europe either: old song settings of this type are becoming alive again in 'singing communities' and in other similar attempts" (Sie ist uns übrigens auch in Europa durchaus nicht mehr so fremd: alte Liedsätze dieser Art leben wieder auf den "Singgemeinden" und ähnlichen Bestrebungen, 72).

121. I would like to thank Reinhard Strohm for this observation. In Ringmann's 1936 edition of the *Glogauer Liederbuch (Das Erbe deutscher Musik*, Ser. I, vol. 4, no. 123), it appears with the text "Nu bitten wir den heiligen Geist."

122. For Mbunga, see Kornder, *Die Entwicklung der Kirchenmusik*, 174–75. Mbunga studied ethnomusicology for one semester with Marius Schneider in Cologne. See also chap. 13 on Missionsbenediktiner.

123. Kubik, *Theory of African Music*, 1:173, 202.

124. Rietzsch gives a detailed account of the quarrel in his letter to Baudert of 16 February 1933. See also Kornder's excellent summary of the issues in *Die Entwicklung der Kirchenmusik*, 114–20.

125. "Erinnerungen des Missionars Alexander Ferdinand Jansa" (1868–1957), typescript (1987–88) after handwritten orignal (ca. 1945–1950, here 1949), 239–41, UA.

126. "Denn der Neger, und leider der Christ in ganz besonderer Weise verachtet seine eigne Musik. Der gebildete Christ hält die eigene Volksmusik für ungebildet und darum verwerflich. Über diese Feststellung bin ich recht erschrocken. Ist diese Tatsache schon sehr traurig, da hier wertvolle Volksgüter vernichtet werden." Letter from Rietzsch to Baudert, 10 August 1932, 38.

127. "Natürlich waren sie diesen Liedern gegenüber nur unsicher, weil die Europäer von Anfang an sie mehr oder weniger abgelehnt hatten." Letter from Rietzsch to Baudert, 16 February 1933, 11.

128. Only the chair of the mission station in Rungwe, Walter Marx, commented on the fact that the Wanyakyusa were unable to sing Western music; *Missionsblatt* (1931): 252–53. My thanks to Adam Jones for calling the passage to my attention.

129. Sankey hymns continue to be extremely popular all over Africa. According to Tobias Robert Klein, five African national anthems are based on the hymn "Jesus, Lover of My Soul."

130. Letter to his sister Marianne, 23 September 1935, 5. Rietzsch mentions that they learned staff notation within six months, the same amount of time it usually takes to learn tonic *sol-fa*.

131. In a conversation I had on 12 July 2011 with the Reverend Amoni Mwambande, retired secretary of the Southern Province for Music of the Moravian Church, he explained to me that African students find tonic *sol-fa* much easier to learn than staff notation.

132. For a discussion of this issue see Kornder, *Die Entwicklung der Kirchenmusik*, 120–25. Hollinger, *Protestants Abroad*, reports similarly that in the 1920s and '30s American Protestant missionaries in Asia became less convinced of their religious calling and turned increasingly to help the local population through other means.

133. "Nun sind wir also nicht mehr zufrieden mit dem Kirchengesang. Und darum stürzen wir uns auf die Neger, sagen ihnen daß sie besser singen müssen, üben mit ihnen, setzen ihnen gar, wie ich, neue Notensysteme vor. Und er weiß absolut nicht, was wir eigentlich von ihm wollen, warum wir von ihm plötzlich verlangen, das, wie er instinktsicher fühlt, wir ja selber garnicht machen. . . . In vielen Dingen, besonders auch in der kirchenmusikalischen Arbeit, gleichen wir auf der Mission einer Art Wohltätigkeitsverein. . . . Von einer überlegenen Warte aus bringen wir dem 'armen' Neger so allerhand bei, was ihm irgendwie guttun soll und was er ja auch gern haben will und annimmt. Und wie der bewohlätitgte Arme zuhause dann oft die empfangene Gabe zum Ärger des Wohltäters unsinnig gebraucht oder gar verschleudert, so tuts auch der Neger." Letter from Rietzsch to his sister Marianne, 19 January 1936, 3. Similarly, the principal of the Teacher's Training College in Rungwe, Joseph Busse, was disturbed by the feeling of cultural superiority exhibited by the black leaders who had been educated by the Moravian missionaries. Kornder, *Die Entwicklung der Kirchenmusik*, 121–22.

134. They have been published with a detailed introduction; see Berger, *Walzenaufnahmen von Franz Rietzsch—Tanzania 1931–37*.

135. Letter from Rietzsch to his sister Marianne, 11 January 1932, 5–7, 10: "The soloist creates his text and demands, if I understood him correctly, that all kinds of people should praise Jesus: the Europeans, the Wanyakyusa, or he might call all singers and people present one after another by name, and the chorus responds every time with the same text: Praise, praise Jesus!" (Der Vorsänger dichtet seinen Text aus dem Stegreif. Er fordert da, so weit ichs verstanden habe, alle möglichen Leute auf, Jesus zu loben: die Europäer, die Wanyakyusa, oder er nennt der Reihe nach alle Sänger oder Anwesenden mit Namen, und der Chor antwortet jedesmal mit demselben Text: Lobt, lobt Jesus!). Rietzsch believed it would make a great Gloria.

136. Letter from Rietzsch to his sister Marianne, 27 April 1936. The recordings that Rietzsch had sent to Heinitz were still in the musicology department of Hamburg University after the war but seem to be lost now. Thanks to Albrecht Schneider for this information.

137. Kornder, *Die Entwicklung der Kirchenmusik*, 76–78.

138. "Ist es aber eine Tatsache, daß die Missionen eine Einbeziehung afr. volksmäßiger Musik in die christl. Gottesdienste ablehnen—und von ihrem aufgeklärt-pietistischen Standpunte aus wohl auch immer werden ablehnen müssen." Letter from Rietzsch to his sister Marianne, 10 November 1938, 1. See also the letter from Rietzsch to his sister Marianne, 11 May 1932, 16, where he comments that the church elders would not be in favor.

139. "Die eingeborenen Musik muss möglichst ergründet werden und ihr Verhältnis zu der unseren aufgezeigt werden." Letter from Rietzsch to Marianne Rietzsch, 23 September 1935, 4.

140. Protocol of the Provinzial Konferenz, 1935, section 5, no. 13, "Musikalische Arbeit von Bruder Rietzsch" (Musical work of Brother Rietzsch), UA.

141. Kornder, *Die Entwicklung der Kirchenmusik*, 246 n. 84. The missionary Otto Hagena, from the Bethel Mission, took over from Rietzsch. See chap. 12, pp. 305–6n98.

142. Private communication, Elisabeth Rietzsch, 22 September 2011.

143. Letter from Rietzsch to Baudert, 17 February 1936; and letter from Baudert to Rietzsch, 7 April 1936.

144. The vast majority of Moravian missionaries in Africa of Rietzsch's generation were members of the party. The older missionaries and Baudert were not. It seems that most missionaries joined the party in Tanganyika and had left Germany for Africa before Hitler came to power. Many did not understand what was going on and were deeply ashamed later on, although Rietzsch remained unrepentant; private communication with Rietzsch's son-in-law, the Lutheran superintendent Andreas Voigt, Leipzig, 4 September 2012. See also Meyer, "Ein Stachel im Herzen"; and Wright, *German Missions in Tanganyika, 1891–1941*.

145. Marx wrote to the mission director Vogt on 27 January 1942; Letter from Gemuseus to Vogt, 29 January 1942; and letter from Tietzen to Vogt, 30 January 1942, Folder Rietzsch, UA.

146. Confidential letter from Marx to Baudert, 24 December 1936, Folder Rietzsch, UA.

147. Private communication, Elisabeth Rietzsch, 26 February 2012.

CHAPTER ELEVEN

1. For a detailed discussion of the connection of Prussion mission societies with colonialism, see Gründer, *Christliche Mission und deutscher Imperialismus;* Altena, *Ein Häuflein Christen mitten in der Heidenwelt des dunklen Erdteils,* 66–70, 317–29.

2. The Leipzig missionaries were active in three areas: first, the Kilimanjaro area, inhabited by the Wachagga (the Kichagga language has two dialects, Kimoshi and Kimamba); second, the Pare mountains, inhabited by the Pare (the Pare consist of two tribes, the Wagueno and Wasangi, the languages are Kigueno and Chasu); and third, the area around Mount Meru, inhabited by the Waro (whose language is Kiro) and Maasai (who speak Maasai).

3. Bennett, "The British on Kilimanjaro." For more background on the Chagga, see Moore and Puritt, *The Chagga and Meru of Tanzania;* and Perras, *Carl Peters and German Imperialism,* 188–204. The Kilimanjaro area was already a tourist attraction in the late nineteenth century: in the 1880s alone almost fifty Germans visited the area. Perras, *Carl Peters and German Imperialism,* 191.

4. Perras, *Carl Peters and German Imperialism,* 190.

5. Gründer, *Christliche Mission und deutscher Imperialismus,* 220–24.

6. See also Perras, *Carl Peters and German Imperialism,* 81–86.

7. Ibid., 191–92.

8. Ibid., 200.

9. Peters's behavior did not go unnoticed in Germany. The 1892 atrocities in African colonies were discussed at a Reichstag meeting on 13 March 1896. Tipped off by Protestant missionaries, the Social Democratic leader August Bebel gave a detailed account of Peters's activities in the Kilimanjaro area (ibid., 205–30). However, what shocked people the most was the fact that Peters had an African mistress whom he subsequently had hanged because she was not faithful to him. In other words, he had "gone native." Peters was discharged from his commission and lost his pension. See also the excellent discussion of the matter in Marchand, *German Orientalism,* 346ff.

10. See also Gründer, *Christliche Mission und deutscher Imperialismus,* 41, 201, 220ff.

11. For more on this topic, see ibid., 221–22. After 1904 German plantation owners settled increasingly in the area, and missionaries were unhappy that Chagga children were employed and missing school. They tried to institute compulsory school attendance, but their ability to criticize was limited because the mission also had a number of plantations that employed Wachagga. Ibid., 236.

12. Ibid., 200–201, 24–26. They clarified their position from the beginning: "It hardly needs to be said that even though we are starting to work in a new area as missionaries we are certainly not working for the colonial government and mix secular and sacred items; we are not serving the German Empire instead of God." Ibid., 41.

13. Gutmann's great-grandson Tilmann Prüfer, a journalist who has written a book about his ancestor, recounts a story told to him when he visited the area: during World War I Gutmann's confirmation students were drafted into the army; however, they did not appear for instruction. He marched angrily to the place where the military exercises were taking place and ordered his students to follow him, and they did. He also told the commander that his students needed to be confirmed first. The next day the confirmation classes were filled to capacity. Prüfer, *Der heilige Bruno,* 183.

14. Von Schwarz wrote: "We do have to realize that that the acquisition of colonies is in no way attached to a moral blemish." Gründer, *Christliche Mission und deutscher Imperialismus*, 326–27. See also 239–46, where Gründer describes how virtually all mission societies, both Catholic and Protestant, had children working on plantations at least part-time.

15. Winter, *Bruno Gutmann*, 10.

16. Evans-Pritchard, *Social Anthropology and Other Essays*, 111.

17. Moore, *Social Facts and Fabrications*.

18. Winter, *Bruno Gutmann*, 15.

19. Hornbostel's letter was written on 9 July 1913, and Gutmann responded on 8 August. Elisabeth Seesemann did all the Wachagga recordings for Hornbostel, which are transcribed in Schneider, *Geschichte der Mehrstimmigkeit*. Born in 1869 in what is now Latvia, she was a superior student at the Berlin Musikhochschule and worked in Africa as a teacher from 1905 to 1910; after she became a deaconess during a leave in Germany (1910–14), she worked as a nurse in the Kilimanjaro area. Eventually she became mother superior of her diaconal order, a position she held until her death in 1957. Her notes on and translations of the Chagga songs, now in the Berlin Phonogramm-Archiv, are detailed and impressive.

20. Kornder, *Die Entwicklung der Kirchenmusik*, 220.

21. "Möglichste Schonung der einheimischen Sitte, Unterscheidung von Sündlichem und rein Menschlichem und der Geduldsweg der Heiligung der Volkssitten durch den Unterricht aus Gottes Word und den ganzen erhebenden Einfluss eines christlichen Vorbildes." "Die Stellung der evangelischen Mission in Afrika zur Volkssitte," 293.

22. See Dorschel, "Die Idee des Konservatoriums."

23. Albin Bickrodt was the music teacher at the Leipzig Missionsschule from 1892 to 1932. Upon his retirement, an article was written about him and his teaching philosophy. His goal was to impart a love of music to generations of future missionaries. But more than that, he brought the students up to a "superior appreciation of music according to Luther's saying: 'Music is a marvelous gift of God and close to theology.'" Bickrodt, "Am Feierabend," 334.

24. Küchler, "D. Dr. Bruno Gutmann: Lebenslauf und Würdigung der Lebensarbeit D. Dr. Gutmanns." See also Prüfer, *Der heilige Bruno*, 108–9.

25. Like Bachmann, Gutmann also left his children in Germany from the 1920s on. Prüfer, *Der heilige Bruno*, 23–24. And like Bachmann's, Gutmann's children were extremely unhappy.

26. Rother, "Wie ich das 'Waldfest' der Wapare sah," 468–73. Rother was active in German East Africa from 1901 to 1917, and then again from 1925 to 1939. He founded the Teacher Training Seminary in Marangu and was an excellent musician. Rother was probably the most musically educated of the Leipzig missionaries. From the beginning he published a number of interesting articles on Chagga music, such as "Das Musikinstrument der Wapare," on the mouthbow or ipango. After discussing how the sound is produced, he describes the playing of a young boy, a true artist, who narrates the true story of a man dying and being carried off by laughing hyenas. His account shows a real appreciation for the music. Unfortunately, he ends his article with a plea to donate money to purchase trombones for the Wapare. Similarly, Rother's book *Afrikanischer Sang und Klang* has a lot of interesting observations on Chagga and Pare music and rituals. For a discussion of

Rother's description of Chagga music, see Kornder, *Die Entwicklung der Kirchenmusik*, 32–39, 87–91. Rother's Chagga name was Mwimbi, which means singer.

27. Widenmann, *Die Kilimandscharo-Bevölkerung*, 47. A more recent description of the ritual is Raum, "Female Initiation among the Chaga." O. F. Raum, son of the Leipzig missionary Johannes Raum, became an anthropologist. He wrote his dissertation under Bronislaw Malinowski; it concentrates largely on the instruction connected with the initiation.

28. "All die Lieder und die häßlichen, widerlichen Tänze, von den nackten, nur mit Schellen, Ketten, und Perlen geschmückten, mit Fett eingesalbten Mädchen getanzt,— all das ist unsäglich traurig. . . . die Zeremonie wird begleitet von Tänzen und Liedern, Liedern, die zum Teil sich wegen ihres schmutzigen Inhalts kaum aufzeichnen lassen, und andere, die eine unbeschreibliche Traurigkeit und Wehmut atmen." Seesemann, "Frauennot und Frauenhilfe," 105–6.

29. Rother, *Meine afrikanischen Jungen*, 12. See also Klein, "Bach in Afrika," who cites a passage by Rothert from 1936 where he still recommends only the singing of Western chorales accompanied on the harmonium.

30. "Zwar haben die Dschagganeger von jeher gesungen, aber sie haben nicht Lieder in unserem Sinne. Es ist ähnlich wie mit den Singvögeln der afrikanischen Vogelwelt. Die afrikanischen Vögel singen, aber sie haben keine Lieder wie unsere Singvögel daheim. Der Gesang unserer Neger ist mehr rein melodisch und rhythmisch stark bewegtes Sprechen, zumeist in Wechselchören, das sich vielleicht einmal für epische Stoffe auch biblischen Inhaltes verwenden liesse." Fritze, "Die Geschichte eines Gesangbuches," 298.

31. Kornder, *Die Entwicklung der Kirchenmusik*, 199–202, has a complete list of Chagga hymnbooks.

32. "An zwei Nachmittage in der Woche übe ich den Gesang mit meinen 24 Singbuben, um allmählich hier den Kirchengesang zu heben. Sie bekommen dafür 1 Rupie zu Weihnachten und außerdem Zeug zur Kleidung. Aber obwohl ich hierzu die besten Sänger ausgewählt habe, ist mirs doch bis jetzt nicht gelungen, einen völlig reinen Gesang herauszubringen. . . . Es ist mir schier unbegreiflich, dass gerade unsere Madschameleute so schlechte Sänger sind, aber die Tatsache besteht. . . . Bei ihren eigenen Gesängen tritt das nicht so auffällig in Erscheinung, weil die meist mit der Fistel gesungen werden. Nun, mag es gut oder schlecht klingen, daß unseren Leuten das Singen geistlicher Lieder Herzensbedürfnis und Herzensfreude werde, dann ist es allewege gut gesungen vor unserem Gott." Gutmann, "Der erste Bericht aus der Station Masama," 37.

33. Knittel, "Unser Lehrergehilfen und Mittelschule," 561.

34. Winter, *Bruno Gutmann*, includes a complete bibliography of all of Gutmann's publications, which amounts to 148 items.

35. As quoted in Prüfer, *Der heilige Bruno*, 225. The letter is not dated, but it must come from the 1920s.

36. See Winter, *Bruno Gutmann*, 158–61, for a detailed explanation of Gutmann's interpretation of Tönnies. For Tönnies, see also Merz-Benz, "Die begriffliche Architektonik von 'Gemeinschaft und Gesellschaft,'" 31–64.

37. Gutmann, "Das Herauswachsen christlicher Sitte aus dem Volksboden der Wadschagga," 307.

38. In Germany in the 1920s and '30s Rother was a frequent lecturer on African music. See Kornder, *Die Entwicklung der Kirchenmusik*, 90.

39. The books are *Freies Menschentum aus ewigen Bindungen, Schildwacht am Kilimanjaro,* and *Zurück auf die Gottesstraße.*

40. Gutmann includes an entertaining story he heard about an artist on the instrument whose playing and reciting of stories was so magnificent that everyone came to listen and to learn: "And players of the musical bow not only became better warriors, but they also had magical powers. But now that civilization has entered the country, warriors are no longer needed and the art of the musical bowing is for children, who get addicted to playing and don't do their work anymore. So the chief has forbidden the playing of the musical bow, and then mothers and fathers were happy." Gutmann, "Der Brummbogen," 73.

41. "Die Grußlieder der Wadschagga sind dem Untergang geweiht. Mit ihnen vergeht wieder ein Stück der inneren Beherrschtheit, unter deren Einflusse der Afrikaner das umgängliche Wesen gewann, das ihn auszeichnete. Nun überfällt und überwältigt ihn mehr und mehr die Formlosigkeit des modernen Europäers, an der er entarten muß." Gutmann, "Grußlieder der Wadschagga," 22.

42. "Sie kannten also gewissermaßen schon die Elemente und fanden sie bei uns nur in einer höheren und reineren Ordnung wieder." Gutmann, *Gemeindeaufbau aus dem Evangelium,* 92–93.

43. "Unvergleichlich wertvoll aber für die Einstimmung einer Menge zu gleichem Fühlen und zu freiem Mitschwingen aller Seelen zu einem Ziele sind unsere Choräle. Sie sind von unseren Leuten gern und leicht aufgenommen worden." Ibid., 92.

44. *Kitabu kya Fiimbo, Gesangbuch in der Sprache von Madschame* and *Kitabu kya siri ya ndumi ya sia ya okio* . . . . This hymnbook was used in Moshi. See also Kornder, *Die Entwicklung der Kirchenmusik,* 199–202.

45. Rosenkranz, *Das Lied der Kirche in der Welt,* 112.

46. Gutmann, *Gemeindeaufbau aus dem Evangelium,* 92.

47. Gutmann, "Deutsche Weihnachtssitten und Weihnachtslieder in Ostafrika."

48. "Der Choral ist auch die stärkste Missionsmacht in der lutherischen Kirche." Gutmann, *Gemeindeaufbau aus dem Evangelium,* 93.

49. "In den deutschen Chorälen, die wir hier singen, ist es, als ob ihre Stimmen noch unter uns wären. . . . So gehört noch heute zur Mission des Evangeliums das Gemeinde-lied." Gutmann, "Der Choral in der Dschaggagemeinde," 142.

50. "Wieder fließt das Wasser nieder im Kanal. Geht ihms Geleit! / Sagen sollen unsre Lieder: Nehmt es auf, macht euch bereit. / Ist der Väter Speisemuld, die sie gruben mit Geduld. / Hütet sie vor allem Schmutze! Jeder schöpfe sich zu Nutze." Ibid., 144.

51. There is a recent film on these choir competitions by Julia Irene Peters called *Sing It Out Loud.* The first required piece is Luther's chorale "Ein' feste Burg." The second is a traditional African piece, and the third is chosen by the choir. The choirs take at least two years to prepare for this competition. See Barz, *Performing Religion,* 23, 29–51, and "Politics of Remembering."

CHAPTER TWELVE

1. On Peters, see Craig, *Deutsche Geschichte, 1866–1945,* 116; and Conrad, *Deutsche Kolonialgeschichte,* 91. See also Gründer, *Christliche Mission und deutscher Imperialis-mus,* 36–38.

2. For a detailed discussion of the history of the Bethel Mission, see Menzel, *Die Bethel-Mission*, 1–45. See also Altena, *Ein Häuflein Christen mitten in der Heidenwelt des dunklen Erdteils*, 53–59; for a detailed account of Carl Peters's involvement in Africa, see Perras, *Carl Peters and German Imperialism*, 82ff. It is worth noting that Warneck, the prominent missionary publicist and editor of *AMZ*, did not approve of the close connection between missionary societies and politicians. See ibid., 83.

3. See chap. 13.

4. Menzel, *Die Bethel-Mission*, 17.

5. Ibid., 47–48.

6. Deaconesses, the Protestant equivalent of nuns; they are generally unmarried nurses. Deacons have many professions, among them also nursing, and they do marry. For a critical if unconvincing account of the Bethel Mission, see Conrad, "'Eingeborenenpolitik' in Kolonie und Metropole," 107–28.

7. Pohl, "Dankbarkeit leben: Öffenlichkeitsarbeit in den von Bodelschwinghschen Anstalten Bethel," 101–16.

8. See part II, chap. 8, pp. 103–4.

9. Menzel, *Die Bethel-Mission*, 55–56.

10. Menzel, "'Pastor Fritz' und die Bethel Mission," ibid., 11.

11. See Conrad, "'Eingeborenenpolitik' in der Kolonie," 117.

12. The Usambara station Lutindi, founded in 1893, became the first hospital for mental patients. It was called "Klein-Bethel" and is to this day considered one of the best mental hospitals in Tanzania. See Menzel, *Die Bethel-Mission*, 111–14.

13. Löffler, "Sozialer Protestantismus in Übersee," 321–36.

14. Sundkler and Steed, *A History of the Church in Africa*, 541–42; Menzel, *Die Bethel-Mission*, 82–85.

15. Menzel, *Die Bethel-Mission*, 250–52.

16. Ibid., 232.

17. Ibid., 216–22.

18. Anna Rascher, a schoolteacher, translated various parts of the Bible into Haya and wrote a Haya grammar in which she notated every single pitch. It was from this work that many later missionaries learned the language.

19. Kajerero played a major role in the Buhaya church. After World War I German missionaries were not allowed to work in Tanganyika. When the Anglican missionary Harry Leakey decided to leave the area in 1924 to the Methodists, Kajerero and Joel Kibira refused to join the new church and wrote to their old Bethel missionary Johanssen asking him to return. The matter was discussed at the mission conference in Le Zoute, and Bethel missionaries duly returned. Menzel, *Die Bethel-Mission*, 274–79. For a study of Christian revival in Africa, especially among the Haya, see Günther, *Erweckung in Afrika*, 73–87. Günther, one of the most important leaders of the German *Jugendbewegung* who came out of the Stefan George circle, talks about a "Christian *Jugendbewegung* in East Africa" (77).

20. Only one missionary couple, Ernst von der Heyden and his wife, were allowed to stay in Rwanda after the war because, coming from Lorraine, they held French citizenship. Menzel, *Die Bethel-Mission*, 251.

21. Sundkler and Steed, *A History of the Church in Africa*, 546.

22. G. Menzel, *Die Bethel-Mission*, 168–69.

23. Ibid., 169.

24. Ronicke, "Kleine Erinnerungen an einen großen Mann," 25.

25. See part II, chap. 8, pp. 103–4.

26. Rundbrief, 24 January 1933, 9, Akte Trittelvitz, VEM. He mentions that he plays viola in a string quartet and talks about all the music making at their home.

27. Trittelvitz was also a close friend of Johannes Kuhlo (1856–1941), who was called "Posaunengeneral." Kuhlo, an important member of the *Singbewegung*, established brass ensembles not only all over Germany, but also, with Trittelvitz's help, in Bethel mission stations in Africa.

28. He and Felix von Luschan, director of the Ethnography Museum in Berlin, were in total agreement on this at the Kolonialkongreß of 1910. Gründer, *Christliche Mission und deutscher Imperialismus*, 112.

29. The best discussion is in Kornder, *Die Entwicklung der Kirchenmusik*, 56–57, 197–98.

30. Letter from Paul Döring, 15 August 1913, Akte M III 2.2, VEM.

31. See chap. 6 for a detailed discussion of Ballanta. The conference was held from 14 to 21 September.

32. Smith, *The Christian Mission in Africa*, 43.

33. For Bachmann, see chap. 10, pp. 139–40.

34. For the German, see p. 179n1, letter from Trittelvitz to Martha Hosbach, 17 January? [month illegible] 1927, Akte Hosbach, VEM.

35. Marie Müller had studied music and was a good pianist.

36. "Aber wenn nun auch unsere Gemeinden sich längst an Halbtöne gewöhnt haben, so können wir doch aus den Heften [Negro Spirituals] etwas lernen, das ist die Vortragsweise. Dabei wechselten Solo und Chor immer miteinander ab. Auch in den afrikanischen Liedern spielt, soviel ich weiss, der Wechselgesang eine Rolle." Letter from Trittelvitz to Martha Hosbach and Marie Müller, 17 November? [month illegible] 1926, Akte Hosbach, VEM.

37. Letter from Martha Hosbach, 20 June 1927, Akte Hosbach, VEM.

38. Letter from Samuel Müller to Trittelvitz, 11 May 1927, Akte Müller, VEM.

39. Letter from Trittelvitz to Samuel Müller, 8 March 1927, Akte Müller, VEM.

40. "Ich bin aber immer noch nicht zu meinem Dank gekommen-es handelt sich um die amerikanischen Negerlieder. Frau Pastor Wohlrab war so lieb, mir von den drei Exemplaren, die nach Usambara gegangen sind, eins zu schicken-und sie sind mit Begeisterung hier aufgenommen. Im Nu haben meine Sänger die Melodien weg und schmettern sie aus tiefstem Herzen am Sonntag von der Empore hinunter. Ebenso dankbar werden sie unten unter den Zuhörern aufgenommen. Die alten Bakehuru (Frauen) haben mir sagen lassen, das wäre das erste Mal gewesen, dass sie wirklich gesungen hätten." Letter from Trittelvitz to Hagena, 20 January 1930, 2 Akte Hagena, VEM. Kornder, in an otherwise excellent book, attributes this account to the Usambara missionary Paul Wohlrab, but Trittelvitz is quoting the wife of Ernst von der Heyden. Kornder, *Die Entwicklung der Kirchenmusik*, 95.

41. Maneromango is a mission station of the Berlin Mission.

42. "Besonders unmittelbar trat uns das bei einem Besuch auf der Missionsstation Maneromango entgegen. Als die Missionare der unterschiedlichen Arbeitsgebiete

die Gemeinde begrüßten, antwortete diese mit mancherlei Liedern. Zuerst sangen sie Choräle, dann eingeborene Lieder. Das war ein überraschender Unterschied. Die Choräle klangen etwas schleppend und farblos, mit dem ersten einheimischen Liede kam sofort eine starke Bewegung in die ganze Schar. Männer, Frauen und Kinder sangen mit großer Frische; man spürte es den Leuten an, daß ihr gesangliches Empfinden in diesen Liedern lebendig wurde." Wohlrab, "Die dritte lutherische Missionskonferenz in Ostafrika," 20–21.

43. "Eine Wiedergabe dieser Lieder in unserer Notenschirft wird—wenn überhaupt möglich—sehr schwierig sein, weil man die eigenartige Klangfarbe durch die Noten nicht darstellen kann." Ibid., 21.

44. "Aber ist es denn recht, dass wir den Eingeborenen unsere Musik bringen? Ueberall auf dem Missionsfelde ist jetzt die Frage aufgetaucht, ob wir die Bewohner Afrikas nicht allzusehr europäisieren; sie sollen doch Afrikaner bleiben. Warum lassen wir ihnen nicht ihre alte afrikanische Musik? Lange Zeit haben die Missionare gemeint, afrikanische Musik eigne sich nicht für den Gottesdienst. Seit vielen Jahren habe ich immer wieder gebeten: Sammelt doch Lieder der Eingeborenen und schreibt ihre einheimischen Weisen auf! . . . Nun erwacht dieser Gedanke überall in Afrika." Trittelvitz, "Der Geiger von Bumbuli," 43.

45. "Wir hatten vor Monaten jedes Land um eine Trommel gebeten. Sie waren auch alle acht eingetroffen. . . . Kurz vor Gottesdienstbeginn kamen die Europäer und die Häuptlinge. Auf dem Kirchplatz versammelte sich eine unübersehbare Masse von Menschen. Wir mußten einen Nebengottesdienst unter den Bäumen einrichten. . . . Auf der Empore saßen gedrängt die Seminaristen aus Kigarama mit ihren Posaunen. Vor der Kanzel standen die zwei Trommelständer mit den acht Buhajatrommeln festlich geschmückt und um diese gruppiert die acht ausgewählten Gemeindevertreter. . . . Nach der Predigt wurden die acht Trommeln geweiht. Jeder Trommler sprach ein Bibelwort, dann schlug er mit einigen kräftigen Schlägen seine Landestrommel." Scholten, "Die Einweihung der Erlöserkirche in Bukoba," 220–21.

46. Personalakte Otto Hagen, SU 4834–72, VEM.

47. Daniels, *Nietzsche and the Birth of Tragedy*, 9.

48. "Lebenslauf," 1, Akte Hagena, VEM.

49. Ibid., 2.

50. I would like to thank his daughters, Ruth Köhne and the late Elisabeth Hagena Wulczyn, for giving me access to all the family letters.

51. Hagena, "Lieder der Bahaya," (1939), MS, 10 pp., VEM.

52. Rosenkranz, *Das Lied der Kirche in der Welt*.

53. "Die Haja haben in ihrer Sprache nur das kleine Liederbuch von Döring, und die Lieder klingen entsetzlich, wo man auch einen Gottesdienst hält. . . . Das Volk hier, jedenfalls die Erwachsenen, haben kein Ohr für unsere Melodien." Johanssen, *In der Heimat und im Dienst am Wiederaufbau*, 191.

54. "Plötzlich kommt . . . ein festlich gekleideter Trupp Menschen unter lautem Gesang. Ich dachte: was haben die Katholiken für einen eigentümlichen Gesang. Plötzlich verstehe ich etwas vom Text, und es schiesst mir blitzschnell der Gedanke durch den Kopf: die haben ja denselben Text wie wir. Natürlich war es mir dann auch sofort klar, wen ich vor mir hatte. Nun ging es unter fröhlichem Singen weiter, und ich hatte Musse

darüber nachzudenken. Wie diese eigtümlichen Melodien wohl zustandegekommen sein mögen, wieviel davon auf Englands Konto kommt, und wieviel für unser Konto übrigbleibt. Ich konnte nicht mitsingen, meine Begleitung hatte sich aber bald in die neuen Melodien hineingefunden. Öfters war es, als sänge sie die 2. Stimme. Grosse Sänger müssen die Baganda nicht sein, denn auch die ihnen von früher her bekannten Melodien wie Kommet zum Heiland und Sicher in Yesu Armen singen sie nicht weniger entstellt." Report by Paul Döring, "Wieder in Kigarama," 15 August 1913 or 1916, Akte M III 2.2, VEM.

55. Kornder, *Die Entwicklung der Kirchenmusik*, 58–59. Baganda music is closely related to Haya music.

56. "Nur eine wirklich volkstümliche Missionsarbeit wird in die Volksseele eindringen. In letzter Zeit ist für Afrika der Name von Gutmann bei diesem Problem oft genannt worden. Dein lieber Schwiegervater hat aber von Anfang an mit der gleichen Aufmerksamkeit diese Frage studiert. Wenn Du nun meine Gedanken aufnimmst, so freue ich mich und wenn Du dann gerade im Blick auf die afrikanische Musik das tun kannst, so freue ich mich besonders, denn ich habe immer den Wunsch gehabt, dass dieses Gebiet noch einmal gründlicher bearbeitet werden möchte. Du wirst, wenn Du darüber einmal etwas mitzuteilen hast, bei mir immer ein teilnehmendes Aufmerken finden . . . Nun sind nicht alle unsere Mitarbeiter in Usambara hierfür besonders offen." Letter from Trittelvitz to Hagena, 14 January 1929, Akte Hagena, VEM.

57. Letter from Trittelvitz to Hagena, 3 August 1929, Akte Hagena, VEM.

58. "Was die Musik anbetrifft, so versuche ich zunächst einmal selbst bei allen möglichen Gelegenheiten, afrikanische 'Melodien' oder besser Singarten in mich aufzunehmen so daß ich sie auch singen kann. Das ist aber garnicht so einfach. Es fehlt auch manchmal einfach an Zeit. Aber wenn ichs noch nicht selbst wirklich kann, übersehe ich noch nicht Konsequenzen und Möglichkeiten einer kirchlichen Verwendung. Es wird auch einer größeren wissenschaftlichen und praktischen Erforschung der Sprache bedürfen, um die Zusammenhänge die *vielleicht* zwischen dem musikalischen Ton beim Sprechen und der Tonführung in der Melodie bestehen, zu erkennen. Welche Literatur gibt es darüber?" Letter from Hagena to Trittelvitz, 26 September 1929, 1, Akte Hagena, VEM.

59. "Das Singen mit diesen anfangs als unmusikalisch geltenden Jungen macht Freude. Du wirst nicht in jeder Schule aus 40 Jungen einen so sauber singenden (4stimmigen) Chor zusammenbringen. Etwa 8 Schüler der Oberklasse sind imstande eine unbekannte, ihnen langsam vorgesungene Melodie in Noten aufzuschreiben. Wir haben schon Bach Choräle gesungen." Letter from Hagena to Johannes Richter, 22 September 1920, private possession.

60. "Übrigens ist Deine Annahme, dass die Haya nicht für Musik zu haben sind, doch falsch. Ich glaube von vorneherein nicht daran und kann nur sagen, dass sich unser Chor durchaus neben dem Chor des Eislebener Gymnasiums sehen lass kann." Letter from Hagena to Trittelvitz, 17 December 1931, Akte Hagena, VEM.

61. "Ich glaube ja auch nach meinen Erfahrungen, dass der Eindruck, der zuerst immer berichtet wurde, revidiert werden muss und wir nur von—in europäischem Sinne—ungeschultem Singen sprechen müssen. Sie sind in ihrer Gesamtheit durchaus fähig auch europäische Kunst aufzunehmen und wiederzugeben. Als ich das erste Mal mit meinem Chor in der Kirche vierstimmig gesungen hatte: 'Ach bleib mit deiner Gnade,' da bekam ich einige Tage später einen Brief unseres Lehrers Petelo—die Eingeborenen machen so

etwas gern brieflich-mit der dringenden Bitte, die Jungen doch jeden Sonntag singen zu lassen. Wenn er das hörte, dann würde ihm so warm ums Herz. Doch steht es als Aufgabe vor uns ihre eigene Musik, befruchtet gewiss mit einer Ausdruckstiefe zu einem Instrument zu machen Gott nun wirklich auf Hajaweise zu loben." Hagena, "Aus dem Wachsen und Werden einer Hayagemeinde," 3.

62. "Übrigens gibt es keine korrekte Notierung (soweit sie überhaupt nach unserem System möglich ist), noch lange kein richtiges Tonbild der Wirklichkeit. Das eigentümliche Fallen der Stimmen, dies scheinbare oder wirkliche Abgleiten von der gefundenen Tonhöhe und doch niemals Herunterziehen ist uns ungeheuer fremd. Eine Folge von 8 Tönen muß ich mir mindestens 10 mal vorsingen lassen, ehe ich sie nachsinge. Studien darüber werde ich wohl nicht so en passant machen können." Letter from Hagena to Trittelvitz, 17 December 1931, 2, Akte Hagena, VEM.

63. Letter from Trittelvitz to Hagena, 7 November 1931, Akte Hagena, VEM. I have been unable to find the melody.

64. "Jeder Missionar fühlt die Schwierigkeit im Gebrauch europäischer Weisen und zugleich, daß es wünschenswert ist in steigendem Maße eingeborene Melodien zu verwenden. Die Schwierigkeit im Gebrauch europäischer Melodien sind gegeben durch die völlige Andersartigkeit afrikanischer Musik. Diese Andersartigkeit ist 1. eine solche des Tonsystems überhaupt. Wohl haben wir bei unseren Eingeborenen Melodien im Gegensatz zu anderen Bantustämme Halbtöne, doch ist trotzdem ihr Tonsystem doch nicht unserer Heptatonik entsprechend." Hagena, "Musik in der Evangelischen Heidenmission," VEM, 1.

65. "Der Eingeborene kennt nur selten längere Strophen, die einen geschlossenen Gedankengang zulassen. Die Regel ist bei ihm der im Wechsel unermüdlich wiederholte *Zweizeiler*." Ibid., 1.

66. "Der völlig andere Sprachrhythmus der Bantusprachen paßt fast niemals ohne Vergewaltigung zu den für unserem deutschen Sprachrhythmus geschaffenen Melodien. Europäischer Melodieakzent und afrikanischer Wortakzent sind kaum auf einen Nenner zu bringen." Ibid.

67. Ibid., 2.

68. "Irgendwie nasal. Dadurch bekommt der Gesang etwas Verhaltenes, Schwebendes." Hagena, "Musik in der evangelischen Heidenmission," 2.

69. "Mein Eindruck, den ich allerdings noch nicht genügend belegen kann, ist dieser, daß dem Eingeborenen mehr eine fallende Melodie als eine aufsteigende liegt." Ibid., 2.

70. The only description of their music can be found in Brose, "Musik der Kagera Region in Tansania." The typescript can be accessed in the VEM archive. I would like to thank Martin Brose, a former missionary, for giving me a copy of his text.

71. Hosbach, "Bericht eines Hofmusikers von Ihangiro," 38. Also found in Brose, "Musik der Kagera Region," 59.

72. For a description of an amakondele orchestra at the royal court in Bugabo, see Döring, "Bei den Songo und Mutahangarwa," 10.

73. What has received considerable scholarly attention in the last years is Haya epics that are performed with an enanga, a zither associated with the ruling class. For Haya epics, see Schmidt, *Historical Archeology in Africa*, 73–96; and Mulokozi, *The African Epic Controversy*; see also Kubik, "Tanzania: North-Western Tanzania." Klaus Wachsmann has published an excellent article on the neighboring Buganda instruments,

several of which are also used among the Haya. Most important among these are the endingidi (bowed lute or fiddle), the enanga, drums, and the amakondele (or eikondele). Wachsmann, "Musical Instruments in Kiganda Tradition and Their Place in the East African Scene," in Wachsmann, *Essays on Music and History in Africa*, 93–134. See also Wachsmann's fundamental discussion of East African instruments, which includes a detailed description of the enanga and endingidi in Trowell and Wachsmann, *Tribal Crafts of Uganda*, 389–90, 405–7.

74. Tracey, "Towards an Assessment of African Scales," 15–20. Gerald W. Hartwig wrote an article on music instruments in Bukerebe, an island on Lake Victoria. The music is closely related to the Haya and gives important historical details about the origins of their instruments. However, he does not describe the tonal system. Hartwig, "The Historical and Social Role of Kerebe Music."

75. Rehse, *Kiziba: Land und Leute*, 69.

76. See http://www.sternsmusic.com/popup_player.php?CAT_NAME=&track=&SONG _ID=61299.

77. See http://missionmusicafrica.com/. Both's recordings have just been given to the Berlin Phonogramm-Archiv.

78. The endingidi (in German *Röhrenfiddel*) came from the East African coast and shows a clear Arab influence, hence the chromaticism. See Kubik, "Musikgestaltung in Afrika," 30. Kubik also writes about the amakondere Orchestra (*abgestimmte Zweihörner* at the court of the Kabaka (king of Buganda) and the Omukama (king of Bunyoro). In the amakondere orchestra and the Kiganda xylophone the only interval permitted is the octave.

79. See this chapter, note 76.

80. Kubik, *The Theory of African Music*, 2:186–87.

81. See, for example, Kubik, "Die Amadinda-Musik von Buganda," 141.

82. Note, though, that he never mentions that also the text should be adapted to Haya culture, as Gutmann did with the Chagga or Bachmann with the Nhiha (see part III, chaps. 10 and 11). The most likely reason is that he was simply not in Africa long enough to also address this difficult issue.

83. The translation of New Testatment was a long process. The first translations had been done by Paul Döring, who had worked on the Gospels, Acts, and the Epistles. Major revisions were done by Ernst Johanssen. Then Anna Rascher, wife of Wilhelm Rascher and by training a teacher, contributed in a major way before Hagena started to work on the translation. The translation was eventually finished by the Swedish mission society in 1951 and published in 1952. Menzel, *Die Bethel-Mission*, 319. Trittelvitz Rundbrief, 24 April 1934, VEM.

84. "Lebenslauf," 4, Akte Hagena, VEM. I found a moving letter dated 1952 from the mission inspector, Curt Ronicke, to Hagena's widow, Adelheid, after her husband's death. This letter accompanied the translation of the New Testament. Akte Hagena, VEM.

85. Hagena's daughter, Ruth Köhne, has informed me that she sent both the Haya and German versions to the music school Ruhija in Buhaya.

86. "Wie groß muß nun erst das Verwundern sein, wenn die Beschäftigung dem geistigen Besitz eines Volkes gilt, das nach immer noch üblichem Urteil als ein Negervolk auf halbtierischer Stufe steht, und dessen Glieder nur triebhaft, als Kollektivwesen mit denkbar geringem seelischem Eigenleben ihre Tage dahindämmern. Wohl niemand, der in der

Missionsarbeit steht, wird in Gefahr sein, solcher Meinung zuzustimmen. Aber gerade darum wird die Freude groß sein, aus eigener Begegnung mit dem Volke und seiner Seele den Beweis erbringen zu können, wie ahnungslos die eben erwähnten 'Urteile' sind. . . . Die folgenden Zeilen sind als ein Versuch gemeint, an solcher Freude und an solchem Verwundern teilnehmen zu lassen. Es sollen einige Lieder, wie sie unsere Eingebornen, die Haja, am Westufer des Viktoria-Sees im alten Deutsch-Ostafrika bei ihren amayaga singen, wiedergegeben werden." Hagena, "Lieder der Haja," 238–39.

87. Ibid., 238–39.

88. Private communication, Werner Both, 16 January 2016.

89. Pastor Fritz von Bodelschwingh had been elected bishop of the Confessing Church but stepped down very quickly because of pressure from the NSDAP.

90. On Ernst Wilm, see Brinkmann, "Ernst Wilm, 1901–1989"; on Bodelschwingh, see Bautz, "Bodelschwingh, Friedrich von."

91. Letter to Adelheid Hagena from 12 March 1943. All of these letters are in the possession of the Hagenas' daughter, Ruth Köhne.

92. "Heute abend hörte ich auch die Nachricht, daß schon wieder über Bethel Bomben abgeworfen wurden mit dem traurigen Ergebnis. Aber hat unser Volk ein Recht, sich darüber zu erregen, wo doch das Leben der Kranken in Bethel nicht mehr als 'lebenswert' gilt? Der Feind nimmt ihnen damit nur eine Arbeit ab, die sie selbst gerne tun wollen." Letter to Adelheid Hagena, 1 April 1941. Most mental patients in Germany were killed, but not in Bethel. Even though Hitler announced in late 1941 after massive protests that the killing would stop, it continued until the end of the war.

93. "Es ist vieles, was auf das Ende hindeutet. Und doch scheint mir die Welt noch nicht reif zum Gericht. Es mag aber sein, daß der Wahnsinn dieses Krieges noch größer wird und Gottes Gericht in allem offenbar. Jedenfalls ist es vor allem die Lüge, die ins ungeheure wächst." Letter to Adelheid Hagena, 3 March 1940.

94. "Du weißt ja, wie sehr ich in allem immer darum bemüht bin, in innerster Übereinstimmung mit Dir zu handeln. Ich möcht mich nach Afrika melden, weil mir eine Verwendung in Rußland aus mancherlei Gründen doch schwer werden würde. Die Form, die der Krieg dort angenommen hat, ist so, daß ich dort wohl, wenn ich hinbefohlen werde, mit ganzem Einsatz meine Pflicht tun würde, aber freiwillig mich dorthin zu melden, wo der Krieg doch mit Ausdehnung auf die Zivilbevölkerung geführt wird und im eigentlichen Sinne ein Vernichtungskrieg ist, das möchte ich nicht." Letter to Adelheid Hagena, 18 March 1942.

95. "Es ist so grauenhaft, was jetzt geschieht. Es ist fast, als ob—wie bei schwersten Verwundungen der Körper unempfindlich wird, so auch jetzt die Seele den ungeheueren Umfang des Leidens und der Not nicht zu fassen mag." Letter to Adelheid Hagena, 30 May 1943.

96. The main archive of Bethel has an account by Hauptmann Köhler of the plane crash; Köhler, "Bericht von Herrn Hauptmann Köhler," Akte Hagena. They also have the sermon given at the memorial service in Bethel's Zionskirche by his missionary colleague Heinrich Scholten ("Gedächtnisrede für Oberleutnant Pastor Missionar Otto Hagena," 24 August 1943, Zionskirche, Akte Hagena). Thanks to Dorothea Woydack for checking the report.

97. Stargardt, *The German War*, shows in his fascinating book that a great part of the German population knew what was going on; Hagena was by no means the only one.

98. Note esp. Weman, *African Music and the Church in Africa.* One of the letters of condolence found in Hagena's file at the VEM is from the Moravian mission director

Vogt, who remembers all the help Hagena gave them in completing a music project that Rietzsch was unwilling to finish.

99. Kornder, *Die Entwicklung der Kirchenmusik*, 165–67, has a discussion of Both's work in Africa. See also Menzel, *Die Bethel-Mission*, 461. I would also like to thank Both for a long conversation we had on 16 January 2016. Brose met with me several times in Berlin and was also extremely helpful.

100. Ehmann was the son of a Bethel deacon; he earned his PhD under Gurlitt in Freiburg, took over all musical NSDAP events there beginning in 1935, joined the NSDAP in 1937, and published extensively on Nazi topics. In this he is quite typical of many leaders of the *Singbewegung*. See John, "Der Mythos vom Deutschen in der deutschen Musik," and Bockstiegel, "Ehmann, Wilhelm."

101. Personal communication, 16 January 2016.

102. Blasio Mulyowa wrote a thesis on how to build amadindas and akadindas, and Joas Kijugo wrote one on how to play them, both for Ruhija Music Center. I would like to thank Werner Both for allowing me to see these theses.

103. The recordings can be heard at http://missionmusicafrica.com/, accessed 5 February 2020.

104. See https://dacb.org/stories/tanzania/kibira2/, accessed 5 February 2020.

105. For more information on Kibira, see http://www.bu.edu/sth-history/prophets/josiah-kibira/, accessed 5 February 2020.

106. Martin Brose, private communication, 19 February 2016.

107. Brose stayed in Ruhija from 1968 to 1971.

108. Thanks to the VEM archivist, Wolfgang Apelt, for this information.

109. Martin Brose told me that Kibira told him that this is the main reason he would like Kijuga to study in Herford. Private communication, 17 February 2016.

110. Martin Brose, private communication, December 2011.

111. Nannyonga-Tamusza and Solomon, *Ethnomusicology in East Africa*, 120.

112. Agawu, *Representing African Music*, 148.

CHAPTER THIRTEEN

1. For an overview of all African mission activities, see Sundkler and Steed, *A History of the Church in Africa*. For a recent biography on St. Ottilien, see Egger, *Transnationale Biographien*, which only deals with the later period.

2. For their work in East Africa including purchasing men and women out of slavery, see also Koren, *To the Ends of the Earth*.

3. See Renner, *Vom Missionshaus Reichenbach zur Benediktinerkongregation von St. Ottilien 1971*, 15–92, 93–111, 132–36; Auf der Maur, "Beitrag der Benediktiner-Missionare"; and Gründer, *Christliche Mission und deutscher Imperialismus*, 53–55.

4. Perras, *Carl Peters and German Imperialism*, 83–85.

5. Gründer, *Christliche Mission und deutscher Imperialismus*, 205–6.

6. Ibid., 229–30. The Benedictines also had extensive plantations where many children between the ages of five and fifteen were put to work. Ibid., 243. See also "Aus dem Tagebuch des Hochwürdigen Apostolischen Präfekten P. Maurus."

7. For a map of the locations of St. Ottilien activities in Tanzania, see http://www .ottilien.org/ and https://erzabtei.de/mission, accessed 5 February 2020. For an excellent overview, see Kornder, *Die Entwicklung der Kirchenmusik*, 144–55; Hertlein, "Die Entwicklung katechetischer Literatur; and Hertlein, *Ndanda Abbey: Part 1*. Peramiho had an abbey church built in Romanesque style built during World War II; the monastery had 150 monks and 100 sisters. It also included a hospital, schools, and agricultural schools. Apparently when the first Tanzanian prime minister, Julius Nyere, a Catholic, visited Peramiho in 1960, he said, "You have got everything—except a prison." Sundkler and Steed, *The History of the Church in Africa*, 877.

8. Dyer, "Roman Catholic Church Music."

9. "Da sehe ich die Wangoni und die anderen Stämme des Missionsgebietes von Peramiho und weit, weit darüber hinaus Wege gehen, die einst unsere eigenen Vorfahren gegangen sind. Ich sehe sie von der Kirche nicht nur den Glauben empfangen, sondern auch Güter höherer Kultur und darunter vor allem Gesang und Musik übernehmen, innerlich verarbeiten, zum Eigenbesitz umgestalten und zu einer individuellen Entwicklung bringen." Iten, "Über Neger-Musik," 343.

10. Berg, *Die katholische Heidenmission als Kulturträger*, 172.

11. Richter, *Die Einwurzelung des Christentums in der Heidenwelt*, 192.

12. Berg, *Die katholische Heidenmission als Kulturträger*, 191.

13. He wrote this article for a festschrift in honor of the St. Ottilien abbot Norbert Weber; see Drinkwelder, "Die Bedeutung der Liturgie für Missionär und Mission," 74.

14. I would like to thank Barbara Boisits for information on Vivell. For a detailed discussion of his life and work, see Boisits, *Coelestin Vivell*.

15. Vivell, "Musik und Gesang der Neger in der apostolischen Präfektur Süd-Sansibar."

16. Ibid., 72.

17. Ibid., 73.

18. Ibid., 74.

19. Ibid.

20. Ibid.

21. We know that he sang in the choir in the Vincentium in Bressanone, since he is listed among the choir singers. The repertoire there included works by Orlando di Lassus. "Erinnerungen an Missionsbischof Cassian Spiess," bk. 3, 13–14, St. O.

22. Sundkler and Steed, *A History of the Church in Africa*, 534; and Mapunda, "Reexamining the Maji," 230.

23. Doerr, *Peramiho, 1898–1998*, 35.

24. This account is based on Mapunda, "Reexamining the Maji," and relies on both written documents and oral history, as indicated by the title.

25. He was also a close friend of Amrhein, but I am not sure that this played a role in the murder.

26. Hans Paasche, a leader of the *Jugendbewegung* (see part II, chap. 8), participated in putting down the uprising as an officer in the imperial navy. The experience turned him into a lifelong pacifist and an admirer of Africans.

27. Sundkler and Steed, *A History of the Church in Africa*, 534. Later, during the Nazi years, the Catholic Church did not allow their priests and monks to join NSDAP.

As a result, although the German priests were interned and the abbey was run by Swiss priests, the German priests generally did not have to go back to Germany but were interned in Tanzania. See Hertlein, *Ndanda Abbey*, part II, 345–61. All Catholic clerics were prohibited from joining political parties because of the so-called *Entpolitisierungsklause des Reichskonkordats*. See Scholz, *Die Kirchen und der deutsche Nationalstaat*, 321. The *Konkordat* between Hitler and the pope was signed on 20 July 1933.

28. St. Ottilien did not have a copy of the 1901 or 1923 hymnbook, so I am relying on the description in Kornder, *Die Entwicklung der Kirchenmusik*, 147–48.

29. Festchronik von St. Ottilien, Bischofsweihe des ersten Apost. Vicars von Süd Sansibar, RMI P, St. O; Cassian Spiess, OSB, 16 November 1902, 4, St. O.

30. Auf der Maur, "Beitrag der Benediktiner-Missionare," 127.

31. Renner, *Die Benediktinermission*, 131.

32. Spiess, *Kihehe Wörtersammlung*.

33. Spiess, *Kingoni und Kisutu Mitteilungen*; also Sieber, "Cassian Spiess," 342.

34. Akte Künster, St. O. He must have also been an ardent Karl May fan in his younger years, because he composed an Ave Maria for Winnetou's death. Kühne and Lorenz, *Karl May und die Musik*, 332–33.

35. "P. Klemens Künster D.S.B. †."

36. St. O, 028.

37. In contrast, the Leipzig Mission did not send Bruno Gutmann back even though he was in constant conflict with colonial authorities (see part III, chap. 11). But the Catholics in Dar es Salaam were close to colonial officers, while the Protestant missionaries tried to get out of the way of the colonial government.

38. Künster, "Etwas über afrikanische Musikinstrumente," and *Harmonisches System zur Begleitung der gregorianischen Choralmelodien*.

39. Rühl, "Die missionarische Akkommodation," 129–30.

40. All of these instruments are now in St. Ottilien in Bavaria, which has just re-opened its museum; http://www.missionsmuseum.de/museum/aktuelles.html.

41. "Das längste Stäbchen steht, wie das Bild zeigt, in der Mitte und gibt naturgemäß den tiefsten Ton des Instrumentes an, also den Grundton. Die rechts von diesem Grundton sich befindenden drei kürzeren Stäbchen geben zu diesem Grundton die kleine Terz, reine Quinte und reine Oktav an, und die links stehenden drei Stäbchen die noch übrigen Töne der auf dem Grundton sich aufbauenden diatonischen Tonleiter, mit Ausnahme des sechsten Tones; dabei ist noch zu merken, daß der zweite Ton dieser Tonleiter nur in der Oktave vorhanden ist, welche das auf der linken Seite stehende kürzeste Stäbchen angibt. . . . Vom musikalischen Standpunkte aus also können wir, wenn wir alle Töne zusammenfassen, sagen, wir haben hier vor uns die auf dem Grundton d aufgebaute, im Mittelalter mit dem Namen dorische und in den Kirchentonarten oder Tonleitern als erste bezeichnete Tonleiter mit Auslassung des sechsten Tones h oder b." Künster, "Etwas über afrikanische Musikinstrumente," 85–86.

42. "Wie sie das natürliche, unverdorbene musikalische Gefühl, unbeeinflußt von allem Konventionellem und Gewohnheitsmäßigen eingegeben hat." Ibid., 86.

43. Ibid. The phrase "recedite ad fontes" clearly refers to the pope's *motu proprio*.

44. St. O, 1906.

45. Künster, *Harmonisches System*, 3–4.

46. Ibid., 11.

47. ". . . der menschlichen Natur angepaßt, ja noch mehr ihr eigen ist und immer bleiben wird und daß er nicht eine vorübergehende künstlerische Erfindung, sei es nun der Griechen oder irgend eines anderen Volkes oder auch der katholische Kirche ist, und daß seine Tonarten (so fremd sie auch manchmal dem Uneingeweihten klingen mögen) in der Natur des Menschen begründet und aus ihr hervorgegangen sind." Ibid.

48. "Wir sehen, alle diese Melodien der unkultivierten und auch teilweise kultivierten Völker sind fast ausschließlich in den alten Tonarten verfaßt." Künster, *Harmonisches System*, 16.

49. Ibid., 14.

50. Letter from Künster to Abbot Gallus, 25 April 1929, 5, St. O.

51. Rühl, "Die missionarische Akkomodation," 128–29.

52. "P. Clemens M. Künster O.S.B. schreibt: Was ich in dem Buche (*Harmonisches System für die Choralbegleitung*, St. Ottilien, 1906) über die Natürlichkeit des Chorals gesagt habe, dem habe ich aus meinen persönlichen Erfahrungen in Deutsch-Ost-Afrika (jetzt englisch) noch hinzuzufügen, daß ich bei meinem letzten Aufenthalt am Nyassasee den Choral auf meiner Station in drei bis vier Monaten eingeführt habe ohne ein anderes Hilfsmittel als mein einziges Graduale. Nach 3 Monaten konnte die Gemeinde (100 Christen und 1000 Katechumenen und Heiden) das ganze leichte Commune (Kyrie, Gloria, Kredo, Sanctus und Agnus Dei) singen. 20–30 Knaben sangen vor, und die ganze Gemeinde, Knaben, Mädchen, Männer und Frauen, sangen abwechselnd mit diesen. Die Kirche war nur von Bambus gebaut. Ich habe dazu jeden Sonntag nach dem Amt eine Viertelstunde an die ganze Gemeinde Gesangsunterricht gegeben. . . . Nach 3 oder 4 Monaten äußerte ich meinem schwarzen Hauptlehrer die Ansicht, jetzt aufhören zu wollen mit dem Gesangunterricht nach dem Amte, weil es den Leuten, besonders den älteren, zu viel werden könnte . . . Darauf sagte mir der Lehrer: 'Nein, das darfst du nicht tun; denn die Leute kommen ja eben so fleißig in den Gottesdienst, weil sie das Singen des Chorals so lieben' Die Leute mußten (wenigstens die größere Anzahl) über den Krokodilfluß mit dem Einbaum setzen, was nicht ohne Gefahr war." Ibid., 129–30.

53. I would like to thank Johannes van Ooyen, a grandnephew of Meinulf Küsters, for information on his relative.

54. The main authority on Küsters is the art historian Maria Kecskési. His biographical information is summarized in her article "Der Afrikanist P. Meinulf Küsters."

55. Schmidt is the founder of the Vienna Kulturkreislehre. He founded the journal *Anthropos* in 1906 and also the Anthropos Institute.

56. For Küsters's view of Wundt's relevance for missionaries, see his "Wilhelm Wundts Bedeutung für die katholischen Missionare."

57. See esp. Küsters, "Afrikanische Negerkunst und ihre Beziehungen zur Hochkultur," 1–16, and "Die figürliche Darstellung auf den Beninzähnen des Linden-Museums, Stuttgart."

58. Numerous anecdotes circulate about him; he must not have been a typical cleric. He regularly participated in the Munich carnival in his clerical uniform and was greatly amused when people accused him of dressing up as a priest. See Kecskési, "Das Lied, der Mönch und die 'Lippennegerinnen,'" 1491. And in a letter dated 26 November 1928, Bishop Bonifaz Sauer asked Abbot Primas Fidelis v. Stotzingen to send P. Meinulf Küsters

back to Africa "because he is introducing free customs to the clerical students of St. Ot-tilien in Munich." I would like to thank Johannes van Ooyen, grandnephew of Meinulf Küsters, for this information (e-mail, 9 October 2014).

59. In 1928 he wrote about his Peramiho students in the St. Ottilien Monatsblatt: "But, very much in his own way, he [the African student] tortures himself to satisfy the European. He still needs to be taught accurate observation and exact working methods. He does everything more or less as he is told, writes roughly as he has been directed to write. One has to check every word that one has written on the blackboard in the book-let, and when one does this one can see the most astonishing word transformations, which can be very amusing for an observer, but for the upright schoolteacher they can be quite hair-raising. . . . Awful also are the leaps that a grown-up Negro brain can do. Where we contemplate, the Negro does not see any reason whatsoever to torture him-self. One thing happens after the other, thus the second thing follows from the first. Why was Joseph sold by his brothers? Because he went to the desert with them. . . . They also constantly mix up form and content. When something looks roughly the same and sounds roughly the same, then it also is the same, and they are very astonished when we place a fat red line under their work because of a few shabby letters." (Aber er quält sich red-lich, den Europäer zu befriedigen. Freilich nach seiner Art. Genaues Zusehen, exaktes Ar-beiten muß ihm erst beigebracht werden. Er macht alles ungefähr so wie man ihm sagt, schreibt alles so ungefähr so wie man ihm sagt, schreibt alles ungefähr so wie man es ihm vorschreibt. Man muß jedes Wort, das man an die Wandtafel schreibt, im Heft nachsehen, und kann dann die wunderbarsten Wortwandlungen studieren, die für die Fernstehenden äußerst lustig, für den biederen Schulmeister aber geradezu haarsträubend anzusehen sind. Schlimm sind auch die gedanklichen Sprünge, die ein ausgewachsenes Negerhirn machen kann. Wo wir überlegen, da sieht der Neger wirklich keinen Grund zu solcher Selbstquälerei. Es ist eins nach dem anderen geschehen, also war das Erste die Ursache des Letzteren. Warum wurde Joseph von seinen Brüdern verkauft? Weil er zu ihnen in die Wüste ging. . . . Nicht minder ist ihre andere Eigenart, Inhalt und Form zu verwechseln. Wenn etwas ungefähr gleich aussieht, sich ungefähr gleich anhört, dann ist es eben auch dasselbe, und grosses Staunen hebt an, wenn wir um ein paar lumpige Buchstaben willen einen dicken roten Strich unter die Geistesarbeit setzen.) Küsters, "Von München nach Peramiho" and "Die Missionsschule in Peramiho," 228–29. The historian Richard Hölzl finds that Küsters is among the missionaries who is more concerned with developmental aid than simple missionary activity. Holzl, "Rassismus, Ethnogenese und Kultur," 33.

60. Küsters, *Myrtenblume der christlichen Braut und Ehefrau*; and Reichart and Küsters, *Elementary Kiswaheli Grammar of Introduction*.

61. Kecskési, *Die Mwera in Südost-Tansania*. Kecskési untangles the various sources of the book. It seems that Küsters's missionary colleague Joachim Ammann gave his manuscript to Küsters and expected him to finish the book (14). Of interest to music scholars is the description of music and dance and the musical instruments. In addition, there are detailed notes in the St. Ottilien archive on two other tribes: the Matengo and the Pangwa. The Matengo material includes an especially rich description of music, dance, and musical instruments.

62. "Es glang mir unter anderm die uralten Lieder, die bei den Beschneidungsfeiern oder Mädchenweihen besser gesagt, bebraucht werden, zu erlangen. Moderne Einflüsse

machen sich hier nur vom Kongo aus geltend, von woher vor allem die Marimba eingeführt wurde und einzelne Tänze." Letter from Küsters to Hornbostel, 7 May 1927, Berlin
Phonogramm-Archiv. In contrast to the Leipzig missionaries, Küsters does not express
any dismay about female genital mutilation.

63. "Sehr wichtig wäre die Feststellung, ob bei Blasinstrumenten mit Grifflöchern
(Flöten, Klarinetten usw.) die Instrumente und die Anordnung der Löcher willkürlich
hergestellt werden, oder nach älteren Modellen kopiert, oder nach bestimmten überlieferten Regeln durch Abmessung (nach Pannen, Fingerbreiten usw.) und im letzten Fall die
Regeln genau zu erkunden.—Dass Panpfeifen jeder Art für uns das größte Interesse haben,
brauche ich wohl nicht zu erwähnen. Auch die Feststellung, daß sie fehlen, ist natürlich
wichtig." Letter from Hornbostel to Küsters, 4 March 1928, Berlin Phonogramm-Archiv.

64. Letter from Küsters to Hornbostel, 14 February 1929, 1, Berlin Phonogramm-
Archiv. Equally interesting is a description by Küsters's teacher Karl Weule from his
1906 trip to East Africa; Weule. "Negerleben in Ostafrika," 56. Hornbostel, in his letter
to Küsters of 4 March 1928, again tells him that he wants purely African music. Küsters
also writes to Marius Schneider about the phonograph Hornbostel sent him, saying that
he can only record a few people at a time and not large groups of singers. He wonders if
he could not be sent a phonograph with a larger speaking tube. "I am thankful for the
old Edison. Would it be possible to send me a larger funnel, because with the present
funnel the people have to stand very close if one wants to hear them at all. I have tried to
have fifty people sing, but all we heard was a small sound. And since the songs are often
polyphonic, it would be great if one could make the choir heard." Letter from Küsters to
Schneider, 16 July 1934, Berlin Phonogramm-Archiv.

65. "So habe ich bemerkt, dass bei allen Tänzen die Tänzer zu erneuter Kraftleistung
durch das Trillern angespornt werden." Letter from Küsters to Hornbostel, 14 February
1929, Berlin Phonogramm-Archiv.

66. "Die Art des Trillerns hat mit dem Lippenflock, so weit ich es beurteilen kann,
nichts zu tun. Denn ich habe das Trillern sowohl von den Wamuera als auch von den
Wangoni und Wanyassa aufgenommen, bei welch letzteren Völkern der Lippenpflock
nicht gebraucht wird. Beim Triller vibriert die Zungenspitze an dem vorderen Gaumen.
Um eine Tondifferenz hervorzubringen, wird mitunter der Mund von der rechten Hand
bedeckt. Immer ist der Ton sehr durchdringend, weshalb oft eine einzige Frau eine ganze
Menge durch ihr Trillern übertönen kann. Es kommt das bei verschiedenen Liedern, am
Nyassasee aufgenommen, vor. Dabei standen die Hauptsänger vor dem Phonographen,
während die trillernde Frau weit weg war." Letter from Küsters to Hornbostel, 14 February 1929, Berlin Phonogramm-Archiv.

67. St. O. On this photograph see also Kecskési "Das Lied, der Mönch und die
'Lippennegerinnen.'"

68. "The term tonality is a general term . . . while the selection of possible modes
within tonality is dependent on the culture. Thus it is possible to find tonality circles in
the Middle Ages as well as in antiquity, but the *modi* are nevertheless quite different. I
am currently working a lot on these comparative questions. The second volume of my
polyphony volume will appear soon and will discuss the church modes from this point
of view. In the course of spring I hope to start a comparative study of the ancient tone
systems" (Der Begriff Tonalität aber ist etwas Allgemeines . . . , während die Auswahl der

in der Tonalität möglichen Modi von der jeweiligen Kultur abhängt. Die Tonalitätskreise lassen sich also ebenso wie bei der Antike im Mittelalter wiederfinden, die Modi aber sind doch reichlich verschieden. Ich beschäftige mich ziemlich viel mit diesen vergleichenden Fragen. Der 2. Band meiner Mehrstimmigkeit, der in Kürze erscheint, lässt sich von diesem Gesichtspunkte aus mit den Kirchentonarten auseinander. Im Laufe des Frühjahrs hoffe ich zu einer vergleichenden Studie über antike Tonsysteme zu kommen). Letter from Schneider to Küsters, 28 January 1935, Berlin Phonogramm-Archiv.

69. "Bei den alten Platten, die ich seinerzeit aufgenommen hatte, ist auch ein Märchen von den Wangoni. . . . Die Melodie erinnert so auffällig an Choralmelodie, dass ich Sie besonders darauf aufmerksam machen möchte." Letter from Küsters to Schneider, 8 March 1935, Berlin Phonogramm-Archiv.

70. Hornbostel included much more information in his article on African music, such as on texts and instruments.

71. Kecskési, *Die Mwera in Südost-Tansania*, 184.

72. The theologian Romano Guardini was one of the leaders and edited the Catholic journal *Die Schildgenossen*. Not surprisingly, also Guardini had a particular fondness for the Middle Ages.

73. Typescript, 1936, St. O.

74. Küsters, "Neger feiern Ostern," 1.

75. "Als ich das Weihwasser über die Palmen sprengte, da hielt die Menge nicht länger still, da fuhren die Hände mit den Palmwedeln hoch und ein Rauschen ging durch die Kirche, begeisternd, verbindend, der gemeinsamen Stimmung den rechten Ausdruck verleihend. Ich konnte es mir sehr gut vorstellen, wie einst die Juden in ihrer Begeisterung die Zweige von den Bäumen rissen und die Kleider auf den Weg breiteten. Hier würde Christus heute einen ähnlichen Empfang finden." Ibid., 2.

76. "P. Dr. Johannes Baptist Wolf OSB machte sogar neue Melodien für ein neues 'Ordinarium' in Swahili (d.h. zum Kyrie, Gloria, Sanctus und Agnus Dei). Der Anlaß war viel mehr das Buch von Marius Schneider (1934/1969:81–87, 90–91, 100) in dem P. Dr. Wolf Melodien der WaNgoni (Angone und WaNyasa (b.w. WaManda) fand, die P. Dr. Meinulf Küsters gesammelt hatte. Er fand in den Kingoni Liedern vor allem die Intervalle von Prim und Sekunde und bei den Wanyasa auch die Quint. Danach suchte er die entsprechenden Choralmelodien mit diesen Intervallen und achtete auch darauf, daß die Wort- und Melodieakzente gleich sind. Die Leute hatten dieses "Ordinarium" sehr gern und wir Kinder sangen sie auch zu Hause und überall." Mbunga, "Afrikanische Musik im Gottesdienst," 57.

77. The first edition, by Johann Baptist Wolf and P. C. Balbo, is from 1933–34 and is entitled *Chiriku*. See the detailed discussion of these hymnbooks in Kornder, *Die Entwicklung der Kirchenmusik*, 210–11. According to Kornder, this edition is lost, but it was reprinted many times. I was able to see the 1961 edition by Gerold Ruper and J. B. Wolf.

78. See Kornder, *Die Entwicklung*, 155, 258n97.

79. Kornder has identified a number of hymns by Wolf in "Tumsifu Mungu" (1985). Kornder, *Die Entwicklung*, 258n99. Wolf's liturgical pieces were not universally popular. When he had composed the Mass he first sent it to the education secretary Fr. MacCarthy, who judged the pieces too "Protestant." But it was approved by Abbot Gallus Steiger, and various similar volumes appeared. Auf der Maur, "Beitrag der Benediktiner-Missionare," 133n89.

80. Dyer, "Roman Catholic Church Music."

81. The best biographies of Mbunga are Kornder, *Die Entwicklung*, 172–75, and Klein, *Meßkompositionen in Afrika*.

82. Mbunga, *Church Law and Bantu Music*, 19.

83. Ibid.

84. Giorgetti, *Musica Africana*, 14–15; Marfurt, *Music in Africa*; Chambers, *Folksong—Plainsong*; Herzog, "General Characteristics of Primitive Music"; and Nadel, "The Origins of Music."

85. Wachsmann wrote an important dissertation in Fribourg on tonaries entitled *Untersuchungen zum vorgregorianischen Gesang*. He then emigrated to Uganda and did fundamental work on African music. Remarkably, even though he started out as a medievalist, he never compared medieval music to African music.

86. The library volume of Mbunga's article that I used in Berlin had been owned previously by the *Singbewegung* musicologist Konrad Ameln, who was also interested in the subject.

87. Mbunga, "Afrikanische Musik im Gottesdienst," 54.

88. "Man kann sich leicht vorstellen, daß das Ergebnis, außer im Bereich der Seminarien und Klöster, im allgemeinen eher unbefriedigend war; die Musik blieb ein fremdes Element und der Text war unverständlich. Die Fremdheit blieb eine grundsätzliche, obwohl jene Einfachhiet, dem Choral streckenweise eigen, eine gewisse Ähnlichkeit mit bestimmten Arten einheimischer Musik aufwies. Es wäre aber verfehlt, aus dieser Ähnlichkeit den Chrakter der Universalität des Chorals herzuleiten." Ibid., 57.

89. Ibid., 59.

90. Ibid., 62. Similarly, Joseph Kyagambiddwa's composition *Ugandan Martyrs: African Oratorio* was performed in 1964 in the Vatican by a large Ugandan choir. Both signal the synod's new openness to singing in East African languages.

91. Mbunga, "Afrikanische Musik im Gottesdienst," 66.

92. "Negativ reagierten manche Missionare und Katechisten; sie warfen dem Urheber vor, die einheimischen Melodien in der Kirche würden bei den Gläubigen eine heidnische Atmosphäre hervorrufen. Diese Einstellung der Katechisten basiert auf der Überzeugung, daß ihnen das Europäertum schlechthin als erstrebenswertes Statussymbol erschien und weil sie außerdem europäische Geisteswelt mit moderner Lebenshaltung gleichsetzten. So begann in den Sitzungen der liturgischen Kommission die mühevolle Auseinandersetzung mit der fragwürdigen Haltung der früheren Missionsepoche, mit einer Zeit, in der man aus allgemeiner Angst vor heidnischen Einflüssen den Wert ursprünglicher, einheimischer Musikelemente nicht zu erkennen vermochte und die autochtone Musik mit den dazugehörten Musikinstrumenten und Tänzen zugunsten unechter Importware verkommen ließ." Ibid., 60–61.

93. Private communication, 7 September 2015. Many thanks to Sister Barbara Ruckert of Bernried, Tutzing, for talking to me at great length.

BIBLIOGRAPHY

ABBREVIATIONS

Allgemeine Missionszeitschrift (*AMZ*)
Evangelisch-lutherisches Missionsblatt (*ELMB*)
Missionsblatt der Brüdergemeinde (*MBBG*)
Missionsblätter von St. Ottilien (*Mbl*)
Die Musik in Geschichte und Gegenwart, 1st ed. (*MGG*, ed. Blume)
Die Musik in Geschichte und Gegenwart, 2nd ed. (*MGG Online*)
Nachrichten aus der ostafrikanischen Mission (*NOAM*)

ARCHIVAL COLLECTIONS

Unitätsarchiv Herrnhut, Germany (UA)
Archiv der Leipziger Mission (LM)
Archiv der Vereinigten Evangelischen Mission, formerly Bethel Mission (VEM)
Archiv St. Ottilien (St. O)
Archiv der Jugendmusikbewegung, Burg Ludwigstein (AJ)
Guggenheim Foundation (GF)
Nachlass Franz Ferdinand Rietzsch (privately owned)
Letters of Otto Hagena (privately owned)
Letters of Adelheid Hagena (privately owned)
Letters of Franz Ferdinand Rietzsch to his family (Elisabeth Rietzsch, Spremberg, Saxony)
Berlin Phonogramm-Archiv
Universität der Künste, Berlin (UdK)
Jean Hargrove Music Library, University of California, Berkeley
Warburg Institute, London

WORKS CITED

Abraham, Otto, and Erich M. von Hornbostel. "Studien über das Tonsystem und die
Musik der Japaner." *Sammelbände der Internationalen Musikgesellschaft* 4 (1903):
302–60.

——. "Phonographierte indische Melodien." *Sammelbände der Internationalen Musikgesellschaft* 5 (1904): 348–401.

——, and Erich M. von Hornbostel. "Vorschläge für die Transkription exotischer Melodien." *Sammelbände der Internationalen Musikgesellschaft* 11 (1909): 1–25.

Adler, Guido. "Umfang, Methode und Ziel der Musikwissenschaft." *Vierteljahrsschrift
für Musikwissenschaft* 1 (1885): 5–20.

Adorno, Theodor W. *Dissonanzen: Musik in der verwalteten Welt.* Frankfurt: Suhrkamp,
1956.

——, and Walter Benjamin. *The Complete Correspondence, 1928–1940.* Cambridge, MA:
Harvard University Press, 2001.

Agawu, Kofi. "Tone and Tune: The Evidence for Northern Ewe Music." *Africa* 58 (1988):
127–46.

——. *Representing African Music: Postcolonial Notes, Queries, Positions.* New York:
Routledge, 2003.

——. "Tonality as a Colonizing Force in Africa." In *Audible Empire: Music, Global
Politics, Critique*, edited by Ronald Radano and Tejumola Olaniyan, 334–55. Durham,
NC: Duke University Press, 2015.

Agnew, Vanessa. "The Colonial Beginnings of Comparative Musicology." In *Germany's
Colonial Pasts: An Anthology in Memory of Susanne Zantop*, edited by Eric Ames,
Marcia Klotz, and Lora Wildenthal, 41–60. Lincoln: University of Nebraska Press, 2005.

Allgayer, Regine. "Heinitz, Wilhelm." *MGG Online.* Accessed 7 February 2020. https://
www.mgg-online.com/article?id=mgg06120&v=1.0&rs=mgg06120&q=Heinitz.

Altena, Thorsten. *Ein Häuflein Christen mitten in der Heidenwelt des dunklen Erdenteils.* Münster: Waxmann, 2003.

Althaus, Gerhard. *Mamba-Anfang in Afrika.* Edited by Hans Ludwig Althaus. Erlangen:
Verlag der ev.-luth. Mission Erlangen, 1968.

"Am Feierabend." *ELMB* 87 (1932): 334–35.

Antholz, Heinz. "Jugendmusikbewegung." *MGG Online.* Accessed 7 February 2020.
https://www.mgg-online.com/article?id=mgg15540&v=1.0&rs=mgg15540&q=Jugend
musikbewegung.

Arens, Hans. *Sprachwissenschaft: Der Gang ihrer Entwicklung von der Antike bis zur
Gegenwart.* Freiburg: Karl Alber, 1955.

Arnim, Achim von, and Clemens Brentano. *Des Knaben Wunderhorn.* 3 vols. Heidelberg:
Mohr & Zimmer, 1805 and 1808.

Arom, Simha, and Frédéric Voisin. "Theory and Technology in African Music." In *Africa:
The Garland Encyclopedia of World Music*, edited by Ruth Stone, 254–70. New York:
Garland, 1997.

Auf der Maur, Ivo. "Beitrag der Benediktiner-Missionare von St. Ottilien in Tansania zur
liturgischen Erneuerung (1887–1970)." *Neue Zeitschrift für Missionswissenschaft* 27
(1971): 126–35, 188–200.

"Aus dem Tagebuch des Hochwürdigen Apostolischen Präfekten P. Maurus." *Mbl* 101 (1997): 338–42.

Bachmann, Traugott. "Praktische Lösungen missionarischer Probleme auf einem jungen Arbeitsfelde (Nyassagebiet, Deutsch-Ostafrika)." In *Hefte zur Missionskonferenz der Brüdergemeine*, 1–35. Herrnhut, 1912.

———. "Nyiha-Märchen: Gesammelt und übersetzt von Missionar Tr. Bachmann." *Zeitschrift für Kolonialsprachen* 6 (1915–16): 81–101.

———. *Ich gab so manchen Anstoss*. Edited by Hans-Windekilde Jannasch. Leipzig: Koehler & Amelang, 1957.

Bakker, Egbert J., ed. *A Companion to the Ancient Greek Language*. Oxford: Wiley, 2010.

Ballanta, Nicholas G. J. "An African Scale." *Musical Courier*, 29 June 1922, 6.

———. *Saint Helena Spirituals*. New York: Schirmer, 1925.

———. "Gathering Folk Tunes in an African Country." *Musical America* 27 (1926): 3–11.

———. "Music of the African Races." *West Africa* 14 (1930): 752–53.

Barker, Andrew. "*Heterophonia* and *Poikilia*: Accompaniments to Greek Melody." In *Mousike: Metrica, ritmica e musica greca; In memoria di Giovanni Comotti*, edited by Bruno Gentili and Franca Perusino, 41–60. Studi di metrica classica 11. Pisa: Istituto Editoriali e Poligrafici Internazionale, 1990.

Barz, Gregory. "Politics of Remembering: Performing History(ies) in Youth Kyaya Competitions in Dar es Salaam, Tanzania." In *Ub Mashindano! Competitive Music Performance in East Africa*, edited by Frank Gunderson and Gregory Barz, 379–405. Dar es Salaam: Mkuki na nyota, 2000.

———. *Performing Religion: Negotiating Past and Present in Kwaya Music of Tanzania*. Amsterdam: Rodopi, 2003.

Baudert, Samuel. *The Advance Guard: 200 Years of Moravian Missions, 1732–1932*. London: Moravian Book Room, 1932.

Baum, Richard, and Dietrich Berke. "Bärenreiter." *Grove Music Online*. Accessed 7 June 2012. https://www.oxfordmusiconline.com/grovemusic/view/10.1093/gmo/978156 1592630.001.0001/omo-9781561592630-e-0000002041.

Bautz, Friedrich Wilhelm. "Bodelschwingh, Friedrich von." In *Biographisch-Bibliographisches Kirchenlexikon* 1 (1975), cols. 649–51.

Bayreuther, Rainer. "Die Situation der deutschen Kirchenmusik um 1933 zwischen Singbewegung und Musikwissenschaft." *Archiv für Musikwissenschaft* 67 (2010): 1–35.

Beck, Hartmut. *Brüder in vielen Völkern: 250 Jahre Mission der Brüdergemeine*. Erlangen: Verlag der evangelischen Mission, 1981.

Becking, Gustav. "Der Gegenwartswert mittelalterlicher Musik." *Melos* 4 (1925): 347–52.

———. "Der musikalische Bau des montenegrinischen Volksepos." *Archives néerlandaises de phonétique expérimentale* 8–9 (1933): 144–53.

Beckley, Joseryl. "African and Western Aspects of Ballanta's Opera *Afiwa*." DMA diss., University of British Columbia, 2016.

Bennett, Norman R. "The British on Kilimanjaro, 1884–1892." *Tanganyika Notes and Records* 63 (1964): 229–44.

Beregovski, Moshe. "The Altered Dorian Scale in Jewish Folk Music." In *Old Jewish Folk Music: The Collections and Writings of Moshe Beregovski*, edited and translated by Mark Slobin, 549–68. Syracuse, NY: Syracuse University Press, 2000.

Berg, Ludwig. *Die kath. Heidenmission als Kulturträger*. Aachen: Xaverius-Verlagsbuchhandlung, 1923–28.

Berger, Anna Maria Busse. *Medieval Music and the Art of Memory*. Berkeley and Los Angeles: University of California Press, 2005.

———. "Wann wurde das Notre Dame Repertorium kanonisch?" In *Der Werkekanon in der Musik-Werturteil, Konstrukt, historiographische Herausforderung*, edited by Klaus Pietschmann and Melania Wald, 254–79. Munich: Edition Text + Kritik, 2013.

———. "Tonic Sol-Fa in Africa." In *"Unser Land"? Lesothos schweizerische Nationalhymne/"Our Land"? Lesotho's Swiss National Anthem*, edited by Matthias Schmidt and Andreas Baumgartner, 150–58. Basel: Merian, 2018.

———. *Walzenaufnahmen von Franz Rietzsch: Tanzania, 1931–37*. Berliner Phonogramm-Archiv-Historische Klangdokumente/Berlin Phonogramm-Archiv Historical Sound Documents. Berlin: Berlin Phonogramm-Archiv, 2017.

Berger, Karol. *A Theory of Art*. New York: Oxford University Press, 2000.

Berlin, Isaiah. *Three Critics of the Enlightenment*, edited by Henry Hardy. Princeton, NJ: Princeton University Press, 2000.

Berliner, Paul. *The Soul of Mbira*. Berkeley and Los Angeles: University of California Press, 1978.

———. *Thinking in Jazz: The Infinite Art of Improvisation*. Chicago: University of Chicago Press, 1994.

Besseler, Heinrich. "Studien zur Musik des Mittelalters: I. Neue Quellen des 14. und beginnenden 15. Jahrhunderts." *Archiv für Musikwissenschaft* 7 (1925): 167–252.

———. "Musik des Mittelalters in der Hamburger Kunsthalle, 1.-8. April, 1924." *Zeitschrift für Musikwissenschaft* 8 (1926): 42–54.

———. "Studien zur Musik des Mittelalters: II. Die Motette von Franko von Köln bis Philipp von Vitry." *Archiv für Musikwissenschaft* 8 (1926): 131–258.

———. *Die Musik des Mittelalters und der Renaissance*. Potsdam: Akademische Verlagsgesellschaft Athenaion, 1931.

———. "Umgangsmusik und Darbietungsmusik im 16. Jahrhundert." *Archiv für Musikwissenschaft* 16 (1959): 21–43.

———. "Zum Tode Wilibald Gurlitts." *Acta musicologica* 36 (1964): 48–50.

Blacking, John. "Some Notes on a Theory of African Rhythm Advanced by Erich von Hornbostel." *African Music* 1 (1955): 12–20.

Blankenburg, Werner. "Was war die Singbewegung? Dank des siebzigjährigen Schriftleiters." *Musik und Kirche* 43 (1973): 258–60.

———. "The Music of the Bohemian Brethren." In *Protestant Church Music: A History*, edited by Friedrich Blume, 591–608. New York: Norton, 1974.

Bleibinger, Bernhard. *Marius Schneider und der Simbolismo: Ensayo musicológico y etnológico sobre un buscador de símbolos*. Munich: Alteritas, 2005.

Blüher, Hans. *Wandervogel: Geschichte einer Jugendbewegung. Erster Teil: Heimat und Aufgang*. 3rd ed. Berlin: Hans Blüher, 1913,

Blum, Stephen. "European Musical Terminology and the Music of Africa." In *Comparative Musicology and Anthropology of Music: Essays on the History of Ethnomusicology*, edited by Bruno Nettl and Philip V. Bohlman, 3–36. Chicago: University of Chicago Press, 1991.

———. "Composition." *Grove Music Online.* Accessed 7 February 2020. https://www
.oxfordmusiconline.com/grovemusic/view/10.1093/gmo/9781561592630.001.0001
/omo-9781561592630-e-0000006216.

———. "E. M. von Hornbostel as Listener and Scientist." Paper read at the Captured
Sounds—Collecting, Storing, Sharing conference, Humboldt Forum, 15–16 May 2018.

Blume, Friedrich. *Das Rasseproblem in der Musik: Entwurf einer Methodologie musik-
wissenschaftlicher Rasseforschung.* Wolfenbüttel: Kallmeyer, 1939.

———. "The Period of the Reformation." In *Protestant Church Music: A History,* edited
by Blume, 1–124. New York: Norton, 1974.

Boas, Franz. *The Central Eskimo.* Sixth Annual Report of the Bureau of Ethnology to the
Secretary of the Smithsonian Institution, 1884–1885, 399–670. Washington: Government Printing Office, 1888.

———. "Changes in the Bodily Form of Descendants of Immigrants." *American Anthropologist* 14 (1912): 530–60.

———. *The Mind of Primitive Man.* New York: Macmillan, 1911. Revised ed., 1938.

Bockstiegel, Heiko. "Ehmann, Wilhelm." In *Biographisch-Bibliographisches Kirchenlexikon,* 20:444–50. Nordhausen, 2002.

Bohlman, Philip V. *Song Loves the Masses: Herder on Music and Nationalism.* Berkeley
and Los Angeles: University of California Press, 2017.

Boisits, Barbara. *Coelestin Vivell: Ein Choralforscher aus dem Stift Seckau (Steiermark).*
Ph.D. diss., Karl-Franzens-Universität, Graz, 1995.

Bopp, Franz. *Über das Conjugationssystem der Sanskritsprache in Vergleichung mit
jenen der griechischen, lateinischen, persischen und germanischen Sprache.* Frankfurt: Andreäischen Buchhandlung, 1816.

———. *Vergleichende Grammatik des Sanskrit, Zend, Griechischen, Lateinischen, Litauischen, Altslavischen, Gotischen und Deutschen.* Berlin: Königliche Akademie
der Wissenschaften, 1833.

———. *Vocalismus, oder sprachvergleichende Kritiken.* Berlin: Nicolai, 1836.

Bredekamp, Horst. *Aby Warburg, der Indianer.* Berlin: Wagenbach, 2019.

Brenner, Klaus-Peter. *Die kombinatorisch strukturierten Harfen- und Xylophonpattern
der Nzakara (Zentralafrikanische Republik) als klingende Geometrie: Eine Alternative zu Marc Chemilliers Kanonhypothese.* Bonn: Holos, 2004.

Breuer, Hans, Editor. *Der Zupfgeigenhansl.* Darmstadt: Heinrich Hohmann, 1909.

Brinkmann, Ernst. "Ernst Wilm, 1901–1989." *Jahrbuch für Westfälische Kirchenge-
schichte* 82 (1989): 11–28.

Brose, Martin. "Musik der Kagera Region in Tansania." Typescript, 1998, VEM.

Brown, Howard Mayer. "Sachs, Curt." *Grove Music Online.* Accessed 7 February 2020.
https://www.oxfordmusiconline.com/grovemusic/view/10.1093/gmo/9781561592630
.001.0001/omo-9781561592630-e-0000024256.

"Die Brust aufgeschlitzt." *Der Spiegel,* 27 July 1950, 36–37.

Bukofzer, Manfred. "Präzisionsmessungen an primitive Musikinstrumenten." *Zeitschrift
für Physik* 99 (1936): 643–65.

———. "Kann die 'Blasquintentheorie' zur Erklärung exotischer Ton-Systeme beitragen?"
Anthropos 32 (1937): 402–18.

———. "Popular Polyphony in the Middle Ages." *Musical Quarterly* 26 (1940): 31–49.

————. "Blasquinte." In *MGG*, ed. Blume (1949–51), 1:1918–24.

Bunzl, Matti. "Franz Boas and the Humboldtian Tradition." In *Volksgeist as Method and Ethic: Essays on Boasian Ethnography and the German Anthropological Tradition*, edited by George W. Stocking, 17–78. Madison: University of Wisconsin Press, 1996.

Burridge, Kate. "Nineteenth-Century Study of Sound Change from Rask to Saussure." In *The Oxford Handbook of Linguistics*, edited by Keith Allen, 141–67. Oxford: Oxford University Press, 2013.

Buschmann, Eduard. *Über die Kavi-Sprache auf der Insel Java, nebst einer Einleitung über die Verschiedenheit des menschlichen Sprachbaues und ihren Einfluss auf die geistige Entwicklung des Menschengeschlechtes.* 3 vols. Berlin: F. Dümmler, 1836–39.

Busse, Joseph. *Die Nyakyusa: Wirtschaft und Gesellschaft.* Münster: LIT Verlag, 1995.

————. *Die Nyakyusa: Religion und Magie.* Bonn: Holos Verlag, 1998.

Busse Berger, Anna Maria. *See* Berger, Anna Maria Busse.

Cantor, Norman F. *Inventing the Middle Ages: The Lives, Works and Ideas of the Great Medievalists of the Twentieth Century.* New York: Morrow, 1991.

Carl, Florian. *Was bedeutet uns Afrika? Zur Darstellung afrikanischer Musik im deutschsprachigen Diskurs des 19. und frühen 20. Jahrhunderts.* Münster: LIT Verlag, 2004.

Chailley, Jacques. *Formation et transformation du langage musical.* Paris: Centre de Documentation Universitaire, 1955.

Chambers, G. B. *Folksong—Plainsong: A Study in Musical Origins.* London: Merlin Press, 1956.

Charles, Sydney Robinson. "Bukofzer, Manfred." *Grove Music Online.* Accessed 7 February 2020. https://www.oxfordmusiconline.com/grovemusic/view/10.1093/gmo/978 1561592630.001.0001/omo-9781561592630-e-0000004284.

Christensen, Thomas. *Stories of Tonality in the Age of François-Joseph Fétis.* Chicago: University of Chicago Press, 2019.

Conrad, Joachim. *Richard Gölz (1887–1975): Der Gottesdienst im Spiegel seines Lebens.* Göttingen: Vandenhoeck & Ruprecht, 1995.

————. *Liturgie als Kunst und Spiel: Die Kirchliche Arbeit Alpirsbach, 1933–2003.* Heidelberger Studien zur Praktischen Theologie 8. Hamburg: LIT Verlag, 2003.

Conrad, Sebastian. "'Eingeborenenpolitik' in Kolonie und Metropole: 'Erziehung zur Arbeit' in Ostafrika und Ostwestfalen." In *Das Kaiserreich transnational: Deutschland in der Welt 1871–1914*, edited by Sebastian Conrad und Jürgen Osterhammel, 107–28. Göttingen: Vandenhoeck & Ruprecht, 2004.

————. *Deutsche Kolonialgeschichte.* Munich: Beck, 2008.

Craig, Gordon. *Deutsche Geschichte, 1866–1945: Vom Norddeutschen Bund bis zum Ende des Dritten Reiches.* Munich: Beck, 1985.

Crocker, Richard. "No Polyphony before AD 900!" In *Strings and Threads: A Celebration of the Work of Anne Draffkorn Kilmer*, edited by Wolfgang Heimpel and Gabriella Frantz-Szabó, 45–58. Winona Lake, IN: Eisenbrauns, 2011.

Dahlhaus, Carl. *Die Musiktheorie im 18. und 19. Jahrhundert. Zweiter Teil: Deutschland; Geschichte der Musiktheorie.* / Vol. 11. Edited by Ruth E. Müller. Darmstadt: Wissenschaftliche Buchgesellschaft, 1989.

Daniels, Paul Raymond. *Nietzsche and the Birth of Tragedy*. New York: Routledge, 2014.

Day-O'Connell, Jeremy. "Pentatonic." *Grove Music Online*. Accessed 7 February 2020. https://www.oxfordmusiconline.com/grovemusic/view/10.1093/gmo/9781561592630.001.0001/omo-9781561592630-e-0000021263.

Dietrich, Fritz. "Zur Kultmusikfrage." *Musik und Kirche* 8 (1936): 1–7.

Doerr, Lambert. *Peramiho, 1898–1998, in the Service of the Missionary Church*. Vol. 1. Ndanda-Peramiho: Benedictine Publications, 1998.

Donat, Helmut. "Auf der Flucht erschossen." *Zeit Online*, 3 April 1981. Accessed 5 February 2020. https://www.zeit.de/1981/15/auf-der-flucht-erschossen.

Döring, Paul. "Bei den Songo und Mutahangarwa." *NOAM* 29 (1915): 10.

Dorschel, Andreas. "Die Idee des Konservatoriums." In *Mendelssohns Welten*, edited by Laurenz Lütteken, 89–108. Kassel: Bärenreiter, 2010.

Drinkwelder, P. Erhard. "Die Bedeutung der Liturgie für Missionär und Mission." In *Lumen caecis: Festschrift zum silbernen Abts-Jubiläum des hochwürdigsten Herrn Dr. Norbert Weber O.S.B*, edited by Romuald Heiss, Leander Bopp, et al., 70–83. St. Ottilien: EOS Verlag, 1928.

Dyer, Joseph. "Roman Catholic Church Music," VII.1., 'The "motu proprio" of Pope Piux X.'" *Grove Music Online*. Accessed 1 November 2018. https://www.oxfordmusiconline.com/grovemusic/view/10.1093/gmo/9781561592630.001.0001/omo-9781561592630-e-0000046758.

Ebel, P. Basilius. *Das älteste alemannische Hymnar mit Noten: Kodex 386*. Veröffentlichungen der gregorianischen Akademie zu Freiburg in der Schweiz. Benziger: Einsiedeln, 1931.

Eggebrecht, Hans-Heinrich. "Polyphonie." In *Riemann Musiklexikon*, 3:740. 12th ed. Mainz: Schott, 1967.

Eggebrecht, Hans Heinrich, David Hiley, and Pamela Potter. "Husmann, Heinrich." *Grove Music Online*. Accessed 7 June 2012. https://www.oxfordmusiconline.com/grovemusic/view/10.1093/gmo/9781561592630.001.0001/omo-9781561592630-e-0000013606.

Egger, Christine. *Transnationale Biographien: Die Missionsbenediktiner von St. Ottilien in Tanganyika, 1922–1965*. Weimar: Böhlau, 2016.

Einstein, Alfred. "Der musikhistorische Kongress in Wien (March 26–31, 1927)." *Zeitschrift für Musikwissenschaft* 9 (1926–27): 498–99.

Elftmann, Heike. *Georg Schünemann, 1884–1945: Musiker, Pädagoge, Wissenschaftler, Organisator; Eine Situationsbeschreibung des Berliner Musiklebens*. Berliner Musik Studien 19. Sinzig: Studio, 2001.

Eskew, Harry. "Gospel Music." *Grove Music Online*. Accessed 7 June 2012. https://www.oxfordmusiconline.com/grovemusic/view/10.1093/gmo/9781561592630.001.0001/omo-9781561592630-e-1002224388?rskey=KeufTY&result=1.

Evans-Pritchard, Edward E. *Social Anthropology and Other Essays*. New York: Free Press, 1962.

Eyerly, Sarah Justina. "'Der Wille Gottes': Musical Improvisation in Eighteenth-Century Moravian Communities." In *Self, Community, World: Moravian Education in a Transatlantic World*, edited by Heikki Lempa and Paul Peucker, 201–27. Lehigh, PA: Lehigh University Press, 2010.

———. *Moravian Soundscapes: A Sonic History of the Moravian Missions in Early Penn-sylvania (Music, Nature, Place)*. Bloomington: Indiana University Press, 2020.

Fauser, Annegret. *Musical Encounters at the 1889 World's Fair*. Rochester, NY: University of Rochester Press, 2005.

Ferand, Ernest. *Die Improvisation in der Musik: Eine Entwicklungsgeschichte und psychologische Untersuchung*. Zurich: Rhein, 1938.

Ficker, Rudolf von. *Musik der Gotik: Perotinus; Organum Quadruplum; "Sederunt Principes."* Edited by Rudolf Ficker. Klavierauszug mit Text und kritischer Übertragung. Vienna: Universal, 1930.

———. "Der Organumtraktat der vatikanischen Bibliothek." *Kirchenmusikalisches Jahrbuch* 27 (1932): 65–74.

Fiedler, Klaus. *Christentum und afrikanische Kultur: Konservative deutsche Missionare in Tanzania, 1900–1940*. Missionswissenschaftliche Forschungen 16. Gütersloh: G. Mohn, 1982. Revised ed., Mzuzu: Luviri Press, 2017; English trans., *Christianity and African Culture: Conservative German Protestant Missionaries in Tanzania, 1900–1940* (Leiden and New York: E. J. Brill, 1996).

Fleischer, Oskar. *Neumen-Studien: Abhandlungen über mittelalterliche Gesangs-Tonschriften*. 3 vols. Leipzig: F. Fleischer, 1895–1904.

Forster, Michael. "Herder's Role in the Birth of Linguistics and Anthropology." *Stanford Encyclopedia of Philosophy*. Accessed 8 March 2016. http://plato.stanford.edu /entries/herder/#toc.

Freedberg, David. "Warburg's Mask: A Study in Idolatry." In *Anthropologies of Art*, edited by Mariët Westermann, 3–25. Williamstown, MA: Sterling and Francine Clark Institute in association with Yale University Press, 2005.

Fritze, Georg. "Die Geschichte eines Gesangbuches." *ELMB* 86 (1931): 296–306.

Funck, Eike. "Alte Musik und Jugendmusikbewegung." *Die Jugendmusikbewegung: Impulse und Wirkung*, edited by Karl-Heinz Reinfandt, 63–91. Wolfenbüttel: Möseler, 1987.

Garcia, David F. *Listening for Africa: Freedom, Modernity, and the Logic of Black Music's African Origins*. Durham, NC: Duke University Press, 2017.

Gelbart, Matthew, and Alexander Rehding. "Riemann and Melodic Analysis: Studies in Folk-Musical Tonality." In *The Oxford Handbook of Neo-Riemannian Music Theories*, edited by Edward Gollin and Alexander Rehding, 141–64. New York: Oxford University Press, 2011.

George, Stefan. *Blätter für die Kunst* [1892–1919]. Edited by Carl August Klein. Facsimile ed., Düsseldorf: Küpper, previously Georg Bondi, 1968.

Gerhard, Anselm. "Musikwissenschaft." In *Die Rolle der Geisteswissenschaften im Dritten Reich, 1933–1945*, edited by Frank-Rutger Hausmann, 165–92. Munich: Oldenbourg, 2002.

Gerold, P., ed. *Chiriku: Kitabu cha Nyimbo*. London: Macmillan, 1961.

Geyer, Christopher. "From the Arctic North to the Desert Southwest: Laura Boulton's Music Collecting Expeditions among Native North Americans." *Resound: A Quarterly of the Archives of Traditional Music* 21 (2002): 1–8.

Giorgetti, Filiberto. *Musica Africana: Sua tecnica e Acustica*. Bologna: Nigrizia, 1957.

Graetzer, Wolfgang. "Bearbeitung der Bearbei . . . Zu Rudolf Fickers editorischen Bemüh-ungen um einen 'Epochetermin der Musikgeschichte.'" In *Festschrift Gerhard Croll zum 65. Geburtstag*, edited by Wolfgang Graetzer and Andrea Lindmayr, 27–50. Regensburg: Laaber,1992.

Grimm, Jacob, *Über den Ursprung der Sprache*. Berlin: Dümmler, 1851.

Gründer, Horst. *Christliche Mission und deutscher Imperialismus: Eine politische Geschichte ihrer Beziehungen während der deutschen Kolonialzeit (1884–1914) unter besonderer Berücksichtigung Afrikas und Chinas*. Paderborn: Schöningh, 1982.

Grupe, Gerd. "E. M. von Hornbostel und die Erforschung afrikanischer Musik aus der armchair-Perspektive." In *Vom tönenden Wirbel menschlichen Tuns: Erich M. von Hornbostel als Gestaltpsychologe, Archivar und Musikwissenschaftler*, edited by Edited by Sebastian Klotz, 105–15. Berlin: Schibri, 1998.

Günther, Gerhard. *Erweckung in Afrika: Vom Aufbruch junger Kirchen im östlichen Afrika*. 2nd ed. Stuttgart: Evangelischer Missionsverlag, 1961.

Günther, Ursula. "Friedrich Ludwig in Göttingen." In *Musikwissenschaft und Musikpflege an der Georg-August-Universität inf Göttingen*, edited by Martin Staehelin, 152–75. Göttingen: Vandenhoeck & Ruprecht, 1987.

Gutknecht, Dieter. "Universitäre Musikwissenschaft in nationalsozialistischer Zeit: Die Universität zu Köln als Beispiel." In *Musikforschung—Faschismus— Nationalsozialismus: Referate der Tagung Schloß Engers (8. bis 11. März 2000)*, edited by Isolde v. Foerster, Christoph Hust, and Christoph-Hellmut Mahling, 211–22. Mainz: Are Edition, 2001.

Gutmann, Bruno. "Der erste Bericht aus der Station Masama." *ELMB* 22 (1907): 36–37.

———. "Das Herauswachsen christlicher Sitte aus dem Volksboden der Wadschagga." *AMZ* (1922–23): 300–11.

———. "Der Choral in der Dschaggagemeinde." In *Das Dschaggaland und seine Christen*, 141–47. Leipzig: Ev.-Luth. Mission, 1925.

———. *Gemeindeaufbau aus dem Evangelium: Grundsätzliches für Mission und Heimatkirche*. Leipzig: Verlag der evangelisch-lutherischen Mission, 1925.

———. "Grußlieder der Wadschagga." In *Festschrift Carl Meinhof*, 228–32. Glückstadt, Hamburg: L. Friederson, 1927.

———. *Freies Menschentum aus ewigen Bindungen*. Kassel: Bärenreiter, 1928.

———. *Schildwacht am Kilimanjaro*. Book I of *Der Baugrund*. Kassel: Bärenreiter, 1929.

———. "Deutsche Weihnachtssitten und Weihnachtslieder in Ostafrika." *Die Singgemeinde* 6 (1929–30): 44–48.

———. *Zurück auf die Gottesstraße*. Kassel: Bärenreiter-Verlag, 1934.

Hagena, Otto. "Aus dem Wachsen und Werden einer Hayagemeinde." Manuscript, 29 April 1932. Akte Otto Hagena, VEM.

———. "Musik in der evangelischen Heidenmission." Manuscript. Akte Otto Hagena, VEM.

———. "Lieder der Bahaya" (1939). Unpublished manuscript. 10 pp. Akte Otto Hagena, VEM Archiv.

Haines, John. "The Arabic Style of Performing Medieval Music." *Early Music* 29 (2001): 369–78.

Haken, Boris von. "Der Einsatzstab Rosenberg und die Erfassung musikalischer Kulturgüter in Westeuropa während des Zweiten Weltkrieges." *Acta Musicologica* 91 (2019): 101–25.

Halbig, Hermann. *Kleine gregorianische Formenlehre.* Kassel: Bärenreiter, 1930.

Handschin, Jacques. "Marius Schneider, Geschichte der Mehrstimmigkeit. Erster Teil: Die Naturvölker mit 289 Notenbeispielen, Berlin, 1934 (Verlag J. Bard)"; and "Zweiter Teil: Die Anfänge in Europa mit 172 Notenbeispielen und 4 Handschriften Wiedergaben (Berlin, 1935)." *Acta Musicologica* 11 (1939): 146–50 and. 150–51.

———. "Aus der alten Musiktheorie." *Acta musicologica* 15 (1943): 15–23.

———. *Musikgeschichte im Überblick.* Lucerne: Räber, 1948.

———. *Der Toncharakter.* Zurich: Atlantis, 1948.

———. "Die Musik der deutschen Jugendbewegung." In *Gedenkschrift Jacques Handschin: Aufsätze und Bibliographie,* edited by Hans Oesch, 348–54. Bern: Haupt, 1957.

Hansen, Finn Egeland. *The Grammar of Gregorian Tonality: An Investigation Based on the Repertory in Codex H 159, Montpellier.* Copenhagen: Dan Fog Musikforlag, 1979.

Hartwig, Gerald W. "The Historical and Social Role of Kerebe Music." *Tanzania Notes and Records: The Journal of the Tanzania Society* 70 (1969): 41–56.

Heinitz, Wilhelm. *Strukturprobleme in primitiver Musik.* Hamburg: Friederichsen, 1931.

———. "Musikwissenschaft und Völkerkunde." *Mitteilungsblatt der Gesellschaft für Völkerkunde* 8 (1938): 43–54.

Heins, Ernst. "On Jaap Kunst's Music in Java." *Ethnomusicology* 20 (1976): 97–101.

Helms, Richard, and William Hood. *A Look Over My Shoulder: A Life in the Central Intelligence Agency.* New York: Random House, 2002.

Hensel, Walter. "Von gregorianischen Melodien." In Jonas-Corrieri and Scholz, *Die deutsche Jugendmusikbewegung in Dokumenten ihrer Zeit,* 337–38.

———. "Zur Musikerziehung." In Jonas-Corrieri and Scholz, *Die deutsche Jugendmusikbewegung in Dokumenten ihrer Zeit,* 211–15.

Herder, Johann Gottfried. *Adastrea.* Edited by Bernhard Suphan. Vol. 4 of *Sämtliche Werke.* Berlin: Weidmann, 1886.

———. *Abhandlung über den Ursprung der Sprache in Herders sämtliche Werke.* Edited by Bernhard Suphan. Vol. 5 of *Sämtliche Werke,* 1–156. Berlin: Weidmann, 1891.

Hering, Rainer. "Konservative Ökumene." In *Preussische Katholiken und katholische Preussen im 20. Jahrhundert,* edited by Richard Faber and Uwe Puschner, 63–88. Würzburg: Königshausen & Neumann, 2011.

Hertlein, Siegfried. "Die Entwicklung katechetischer Literatur in der ostafrikanischen Benediktinermission (1888–1968)." *Zeitschrift für Missionswissenschaft und Religionswissenschaft* 53 (1969): 279–89.

———. *Die Kirche in Tanzania: Ein kurzer Überblick über Geschichte und Gegenwart.* Münsterschwarzacher Studien no. 1. Münsterschwarzach: Vier Türme Verlag, 1971.

———. *Ndanda Abbey: The History and Work of a Benedictine Monastery in the Context of an African Church; Part 1: Beginning and Development up to 1932.* St. Ottilien: Eos Verlag, 2008.

Herzog, George. "General Characteristics of Primitive Music." *Bulletin of the American Musicological Society* 7 (1943): 23–26.

———. Review, "Marius Schneider: 'A propósito del influjo arabe: Ensayo de etnografía musical' . . . ; *El origen musical de los animales-simbolos en la mitología y las escultura antiguas . . . ." Journal of the American Musicological Society* 4 (1951): 43–47.

Hinton, Stephen. "Alte Musik als Hebamme einer neuen Musikästhetik der zwanziger Jahre." In *Alte Musik als ästhetische Gegenwart: Bach, Händel, Schütz. Bericht über den internationalen Musikwissenschaftlichen Kongreß Stuttgart, 1985,* edited by Dietrich Berke and Dorothee Hanemann, 2:325–31. Kassel: Bärenreiter, 1987.

———. *The Idea of Gebrauchsmusik. A Study of Musical Aesthetics in the Weimar Republic (1919–1933).* Outstanding Dissertations in Music from British Universities. New York: Garland, 1989.

Hodek, Johannes. *Musikalisch-pädagogische Bewegung zwischen Demokratie und Faschismus: Zur Konkretisierung der Faschismus-Kritik Th. W. Adornos.* Weinheim: Beltz, 1977.

Hoekendijk, Johannes. *Kirche und Volk in der deutschen Missionswissenschaft* (1948). Translated by Erich-Walter Pollmann. Munich: Chr. Kaiser Verlag, 1967.

Hoenigswald, Henry M. "On the History of the Comparative Method." *Anthropological Linguistics* 5 (1963): 5–11.

Hoffmann, Hans. "1. Schleswig-Holsteinische Jugendmusikwoche." In Jonas-Corrieri and Scholz, *Die deutsche Jugendmusikbewegung in Dokumenten ihrer Zeit,* 182–83.

Hollinger, David A. *Protestants Abroad: How Missionaries Tried to Change the World but Changed America.* Princeton, NJ: Princeton University Press, 2017.

Hölzl, Richard. "Rassismus, Ethnogenese und Kultur: Afrikaner im Blickwinkel der deutschen katholischen Mission im 19. und frühen 20. Jahrhundert." *Klartext, Sichtbar/verborgen, Werkstattgeschichte* 59 (2012): 7–34.

Hood, Mantle. *The Ethnomusicologist.* New York: McGraw-Hill, 1971.

Hornbostel, Erich M. von. "Über die Verbreitung des Phonographen für die vergleichende Musikwissenschaft" (1904). In *Opera Omnia,* edited by Klaus Wachsmann, Dieter Christensen, and Hans-Peter Reinicke, translated by Ray Giles, 183–202. The Hague: Nijhoff, 1975.

———. "Die Probleme der vergleichenden Musikwissenschaft." *Zeitschrift der Internationalen Musikgesellschaft* 7 (1905–6): 85–97. In *Tonart und Ethos: Aufsätze zur Musikethnologie und Musikpsychologie,* edited by Christian Kaden, 40–58. Reprint, Wilhelmshaven: Noetzel, 1999.

———. "Wanyamwezi-Gesänge." *Anthropos* 4 (1909): 781–800, 1033–52.

———."Über die Mehrstimmigkeit in der aussereuropäischen Musik." In *Kongressbericht der Internationalen Musikwissenschaftlichen Gesellschaft, Wien* (1909): 298–303.

———. "Über vergleichende akustische und musikpsychologische Untersuchungen." *Beiträge zur Akustik und Musikwissenschaft* 5 (1910): 143–67.

———. "Musikpsychologische Bemerkungen über Vogelgesang." *Zeitschrift der Internationalen Musikgesellschaft* 12 (1911): 10–28.

———. "Melodie und Skala." *Jahrbuch der Musikbibiliothek Peters* 19 (1912–13): 11–23.

———. "American Negro Songs." *International Review of Missions* 15 (1926): 748–53.

———. "Musikalische Tonsysteme." In *Handbuch der Physik,* edited by H. Geiger und K. Scheel, 8:425–40. Berlin: Springer, 1927.

———. "African Negro Music." *Africa: Journal of the International African Institute* 1 (1928): 30–62.

———. "Phonogrammierte isländische Zwiegesänge." In *Deutsche Islandforschung*, edited by W. H. Vogt, 300–320. Breslau: Hirt, 1930.

———. "Fuegian Songs." *American Anthropologist* 38 (1936): 357–67.

———. *Opera Omnia*. Edited by Klaus P. Wachsmann, Dieter Christensen, and Hans-Peter Reinicke. The Hague: Martinus Nijhoff, 1976.

Hornbostel, Erich Moritz von, and Robert Lachmann. "Das indische Tonsystem bei Bharata und sein Ursprung." *Zeitschrift für vergleichende Musikwissenschaft* 1 (1933): 73–91.

Hosbach, Wilhelm. "Das Lied der Sehnsucht." In *Geschichten aus dem Hayaland in Afrika*. Bethel: Verlagshandlung Bethel, n.d.

———. "Bericht eines Hofmusikers von Ihangiro." In *Geschichten aus dem Hayaland in Afrika*. Bethel: Verlagshandlung Bethel, n.d.

Humboldt, Wilhelm von. *Prüfung der Untersuchungen über die Urbewohner Hispaniens vermittelst der vaskischen Sprache*. Berlin: Ferdinand Dümmler, 1821.

———. *Gesammelte Schriften*. Edited by Königlich Preussische Akademie der Wissenschaften. Berlin: Behr, 1903–36.

———. *Ueber die Verschiedenheit des menschlichen Sprachbaus und ihren Einfluss auf die geistige Entwicklung des Menschengeschlechts*. Berlin: Königliche Akademie der Wissenschaften, 1836. Modern ed. in Humboldt, *Gesammelte Werke* (Darmstadt: Wissenschaftliche Buchgesellschaft, 1960), vol. 6.7; also, edited by Donatella Di Cesare, (Paderborn: Schöningh, 1998); and translated into English by Michael Losonsky as *The Heterogeneity of Language and Its Influence on the Intellectual Development of the Human Species*, 2nd ed. (Cambridge: Cambridge University Press, 1999).

Hurch, Bernhard, ed. *Die baskischen Materialien aus dem Nachlass Wilhelm von Humboldt*. Paderborn: Schöningh, 2002.

———, ed. *Wilhelm von Humboldt: Schriften zur Anthropologie der Basken*. Paderborn: Schöningh, 2010.

Hüsgen, Jan. *Mission und Sklaverei: Die Herrnhuter Brüdergemeine und die Sklavenemanzipation in British und Danisch-Westindien*. Stuttgart: Steiner, 2016.

Husmann, Heinrich. *Grundlagen der antiken und orientalischen Musikkultur*. Berlin: de Gruyter, 1961.

Idelsohn, Abraham Zvi. "Parallelen zwischen gregorianischen und hebräisch-orientalischen Gesangsweisen." *Zeitschrift für Musikwissenschaft* 4 (1921–22): 515–24.

Ilivangeli lya ku Mataji: Xinyiha [The Gospel of Saint Matthew]. Berlin: Müller, 1903.

Immel, Stephen C. "The Vatican Organum Treatise Re-Examined." *Early Music History* 20 (2001): 121–72.

Ingólfsson, Arni Heimir. *Jón Leifs and the Musical Invention of Iceland*. Bloomington: Indiana University Press, 2019.

Inimbo sya kipanga kya kilisiti basitendekisye na Baputi [Hymnbook for Berlin and Moravian Mission]. Herrnhut: Missions Verlag Winter, 1930.

Inongwa izya mwa Tesitamenti mukali Shiniha [Stories from the Old and New Testament]. Herrnhut: Winter, 1913.

Institut für Musikwissenschaft der Karl-Marx Universität, ed. *Festschrift Heinrich Besseler zum sechzigsten Geburtstag*. Leipzig: VEB Deutscher Verlag für Musik, 1961.

Iten, Beatus."Über Neger-Musik." *Mbl* 37 (1933): 338–43.

Jäschke, Ernst. "Bruno Gutmann's Legacy." *International Bulletin of Missionary Research* 4 (1980): 165–69.

———. *Bruno Gutmann: His Life, His Thoughts, His Work; An Early Attempt at a Theology in an African Context.* Erlangen: Verlag der Ev.- Luth. Mission, 1985.

Jannasch, Hans Windekilde. *Unter Hottentotten und Eskimos: Das Leben meines Vaters.* Lüneburg: Heliand Verlag, 1950.

Jansa, Ferdinand. "Erinnerungen des Missionars Alexander Ferdinand Jansa (1868–1957)." Typescript (1987–88) after handwritten original (ca. 1945–50, here 1949). UA Herrnhut.

Johanssen, Ernst. *In der Heimat und im Dienst am Wiederaufbau von 1918–34.* Vol. 3 of *Führung und Erfahrung im 40jährigen Missionsdienst.* Bethel bei Bielefeld: Verlagsanstalt der Anstalt Bethel, 1936.

John, Eckhard. "Der Mythos vom Deutschen in der deutschen Musik: Die Freiburger Musikwissenschaft im NS-Staat." *Musik in Baden-Würtenberg* 5 (1998): 57–84.

Johner, Dominicus. *Cantus ecclesiastici, juxta editionem vaticanam.* 5th ed. Regensburg: Pustet, 1926.

Jonas-Corrieri, Waltraut, and Wilhelm Scholz, eds. *Die deutsche Jugendmusikbewegung in Dokumenten ihrer Zeit von den Anfängen bis 1933.* Edited from Archiv der Jugendmusikbewegung e. V. Hamburg. Wolfenbüttel: Möseler Verlag, 1980.

Joncus, Berta. "Jöde, Fritz." *Grove Music Online.* Accessed 7 June 2012. https://www .oxfordmusiconline.com/grovemusic/view/10.1093/gmo/9781561592630.001.0001 /omo-9781561592630-e-0000014341.

Jones, Arthur M. *Evangelisation: Report of the General Missionary Conference of Northern Rhodesia Held in Broken Hill.* Lovedale, South Africa: Lovedale Press, 1931. Summarized in "Hymns for the African," *Books for Africa* 2 (1932): 20–21.

———. "African Drumming: A Study of the Combination of Rhythms in African Music." *Bantu Studies* 8 (1934): 1–16.

Kaden, Christian. "Hornbostels akustische Kriterien für Kulturzusammenhänge." In *Vom tönenden Wirbel menschlichen Tuns: Erich M. Von Hornbostel als Gestaltspsychologe, Archivar und Musikwissenschaft,* edited by Sebastian Klotz, 89–95. Milow: Schibri, 1998.

Kaden, Christian, and Erich Stockmann, eds. *Tonart und Ethos: Aufsätze zur Musikethnologie und Musikpsychologie.* Leipzig: Reclam, 1986. Reprint, Wilhelmshaven, 1999.

Kallmeyer, Georg. *25 Jahre deutscher Verlagsbuchhändler: Ein Rückblick.* Wolfenbüttel: Kallmeyer, 1938.

Kantorowicz, Ernst. *Kaiser Friedrich der Zweite.* Berlin: Georg Bondi, 1927.

———. *Laudes regiae: A Study in Liturgical Acclamations and Medieval Ruler Worship.* Berkeley and Los Angeles: University of California Press, 1946.

Karina, Lilian, and Marion Kant. *Hitler's Dancers: German Modern Dance and the Third Reich.* Oxford: Berghahn Books, 2003.

Kecskési, Maria. "Der Afrikanist P. Meinulf Küsters O.S.B. (1890–1947)." *Münchner Beiträge zur Völkerkunde* 3 (1990): 331–33.

———. "Das Lied, der Mönch und die 'Lippennegerinnen.'" *Aviso* 1 (2009): 1461–1501.

———. *Die Mwera in Südost-Tansania.* Munich: Herbert Utz, 2012.

Kindt, Werner, ed. *Dokumentation der Jugendbewegung, Band II: Die Wandervogelzeit—Quellenschriften zur deutschen Jugendbewegung 1896 bis 1919.* Düsseldorf: Diederichs, 1968.

Kirby, Percival. "The Recognition and Practical Use of the Harmonics of Stretched Strings by the Bantu of South Africa." *Bantu Studies* 6, no. 1 (1932): 31–46.

Kitabu kya siri ya ndumi ya sia ya okio . . . . Nördlingen, 1931.

Klautke, Egbert. *The Mind of the Nation:* Völkerpsychologie *in Germany, 1851–1955.* New York: Berghahn Books, 2010.

Klein, Christopher. *Meßkompositionen in Afrika: Ein Beitrag zur Geschichte und Typologie der katholischen Kirchenmusik Afrikas.* Göttingen: Edition Re, 1990.

Klein, Tobias Robert. "Lied und musikalische Lyrik in Afrika." In *Musikalische Lyrik,* edited by Hermann Danuser, vol. 8, no. 2 of *Handbuch der musikalischen Gattungen,* 385–407. Laaber: Laaber, 2004.

———. "Bach in Afrika: Eine Rezeptionsskizze." In *Johann Sebastian Bach und die Gegenwart: Beiträge zur Bach-Rezeption, 1945–2005,* edited by Michael Heinemann and Hans-Joachim Hinrichsen, 19–34. Cologne: Dohr, 2007.

———. "'Proud Possesions of the African': N. G. Ballanta und die frühe westafrikanische Musikhistoriographie." In *Moderne Traditionen Studien zur postkolononialen Musikgeschichte Ghanas,* 25–68. Frankfurt: Peter Lang, 2008.

———. "Ballanta, Nicholas George Julius." *MGG Online.* Accessed 7 February 2020. https://www.mgg-online.com/article?id=mgg16323&v=1.0&rs=mgg16323&q=Ballanta.

———. "Leading Notes, Leading Culture: On African National Anthems." In *"Unser Land"? Lesothos schweizerische Nationalhymne/"Our Land"? Lesotho's Swiss National Anthem,* edited by Matthias Schmidt and Andreas Baumgartner, 171–84. Basel: Merian, 2018.

Klotz, Sebastian. *"Vom tönenden Wirbel menschlichen Tuns": Erich Moritz von Hornbostel als Gestaltpsychologe, Archivar und Musikwissenschaftler; Studien und Dokumente.* Berlin: Schibri, 1998.

———. "Hornbostel, Erich Moritz, Ritter von." *MGG Online.* Accessed 7 February 2020. https://www.mgg-online.com/article?id=mgg06496&v=1.0&rs=mgg06496&q =Hornbostel.

Kniazeva, Janna. *Jacques Handschin in Russland: Die neu aufgefundenen Texte.* Basel: Schwabe, 2011.

Knittel, Karl. "Unsere Lehrergehilfen und Mittelschule." *ELMB* 24 (1913): 560–67.

Koch, Lars-Christian. "Images of Sound: Erich M. von Hornbostel and the Berlin Phonogram Archive." In *The Cambridge History of World Music,* edited by Philip V. Bohlman, 475–97. Cambridge: Cambridge University Press, 2013.

Kolland, Dorothea. *Die Jugendmusikbewegung: "Gemeinschaftsmusik"—Theorie und Praxis.* Stuttgart: Metzler, 1979.

Koren, Henry. *To the Ends of the Earth.* Pittsburgh, PA: Duquesne University Press, 1983.

Kornder, Wolfgang. *Die Entwicklung der Kirchenmusik in den ehemals deutschen Missionsgebieten Tanzanias.* Erlangen: Verlag der evangelischen Mission, 1990.

Kreutziger-Herr, Annette. *Ein Traum vom Mittelalter: Die Wiederentdeckung mittelalterlicher Musik in der Neuzeit.* Cologne: Böhlau, 2003.

Kubik, Gerhard. "Probleme der Tonaufnahme afrikanischer Musiker." *Afrika heute* 15–16 (1966): 227–33.

———. "The Traditional Music of Tanzania." *Afrika* 8, no. 2 (1967): 29–32.

———. *Mehrstimmigkeit und Tonsysteme in Zentral- und Ostafrika*. Vienna: Österreichische Akademie der Wissenschaften, 1968.

———. *Ostafrika in Musikgeschichte in Bildern*. Leipzig: VEB Deutscher Verlag für Musik, 1982.

———. "Musikgestaltung in Afrika" (27–40), "Die Amadinda-Musik von Buganda" (139–65), and "Sozialisierungsprozeß und Gesänge der Initianden in Mukanda Schulen" (343–60). In *Musik in Afrika*, edited by Artur Simon. Berlin: Museum für Völkerkunde, 1983.

———. "Lamellaphone." *Grove Music Online*. Accessed 7 February 2020. https://www.oxfordmusiconline.com/grovemusic/view/10.1093/gmo/9781561592630.001.0001/omo-9781561592630-e-0000040069.

———. "Tanzania: North-Western Tanzania." *Grove Music Online*. Accessed 7 February 2020. https://www.oxfordmusiconline.com/grovemusic/view/10.1093/gmo/97815615 92630.001.0001/omo-9781561592630-e-0000027485.

———. "Multipart Singing in Sub-Saharan Africa: Remote and Recent Histories Unravelled." In *Mehrstimmigkeit und Heterophonie*, edited by Gernot Gruber, August Schmidhofer, and Michael Weber, 181–209. Frankfurt: Peter Lang, 2005.

———. *Theory of African Music*. 2 vols. Chicago: University of Chicago Press, 1994, 2010.

Küchler, Martin. *D. Dr. Bruno Gutmann: Lebenslauf und Würdigung der Lebensarbeit D. Dr. Gutmanns* [pamphlet published in honor of Gutmann's seventy-fifth birthday]. Erlangen: Verlag der evangelisch-lutherischen Mission, 1951.

Kühne, Hartmut, and Christoph F. Lorenz. *Karl May und die Musik*. Bamberg: Karl May Verlag, 1999.

Kunst, Jaap. *Around von Hornbostel's Theory of the Cycle of Blown Fifths*. Koninklijke Vereeniging Indisch Instituut 76. Amsterdam: Indisch Instituut, 1948.

———. *Ethnomusicology: A Study of Its Nature, Its Problems, Methods, and Representative Personalities, to Which Is Added a Bibliography*. Netherlands: Springer, 1953. Reprint, 2012.

———. *Music in Java: Its History, Its Theory, and Its Technique*. Netherlands: Springer, 2013.

Künster, P. Clemens, O.S.B. "Etwas über afrikanische Musikinstrumente." *Mbl* 9 (1904–5): 84–86.

———. *Harmonisches System zur Begleitung der gregorianischen Choralmelodien*. St. Ottilien: Missionsverlag St. Ottilien, 1906.

Küsters, Meinulf. "Das Grab der Afrikaner." *Anthropos* 14–15 (1919–20): 639–728; 16–17 (1921–22): 183–229, 913–59.

———. "Wilhelm Wundts Bedeutung für die katholischen Missionare." *Zeitschrift für Missionswissenschaft* 4 (1921): 202–12.

———. *Myrtenblume der christlichen Braut und Ehefrau: Ein Gebet- und Belehrungsbuch für den Braut- und Ehestand*. Kevelaer: M. van Wyenbergh, 1922.

———. "Von München nach Peramiho" and "Die Missionsschule in Peramiho." *Mbl* 32 (1928): 226–32.

————. "Afrikanische Negerkunst und ihre Beziehungen zur Hochkultur." In *Einführung zu der Sonderausstellung der Sammlung Coray-Lugano im Staatlichen Museum für Völkerkunde*, edited by Lucian Scherman, 1–16. Munich: Staatliches Museum für Völkerkunde, 1931.

————. "Die figürliche Darstellung auf den Beninzähnen des Linden-Museum, Stuttgart." In *Jahresbericht 1931–32 des Würtembergischen Vereins für Handelsgeographie e.V.*, 116–20. Stuttgart: Lindenmuseum, 1931–32.

Kurth, Ernst. *Grundlagen des linearen Kontrapunktes: Bachs melodische Polyphonie*. Bern: M. Drechsel, 1917.

Lach, Robert. "Vorläufiger Bericht über die im Auftrage der Kais. Akademie der Wissenschaften erfolgte Aufnahme der Gesänge russischer Kriegsgefangener im August und September 2016." In *46. Mitteilung der Phonogrammarchivs-Kommission*. Vienna: Hölder, 1917.

————. "Die Musik der turk-tartarischen, finnisch-ugrischen und Kaukasus-völker in ihrer entwicklungsgeschichtlichen und psychologischen Bedeutung für die Entstehung der musikalischen Form." *Mitteilungen der Anthropologischen Gesellschaft in Wien* (1920): 22–50.

————. *Die vergleichende Musikwissenschaft: Ihre Methoden und Probleme*. Vienna: Hölder-Pichler-Tempsky, 1924.

Lachmann, Robert. *Musik des Orients*. Breslau: Ferdinand Hirt, 1929.

————. "Musiksysteme und Musikauffassung." *Zeitschrift für vergleichende Musikwissenschaft* 3 (1935): 1–23.

Laqueur, Walter. *Die deutsche Jugendbewegung: Eine historische Studie*. Cologne: Verlag Wissenschaft und Politik, 1962.

Leech-Wilkinson, Daniel. *The Modern Invention of Medieval Music: Scholarship, Ideology, Performance*. Cambridge: Cambridge University Press, 2002.

Lerner, Robert E. "Ernst Kantorowicz and Theodor E. Mommsen." In *An Interrupted Past: German-Speaking Refugee Historians in the United States after 1933*, edited by Hartmut Lehmann and James J. Sheehan, 188–205. Cambridge: Cambridge University Press, 1991.

————. *Ernst Kantorowicz: A Life*. Princeton, NJ: Princeton University Press, 2017.

Lessing, Gotthold Ephraim. "Gedanken über die Herrnhuter." In *Gotthold Ephraim Lessings sämtlichen Schriften*, vol. 14, edited by Karl Lachmann, 154–63. Berlin: Voß'schen Buchhandlung, 1839.

Levy, Kenneth. *Gregorian Chant and the Carolingians*. Princeton, NJ: Princeton University Press, 1998.

Lochter, Karl-Heinz. "Brüdergemeinde und Singgemeinde." *Unitas Fratrum: Zeitschrift für Geschichte und Gegenwartsfragen der Brüdergemeine* 13 (1983): 3–44.

Löffler, Roland. "Sozialer Protestantismus in Übersee. Ein Plädoyer für die Integration der Äußeren in die Historiographie der Inneren Mission." In *Sozialer Protestantismus im Kaiserreich: Problemkonstellationen-Lösungsperspektiven-Handlungsprofile*, edited by Norbert Friedrich and Traugott Jähnichen, 321–53. Münster: LIT Verlag, 2005.

London Sacred Songs and Solos: Revised and Enlarged, with Standard Hymns. Compiled under the direction of Ira D. Sankey. London: Morgan and Scott, 188[?].

Lord, Albert. *The Singer of Tales*. Cambridge, MA: Harvard University Press, 1960.

Ludwig, Friedrich. Review of Johannes Wolf, *Geschichte der Mensuralnotation von 1250–1460. Sammelbände der Internationalen Musikgesellschaft* 6 (1904–5): 597–641.

———. *Repertorium organorum recentioris et motetorum vetustissimi stili: Vol. 1, Catalogue raisonné der Quellen.* Pt. 1: *Handschriften in Quadratnotation.* Halle: Niemeyer, 1910. Reprint, edited by Luther Dittmer, New York: Institute of Medieval Music and Hildesheim: Georg Olms, 1964. Pt. 2: *Handschriften in Mensuralnotation*, edited by Friedrich Gennrich, Summa musicae medii aevi 7. Langen bei Frankfurt, 1961.

———. "Perotinus Magnus." *Archiv für Musikwissenschaft* 5 (1921): 361–70.

———. "Musik des Mittelalters in der Badischen Kunsthalle Karlsruhe, 24.–26. September, 1922." *Zeitschrift für Musikwissenschaft* 5 (1922–23): 434–60.

———. "Die geistliche nichtliturgische/weltliche einstimmige und die mehrstimmige Musik des Mittelalters bis zum Anfang des 15. Jahrhunderts." In *Handbuch der Musikgeschichte*, edited by Guido Adler, 2nd ed., 157–295. Berlin: Keller, 1930.

Lütteken, Laurenz. "Wiora, Walter." *MGG Online.* Accessed 7 February 2020. https://www.mgg-online.com/article?id=mgg13922&v=1.0&rs=mgg13922&q=Wiora.

Machaut, Guillaume de. *Mass of Notre Dame.* In *Collected Works of Guilaume de Machaut*, vol. 4, edited by Heinrich Besseler. Leipzig: Breitkopf & Härtel, 1954.

———. *Musikalische Werke.* Edited by Friedrich Ludwig. 3 vols. Publikationen älterer Musik. Leipzig: Breitkopf & Härtel, 1926–29.

Madschame Congregation, ed. *Kitabu kya Fiimbo: Gesangbuch in der Sprache von Madschame.* N.p., 1927.

Mapunda, Bertram B. B. "Reexamining the Maji in Ungoni with a Blend of Archeology and Oral History." In *Maji, Maji: Lifting the Fog of War*, edited by James Giblin and Jamie Monson, 221–41. Leiden: Brill, 2010.

Marchand, Suzanne. *German Orientalism in the Age of Empire: Religion, Age, and Scholarship.* New York: Cambridge University Press, 2009.

Marfurt, Luitfred. *Music in Africa.* Munich: Nymphenburger Verlagsbuchhandlung, 1957.

Marti, Andreas. "Konrad Ameln: Der hymnologische Lehrmeister; Persönliche Erinnerungen." *Jahrbuch für Liturgik und Hymnologie* 50 (2011): 35–39.

Maurer Zenck, Claudia, and Peter Peterson, eds. *Lexikon verfolgter Musiker und Musikerinnen der NS Zeit.* Accessed 8 March 2019. https://www.lexm.uni-hamburg.de/content/index.xml.

Meyer-Kalkus, Reinhart. *Stimme und Sprechkünste im 20. Jahrhundert.* Berlin: Akademie-Verlag, 2001.

Mazo, Margarita. "Russia, the USSR and the Baltic States." In *Ethnomusicology: Historical and Regional Studies*, edited by Helen Myers, 195–212. New York: Norton, 1993.

Mbunga, Stephan B. G. *Church Law and Bantu Music: Ecclesiastical Documents and Law on Sacred Music as Applied to Bantu Music.* Schöneck-Beckenried, Switzerland: Nouvelle Revue de Science Missionnaire, 1963.

———. "Afrikanische Musik im Gottesdienst." In *Musica indigena. Einheimische Musik und ihre mögliche Verwendung in Liturgie und Verkündigung*, edited by Josef Kuckertz und Johannes Overath, 51–71. Musikethnologisches Symposium, Rom, 1975. Rome: Consociatio Interationalis Musicae Sacrae, 1976.

McGuire, Charles E. *Music and Victorian Philanthropy: The Tonic Sol-fa Movement.* Cambridge: Cambridge University Press, 2009.

Mehl, Johannes G. "Walther Hensel" [obituary]. *Gottesdienst und Kirchenmusik* 7 (1957):
3–5.

Menzel, Gustav. *Die Bethel-Mission: Aus 100 Jahren Missionsgeschichte.* Neukirchen:
Neukirchener Verlag, 1986.

———. "'Pastor Fritz' und die Bethel Mission." In *Die diakonische Dimension der Mission: Vorträge zum 100jährigen Jubiläum der Bethel Mission,* edited by Vereinigte
Evangelische Mission, 21–35. Bielefeld: Verlagsbuchhandlung, 1987.

Merensky, Alexander, ed. *Deutsche Arbeit am Njaßa, Deutsch-Ostafrika.* Berlin: Buchhandlung der Berliner evangelischen Missionsgesellschaft, 1984.

Merriam, Alan P. "From the Editor." *Ethnomusicology* 7 (1963): iv.

———. *The Anthropology of Music.* Evanston, IL: Northwestern University Press, 1964.

Merz-Benz, Peter-Ulrich. "Die begriffliche Architektonik von 'Gemeinschaft und Gesellschaft.'" In *Hundert Jahre "Gemeinschaft und Gesellschaft": Ferdinand Tönnies in
der Internationalen Diskussion,* edited by Lars Clausen and Carsten Schlüter, 31–64.
Opladen: Leske + Budrich, 1991.

Mettele, Gisela. *Weltbürgertum oder Gottesreich: Die Herrnhuter Brüdergemeine als
globale Gemeinschaft, 1727–1857.* Göttingen: Vandenhoeck & Ruprecht, 2009.

Meyer, Dietrich. "Ein Stachel im Herzen: Der Einfluss der nationalsozialistischen
Judenpolitik auf die Brüdergemeine von 1933 bis 1945." In *Freikirchen und Juden
im "Dritten Reich,"* edited by Daniel Heinz, 245–80. Göttingen: Vandenhoeck &
Ruprecht, 2011.

Meyer, Theodor. *Die Konde: Ethnografische Aufzeichungen (1891–1916) des Missionssuperintendenten Theodor Meyer von den Nyakyusa.* Hohenschäftlarn: K. Renner,
1989.

Möckel, Andreas. *Umkämpfte Volkskirche: Leben und Wirken des evangelisch-sächsischen Pfarrers Konrad Möckel (1892–1965).* Cologne: Böhlau, 2011.

Moore, Sally Falk, and Paul Puritt. *The Chagga and Meru of Tanzania.* London: International African Institute, 1977.

———. *Social Facts and Fabrications: "Customary" Law on Kilimanjaro, 1880–1980.*
Cambridge: Cambridge University Press, 1986.

Moran, John H., and Alexander Gode, trans. *On the Origin of Language.* Chicago: University of Chicago Press, 1986.

Moser, Hans Joachim. *Die Melodien der Luther Lieder.* Leipzig: Schloeßmanns Verlagsbuchhandlung, 1935.

Motel, Hans-Beat. *"Mama, mein Herz geht kaputt": Das Schicksal der Herrnhuter Missionskinder.* Herrnhut: Comenius Buchhandlung, 2013.

Mücke, Dorothea E. von. "'The Entirety of Scripture Is Within Us.'" In *A New History of
German Literature,* edited by David E. Wellbery and Judith Ryan, 320–24. Cambridge,
MA: Harvard University Press, 2004.

Mueller-Vollmer, Kurt. "Wilhelm von Humboldt." *Stanford Encyclopedia of Philosophy.*
Accessed 7 February 2019. http://plato.stanford.edu/entries/wilhelm-humboldt/.

———. "Von der Poetik zur Linguistik: Wilhelm von Humboldt und der romantische
Sprachbegriff." In *Universalismus und Wissenschaft im Werk und Wirken der
Brüder Humboldt,* edited by Klaus Hammacher, 224–40. Frankfurt: Klostermann,
1976.

———. "Wilhelm von Humboldt und der Anfang, der amerikanischen Sprachwissenschaft: die Briefe an John Pickering." In *Universalismus und Wissenschaft im Werk und Wirken der Brüder Humboldt*, edited by Klaus Hammacher, 259–334. Frankfurt: Klostermann, 1976.

———. "Wilhelm von Humboldts sprachwissenschaftlicher Nachlaß: Probleme seiner Erschließung." In *Wilhelm von Humboldts Sprachdenken: Symposium zum 150. Todestag*, edited by Hans-Werner Scharf, 181–204. Essen: Hobbing, 1989.

———. "Mutter Sanskrit und die Nacktheit der Südseesprachen: Das Begräbnis von Humboldts Sprachwissenschaft." In *Athenäum: Jahrbuch für Romantik*, 109–33. Paderborn: Schoeningh, 1991.

———. *Wilhelm von Humboldts Sprachwissenschaft*. Paderborn: Schöningh, 1993.

Müller, Karl, and Adolf Schulze. *200 Jahre Brüdermission*. 2 vols. Herrnhut: Verlag der Missionsbuchhandlung, 1931–32.

Müller-Blattau, Joseph. "Die Tonkunst in altgermanischer Zeit." In *Germanische Wiedererstehung*, edited by Hermann Nollau, 423–85. Heidelberg: Winter, 1926.

Mulokozi, Mugyabuso M. *The African Epic Controversy: Historical, Philosophical and Aesthetic Perspectives on Epic Poetry and Performance*. Dar es Salaam: Fourth Dimension, 2002.

Die Musik in Geschichte und Gegenwart: Allgemeine Enzyklopädie der Musik. 1st ed. Edited by Friedrich Blume. 17 vols. Kassel: Bärenreiter-Verlag, 1949–87.

Die Musik in Geschichte und Gegenwart: MGG Online. 2nd ed. Kassel: Bärenreiter-Verlag, and Stuttgart: J. B. Metzler Verlag, in partnership with RILM, 1994–2008. www.mgg -online.com.

Myers, Helen. "Ethnomusicology, II, Pre-1945." *Grove Music Online*. Accessed 7 February 2020. https://www.oxfordmusiconline.com/grovemusic/view/10.1093/gmo/978156 1592630.001.0001/omo-9781561592630-e-0000052178.

Nadel, Siegfried F. "The Origins of Music." *Musical Quarterly* 16 (1930): 531–46.

———. *Georgische Gesänge*. Berlin: Harrassowitz, 1933.

Nannyonga-Tamusza, Sylvia A., and Thomas Solomon. *Ethnomusicology in East Africa: Perspectives from Uganda and Beyond*. Uganda: Fountain, 2012.

Nettl, Bruno. *Theory and Method in Ethnomusicology*. New York: Free Press of Glencoe, 1964.

———. "An Ethnomusicologist Contemplates Universals in Musical Sound and Musical Culture." In *The Origins of Music*, edited by Nils L. Wallin, Björn Merker, and Steven Brown, 463–72. Cambridge, MA: MIT Press, 2000.

———. *Encounters in Ethnomusicology: A Memoir*. Warren, MI: Harmonie Park Press, 2002.

———. "Contemplating Ethnomusicology: What Have We Learned?" *Archiv für Musikwissenschaft* 67 (2010): 173–86.

———. *Becoming an Ethnomusicologist: A Miscellany of Influences*. Lanham, MD: Scarecrow Press, 2013.

———. *The Study of Ethnomusicology: Thirty-One Issues and Concepts*. Urbana: University of Illinois Press, 2015.

Nketia, J. H. Kwabena. "The Scholarly Study of African Music: A Historical Review." In *Africa: The Garland Encyclopedia of World Music*, edited by Ruth Stone, 13–73. New York: Garland, 1997.

Olwage, Grant. "Scriptions of the Choral: The Historiography of Black South African Choralism." *South African Journal of Musicology* 22 (2002): 29–45.

———. "Singing in the Victorian World: Tonic Sol-fa and Discourses of Religion, Science, and Empire in the Cape Colony." *Muziki* 7, no. 2 (2010): 193–215.

Orff, Carl. *Lehrjahre bei den alten Meistern.* Tutzing: Schneider, 1975.

"P. Klemens Künster D.S.B. †." *Monatsschrift der Beneditkinermissionäre von St. Ottilien* 39 (1935): 272–73.

Paasche, Hans. *Im Morgenlicht.* Berlin: Schwetschke & Sohn, 1907.

———. *Die Forschungsreise des Afrikaners Lukanga Mukara ins innerste Deutschland* [1912–13]. Originally published, Hamburg: Verlag Junge Menschen, 1921. Accessed 8 March 2019. http://gutenberg.spiegel.de/buch/die-forschungsreise-des-afrikaners -lukanga-mukara-ins-innerste-deutschland-1915/1.

Parry, Milman. "Studies in the Epic Technique of Oral Verse-Making, I: Homer and Homeric Style." *Harvard Studies in Classical Philology* 41 (1930): 73–143.

"Paul Gerhardt." *MBBG* (1907), 119.

Penny, Glenn. *Objects of Culture: Ethnology and Ethnographic Museums in Imperial Germany.* Chapel Hill: University of North Carolina Press, 2002.

Perras, Arne. *Carl Peters and German Imperialism, 1856–1918: A Political Biography.* Oxford: Clarendon Press, 2004.

Peters, Julia Irene, dir. *Luthers Erben: Sing It Out Loud.* Documentary film. Germany, May 2017.

Petersen, Birte. "Darum." *Evangelisches Missionswerk in Südwestdeutschland e.V.* (April 2000): 18.

Petersen, Peter. "Musikwissenschaften in Hamburg 1933 bis 1945." In *Hochschulalltag im "Dritten Reich": Die Hamburger Universität, 1933 bis 1945,* edited by Eckart Krause, Ludwig Huber, and Holger Fischer, 625–40. Hamburger Beiträge zur Wissenschaftsgeschichte 3. Berlin: Dietrich Reimer Verlag, 1991.

Peucker, Paul. "'In Staub und Asche': Bewertung und Kassation im Unitätsarchiv, 1760–1810." In *"Alles ist euer, ihr aber seid Christi": Festschrift für Dietrich Meyer,* edited by Rudolf Mohr, 127–58. Cologne: Rheinland Verlag, 2000.

———. "Aus allen Nationen: Nicht-europäer in den deutschen Brüdergemeinen des 18. Jahrhunderts." *Unitas Fratrum* 59–60 (2007): 1–35.

Piel, Peter, and Paul Manderscheid. *Harmonielehre (mit Kirchentönen).* Düsseldorf: Schwann, 1923.

Pohl, Ulrich. "Dankbarkeit leben: Öffenlichkeitsarbeit in den von Bodelschwinghschen Anstalten Bethel." In *Elefanten schwimmen und Lämmer waten: Von Tiefen und Untiefen der Kommunikation,* edited by Thomas Kreuzer, 101–16. Münster: Lit Verlag, 2010.

Potter, Pamela. "German Musicology and Early Music Performance, 1918–1933." In *Music and Performance during the Weimar Republic,* edited by Bryan Gilliam, 94–106. Cambridge: Cambridge University Press, 1994.

———. *Most German of the Arts: Musicology and Society from the Weimar Republic to the End of Hitler's Reich.* New Haven, CT: Yale University Press, 1998.

———. "Blume, Friedrich." *Grove Music Online.* Accessed 8 March 2019. https://www .oxfordmusiconline.com/grovemusic/view/10.1093/gmo/9781561592630.001.0001 /omo-9781561592630-e-0000003314.

Price, Richard. *Alabi's World*. Baltimore, MD: Johns Hopkins University Press, 1990.

Prieberg, Fred K. *Musik im NS Staat*. Frankfurt: Fischer, 1982.

———. *Handbuch Deutscher Musiker, 1933–1945*. CD-ROM. Kiel: Oliver Kopf, 2009.

"Proletarische Musikarbeit in Neukölln." *Der Kreis* 6 (1929). Reprinted in Jonas-Corrieri and Scholz, *Die deutsche Jugendmusikbewegung in Dokumenten ihrer Zeit*, 798.

Prüfer, Tilmann. *Der heilige Bruno: Die unglaubliche Gschichte meines Urgrossvaters am Kilimanjaro*. Reinbek: Rowohlt, 2015.

Pugach, Sara. *Africa in Translation: A History of Colonial Linguistics in Germany and Beyond, 1814–1945*. Ann Arbor: University of Michigan Press, 2012.

Ranger, Terence O. *Dance and Society in Eastern Africa, 1890–1970*. Berkeley and Los Angeles: University of California Press, 1975.

Rask, Rasmus. *Undersøgelse om det gamle nordiske eller islandske sproks oprindelse*. Copenhagen, 1818. Partial English translation in *A Reader in Nineteenth-Century Indoeuropean Linguistics*, edited by W. P. Lehmann, 29–37. Bloomington: University of Indiana Press, 1967.

Raum, Otto Friedrich. "Female Initiation among the Chaga." *American Anthropologist* 41 (1939): 554–65.

Rehse, Hermann. *Kiziba: Land und Leute*. With a preface by Felix von Luschan. Edited with support of the Imperial Colonial Office. Stuttgart: Strecker & Schröder, 1910.

Reichart, Athanasius, and Meinulf Küsters. *Elementary Kiswaheli Grammar of Introduction into the East African Negro Language and Life*. Heidelberg: Groos, 1926.

Reichenbach, Herman. "Die Musik der Jugendbewegung." *Melos* (December 1925). Reprinted in Jonas-Corrieri and Scholz, *Die deutsche Jugendmusikbewegung in Dokumenten ihrer Zeit*, 931–35.

———. *Formenlehre der Musik*. Wolfenbüttel: Kallmeyer, 1929.

———. "Singtreffen der Berliner Jugend." *Musik und Gesellschaft* (1930–31). Reprinted in Jonas-Corrieri and Scholz, *Die deutsche Jugendmusikbewegung in Dokumenten ihrer Zeit*, 495–97.

Rein, Walter, ed. *Deutsche Lieder vergangener Jahrhunderte. Vol. 2: Geistliche Lieder*. Wolfenbüttel: Kallmeyer, 1927.

Reinfandt, Karl-Heinz. "Fritz Jödes Schaffen zwischen Idee und Wirklichkeit." In *Die Jugendmusikbewegung: Impulse und Wirkungen*, edited by Karl-Heinz Reinfandt, 277–96. Wolfenbüttel: Möseler, 1987.

———. "Jöde, Fritz." *MGG Online*. Accessed 7 February 2020. https://www.mgg-online .com/article?id=mgg06867&v=1.0&rs=mgg06867&q=Jöde.

Renner, Frumentius. *Vom Missionshaus Reichenbach zur Benediktinerkongregation von St. Ottilien, 1971*. In *Der fünfarmige Leuchter*, vol. 1, *Gründung und Grundlegung der Kongregation St. Ottilien*, edited by Frumentius Renner, 1–336. St. Ottilien: EOS Verlag, 1979.

Retzius, Anders. "Über die Schädelformen der Nordbewohner." *Archiv für Anatomie, Physiologie und wissenschaftliche Medicin* (1845): 84–129.

Reusch, Fritz. "Erziehungsaufgabe im tiefsten Sinn des Wortes." *Musikantengilde* 4 (1926): 2–5.

———. *Musik und Musikerziehung*. Berlin: Zickfeldt, 1938.

Ribera, Julián. *La música de las Cantigas*. Madrid: Tipografía de la Revista de Archivos, 1922.

Rice, Timothy. "Comparative Musicology." *Grove Music Online.* Accessed 26 October 2019. https://www.oxfordmusiconline.com/grovemusic/view/10.1093/gmo/978156 1592630.001.0001/omo-9781561592630-e-0000046454.

Richter, Christoph. "Hensel, Walther." *MGG Online.* Accessed 8 March 2019. https://www.mgg-online.com/article?id=mgg06193&v=1.0&rs=mgg06193&q=Hensel.

Richter, Julius. *Die Einwurzelung des Christentums in der Heidenwelt.* Gütersloh: Bertelsmann, 1906.

Riemann, Hugo. *Folkloristische Tonalitätsstudien.* Leipzig: Breitkopf & Härtel, 1916.

Rietzsch, Franz. "Diesseits und jenseits von Dur und Moll: Unterschiede zwischen europäischer und afrikanischer Musik." *Herrnhut, Wochenblatt aus der Brüdergemeine* (1935): 64–67, 71–73.

———. "Kirchenmusikalische Fragen in der Missionsarbeit." *Musik und Kirche* 8 (1936): 80–81.

———. "Afrikanische Klänge" (1935). Edited by Bernd Arnold as "Notizen zur ostafrikanischen Musik." *Wiener völkerkundliche Mitteilungen* 35 (1993): 23–37.

Roberts, Andrew D. "The Awkward Squad: Arts Graduates from British Tropical Africa before 1949." *Journal of Imperial and Commonwealth History* 44 (2016): 799–814.

Robins, R. H. *A Short History of Linguistics.* 3rd ed. London: Longman, 1990.

Ronicke, Curt, ed. *Kleine Erinnerungen an einen großen Mann: Zum Gedenken an Walther Trittelvitz.* Bethel bei Bielefeld: Verlagshandlung der Anstalt Bethel, 1959.

Roon, Marjolijn van. "Ein Zauberkünstler. Erich Moritz von Hornbostel im Spiegel seiner Biographie und seiner Korrespondenz." In *Vom tönenden Wirbel menschlichen Tuns: Erich M. von Hornbostel als Gestaltpsychologe, Archivar und Musikwissenschaftler,* edited by Sebastian Klotz, 44–77. Berlin: Schibri, 1998.

Rosenkranz, Gerhard. *Das Lied der Kirche in der Welt: Eine missionshymnologische Studie.* Berlin: Verlag Haus und Schule GMBH, 1951.

Ross, Alex. "The Life of Leifs." *New Yorker,* 20 November 2009.

Rother, Paul. "Wie ich das 'Waldfest' der Wapare sah." *ELMB* (1906): 468–73.

———. "Das Musikinstrument der Wapare." *ELMB* (1907): 14–15.

———. *Afrikanischer Sang und Klang.* Leipzig: Verlag der evangelischen Mission, 1925.

———. *Meine afrikanischen Jungen.* Leipzig: Verlag der evangelischen Mission, 1935.

Rühl, Theodor. "Die missionarische Akkommodation im gottesdienstlichen Volksgesang." *Zeitschrift für Musikwissenschaft* 17 (1927): 113–35.

Ryback, Timothy. *Hitler's Private Library: The Books That Shaped His Life.* New York: Knopf, 2008.

Sachs, Curt. *Musik des Altertums.* Breslau: Ferdinand Hirt, 1924.

———. *Die Musik der Antike.* Handbuch der Musikwissenschaft 4. Potsdam: Athenaion, 1928.

Saitoti, Tepilit Ole. *The Worlds of a Maasai Warrior: An Autobiography.* With an introduction by John Galaty. Berkeley and Los Angeles: University of California Press, 1988.

Sandys, John Edwin. *History of Classical Scholarship.* 3rd ed. Cambridge: Cambridge University Press, 1921.

Sapir, Edward. "Herder's 'Ursprung der Sprache.'" *Modern Philology* 5 (1907–8): 100–142.

Schattschneider, David. "Moravians." In *The Encyclopedia of Religion*, edited by Mircea Eliade, 106–8. New York: Macmillan, 1987.

Schenk, Dietmar. *Die Hochschule für Musik zu Berlin: Preussens Konservatorium zwischen romantischem Klassizismus und neuer Musik (1869–1932/33)*. Stuttgart: Franz Steiner Verlag, 2004.

Schenk, Dietmar, and Ulrich Mahlert, *Leo Kestenberg: Gesammelte Schriften*. Vol. 3.2. Freiburg: Rombach, 2010.

Schipperges, Thomas. *Die Akte Heinrich Besseler: Musikwissenschaft und Wissenschaftspolitik in Deutschland 1924 bis 1949*. Munich: Strube, 2005.

Schlegel, Friedrich. *Über das Studium der griechischen Poesie*. Neustrelitz: Michaelis, 1797.

———. *Über die Sprache und Weisheit der Indier*. Heidelberg: Mohr & Zimmer, 1808.

Schleicher, August. *Compendium der vergleichenden Grammatik der indogermanischen Sprachen: Kurzer Abriss einer Laut- und Formenlehre der indogermanischen Ursprache*. Weimar: Böhlau, 1861.

Schlingensiepen, Ferdinand. *Dietrich Bonhoeffer, 1906–1945: Martyr, Thinker, Man of Resistance*. Translated by Isabel Best. London: T. & T. Clark, 2010.

Schmidhofer, August. "Zur Inkulturation liturgischer Musik in Madagaskar im 19. Jahrhundert." *Studien zur Musikwissenschaft* 42 (1993): 451–57.

Schmidt, P. G. "La généalogie des instruments de musique et les cycles de civilisation." *Anthropos* 14–15 (1919): 565–70.

Schmidt, Peter Ridgeway. *Historical Archeology in Africa: Representation, Social Memory, and Oral Traditions*. Lanham, MD: Altamira, 2006.

Schneider, Albrecht. "Marius Schneider, *Geschichte der Mehrstimmigkeit*." *Musica sacra* 94 (1972): 133–34.

———. *Musikwissenschaft und Kulturkreislehre: zur Methodik und Geschichte der vergleichenden Musikwissenschaft*. Bonn: Orpheus, 1976.

———. "Northern and Western Europe." In *Ethnomusicology: Historical and Regional Studies*, edited by Helen Myers, 77–95. New York: Norton, 1993.

———. "Music and Gestures: A Historical Introduction and Survey of Earlier Research." In *Musical Gestures: Sound, Movement, and Meaning*, edited by Rolf Inge Godoy and Marc Leman, 69–100. New York: Routledge, 2010.

Schneider, Marius. "Der Hochetus." *Zeitschrift für Musikwissenschaft* 11 (1928–29): 390–96.

———. *Die Ars nova des XIV. Jahrhunderts in Frankreich und Italien*. Ph.D. diss., Friedrich Wilhelm Universität, 1930. Wolfenbüttel: Kallmeyer, 1930.

———. *Geschichte der Mehrstimmigkeit*. 2 vols. Berlin: Bard, 1934–35. Revised ed. with a supplement, Part III, *Die Kompositionsprinzipien und ihre Verbreitung. Mit 115 Notenbeispielen als Anhang*. Tutzing: Schneider, 1969.

———. "Diskussionen. Zur außereuropäischen Mehrstimmigkeit." *Zeitschrift für vergleichende Musikwissenschaft* 3 (1935): 34–38.

———. "Ethnologische Musikforschung." In *Lehrbuch der Völkerkunde*, edited by Konrad Theodor Preuss, 135–71. Stuttgart: Ferdinand Enke Verlag, 1937.

———. "Kaukasische Parallelen zur mittelalterlichen Mehrstimmigkeit." *Acta Musicologica* 12 (1941): 52–61.

———. *A propósito del influjo árabe-Ensayo del etnografía musical de la España medieval. Annuario musical* 1 (1946): 31–139.

———. "Ist die vokale Mehrstimmigkeit eine Schöpfung der Altrassen?" *Acta Musicologica* 23 (1951): 40–50.

———. "Wurzeln und Anfänge der abendländischen Mehrstimmigkeit." In *Report of the Eighth Congress, New York, 1961*, edited by Jan LaRue, 161–78. Kassel: Bärenreiter, 1961.

Scholl, Inge. *Die weisse Rose*. Frankfurt: Fischer, 1993.

Scholten, Heinrich. "Die Einweihung der Erlöserkirche in Bukoba." *NOAM* 50 (1936): 218–22.

Scholz, Bastian. *Die Kirchen und der deutsche Nationalstaat: Konfessionelle Beiträge zum Systembestand und Systemwechsel*. Wiesbaden: Springer, 2015.

Schulze, Adolf, and Karl Müller. *200 Jahre Brüdermission*. 2 vols. Herrnhut: Missionsbuchhandlung, 1931–32.

Schünemann, Georg. "Zur Geschichte des Taktschlagens und der Textbehandlung in der Mensuralmusik." *Sammelbände der Internationalen Musikgeselleschaft* 10 (1908): 73–114.

———. "Über die Beziehungen der vergleichenden Musikwissenschaft zur Musikgeschichte." *Archiv für Musikwissenschaft* 2 (1919–20): 175–94.

———. *Das Lied der deutschen Kolonisten in Russland*. Munich: Drei Masken Verlag, 1923.

———. "Beziehungen neuer Musik zu exotischer und frühmittelalterlicher Tonkunst." *Zeitschrift für Ästhetik und allgemeine Kunstwissenschaft* 17 (1924): 411–20.

Schwandt, Christoph, and Karl-Werner Gümpel. "Gurlitt, Wilibald." *Grove Music Online*. Accessed 26 October 2019. https://www.oxfordmusiconline.com/grovemusic/view/10.1093/gmo/9781561592630.001.0001/omo-9781561592630-e-0000012044.

Seesemann, Elisabeth. "Frauennot und Frauenhilfe." *ELMB* (1914): 105–11.

Sieber, Abt Godfrey. "Cassian Spiess (1866–1905), Bischof in Ostafrika (1902–1905)." In *Beständigkeit und Sendung: Festschrift St. Ottilien*, edited by Godfrey Sieber and Cyrill Schäfer, 339–44. St. Ottilien: EOS, 2003.

Simon, Artur, ed. *Das Berliner Phonogrammarchiv, 1900–2000: Sammlungen der traditionellen Musik der Welt*. Berlin: Verlag für Wissenschaft & Bildung, 2000.

Skoog, Gabriel. "The Life of George Herzog." *Resound* 18 (1999): 6–8.

Smith, Edwin William. *The Christian Mission in Africa: A Study Based on the Work of the International Conference at Le Zoute, Belgium, September 14ᵗʰ to 21ˢᵗ, 1926*. N.p., 1926.

Spiss, Cassian. "*Kihehe Wörtersammlung: Kihehe-Deutsch und Deutsch-Kihehe.*" *Mitteilungen des Seminars für orientalische Sparchen* 4 (1900): 114–90.

———. "Kingoni und Kisutu." *Mitteilungen des Seminars für orientalische Sprachen* 7 (1904): 270–414.

Stählin, Wilhelm. *Berneuchen: Unser Kampf und Dienst für die Kirche*. Kassel: Staude, 1939.

Stargardt, Nicholas. *The German War*. New York: Basic Books, 2015.

"Die Stellung der evangelischen Mission in Afrika zur Volkssitte." *ELMB* 48 (1893): 291–93.

Stephan, Rudolf. "Die Musik der Zwanzigerjahre." In *Zu Paul Hindemiths Schaffen in den Zwanziger Jahren*, edited by Dieter Rexroth. Frankfurter Studien 2:9–14. Mainz: B. Schotts Söhne, 1978.

Strohm, Reinhard. "Michael Weisse: Transmitting Medieval Melodies to Bach." *Understanding Bach: Web Journal of Bach Network UK* 6 (2011): 56–60.

———. "Sacred Song in the Fifteenth Century: Cantio, Carol, Lauda, Kirchenlied." In *The Cambridge History of Fifteenth-Century Music*, edited by Anna Maria Busse Berger and Jesse Rodin, 755–70. Cambridge: Cambridge University Press, 2015.

Stumpf, Carl. "Lieder der Bellakula-Indianer. " *Vierteljahresschrift für Musikwissenschaft* 2 (1886): 405–26.

———. *Die Anfänge der Musik.* Leipzig: Barth, 1911. Translation into English by David Trippett as *The Origins of Music* (Oxford: Oxford University Press, 2012).

Sühring, Peter. *Gustav Jacobsthal: Ein Musikologe im deutschen Kaiserreich; Musik inmitten von Natur, Geschichte und Sprache; Eine kultur- und ideengeschichtliche Biografie mit Briefen und Dokumenten.* Hildesheim: Olms, 2012.

Sundkler, Bengt, and Christopher Steed. *A History of the Church in Africa.* Cambridge: Cambridge University Press, 2000.

Taruskin, Richard. "On Letting the Music Speak for Itself: Some Reflections on Musicology and Performance." *Journal of Musicology* 1 (1982): 338–49.

Testamenti Umupwa wa mwene witu Yesu Cilisiti umuposhi wa nsi [New Testatment in Shiniha]. London: British and Foreign Bible Society, 1913.

Thamer, Hans-Ulrich, Daniel Droste, and Sabine Happ, eds. *Die Universität Münster im Nationalsozialismus.* Vol. 1. Münster: Aschendorff, 2012.

Tillich, Paul. *Gesammelte Werke: Impressionen und Reflexionen.* Stuttgart: Evangelisches Verlagswerk, 1972.

Titon, Jeff. *The Oxford Handbook of Applied Ethnomusicology.* Oxford: Oxford University Press, 2015.

Trabant, Jürgen. *Apeliotes, oder Der Sinn der Sprache: Wilhelm von Humboldt.* Munich: Fink, 1986.

———. *Traditionen Humboldts.* Frankfurt: Suhrkamp, 1990.

Tracey, Hugh. *Handbook for Librarians.* Roodepoort: African Music Society, 1948.

———. "Towards an Assessment of African Scales." *African Music* 2 (1958): 15–20.

Traub, Andreas, and Susanne Ziegler. "Mittelalterliche und kaukasische Mehrstimmigkeit: Neue Überlegungen zu einem alten Thema." *Beiträge zur Musikwissenschaft* 32 (1990): 214–77.

Treitler, Leo. "Homer and Gregory: The Transmission of Epic Poetry and Plainchant." *Musical Quarterly* 60 (1974): 333–72. Later published as chapter 6 in *With Voice and Pen: Coming to Know Medieval Song and How It Was Made* (Oxford: Oxford University Press, 2007).

Trippett, David. *Wagner's Melodies: Aesthetics and Materialism in German Musical Identity.* Cambridge: Cambridge University Press, 2013.

Trittelvitz, Walther. "Der Geiger von Bumbuli." *Nachrichten aus der Bethel Mission* 47 (1933): 41–47.

Trowell, Brian. "Fauxbourdon." *Grove Music Online.* Accessed 6 December 2019. https://www.oxfordmusiconline.com/grovemusic/view/10.1093/gmo/9781561592630.001.0001/omo-9781561592630-e-0000009373.

Trowell, Margaret, and Klaus P. Wachsmann. *Tribal Crafts of Uganda.* Oxford: Oxford University Press, 1953.

Unwerth, Wolf von, and Viktor Schirmunski, "Sprachgeschichte und Siedlungsmundarten." *Germanisch-Romanische Monatsschrift* 18 (1926): 113–22, 171–88.

Ustorf, Werner. "'Survival of the Fittest': German Protestant Missions, Nazism and Neocolonialism, 1933–1845." *Journal of Religion in Africa* 28 (1998): 93–114.

———. "*Wissenschaft*, Africa, and the Cultural Process according to Johann Gottfried Herder (1744–1803)." In *European Traditions in the Study of Religion in Africa*, edited by Ulrich Berner and Christoph Bochinger, 117–127. Wiesbaden: Harrassowitz, 2004.

———. *Robinson Crusoe Tries Again: Missiology and European Constructions of "Self" and "Other" in a Global World, 1789–2010*. Essays edited by Roland Loeffler. Goettingen: Vandenhoeck & Ruprecht, 2010.

Vallejo, Polo. *Patrimonio musical de los wagogo de Tanzania: Contexto y sistemática*. Madrid: Cyan, 2008.

Varwig, Bettina. *Histories of Heinrich Schütz*. Cambridge: Cambridge University Press, 2011.

"Veni Creator Spiritus." In *Glogauer Liederbuch*. Das Erbe deutscher Musik I, 4, no. 123, edited by Heribert Ringmann. Kassel: Bärenreiter, 1936.

Vikør, Lars S. *The Nordic Languages*. Oslo: Novus Press, 1993.

Vierhaus, Rudolf. *Deutsche biographische Enzyklopädie*. Berlin: de Gruyter, 2007.

Vivell, Coelestin. "Musik und Gesang der Neger in der apostolischen Präfektur Süd-Sansibar." *Mbl* 1 (1897): 70–76.

Vries, Willem de. *Sonderstab Musik. Organisierte Plünderungen in Westeuropa, 1940–1945*. Cologne: Dittrich, 1998.

Wachsmann, Klaus. *Untersuchungen zum vorgregorianischen Gesang*. Regensburg: A. Hopfer, 1935.

———, ed. *Essays on Music and History in Africa*. Evanston, IL: Northwestern University Press, 1971.

Wagner, Peter. *Elemente des gregorianischen Gesangs*. Regensburg: Pustet, 1917.

———. "Germanisches und romanisches im frühmittelalterlichen Kirchengesang." *Musica sacra* 10 (1925): 293–307.

Waldmann, Guido. "Die deutschen Kolonisten und ihr Lied." *Die Singgemeinde* 9 (1932): 98–107.

Wallaschek, Richard. *Anfänge der Tonkunst*. Leipzig: J. A. Barth, 1903.

Walter Hensel Gesellschaft, ed. "Walther Hensel und die Finkensteiner Bewegung: zur Erinnerung an die erste Singwoche in Finkenstein vor vierzig Jahren." N.p., 1963.

Ware, Louise. *George Foster Peabody: Banker, Philanthropist, Publicist*. Athens: University of Georgia Press, 1951.

Warneck, Gustav. *Evangelische Missionslehre*. 3 vols. Gotha: Perthes, 1892–1903.

———. *Abriss einer Geschichte der protestantischen Missionen von der Reformation bis auf die Gegenwart*. 10th ed. Berlin: Martin Warneck, 1913.

Waterman, Christopher A. "The Uneven Development of Africanist Ethnomusicology: Three Issues and a Critique." In *Comparative Musicology and Anthropology of Music: Essays on the History of Ethnomusicology*, edited by Bruno Nettl and Philip V. Bohlman, 169–86. Chicago: University of Chicago Press, 1991.

Weman, Henry. *African Music and the Church in Africa*. Studia Missionalia Upsaliensis. Uppsala: Ab Lundquistka Bokhandeln, 1960.

Weule, Karl. "Negerleben in Ostafrika."*Mbl* 13 (1908–9): 55–75.

Widenmann, August. *Die Kilimandscharo-Bevölkerung: Anthropologisches und Ethno-graphisches aus dem Dschagga-Lande.* Gotha: Perthes, 1899.

Wilson, Monica. *Communal Rituals of the Nyakyusa.* New York: Oxford University Press, 1959.

Winter, Jürgen Christoph. *Bruno Gutmann (1876–1966): A German Approach to Social Anthropology.* Oxford: Clarendon Press, 1979.

Wohlrab, Paul. "Die dritte lutherische Missionskonferenz in Ostafrika." *NOAM* 45 (1931): 18–21.

Wolf, Gunther, ed. *Stupor Mundi: Zur Geschichte Friedrichs II. von Hohenstaufen.* Darmstadt: Wissenschaftliche Buchgesellschaft, 1966.

Wolf, Johannes. "Ein Beitrag zur Diskantlehre des 14. Jahrhunderts." *Sammelbände der Internationalen Musikgesellschaft* 15 (1913–14): 504–34.

———. *Geschichte der Mensuralnotation von 1250–1460.* Leipzig: Breitkopf & Härtel, 2004.

Wright, Josephine. "Ballanta (Taylor), Nicholas George Julius." *Grove Music Online.* Accessed 28 October 2016. https://www.oxfordmusiconline.com/grovemusic/view/10.1093/gmo/9781561592630.001.0001/omo-9781561592630-e-1002087190.

Wright, Logie, ed. *"Shine like de Mornin' Star": N. G. J. Ballanta of Sierra Leone, Composer and Ethnomusicologist.* Freetown, Sierra Leone: United States Information Agency, 1995.

Wright, Marcia. *German Missions in Tanganyika, 1891–1941.* Oxford: Clarendon Press, 1971.

Wundt, Wilhelm. *Völkerpsychologie: Eine Untersuchung der Entwicklungsgesetze von Sprache, Mythos und Sitte.* 10 vols. Leipzig: Kröner, 1900–1920.

Zeisberger, David. *Delaware Grammatik.* Translated into English by Peter Stephen du Ponceau as *Grammar of the Language of the Lenni Lenape or Delaware Indians.* Philadelphia: J. Kay Jr., 1826.

Ziegler, Susanne. "Erich M. von Hornbostel und das Berliner Phonogramm-Archiv." In *Vom tönenden Wirbel menschlichen Tuns: Erich Mortiz von Hornbostel als Gestaltpsychologe, Archivar und Musikwissenschaftler,* edited by Sebastian Klotz, 146–68. Berlin: Schibri Verlag, 1998.

———. *Die Wachszylinder des Berliner Phonogramm-Archivs.* Berlin: Staatliche Museen zu Berlin, 2006.

———. "Polyphony in Historical Sound Recordings of the Berlin Phonogramm-Archiv." *International Research Center for Traditional Polyphony Bulletin* 6 (2008): 8–13.

———. "Siegfried F. Nadel and his contribution to Georgian Polyphony." In *The Fourth International Symposium on Traditional Polyphony. Proceedings,* edited by R. Tsurtsumia and J. Jordania, 97–115. Tbilisi: International Research Center for Traditional Polyphony of Tbilisi State Conservatoire, 2010.

Zimmermann, Walter. *Tonart ohne Ethos: Der Musikforscher Marius Schneider.* Wiesbaden: Steiner, 2003. Accessed 28 October 2016. http://home.snafu.de/walterz/biblio/tonart_ohne_ethos.pdf.

Zoka, Hoda M. *Civil Rights and Politics at Hampton Institute: The Legacy of Alonzo G. Moron.* Urbana: University of Illinois Press, 2006.